3000 800051 78636
St. Louis Community College

S0-AEC-053

Crane

F.V.

WITHDRAWN

 **St. Louis Community
College**

**Forest Park
Florissant Valley
Meramec**

**Instructional Resources
St. Louis, Missouri**

● **Television Violence and Public Policy**

Television Violence
and
Public Policy

Edited by
James T. Hamilton

Ann Arbor
THE UNIVERSITY OF MICHIGAN PRESS

Copyright © by the University of Michigan 1998
All rights reserved
Published in the United States of America by
The University of Michigan Press
Manufactured in the United States of America
⊗ Printed on acid-free paper

2001   2000   1999   1998   4   3   2   1

No part of this publication may be reproduced, stored in a retrieval system,
or transmitted in any form or by any means, electronic, mechanical, or otherwise,
without the written permission of the publisher.

A CIP catalog record for this book is available from the British Library.

Library of Congress Cataloging-in-Publication Data

Television violence and public policy / James T. Hamilton, editor.
    p.   cm.
    Essays originally presented at the Duke Conference on Media
Violence and Public Policy, held at the Sanford Institute of Public
Policy on June 28–29, 1996.
    Includes bibliographical references and index.
    ISBN 0-472-10903-0 (cloth : acid-free paper)
    1. Violence in television—United States—Congresses.
2. Television broadcasting policy—United States—Congresses.
I. Hamilton, James T. (James Towler), 1961–   . II. Duke Conference
on Media Violence and Public Policy (1996 : Terry Sanford Institute
of Public Policy)
PN1992.8V55T46   1998
303.6'0973—dc21   97-45388
                                                       CIP

For Nancy

Contents

Figures

Tables

Preface

These essays were originally presented at the Duke Conference on Media Violence and Public Policy, held at the Sanford Institute of Public Policy on June 28–29, 1996. The conference brought together researchers, interest group participants, government officials, and industry representatives to discuss the implications of academic research from many different disciplines for policies dealing with television violence. The four university research teams participating in the National Television Violence Study (NTVS) funded by the National Cable Television Association presented papers addressing the policy implications of the first year of their research. The full versions of the first year of their research efforts are available in the *National Television Violence Study, Volume 1* (Sage, 1997).

In the papers presented at the Duke Conference, the NTVS researchers from the University of California at Santa Barbara, University of North Carolina at Chapel Hill, University of Texas at Austin, and University of Wisconsin at Madison demonstrated how television violence can be defined and analyzed through content analysis, described in program ratings, and addressed through campaigns such as public service announcements. Cynthia Hoffner presented a content analysis to examine how the media covered the debate about television violence. Matthew Spitzer drew on research from law and economics to examine whether the V-chip provisions of the Telecommunications Act of 1996 would survive court scrutiny. My essay at the conference analyzed how information provision about program content affected the willingness of advertisers to sponsor a given set of programs, prime-time broadcast network movies.

I am indebted to the conference authors and participants for their willingness to discuss how research from different disciplines could be used to develop remedies to deal with television violence. The papers from the conference were sent to Jack Valenti, president of the Motion Picture Association of America, who directed the TV Ratings Executive Committee working on the industry's program rating system. Many of the conference participants met with the industry committee in the fall of 1996 as it developed a ratings system. The essays in this volume were revised after the December 1996 announcement of the industry's ratings system, the TV Parental Guidelines.

In organizing the conference, I was fortunate to benefit from the help of many colleagues from Duke: Phil Cook, Joel Fleishman, Joel Huber, and Redford Williams. Ellen Mickiewicz, the Director of the DeWitt Wallace Center for Communications and Journalism at Duke, provided support throughout the project. I also benefited greatly from discussions with Joel Federman of the NTVS and Julius Genachowski of the Federal Communications Commission. Nancy Torre helped arrange the conference, while Robert Malme helped edit the final essays. Charles Myers provided encouragement throughout the editorial process.

Chapter 1

Media Violence and Public Policy

James T. Hamilton

The First Amendment states clearly that "Congress shall make no law . . . abridging the freedom of speech, or of the press. . . ." Yet since the first congressional hearing on television violence was held in 1954, violence on television has been a topic of legislative debate, agency pronouncement, and presidential commentary. The academic literature surrounding media violence neatly divides into two streams, one asking what types of restrictions on media content are constitutional given the First Amendment and the other asking what evidence exists that violence in the media causes violence in society. The essays in this volume go beyond a rhetorical consideration of these questions, for they are generally aimed at providing empirical evidence on specific policy issues surrounding media violence. Although the authors come from different disciplines, a common theme of media violence as a problem created by information consumption and potentially addressed through information provision unites the papers in this volume. Taken together, the chapters in this volume offer evidence of how television violence can be profitably examined as a public policy issue.

At its core, television violence is a problem of pollution. Many public policies, ranging from zoning to air pollution controls to residential garbage collection, are driven by the notion that individuals do not always fully internalize the costs to society of their actions. Economists define these problems as involving the generation of negative externalities, costs that are borne by people other than the individuals involved in production activities. In environmental pollution, negative externalities arise when firms fail to take into account the potential damage to human health or natural resources from their emissions. Television violence is akin to pollution because programmers and advertisers may not take into account the full costs to society of the shows that they schedule or support. Laboratory research, survey data, and natural experiments created by the introduction of television in new areas point to at least three potential harms from the consumption of violent programming: increases in aggression and/or criminal activity; desensitization; and the generation of fear among viewers.[1] Many of these dangers are highest for children, yet programmers and advertisers do not face many market incentives to incorporate these potential damages in their programming decisions.

In a market where consumers face multiple viewing options across broadcast and cable channels, networks offer products differentiated in part by the level of violence within a show. Programmers use violent programs to attract those distinct marginal viewers with a taste for violent content. Males 18 to 34 are the top adult consumers of violent television and movies, followed by females 18 to 34.[2] Since females 18 to 34 are highly valued by advertisers because of their product purchases, their preferences help account for the popularity of violent programming on broadcast television. Although advertisers aim to reach younger or male viewers through violent shows, children are not a target audience for the violence contained in prime-time network programs. Analysis of advertising rates on network programs indicates, for example, that the number of children viewing a prime-time show does not influence the advertising rates charged for commercials.[3] Children's viewership of prime-time violent programs arises as an unintended by-product of attempts to reach (young) adult viewers. The damages arising from children's exposure to violent programs, such as short-term increases in aggression and long-term increases in the likelihood of criminal activity, create a case for examining media violence as a public policy issue.

Politics offers another explanation for why media violence is a public policy issue. While the entertainment industry uses violence to reach particular viewing audiences, politicians may use the issue of violent television to reach particular voting audiences. In 1996, Republican candidate Bob Dole emphasized television violence during the primary season in an effort to attract cultural conservatives, and President Clinton championed the same issue in the general election in a bid to attract swing voters such as young married women. The conflict between the entertainment industry and government over television violence arises in part because of the differences between the marginal viewers sought by programmers and the marginal voters sought by politicians. Viewers 18 to 34 who consume heavy amounts of violent programming are less likely to see television violence as a major cause of violence in society and are less likely to vote. People identified as swing voters in the 1996 elections (e.g., young married women, 1992 Perot voters, suburban residents) agreed in survey responses that there was too much violence in entertainment programming.[4] The benefits of reducing television violence would be distributed widely across society, so that politicians are unlikely to be lobbied directly by groups dedicated to reducing television violence. The electoral returns at the ballot box for championing this issue, however, mean that election-minded candidates for Congress and the presidency may choose to make television violence a policy issue. Though self-interested behavior in the economic marketplace leads networks to program television violence, self-interested behavior in the political marketplace may lead politicians to try to address the problems posed by violent television content.

If television violence is defined as a problem of pollution, then policies to deal with media violence may parallel those designed to reduce the damages associated with pollution. Legislative proposals to deal with media violence include zoning (e.g., shifting violent programs to times when children are less likely to be in the audience) and taxing (e.g., placing a 25 percent tax on violent "ultimate fighting events" on pay-per-view cable).[5] The most recent attempt to craft a policy remedy in this area involves information provision about violent content. Information provision is frequently used as a regulatory tool to deal with pollution. The U.S. Environmental Protection Agency, for example, has successfully encouraged firms to reduce their toxic emissions through the yearly publication of pollution figures that publicly reveal pollution data about individual plants. The release of the data has attracted scrutiny from investors, company officials, state regulators, and plant neighbors, scrutiny that has led to a large reduction in the pollutants tracked in the public data.

The Telecommunications Act of 1996 embraced information provision as a way to reduce the dangers posed by television violence. The measure required televisions with diagonals 13 inches or greater to be equipped with technology capable of reading a program rating. One year after the passage of the bill, the Federal Communications Commission was required to appoint an advisory committee to develop a program rating methodology unless the industry had developed a credible rating system and was broadcasting signals that contained the ratings. If the industry did develop a program rating system, the act required distributors of video programming to transmit the rating. Entertainment industry executives announced in the wake of the bill a plan to develop a program rating system by January 1997.

The industry committee headed by Motion Picture Association of America (MPAA) president Jack Valenti announced the creation of the industry's *TV Parental Guidelines* in December 1996. This rating system for programs placed shows in six categories, which blended together concerns about content and viewer age. Under these guidelines, broadcasters and cable channels would rate programs designed solely for children with the icon TV-Y (appropriate for all children) and TV-Y7 (program designed for children age 7 or above). Shows aimed at the entire audience (except for news and sports programs) would receive one of four designations: TV-G (general audience); TV-PG (parental guidance suggested); TV-14 (parents strongly cautioned); or TV-MA (mature audience only). The rating would not provide a parent with specific information on the particular types of content (e.g., violence, sexual content, language) that gave rise to the rating. The rating rather represents a summary indicator meant to convey the possible presence of many different types of content. For example, the description of the TV-14 rating reads in the guidelines as:

> TV-14 Parents Strongly Cautioned. *This program may contain some material that many parents would find unsuitable for children under 14 years of age.* Parents are strongly urged to exercise greater care in monitoring this program and are cautioned against letting children under the age of 14 watch unattended. This program may contain sophisticated themes, sexual content, strong language and more intense violence.[6]

Though broadcasters and cable channels began to use these age-based ratings in January 1997, the system was widely criticized by interest groups, academics, and politicians who had been active in the development of the V-chip legislation. Many outside the entertainment industry announced their support for a ratings system that would provide parents more information about the level or intensity of violence, sexual content, or adult language in a program. The essays in this volume refer to the ratings system as implemented in the spring of 1997, so that proposals for changes in the ratings system focus on the age-based ratings used at the time. In July 1997 representatives of the television industry agreed to change the TV Parental Guidelines system, so that starting in October 1997 programs in the TV-Y7 category could be supplemented with an FV for fantasy violence and programs in the TV-PG, TV-14, and TV-MA categories could carry indicators of V for violence, S for sexual situations, L for language, and D for suggestive dialogue. The major broadcast networks, with the exception of NBC, declared their agreement to use these additional program rating indicators. The criticisms of the limitations of the age-based system initially proposed are left unchanged in these essays, in part because these papers as written reflect the debate that led to changes in the ratings system and in part because it remains to be seen how the proposed addition of content indicators for FV, V, S, L, and D will be implemented.

Judging the design and operation of a ratings system, either the original age-based system or the proposed supplement of these guidelines with additional content indicators, involves answering a number of questions about violent television content. How can media violence be defined? How do viewers react to the provision of information about program content? How do advertisers react when programs carry warnings? Can television convey information that reduces the likelihood of violence? What types of information about television violence reach viewers/voters through the media? Are the information provision requirements in the Telecommunications Act such as the V-chip and rating system constitutional? The essays in this book provide answers to these policy questions, drawing upon research from communications, political science, economics, and law.

Chapters 2 through 5 provide a detailed description of how television violence can be defined and measured. In chapter 2, authors from the University of California at Santa Barbara (i.e., Wilson, Donnerstein, Linz, Kunkel, Potter, Smith, Blumenthal, and Gray) provide an overview of the research literature on the negative effects of violent television programming. They identify three main harmful effects from the consumption of violent programming: learning or imitation of aggressive thoughts, attitudes, and behavior; desensitization, the development of a callous view toward real-world violence; and fear. Drawing heavily upon lab experiments where researchers were able to isolate the different program elements that contribute to viewer reactions, the researchers develop an analytical framework that describes the context of how violence is portrayed in a program. They state that at least nine different contextual factors may affect the reaction of viewers to violent portrayals: the nature of the perpetrator; nature of the target; reason for violence; presence of weapons; extent and graphicness of violence; degree of realism of the violence; whether the violence is rewarded or punished; consequences of violence; and use of humor with violence. These contexts may generate harms for both child and adult viewers, although the Santa Barbara researchers are careful to point out that younger children may react differently to at least two contextual factors because of differences in their perceptions of programming. A programming segment featuring fantasy violence that is punished at the end of a program may be more likely to generate imitation among younger children, who may view the violence as realistic and who may not link up a punishment that occurs at the end of the program with earlier violent segments.

Lab experiments have not been conducted that determine how these contextual factors interact in terms of producing synergistic effects (e.g., what is the impact of a violent act committed by an attractive perpetrator who goes unpunished?). Overall, the authors indicate that the framework allows one to make statements about what types of violence portrayals are more likely to generate harms among viewers. As they indicate:

> . . . a portrayal that poses the greatest risk for the learning of aggression would feature an attractive perpetrator who is motivated by morally proper reasons; who engages in repeated violence that seems realistic, is rewarded, and employs conventional weapons; and whose violent actions produce no visible harm or pain and are accompanied by humor.[7]

In chapter 3, the Santa Barbara authors describe how they used the research on the context of violence to develop the methodology to track violent programming in the National Television Violence Study, a three-year television research program funded by the National Cable Television Association.[8] The authors define violence as:

> . . . any overt depiction of a credible threat of physical force or the actual use of such force intended to physically harm an animate being or group of beings. Violence also includes certain depictions of physically harmful consequences against an animate being or group that occur as a result of unseen violent means. Thus, there are three primary types of violent depictions: credible threats, behavioral acts, and harmful consequences.[9]

The violent incident forms the basic unit of analysis for their work, with an incident defined by the perpetrator, act, and target. The authors also develop broader measures at the scene level (with a scene defined by interrelated incidents) and program level. The Santa Barbara researchers used this definition of violence and coded the contextual factors discussed in chapter 2 to develop a snapshot of the type of violent programming available across different channels, genres of programming, and times of day. Chapter 3 describes in detail how the authors developed a sample of 2,500 hours of programming that allows them to investigate differences in content across such programming outlets as broadcast channels, basic cable, and premium cable channels. The chapter demonstrates that their measures of coder reliability indicate that the framework can be consistently applied by different coders, a common concern about any attempt to apply a definition of violent content to many different programs.

Chapter 4 summarizes the results of the Santa Barbara team's first year (1994–95) of monitoring violent content. When an overview of these results was first released in the *National Television Violence Study*, media accounts of the research focused on the fact that the researchers found that 57 percent of all programs in the 23-channel sample contained violence. Chapter 4 emphasizes, however, that the Santa Barbara findings provide much more than a single number to measure violence on television. Their results provide the first representative picture of the context of violent acts and the differences across genre and channel type in the use of violence. Chapter 4 shows that violence on television is often used in contexts that are most likely to simulate learning and imitation. Nearly half of all violent actions on television fail to show a victim's pain/harm and are portrayed as justified, and the majority of violent actions are not followed in the same scene by any sort of punishment. Of those programs that use violence, a third contain nine or more violent interactions. Premium channels, independent stations, movies, and reality-based programs are more likely to contain these high numbers of violent interactions.

In chapter 5, the Santa Barbara authors discuss how their results can be used by television industry decision makers, policymakers, and parents. Although violence is likely to remain central to certain programming genres, the context research indicates that producers can attempt to avoid portrayals likely to encourage imitation and learning of aggression by children. For example, the research literature indicates violent stories are less likely to generate aggression if the violence is punished, if negative consequences such as pain and harm are portrayed, and if the violence is not shown as justified. They urge policymakers to take contextual factors into account when formulating ways to deal with television violence. The authors also urge parents to be aware of the dangers of different contexts of violent television for their children, so that parents can be careful to shield their children from channel types and genres most likely to be violent. With the advent of the V-chip and rating system, they stress that the rating system should take into account variations in the context of violence and that it should take into account differences in the ability of children of different ages to comprehend violent actions. This would mean, for example, a recognition that fantasy violence may be harmful for younger children since they view the interactions as realistic rather than fictional.

A common question that arises in the debate over rating systems is what types of programs will be rated. The February 1996 announcement of the attempt by the entertainment industry to develop a rating system indicated that news and sports programming would not be rated. Chapter 6 implicitly raises the question of what should be considered news programming in a rating system, for the results indicate that problematic portrayals of violence occur in many types of reality-based programs. In chapter 6, researchers from the University of Texas at Austin (i.e., Lasorsa, Danielson, Wartella, Whitney, Klijn, Lopez, and Olivarez) employ the definition of violence applied to entertainment programming earlier by the Santa Barbara researchers and use this to analyze reality-based programming from 1994–95. The researchers explicitly exclude regularly scheduled "bona fide" newscasts, such as network evening news and local news broadcasts. This leaves a wide variety of reality-based programs to examine, including documentaries, entertainment news/review programs, news magazine and public affairs shows, police programs, tabloid news such as *Hard Copy,* talk shows, and other reality programs such as *Rescue 911.* The results indicate some genres of reality-based programming do raise concerns about their use of violence. All of the police reality shows in the sample contained violent acts, and the violence in these programs was more likely to be extreme and be rewarded. Tabloid news programs were also likely to contain violence, although the contexts were less harmful. Entertainment news and review programs were not likely to contain much violence, but the violent segments used were likely to be problematic. News or public affairs programs were not likely to contain violent acts. Overall, the results indicate the importance of explicitly defining news programs. If reality-based programs such as *Cops* are treated as news, this would mean that a genre of programming characterized by frequent use of violence in contexts potentially harmful to viewers would go unrated.

If programs carry warnings, the question arises of how parents and children will use this information to make viewing decisions. In chapter 7, researchers from the University of Wisconsin-Madison and East Carolina University (i.e., Cantor, Harrison, and Krcmar) investigated in experimental settings how children's selection of program choices varied depending on the wording and information content of viewer warnings. If a program carried the label "parental discretion advised" in a viewing guide describing programming, boys were more likely to select the show for viewing. For movies carrying MPAA ratings, boys 10 to 14 were especially attracted to movies if they carried a PG-13 or R rating. If the program warning was phrased as "viewer discretion advised," however, there was no impact on boys' interest in viewing and a decrease in girls' desire to view a program. The authors find that the attraction to restricted programs arises more from an attempt "to reject control over their viewing" than from an explicit seeking-out of violent content. In analyzing the use of MPAA ratings and content indicators in premium channels, the authors establish that it is difficult to determine why movies receive a PG versus PG-13 rating since these categories contain many different combinations of language, violence, and sex.

These findings lead Cantor, Harrison, and Krcmar to a clear set of recommendations about how information provision should be used in labeling television programs. They emphasize that ratings systems should pay attention to the exact wording of warnings or content indicators, since phrasing appears to affect whether children are attracted to a program on the basis of a warning. The potential for some wordings to give rise to a "forbidden fruit" effect where children are attracted to that which is labeled off-limits means that they recommend that the rating system should stress content indicators (e.g., sex, violence, language) rather than viewing prescriptions about who should be able to see a program. They also indicate that the simple importation of MPAA ratings to television would not work since these come with some associations that may attract the interest of viewers such as young teenage boys. Another problem they note with the MPAA ratings is that parents cannot readily determine whether a movie received a PG versus a PG-13 rating because of violence, sexual content, or language use.

Historically, broadcast networks have been reluctant to provide warning labels on programs because of fear that some companies will be less likely to advertise on labeled programs for fear of consumer backlash. Chapter 8 investigates the impact of warning on a particular type of program, prime-time movies on broadcast television. Warnings on television programs reduce the costs to parents of learning what programs they wish to shield their children from on television. If networks provide viewer discretion warnings, then some parents should act to make sure that their children do not watch a particular film. In chapter 8 I discuss how analysis of ratings data from 2,295 prime-time movies shown on broadcast network television indicates that a placement of a warning on a movie resulted in a drop of viewership by children 2 to 11 of approximately 14 percent (i.e., 222,000 fewer children were in the prime-time movie audience). Warning labels had no net impact on the viewing of teens or adults. Despite the fact that adult audiences for films with warnings do not change, chapter 8 demonstrates that the placement of a warning on some prime-time movies can result in changes in advertising purchases that ultimately may lower the returns to networks of showing labeled films.

Chapter 8 draws on analysis of over 19,000 commercials shown on 251 prime-time broadcast network movies in 1995–96. The placement of warnings on theatrical violent films results in fewer general product ads and more network promotions being run on these films. Violent theatrical films with warnings were more likely to have products aimed at younger consumers, males, and those without children, which are all consumer groups that are less likely to view television violence as a significant problem. Products aimed at these consumers, such as sports products and alcoholic beverages, were more likely to advertise on movies with warnings, while products with "family" brand images such as food or kitchen products were less likely to advertise on these theatrical films with warnings. These results underscore that even though the adult audiences for television programs are not changed by the addition of a warning, networks may face incentives not to label violent programs because this changes the willingness of some firms to be associated with sponsoring a program.

As pressure on broadcast and cable networks mounted to take action to mitigate the effects of violent programming, some in the television industry announced plans to use public service announcements to promote antiviolence messages. Researchers from the University of North Carolina at Chapel Hill (i.e., Knight, Kemp, Brown, and Biocca) examine in chapter 9 the potential effectiveness of this use of information provision to provide messages that run counter to those implicit in violent entertainment programming on television. Although their review of the literature on public service announcements (PSAs) concludes that systematic and coordinated use of television could reduce levels of violence, the authors find that the current antiviolence programming and PSAs offered were ineffective. The UNC researchers tested 15 PSAs and one hour-long antiviolence educational program in five different studies involving over 200 youths. They found "no evidence of any significant effect on attitudes about violence" among the prime audience for these antiviolence messages. The ineffectiveness of the current construction of antiviolence messages is not surprising, given that the researchers note that pretesting and evaluation of these commercials within the industry are rare. While the research literature suggests that a coordinated campaign of antiviolence messages could be effective, industry participants currently have little incentive to construct an effective antiviolence campaign.

Chapter 10 indicates that few of the messages from research about television violence are entering the debate in the media over the issue. In this chapter, Hoffner examines coverage of television violence in five major newspapers during 1994–95. Though research emphasizes the importance of context in understanding the potential dangers posed by television violence, the papers examined by Hoffner were much more likely to focus on whether there are "excessive" levels of television violence rather than on the context of television violence. Though researchers on the whole agree on the negative impacts of violent programming, Hoffner finds a sizable percentage of stories that indicate that "effects of televised violence are minimal or controversial." She finds that the papers frame the issue as one of industry self-regulation versus government intervention, with industry officials quoted as minimizing the problems posed by television violence and emphasizing that government action is akin to censorship. Though content analysis cannot demonstrate the impact of media framing on public opinion, Hoffner's results suggest that the journalistic pressures to focus on conflict and entertainment may crowd out discussion of the details of policy research such as the focus on context.

In the book's final chapter, Spitzer examines the legal issues surrounding the V-chip and rating system requirements in the Telecommunications Act of 1996. He notes that although the industry "voluntarily" offered in February 1996 to rate its programming, the actions of President Clinton in encouraging broadcasters to take action and the setup of the administrative system in the legislation, which requires the FCC to develop a methodology if the industry does not act within one year of the bill's passage, make it likely that the rating system will be viewed as "state action" by the courts. He argues that the system may survive a First Amendment challenge in part because it is designed to serve a compelling state interest, that is, "empowering parental control of children's television viewing."[10] The V-chip would probably be found to be a narrowly tailored remedy, since it is less restrictive or costly than having parents watch children with their television or shifting programs to later viewing times. His analysis suggests that, depending on the procedural details such as how ratings could be appealed, the V-chip and rating system would likely survive a constitutional challenge.

Taken together, the essays in this volume demonstrate the benefits of using multiple disciplines and empirical analysis to examine media violence as a policy issue. When the television industry announced its selection of an age-based program rating system in December 1996, many participants in the policy debate voiced their frustration with the failure of the ratings to provide information about specific program content. The chapters in this volume help explain how a rating system could have been designed differently and why the industry initially chose to provide parents with only a summary measure of program content. Chapters 2 through 6 suggest that a content rating system could be constructed based on academic research that categorizes programs based on their use of violence. Although research today cannot determine the specific harms arising from a violent act on a particular television program, evidence from many lab experiments allows one to categorize programs based on the context of how violence is used.

Chapter 7 shows how the industry could have experimented with different types of ways to provide content information to maximize the probability that the information would help parents protect their children from content they viewed as harmful or objectionable.

The industry did not link its rating system to academic research or offer evidence that its system would achieve its stated goals of helping parents make informed viewing decisions. Chapter 8 helps explain why broadcasters faced incentives to minimize the type of content information provided, since warnings reduce the willingness of some companies to advertise on violent programs. Industry participants could have conducted extensive research on how different warnings affect behavior by parents and children and how public service announcements could be used to deliver an antiviolence message. Chapter 9 indicates that research could help the industry develop an effective antiviolence campaign but that there is little evidence that the industry engages in such measures as evaluating the efficacy of its antiviolence public service announcements. Entertainment industry officials may ultimately be reluctant to invest in learning about effective rating systems and information provision programs, however, if they view effectiveness in political rather than social terms.

Under the pressure created by the Telecommunications Act of 1996, the industry has agreed to use information provision in the form of a program ratings system. In a world of limited information about program content and limited time for parents to make their viewing decisions, the summary information provided by the *TV Parental Guidelines* may give some parents a better indication of whether a program is appropriate for their children. Ironically, the increasing complexity of viewing options and viewing technology may eventually provide parents with more detailed program information. As the number of channels expands, viewers will eventually use software to navigate among television channels. The introduction of viewing software may allow consumers to program viewing options based on content ratings from many different groups, so that parents could choose programs based on specific content information and use technology such as the V-chip to screen particular types of shows. The essays in this volume help establish a baseline to examine whose interests the ratings systems that develop will ultimately serve: broadcasters and cable programmers; advertisers; politicians; parents; or children.

NOTES

1. See chapter 2 for a discussion of the literature on the impacts of television violence.

2. Chapter 8 provides more details on the market for violent programming. For an extensive empirical assessment, see James T. Hamilton, *Channeling Violence: The Economic Market for Violent Television Programming,* Princeton University Press, 1998.

3. Hamilton, *Channeling Violence.*

4. Hamilton, *Channeling Violence.*

5. In 1995, Senator Hollings introduced a bill that would have required the Federal Communications Commission to define violent programming and required the agency to develop rules so that violent shows could only be shown on broadcast or cable television at times when children were not likely to be a substantial part of the audience. In 1996, Missouri passed a law placing a 25 percent tax on "gross receipts . . . derived from the sale, lease, or other exploitation in this state of broadcasting, television, closed-circuit and motion picture rights for any ultimate fighting contest." Ultimate fighting events involve no holds barred, bare-knuckle fighting. See Hamilton, *Channeling Violence,* for a discussion of these policies.

6. TV Parental Guidelines Oversight Monitoring Board, 1996. When the TV Parental Guidelines were first announced, the "mature audience only" program category was represented with a TV-M label. This was later changed to TV-MA.

7. See chapter 2, under "Summary: Contextual Patterns."

8. For the results of the first year of the National Television Violence Study see *National Television Violence Study, Volume 1,* Sage, 1997.

9. See chapter 3, under "Definition of Violence."

10. See chapter 11, under "Finding a Good Reason."

REFERENCES

Hamilton, J. T. 1998. *Channeling Violence: The Economic Market for Violent Television Programming.* Princeton: Princeton University Press.
National Television Violence Study, Volume 1. 1997. Thousand Oaks, CA: Sage.
TV Parental Guidelines Oversight Monitoring Board. 1996. *The TV Parental Guidelines.* Washington, DC: TV Parental Guidelines Oversight Monitoring Board.

Chapter 2

Content Analysis of Entertainment Television: The Importance of Context

Barbara J. Wilson, Edward Donnerstein, Daniel Linz,
Dale Kunkel, James Potter, Stacy L. Smith, Eva Blumenthal,
and Tim Gray

Introduction

It is well established by scientific research that exposure to televised violence contributes to a range of antisocial or harmful effects on many viewers. It is also the case that not all research on the impact of violent depictions produces evidence of a negative effect on the audience. We believe that much of the variability in the findings can be traced to differences in the nature of the violent depictions studied.

Obviously, there is a vast array of approaches to presenting violent material. In terms of its visual presentation, the violence may occur on-screen and be shown graphically, or it may occur offscreen but be clearly implied. Violent acts may be shown close-up or at a distance. There are also differences in scripting of characters who commit violence and their reasons for doing so. And there are variations in the portrayals of the results of violence, including both the pain and suffering of victims as well as the outcomes for the perpetrator. Simply put, not all portrayals of violence are the same; they vary in many important ways.

These and other similar variations represent the context of violent. Such contextual features hold important implications for the influence of television violence on the audience. While some depictions of violence are likely to contribute to harmful effects on viewers, others may be prosocial and actually beneficial for the audience.

In this chapter, we seek to identify the contextual features associated with violent depictions that most significantly increase the risk of a harmful effect on the audience. To this end, we have divided the chapter into two major sections.

The first section reviews both theory and research on three documented harmful effects that have been associated with exposure to media violence: aggression, desensitization, and fear. In the second section of this chapter, however, we review all of the existing social scientific research that has examined specific aspects or features of violent portrayals and their influence on individuals' learning of aggressive thoughts and behaviors, becoming desensitized to real-world violence, and developing a short- or long-term fear about becoming a victim of aggression.

Drawing conclusions as warranted from this evidence, we have devised an elaborate framework for evaluating the important contextual elements associated with violent depictions (see *National Television Violence Study, Volume 1* 1997). Our review of the effects literature indicates the importance of at least nine contextual factors that influence audience reactions to violent portrayals: the nature of the perpetrator; nature of the target; reason for the violence; presence of weapons; extent and graphicness of the violence; degree of realism of the violence; whether the violence is rewarded or punished; consequences of violence; and whether humor is involved in the violence. Utilizing this framework, we have established systematic procedures for measuring the presence of these features in television programming. This chapter establishes the research basis for focusing on these contextual elements, while chapters 3 and 4 describe how these elements can be captured in a coding framework and used to analyze a sample of programming.

During the debate over the *TV Parental Guidelines* rating systems, individuals sometimes claimed that specific content ratings would be difficult because it is impossible to define violence. Similarly, placing a content code on a children's cartoon was viewed as problematic since it was claimed that there was little evidence that cartoon images had a negative impact on children. Our results in this chapter contradict these assertions. The review of the literature here indicates that research can provide a basis for defining violent programming, that context can be measured, and that contextual factors such as whether the violent act is presented in a cartoon or other fantastic image can be used to describe potential harms to children of different ages.

The Effects of Exposure to Media Violence

We live in a violent society. As a nation we rank first among all developed countries in the world in homicides per capita. The pervasiveness of violence is staggering, particularly involving children and adolescents. For example, consider the following statistics cited by the American Psychological Association (1993):

1. Every five minutes a child is arrested for a violent crime.
2. Gun related violence takes the life of an American child every three hours.

3. Every day over 100,000 children carry guns to schools.
4. In a recent survey of fifth graders in New Orleans, more than 50 percent report being a victim of violence, and 70 percent have seen weapons being used.
5. Adolescents account for 24 percent of all violent crimes leading to arrest. The rate has increased over time for the age groups 12–19, and is down for age groups 35 and older.
6. Among individuals age 15 to 24 years old, homicide is the second leading cause of death, and for African American youth it is the leading cause.
7. A child growing up in Chicago is 15 times more likely to be murdered than a child growing up in Northern Ireland.

What accounts for these alarming figures? There is universal agreement that many factors contribute to violent behavior, such as gangs, drugs, guns, poverty, and racism. Violence is truly multifaceted, such that these factors may independently and interactively combine to elicit antisocial behavior. Groups like the American Psychological Association, American Medical Association, National Academy of Science, and Centers for Disease Control and Prevention have all examined recently the perplexing problem of the causes of violence. While recognizing the complexity in determining the causes of violent behavior, all of these groups have concluded that the mass media bear some responsibility for contributing to real-world violence. Viewing media violence is not the only, nor even the most important, contributor to violent behavior. Furthermore, it is not every act of violence in the media that raises concern, nor every child or adult who is affected. But there is clear evidence that exposure to media violence contributes in significant ways to violence in society. This conclusion is based on careful and critical readings of the social science research collected over the last 40 years.

While media violence may not be the single most important contributor to aggression, there is wide consensus that it may be the one factor that is the easiest to mitigate. To devise solutions to the problem of media violence, two fundamental issues need to be addressed: what types of violent material are the most problematic; and what types of violence exist on television. This chapter addresses information at both of these levels, providing a detailed analysis of violence on television that is framed according to all existing scientific knowledge that informs us about the effects of media violence on the audience.

Conclusions of the Research Community

Over the past few decades many governmental and professional organizations have conducted exhaustive reviews of the scientific literature on the relationship between media violence and aggressive behavior. These investigations have consistently documented how media violence, across various genres, is related to the aggressive behavior of many children, adolescents, and adults, as well as an influence on perceptions and attitudes about violence.

Two early, major reports from the government's leading public health agencies, the 1972 Surgeon General's Report and the 1982 National Institute of Mental Health (NIMH) review, concluded that television occupied a significant role in the lives of both children and adults. Both of these reports were emphatic in their claim that many types of televised violence can influence aggressive behavior. The Surgeon General's Report concluded that there was a consistent and significant correlation between viewing televised violence and subsequent aggression. This finding emerged across many different measures of aggressive behavior and across different methodological approaches (e.g., experimental evidence, longitudinal field studies) to studying the problem. The Surgeon General's research made clear that there was a direct, causal link between exposure to televised violence and subsequent aggressive behavior by the viewer.

The NIMH report, which followed ten years later, added significantly to the conclusions of the Surgeon General. First, the age range of the effects was extended to include preschoolers and older adolescents, and the findings were generalized to girls as well as to boys. Second, and perhaps more important, it was established that viewers learn more than aggressive behavior. They learn to fear being a victim. Heavy viewing may lead to aggression, but for some individuals it will lead to fear and apprehension about being victimized by aggression. It is more than aggressive behavior, the report concluded, that should be of concern.

In recent years additional reports, particularly from the Centers for Disease Control (1991), National Academy of Science (1993), and the American Psychological Association (1993), have lent further support to the conclusion that the mass media contribute to aggressive attitudes and behavior. The most comprehensive of these reports comes from the American Psychological Association (APA), which established a Commission on Youth and Violence to exhaustively examine the scientific literature on the causes and prevention of violence. Like previous investigations into violence, the role of the mass media was considered, and the conclusions reached were similar. Specifically, the APA report concluded that:

1. Nearly four decades of research on television and other media have documented the almost universal exposure of American children to high levels of media violence.
2. There is absolutely no doubt that those who are heavy viewers of this violence demonstrate increased acceptance of aggressive attitudes and increased aggressive behavior.

This correlation between violence viewing and aggressive behavior is fairly stable over time, place, and demographics (Donnerstein, Slaby, and Eron 1994;

Huesmann and Eron 1986), and also across varieties of television genres (Paik and Comstock 1994). An examination of hundreds of experimental and longitudinal studies supports the position that viewing violence in the mass media is related to aggressive behavior (Huston et al. 1992). Moreover, naturalistic field studies and cross-national studies support the position that the viewing of televised aggression leads to increases in subsequent aggression and that such behavior can become part of a lasting behavioral pattern (Huesmann and Eron 1986). Aggressive habits learned early in life form the foundation for later behavior. Aggressive children who have trouble in school and with relating to peers tend to watch more television; the violence they see there, in turn, reinforces their tendency toward aggression. These effects are both short-term and long lasting. In fact, Huesmann and his colleagues (i.e., Huesmann 1986; Huesmann, Eron, Lefkowitz, and Walder 1984) found a clear and significant relationship between early exposure to televised violence at age eight and adult aggressive behavior (measured by seriousness of criminal acts) 22 years later. As Huesmann (1986) noted:

> Aggressive habits seem to be learned early in life, and once established, are resistant to change and predictive of serious adult antisocial behavior. If a child's observation of media violence promotes the learning of aggressive habits, it can have harmful lifelong consequences. Consistent with this theory, early television habits are in fact correlated with adult criminality. Consequently, children's exposure to violence in the mass media, particularly at young ages, can have lifelong consequences.

In addition to increasing violent behavior toward others, viewing violence on television changes attitudes and behaviors in response to violence in significant ways. Even those who do not themselves behave violently are affected by their viewing of violence in two significant ways.

First, prolonged viewing of media violence can lead to emotional desensitization toward real-world violence and the victims of violence. Such emotional numbing can result in callous attitudes toward violence directed at others and a decreased likelihood to take action on behalf of the victim when violence occurs (Donnerstein, Slaby, and Eron 1994). Research on desensitization to media violence has shown that although observers react initially with relatively intense physiological responses to scenes of violence, habituation can occur with prolonged or repeated exposure and this habituation can carry over to other settings (Thomas et al. 1977). Once viewers are emotionally "comfortable" with violent content, they may also evaluate media violence more favorably in other domains (Linz, Donnerstein, and Penrod 1988).

Second, viewing violence can increase the fear of becoming a victim of aggression, with a resultant increase in self-protective behaviors and mistrust of others. Research by Gerbner and his colleagues (e.g., Gerbner, Gross, Signorielli, and Morgan 1986) has shown that heavy viewers of media violence tend to have a perception of social reality that matches that presented in the media. That is, heavy viewers tend to see the world as more crime-ridden and dangerous, and they are more fearful of walking alone in their own neighborhoods. Furthermore, viewing violence increases viewers' appetites for becoming involved in violence or exposing themselves to violence (APA 1993).

In summary, the research literature over the last three decades has been highly consistent in documenting three major harmful effects associated with exposure to media violence. First, individuals may develop aggressive thoughts, attitudes, and behavior. This is commonly referred to as the *learning or imitation effect*. Second, viewers may become increasingly calloused or hardened toward real-world violence between other individuals. This is typically labeled the *desensitization effect*. Third, individuals may experience short- or long-term fear over becoming a victim of violence. This is usually referred to as the *fear effect*. In the following section, we will address the major theoretical explanations for each of these effects.

Theoretical Models of Media Effects

Learning and Imitation

As we noted earlier, there is general consensus that viewers learn both aggressive attitudes and behaviors from exposure to media violence. From a scientific perspective, that means such relationships can be predicted with strong confidence. It is a separate, but equally important, scientific question to explain the process by which these effects occur. Theoretical models are devised to provide that information.

Social learning theory.   One of the most important models that explains how learning and imitation of violence occur via the media is social learning theory (Bandura 1971). This theory asserts that modes of response are acquired either directly through experience or indirectly through the observation of models, such as those presented in the mass media. Through the observation of mass media models the observer comes to learn which behaviors are "appropriate"— that is, which behaviors will later be rewarded, and which will be punished. Implicit in this approach is the assumption that most human behavior is directed toward attaining some anticipated reward.

Many laboratory studies have demonstrated that children and adults acquire novel behaviors by observing models (Bandura 1965; Bandura, Ross, and Ross 1961, 1963a, 1963b; Berkowitz and Geen 1967; Liebert and Baron 1972). Typically these studies have involved showing children or adults an aggressive model who is either rewarded or punished for aggressive behavior. After watching a model who is positively reinforced for aggression, the observers are more likely to behave in a similar manner. These studies indicate that viewing a model's aggressive behavior disinhibits, or encourages, aggressive behavior.

Research outside the laboratory, primarily field studies, has also supported the social learning model (Comstock and Paik 1991). For example, Huesmann and Eron (1986) suggest that aggression, as a characteristic way of solving problems, is learned at a young age and becomes more impervious to change as the child grows older. In a longitudinal study designed to examine the long-term effects of television violence on aggressive and criminal behavior, Huesmann, Eron, Lefkowitz, and Walder (1984) studied a group of youth over a 22-year period. This study collected data on aggression and television viewing when the subjects were 8, 18, and 30 years old. The researchers found evidence of a longitudinal effect that spanned the entire 22 years. For boys, early television violence viewing at age 8 correlated with self-reported aggression at age 30 and added significantly to the prediction of serious criminal arrests accumulated by age 30. These effects occurred independent of social class, intellectual capability, and parenting variables (Huesmann 1986). Huesmann and Eron (1986) concluded that early exposure to television violence stimulates aggression and that early aggression is a statistical precursor of later criminal behavior. These researchers find a longitudinal relationship between habitual childhood exposure to television violence and adult crime. Their analyses suggest that approximately 10 percent of the variability in later criminal behavior can be attributed to television violence.

A learning approach to explaining mass media effects has gained wide acceptance among media scholars. Most of the research in recent years has centered on particular variables that facilitate the acquisition of aggressive responses through observational learning. A detailed discussion of those "contextual" variables that mediate the influence of aggressive models will be presented later in this chapter.

Priming effects theory.   In the last decade, a new theoretical proposal has emerged that serves to complement the more traditional learning theories' account of the effects of exposure to violent media. Berkowitz (1984) and his colleagues (Berkowitz and Rogers 1986) have proposed that many media effects are immediate, transitory, and relatively short-lived. They have offered an explanation for these effects grounded in cognitive psychology theory (Neisser 1967). In brief, the explanation is that when people witness an event through the media, ideas are "activated" and for a short period of time those ideas prime or evoke other semantically related thoughts. After an idea is activated there is a greater likelihood that it and associated thought elements will come to mind again. This process of thought activation has been termed a "priming effect." Berkowitz suggests, for instance, that aggressive ideas brought on by viewing violence in the mass media can prime other semantically related thoughts. Once these additional thoughts have come to mind they influence aggressive responding in a variety of ways.

Berkowitz's explanation is appealing because it provides a way of unifying several tangents of mass media research by invoking one relatively simple explanation. For example, one of the contextual variables we will examine later is the observer's identification with media characters who commit violence. This theoretical model suggests that viewers who identify with certain actors may be vividly imagining themselves as these characters and thinking of themselves as carrying out the depicted actions. Identification with characters in the mass media should activate high imagery thoughts, and the subsequent priming of these thoughts might influence subsequent behavior. It is as if viewers draw a lesson from what they see: "What happens on the screen might also happen to me if I engage in the same behavior."

Many studies provide evidence that the activation of aggressive ideas through exposure to media violence primes other aggression-related thoughts, which in turn may have important social consequences. For example, a study by Carver et al. (1983) presented participants with a brief film depicting a hostile interaction between a businessman and his secretary; afterward, subjects evaluated an ambiguous person as more hostile than did those who had not seen the film. In another experiment (Berkowitz, Parker, and West; cited in Berkowitz 1973) children who read aggressive comic books were more likely to choose words with aggressive connotations to complete sentences later presented by the experimenters than subjects who had read neutral comics. Other studies have shown that people who have witnessed certain types of violent media (e.g., depictions of sexual violence) are more likely to report they would use violence in interpersonal situations (Malamuth and Check 1981). There is also evidence to suggest that being primed with aggressive thoughts often leads to aggressive acts. Carver et al. (1983) showed that men who were induced to have aggressive thoughts delivered the most intense electric shocks to other men. Other studies (e.g., Worchel 1972) have shown similar results.

Social developmental model. From either the modeling or the cognitive theoretical perspective, media depictions of violence have a high likelihood of being emulated. Issue can be taken with these theories, however, because they are primarily one-directional. Media effects are presumed to arise from the environment and to influence individuals in the audience. There is little attempt to account for audience expectations, more active construal of messages, or the continued interaction of the viewer with the mass media. This one-sided approach leaves many important questions unaddressed. What are the consequences of viewing media violence for future interest in violent media? Or, once the individual has been exposed to media violence, does he or she seek further violence viewing? And finally, how can we explain the fact that some individuals are affected by televised violence differently than others? We can address these questions and many others with a recent theoretical model that emphasizes the reciprocal influence between the viewer, his or her viewing environment, and the type of content he or she views. This model is the developmental theory of media violence proposed by Huesmann (1986).

Huesmann draws upon ideas in social cognition to explain the effects of televised violence, especially the notion that learning the appropriate course of action in a situation involves the retention of behavioral rules or "scripts." In this model, as in social learning theory, behavioral strategies learned through watching violent television are tried in the immediate environment and, if reinforced, are retained and used again. The most important contribution of the social developmental model proposed by Huesmann, however, is the explication of personal and interpersonal factors that intervene and link violence viewing and aggressive behavior.

Past empirical research indicates that five variables are particularly important in maintaining the television viewing–aggression relationship (Huesmann 1986). These key factors are the child's (1) intellectual achievement, (2) social popularity, (3) identification with the television characters, (4) belief in the realism of the violence shown on television, and (5) amount of fantasizing about aggression. According to Huesmann, a heavy diet of television violence sets into motion a sequence of processes, based on these personal and interpersonal factors, that result in many viewers becoming not only more aggressive but also developing increased interest in seeing more television violence.

Research suggests that children who have poorer academic skills behave more aggressively. They also watch television with greater frequency, watch more violent programs, and believe violent programs are more accurate portrayals of real life (Huesmann and Eron 1986). Huesmann speculates that aggressiveness interferes with the social interactions between the viewer and his/her teachers and peers that are needed in order to develop academic potential. Slow intellectual achievement may therefore be related to heightened television violence viewing in two ways. First, heightened television viewing in general may interfere with intellectual achievement (Lefkowitz, Eron, Walder, and Huesmann 1977). It may also be that children who cannot obtain gratification from success in school turn to television shows to obtain vicariously the successes they cannot otherwise achieve. Aggressive children may also be substantially less popular with their peers (Huesmann and Eron 1986). Longitudinal analyses suggest, however, that the relationship between unpopularity and aggression is bidirectional. Not only do more aggressive children become less popular, but less popular children seem to become more aggressive. In addition, less popular children view more television and therefore see more violence on television.

Identification with television characters may also be important. Children who perceive themselves as similar to television characters are more likely to be influenced by the aggressive scripts they observe (Huesmann, Lagerspetz, and Eron 1984). This may be particularly true for boys. At the same time, more aggressive children tend to identify with aggressive characters, and those who identify more with television characters behave more aggressively.

For an aggressive behavioral script to be encoded in memory and maintained, it must be salient to a child. Huesmann speculates that realistic depictions are the most salient depictions. If a violent action is perceived as totally unrealistic, it is likely to receive less attention than material that is more directly pertinent to the viewer. Early investigations of televised violence have emphasized perceived reality as a determinant of imitative effects (e.g., Feshbach 1972). Later investigations by Huesmann and his colleagues have confirmed that the relation between violence viewing and aggression is heightened for children who believe the violence is representative of real life (Huesmann et al. 1984).

Finally, the maintenance of aggressive scripts might be accomplished through the rehearsal of these scripts in the child's mind, which is facilitated by continued exposure to media violence. Research has shown that children's self-reports of violent fantasies are positively correlated with both aggression and greater television viewing (Huesmann and Eron 1986).

Desensitization

Over the years, research on affective reactions to violent messages has been concerned with the possibility that continued exposure to violence in the mass media will undermine feelings of concern, empathy, or sympathy viewers might have toward victims of actual violence. The early research on desensitization to media violence involved exposure to rather mild forms of television violence for relatively short periods of time (Cline, Croft, and Courrier 1973; Thomas 1982; Thomas et al. 1977). These studies indicated that heavy viewers of media violence showed less physiological reactivity to violent film clips compared to light viewers; that general physiological arousal decreases as viewers watched more violent media; and that children as well as adults are susceptible to this effect.

Research on longer-term exposure and more graphic forms of violence has shown further desensitization effects. For example, Linz, Donnerstein, and Penrod (1984, 1987) measured the reactions of college-age men to films portraying violence against women (mostly in a sexual context) viewed across a five-day period. Comparisons of first- and last-day reactions to the films showed that, with repeated exposure, initial levels of self-reported anxiety decreased substantially. Furthermore, subjects' perceptions of the films also changed from the first day to the last day. Material that was previously judged to be violent and degrading to women was seen as significantly less so by the end of the exposure period. Subjects also indicated that they were less depressed and that they enjoyed the material more with repeated exposure. Most importantly, these effects generalized to a victim of sexual assault presented in a videotaped reenactment of a rape trial. Subjects who were exposed to the violent films rated the victim as less severely injured compared to a no-exposure control group. In a similar study (Linz, Donnerstein, and Penrod 1988), subjects were also less sympathetic to the rape victim portrayed in the trial and less able to empathize with rape victims in general, compared to no-exposure control subjects and to subjects who viewed nonviolent films.

Linz et al. (1984, 1988) suggested that the viewers in these studies become increasingly comfortable, or desensitized, to what are initially anxiety-provoking situations. Further, it was suggested that self-awareness of reductions in anxiety and emotional arousal may be instrumental in the formation of new perceptions and attitudes about the violence portrayed in the films. These views may then be carried over to other contexts. This position is similar to that offered in the behavioral treatment of pathological fears from exposure therapy.

In therapy, simply exposing a patient to the situations or objects he or she is frightened of diminishes the anxiety or negative affect that was once evoked by the problem stimulus. Foa and Kozak (1986) have speculated that a patient's perception of his or her own habituation in the presence of a feared stimulus plays an important role in helping the patient become comfortable with that stimulus. Self-awareness of reduced anxiety may provide the patient with information that helps to facilitate a reduction in fear. That awareness might also facilitate changes in the negative valence associated with the feared stimulus. Patients may then begin to evaluate the "badness" of the feared stimuli in a less exaggerated manner.

Similar processes may operate when subjects are exposed repeatedly to graphic media violence. Once viewers are emotionally "comfortable" with the violent content of the films, they may also evaluate the film more favorably in other domains. Material originally believed to be offensive or degrading to the victims of violence may be evaluated as less so with continued exposure. A reduction in the level of anxiety may also blunt viewers' awareness of the frequency and intensity of violence in the films. Reductions in anxiety may serve to decrease sensitivity to emotional cues associated with each violent episode and thereby reduce viewers' perceptions of the amount of violence in the films. Consequently, by the end of an extensive exposure period, viewers may perceive aggressive films as less violent than they did initially. These altered perceptual and affective reactions may then be carried over into judgments made about victims of violence in other more realistic settings.

Fear

The viewing of media violence can lead to fear reactions such as a general fear of crime or victimization that are quite stable over time. There can also be more transitory reactions such as immediate emotional fright when viewing graphic terror. These effects can occur in both children and adults.

One concept that accounts for the more stable, long-term reactions can be grouped under the rubric of "media cultivation effects." Initially developed by George Gerbner (e.g., Gerbner 1969; Gerbner and Gross 1976; Gerbner, Gross, Morgan, and Signorielli 1994), cultivation theory presumes that extensive, cumulative television exposure shapes viewers' perceptions of social reality. The assumption is that individuals develop beliefs about the "real world" from observing the world of television. Researchers have suggested that people store media information automatically (Shapiro 1991) and subsequently utilize it to formulate their perceptions and beliefs about the world (Harris 1994). As Tan (1986) notes, this influence on people's conceptions of social reality may be one of the most important mass media effects.

The media, and in particular television, communicate facts, norms, and values about our social world. For many people television is the main source of information about critical aspects of their social environment. Learning about violence in the news and in fictional programming may lead to the belief that the world is generally a scary and dangerous place. Gerbner and colleagues have presented elaborate evidence that heavy viewers of television believe the world they live in is more violent and unsafe than do light viewers. For example, heavy viewers evidence greater fear of walking alone at night; greater estimations of the prevalence of violence; and greater overall fear of crime (Gerbner and Gross 1976). These results indicate that the media can cultivate fear, and this effect has been found with both children and adult viewers.

While most of the research on cultivation has been correlational in nature, there is also experimental evidence to support the effect. For example, Bryant, Carveth, and Brown (1981) demonstrated that the cultivation effect could be obtained in an experimental situation, even within a short period of time. Subjects in this study were assigned to a six-week television diet of either light or heavy viewing, but with an added twist. Those who were assigned to the heavy viewing condition were divided into two groups: one that saw only justified violence in which the "good guys" won, and the other that saw only unjustified violence in which the "bad guys" got away with their violence. Results indicated that subjects in the heavy viewing/unjustified condition showed the highest increases in anxiety and perceived likelihood of being a victim of crime, in comparison to the other groups. This study suggests that the viewing of media violence can have short- as well as long-term influence on fear reactions.

We should note that cultivation theory has been criticized on both methodological and conceptual grounds (Hirsch 1980, 1981a, 1981b; Newcomb 1978; Potter 1993; Rubin, Perse, and Taylor 1988). Some argue that the theory is simplistic and that a number of mediating factors influence cultivation (Wilson 1995). For example, factors such as experience with crime, motivations for viewing television, and overall cognitive ability seem to be important factors influencing the cultivation effect. Comstock and Paik (1991) note that the effects might not be cumulative at all as suggested by cultivation theory. Instead, they suggest:

> Exposure to violent television stimuli may simply activate or heighten the likelihood of recall of thoughts of a more pessimistic nature. Frequency of exposure in this instance may not be a measure of the history of viewing but the likelihood of recent exposure to violence or distressing events in entertainment, news, or other programming. (185–86)

From another perspective, Gunter (1994) notes that the cultivation effect may be program-specific rather than the result of total television viewing. Specific programs, such as crime-related shows, would be most influential in affecting perceptions of crime. In addition, the effects may be due to how viewers perceive and interpret the content, particularly if they view the program as being more realistic (Potter 1986). Individuals may also selectively attend to programs that reinforce their perception of the world (Gunter 1994).

In a recent overview of cultivation theory, Gerbner and his colleagues address some of these concerns:

> The elements of cultivation do not originate with television or appear out of a void. Layers of social, personal, and cultural contexts also determine the shape, scope, and degree of the contribution television is likely to make. Yet, the meaning of those contexts and factors are in themselves aspects of the cultivation process. That is, although a viewer's gender, or age, or class makes a difference in perspective, television viewing can make a similar and interacting difference. The interaction is a continuous process (as is cultivation) beginning with infancy and going on from cradle to grave. (Gerbner, Gross, Morgan, and Signorielli 1994, 23)

For cultivation theory, television viewing is a lifelong process. Whether television shapes or merely maintains beliefs about the world is not as important as its role in a dynamic process that leads to enduring and stable assumptions about the world, particularly violence.

For children, however, some fear effects may be more specific and urgent. Fright reactions to violent forms of media can be immediate and dramatic, and quite specific to particular content. Child viewers may scream or hide their faces in their hands. Later, nightmares and recurring thoughts may keep both child and parent awake at night (Wilson and Cantor 1985). There is a growing body of evidence that both younger and older children can experience strong emotional reactions, including fear responses, from viewing media depictions of crime, violence, physical injury, or danger (Cantor 1994; Cantor and Wilson 1988; Wilson 1995; Wilson and Smith 1995).

Most research on children's emotional reactions emphasizes immediate impacts, although some evidence suggests that the effects of viewing scary or frightening media can last several days or weeks (Cantor 1994). While most of these longer-lasting effects may be relatively mild, they may sometimes be acute and disabling, like severe anxiety states, lasting up to several weeks (Mathai 1983). As Cantor (1994) notes, transitory fright reactions occur in a large proportion of children, with more enduring reactions affecting an "appreciable" minority of viewers.

To account for these fear reactions, it appears that a stimulus generalization process is operating. Although the viewer is in no "real" danger from viewing a violent media depiction, the reaction is fundamentally the same (although less intense) as if the experience had been encountered in the real world.

Overall, fear reactions to violent portrayals are experienced by both children and adults, and they occur as a function of both immediate exposure as well as the accumulation of viewing over time.

Summary: Three Harmful Effects

In sum, the goal of this section was to review theory and research on the negative effects of exposure to media violence. Specifically, we illustrated that learning aggressive thoughts and behaviors, emotional desensitization, and fear are three harmful effects that have been documented across a variety of empirical investigations using a myriad of methodological approaches. In the following section, however, we shift our focus and begin to examine the specific contextual features of violent portrayals that increase or decrease the risk of one of the aforementioned harmful effects.

The Importance of Context

The research reviewed above indicates that television violence can have at least three types of harmful effects on viewers and that different types of content are capable of producing such effects. However, not all violent portrayals are equal with regard to the risk they might pose. Consider, for example, a documentary about gangs that contains scenes of violence in order to inform audiences about this societal problem. The overall message about violence in such a program is likely to be quite different from that of an action-adventure movie featuring a violent hero. The documentary actually may discourage aggression whereas the action-adventure movie may seem to glamorize it. A comparison of a film like *Schindler's List* about the Holocaust with a film like *The Terminator* illustrates this difference.

Such a contrast underscores the importance of considering the context within which violence is portrayed. Indeed, the television industry itself has long recognized that violence can have different meanings depending upon how it is presented within a program. In a recent policy statement, the National Cable Television Association stipulated that:

> . . . the gratuitous use of violence depicted as an easy and convenient solution to human problems is harmful to our industry and to society. We therefore discourage and will strive to reduce the frequency of such exploitative uses of violence while preserving our right to show programs that convey the real meaning and consequences of violent behavior. (1993, 1)

Similarly, the Network Television Association (1992) issued standards for the depiction of violence that warn against showing, among other things, "callousness or indifference to suffering," "scenes where children are victims," and "portrayals of the use of weapons or implements readily accessible" to children. Most of these programming guidelines focus on contextual cues and the different ways that violence can be portrayed.

The significance of context is highlighted not only by television industry guidelines, but also by academic research. Most of the major theoretical perspectives discussed in the previous section recognize explicitly that contextual cues influence audience reactions to a media portrayal. Bandura's social learning theory, in particular its most recent revisions (Bandura 1986), postulates that a viewer's interpretation of a message mediates imitation and learning. Such interpretations are in part a function of contextual cues like the type of model who engages in violence and the consequences delivered to that model. Berkowitz's priming theory focuses on how specific features of a violent portrayal, such as the type of perpetrator involved, can instigate aggressive thoughts and memories in a viewer.

In addition to theoretical support, several major reviews of social science research demonstrate that some depictions are more likely than others to pose risks for viewers (Comstock and Paik 1991; Gunter 1994; Wilson, Linz, and Randall 1990). For example, Comstock and Paik (1991) examined much of the experimental literature and concluded that three dimensions of a portrayal are important in predicting whether a program is likely to facilitate aggression among viewers: (1) how efficacious or successful the violence is, (2) how normative or justified the violence appears, and (3) how pertinent the violence is to the viewer.

Although such dimensions are useful summary devices, they are too broad to form the basis of a classification scheme that can be used consistently and accurately in a content analysis. Moreover, the dimensions are tied to only one outcome—the learning of aggressive attitudes and behaviors. Unfortunately, most previous reviews of the literature (e.g., Comstock and Paik 1991; Gunter 1994) have paid virtually no attention to how context might influence outcomes such as audience fear and desensitization.

Thus, prior to developing our content coding scheme for the NTVS project, we conducted our own careful and exhaustive search of the social science research. Our goal was threefold: (1) to update previous reviews of the social science research literature, (2) to identify specific features rather than broad dimensions of a violent portrayal that have been consistently documented to influence viewers, and (3) to focus not only on how context influences the learning of aggression but also on how it affects fear and desensitization.

Our search concentrated primarily on experimental studies that manipulated some contextual feature in a violent portrayal and then assessed one of the three outcomes of interest here: subjects' learning of aggression, fear, or desensitization. Although we included correlational and longitudinal evidence in building our framework, we focused most closely on experiments because of their high internal validity and control. With the experimental methodology, we could be most confident in drawing conclusions about the causal effect of a specific context factor. In addition, we scrutinized how each context factor was operationalized or measured in the experiments because these specifications formed the basis for how we defined context in our coding scheme.

Our literature search included books, technical reports, conference papers, journal articles, dissertations, and review pieces. We included studies of adults as well as children. In all, our data base contains over 80 experiments, several review chapters on media violence, and a few metanalyses of the experimental work. As mentioned above, we also relied on several correlational studies to support the experimental evidence. In the next section, we present the context factors that emerged from our review.

Set of Contextual Factors

Our comprehensive review revealed nine contextual factors that influence audience reactions to violent portrayals: (1) the nature of the perpetrator, (2) the nature of the target, (3) the reason for the violence, (4) the presence of weapons, (5) the extent and graphicness of the violence, (6) the degree of realism of the violence, (7) whether the violence is rewarded or punished, (8) the consequences of violence, and (9) whether humor is involved in violence. The research findings regarding each factor are discussed below, with an indication whether a given contextual feature affects learning of aggression, desensitiza-

TABLE 2.1.   Predicted Impact of Contextual Factors on Three Outcomes of Exposure to Media Violence

Contextual Factors	Outcomes of Media Violence		
	Learning Aggression	Fear	Desensitization
Attractive perpetrator	+		
Attractive target		+	
Justified violence	+		
Unjustified violence	−	+	
Presence of weapons	+		
Extensive/graphic violence	+	+	+
Realistic violence	+	+	
Rewards	+	+	
Punishments	−	−	
Pain/harm cues	−		
Humor	+		+

Note: Predicted effects are based on review of social science research on contextual features of violence. Blank spaces are used to indicate that there is inadequate research to make a prediction.
+ = likely to *increase* the outcome
− = likely to *decrease* the outcome

tion, and/or fear, and if so, how. Although some of the factors increase the probability that a violent portrayal will pose risks to viewers, other factors decrease that probability. A summary of these relationships is presented in table 2.1.

Before examining each context factor individually, three overall observations from our literature review should be noted. First, most of the experimental studies have focused on imitation or learning of aggression as the outcome variable. Only a few have used fear or desensitization as the outcome. Thus, we know much more about what types of contextual features pose risks for the learning of aggression than we do about what types facilitate fear or desensitization. Table 2.1 illustrates these gaps in our knowledge.

The second overall observation is that there is a great deal of overlap in the findings regarding adult viewers and child viewers. In other words, the same types of contextual cues that influence older viewers also influence younger viewers. This congruence will be illustrated in the review below.

Third, although the types of factors that affect older and younger viewers are the same, the ways in which these contextual cues operate sometimes differ across age. In particular, several of the contextual cues are interpreted differently by younger children than by older children and adults, resulting in slightly different predicted effects. These developmental differences will be considered later in this chapter.

In the following discussion, we will focus on what we know about each factor rather than what we do not know. Consequently, if fear and/or desensitization are not mentioned in the discussion of a particular factor, then it can be assumed that there is no *controlled* research relevant to this potential outcome, as indicated in table 2.1.

Nature of Perpetrator

When a violent event occurs in a program, typically there is a character or group of characters who can be identified as the perpetrator. The meaning of the violence is closely connected to the characteristics of the perpetrator. For example, viewers are likely to interpret a gunshot from the star of a popular police series differently than a gunshot from a criminal. Indeed, characters are integral to the plot of any program and viewers form strong evaluations of the things that characters do or say in a scene (Hoffner and Cantor 1991). Character evaluations have important implications for how a viewer ultimately will respond to a particular portrayal. Research indicates that both children and adults are more likely to attend to and learn from models who are perceived as attractive (Bandura 1986, 1994). Thus, a perpetrator of violence who is attractive or engaging is likely to be a more potent role model for viewers than is a neutral or unattractive character.

What types of characters are perceived as attractive in entertainment programming? Studies suggest that viewers assign more positive ratings to characters who act prosocially or helpfully than to characters who are cruel (Hoffner and Cantor 1985; Zillmann and Cantor 1977). Moreover, children as young as 4 years of age can distinguish between prototypically good and bad characters in a television program (Berndt and Berndt 1975; Liss, Reinhardt, and Fredriksen 1983).

One exaggerated form of a good character is the superhero who engages in violent means in order to battle evil. Wonder Woman, the Power Rangers, Superman, and the Ninja Turtles are just a few examples of this popular type of protagonist. Liss et al. (1983) found that children who were exposed to a cartoon featuring a violent superhero subsequently were more likely to act aggressively than were those who watched a violent cartoon without a superhero. Interestingly, even adults are susceptible to hero influence. In one experiment (Perry and Perry 1976), male undergraduates who were encouraged to identify with the victor of a filmed prize fight were subsequently more aggressive than those encouraged to imagine themselves as the loser in the film. Other studies also have documented that identification with the hero in a violent portrayal increases aggressive behavior among adult viewers (Leyens and Picus 1973; Turner and Berkowitz 1972).

In addition to heroes, viewers also are attracted to characters who are perceived as similar to themselves. Perceived similarity to a character can be a function of shared demographic characteristics such as sex and age (Jose and Brewer

1984). For example, boys are more likely to attend to and imitate male perpetrators, whereas girls respond more strongly to female characters (Bandura 1986; Bandura, Ross, and Ross 1963a). Furthermore, children are more likely to engage in aggression after watching a violent child character than a violent adult character (Hicks 1965). However, any type of cue in a portrayal that is pertinent to the viewer's own circumstances can prompt aggressive behavior among both children and adults (Berkowitz and Geen 1966, 1967; Geen and Berkowitz 1966; Josephson 1987).

To summarize, the nature of the perpetrator is an important consideration in terms of imitation and learning. Consistent with this assertion, a recent met-analysis of 217 experimental studies found that violent programs have a stronger effect on viewer aggression when they feature perpetrators with whom audiences can identify (Paik and Comstock 1994). Viewers certainly rely on a multitude of cues in determining who is attractive or likable in a program. To date, research has documented that perpetrators who are benevolent, heroic, or demographically similar to the viewer are potent role models in entertainment programming.

Nature of Target

Just as the nature of the perpetrator is an important contextual feature of violence, so is the nature of the target. Once again, viewers are more likely to react strongly to a target who is perceived as likable or attractive. Consider a scene in which a likable star of a detective series is about to be shot. Exchanging the popular detective with a malicious criminal illustrates the importance of the target in terms of audience reactions.

Interestingly, the nature of the target is most likely to influence audience fear rather than learning. Research indicates that viewers feel concern for characters who are perceived as attractive and often share such characters' emotional experiences (Zillmann 1980, 1991). This type of empathic responding has been found with characters who are benevolent or heroic (Comisky and Bryant 1982; Zillmann and Cantor 1977), as well as characters who are perceived to be similar to the viewer (Feshbach and Roe 1968; Tannenbaum and Gaer 1965). Thus, a well-liked character can encourage audience involvement. When such a character is threatened or attacked in a violent scene, viewers are likely to experience increased anxiety and fear.

Reason for Violence

How we interpret an act of violence is dependent to a great extent on a character's motives or reasons for engaging in such behavior (Gunter 1985; Hoffner and Cantor 1991). For example, a father may shoot someone who is trying to kidnap his child. Certain motives such as self-defense and defense of a loved one seem justified, and viewers may even cheer when the character kills the kidnapper. In contrast, a character who shoots a bank teller for not getting the money out of a drawer fast enough is likely to be judged as malicious and not receive much sympathy from a viewer.

Research suggests that motives also can influence a viewer's tendency to learn or imitate aggression. In a series of studies by Berkowitz and others (e.g., Berkowitz and Geen 1967; Berkowitz and Powers 1979), adult subjects were given different descriptions about a perpetrator and target prior to viewing the same violent scene. Those in the justified violence conditions typically were told that a sympathetic perpetrator had been previously harmed or wronged and now is retaliating. In the unjustified violence condition, the perpetrator was cast as someone who attacks innocent people out of hate or greed. The results consistently showed that angered subjects who viewed a film scene portraying violence as justified subsequently behaved more aggressively than did those who viewed less justified violence (Berkowitz and Geen 1967; Berkowitz and Powers 1979; Berkowitz and Rawlings 1963; Geen and Stonner 1973, 1974; Hoyt 1970). Moreover, exposure to unjustified violence actually *reduced* aggressive tendencies compared to a control group receiving no information about the motive (Berkowitz and Powers 1979; Geen 1981).

The impact of justification has been documented with fictional as well as more realistic programming (Meyer 1972), and with adult as well as child viewers (Liss et al. 1983). In fact, a recent metanalysis of 217 media studies documents that a justified portrayal of violence can enhance aggressive behavior among viewers (Paik and Comstock 1994).

Based on this research, we can infer that television violence that is motivated by protection or retaliation, to the extent that it appears to be justified, should facilitate viewer aggression. Researchers have speculated that when violence is portrayed as morally proper or somehow beneficial, it lowers a viewer's inhibitions against aggression (Jo and Berkowitz 1994). The prototypical "justified" scenario is the hero who employs violence to protect society against villainous characters. In contrast, violence that is undeserved or purely malicious should decrease the risk of audience imitation or learning of aggression.

Does the reason or motive for violence have other effects on the audience? It seems reasonable to assume that viewers are more likely to be frightened by television violence that is undeserved or targeted against innocent victims. Such portrayals may make the audience feel more personally vulnerable. One study provides some indirect evidence for this idea (Bryant et al. 1981). In this experiment, adult subjects who viewed action-adventure shows featuring unjust violence were more anxious than were those who viewed violent programs emphasizing justice. The primary difference between these depictions centered on whether violence was punished in the end, but criminals who go unpunished may appear even more unjust in their motives, particularly if they have gotten away with violence against innocent victims. Clearly, further research is needed here but we can tentatively conclude that unjustified violence is likely to be more scary than violence that is socially sanctioned or somehow altruistic.

Presence of Weapons

A variety of methods and tools can be used to enact violence against a target on television. A perpetrator can use natural means such as punching with a fist or slapping with a hand. Alternatively, a perpetrator can use a weapon like a gun or a knife or a more unconventional tool like a frying pan or a chain saw. Berkowitz (1984, 1990) has argued that certain visual cues in a film can activate or "prime" aggressive thoughts and behaviors in a viewer, and that weapons can function as such cues.

In support of this idea, a recent metanalysis of 56 published experiments found that the presence of weapons, either pictorially or in the natural environment, significantly enhanced aggression among angered as well as nonangered subjects (Carlson, Marcus-Newhall, and Miller 1990). In particular, studies have found that exposure to slides or pictures of weapons significantly increased aggressive behavior in male and female adults (Leyens and Parke 1974; Page and O'Neal 1977). Similarly, the mere presence of actual firearms in a naturalistic environment can enhance aggression among adults in controlled studies (Berkowitz and LePage 1967; Turner, Layton, and Simons 1975).

Presumably for ethical reasons, no studies have been done on the impact of weapon cues on young children. However, one experiment found that adolescents became more aggressive against a target when in the presence of weapons than in the presence of neutral stimuli (Frodi 1975). It seems reasonable to assume that conventional weapons can prompt the same types of aggressive tendencies in younger viewers.

According to Berkowitz (1990) and others (e.g., Leyens and Parke 1974), weapons like guns and knives are more likely than unconventional means to instigate or prime aggression in viewers because they are commonly associated with previous violent events stored in memory. Thus, a television portrayal that features traditional weapons poses the greatest risk for the so-called weapons effect on audiences.

Extent and Graphicness of Violence

Television programs and especially movies vary widely in the extent and graphicness of the violence they contain. A violent interaction between a perpetrator and a target can last only a few seconds and be shot from a distance or it can persist for several minutes and involve many close-ups on the action. The media industry recognizes this difference when it provides ratings and advisories for certain programs. As an illustration, the Motion Picture Association of America's film rating system assigns an R rating to a movie when violence is "rough" or "persistent," whereas PG is used when the violence is not "strong" or "cumulative" (Valenti 1987). When other countries such as Great Britain import American movies, they often cut or edit out violence that is considered too extensive or graphic (Gray and Barry 1994).

Research suggests that audiences can be influenced by the extent and explicitness of violent portrayals. Most attention has been devoted to the impact of extensive or repeated violence on viewer desensitization. For example, several early studies on adults showed that physiological arousal to prolonged scenes of brutality steadily declines over time during exposure to a 17-minute film (Lazarus and Alfert 1964; Lazarus, Speisman, Mordkoff, and Davison 1962; Speisman, Lazarus, Mordkoff, and Davison 1964). Moreover, even children have been shown to exhibit such physiological desensitization over time during exposure to a violent film, with the decrement being strongest for those who were heavy viewers of television violence (Cline, Croft, and Courrier 1973).

More recently, studies have examined what happens when subjects are exposed to extensive media violence over several viewing sessions. In a study by Linz, Donnerstein, and Penrod (1988), male undergraduates were exposed to five full-length "slasher" movies (e.g., *Friday the 13th, Part 2; Texas Chainsaw Massacre*) over a period of two weeks. After each film, emotional reactions, perceptions of violence in the films, and attitudes toward female victims in the films were measured. The results revealed that subjects perceived less violence in the films and evaluated the films as less degrading to women after repeated exposure. A subsequent study replicated these findings. Subjects who were shown three slasher films across a five-day period exhibited a progressive decrease in arousal and in sensitivity to the violence in the films across the exposure period (Mullin and Linz 1995). Thus, exposure to extensive violence, either within a single program or across several programs, produces decreased arousal and sensitivity to violence in both children and adults. This is the desensitization effect.

Does extensive or repeated violence influence the other two effects of concern, the learning of aggression and fear? Only one experiment could be found that actually varied the *amount* of exposure to television violence and then measured aggression (Parke et al. 1977). Adolescent juvenile delinquents residing in minimum security institutions were exposed either to five full-length violent films, five neutral films, a single violent film, or a single neutral film. Contrary to expectations, multiple exposures to filmed violence resulted in *less* aggressive behavior than did the single exposure. However, the researchers noted that this unexpected effect was likely due to a substantial difference between the two groups in initial aggressiveness, and thus little information can be gleaned from this study.

Although not experimental, other evidence suggests that exposure to extensive violence in the media should actually promote the learning of aggression. Huesmann and his colleagues have conducted several longitudinal surveys demonstrating that the more television violence children watch in a given year, the more likely they are to behave aggressively in subsequent years (Huesmann 1986; Huesmann et al. 1984). Furthermore, Huesmann's developmental model, social learning theory, and Berkowitz's cognitive script theory all predict that heavy exposure to a variety of violent models and behaviors on television will foster the development of well-established scripts and routines for responding aggressively.

The impact of extent and graphicness of violence on fear, however, is less obvious. One could argue that prolonged exposure to explicit scenes of violence will enhance fright reactions among viewers. Alternatively, if the images are constant and repeated within a program, a viewer could become desensitized and feel *less* upset over time. An experiment by Ogles and Hoffner (1987) suggests that extensive exposure to violence promotes rather than diminishes fear. Male undergraduates were randomly assigned to view five slasher films (e.g., *Toolbox Murders, Maniac*) over a two-week period or two slasher films within a one-week period. Subjects in the extended exposure condition perceived significantly more crime in the real world and felt personally more vulnerable to it, and these perceptions correlated with feelings of fear. These findings taken together with the research reviewed earlier on cultivation effects indicate that viewing extensive violence is likely to be frightening.

Clearly, more research on extent and graphicness is needed, with special attention to the conditions under which fear versus emotional blunting is most likely to occur. For example, are viewers more likely to desensitize if the violent images are redundant rather than constantly changing? Is desensitization more likely if violence is continual and uninterrupted rather than sporadic or interspersed throughout a program? Finally, how long does desensitization persist compared to fear? One recent study suggests that habituation is a relatively short-term effect and that viewers' sensitivity and arousal to violence may rebound fairly quickly (Mullin and Linz 1995). These questions warrant further examination.

Realism of Violence

Another important attribute or contextual factor concerns the degree of realism associated with a violent portrayal. Public reaction to televised images of the Rodney King beatings and the more recent bombing of a federal building in Oklahoma illustrates that realistic scenes of violence can have a significant impact on viewers. But violence in a fictional context also can be differentiated in terms of degrees of realism. Indeed, movies like *The Silence of the Lambs* and

Goodfellas seem to cause more concern about violence in our culture than do movies like *Star Wars* (Plagens et al. 1991), largely because of this factor.

Such public concern is supported by research findings. Several studies indicate that realistic portrayals of violence can pose more risks for viewers than unrealistic ones. For example, Berkowitz and Alioto (1973) found that exposure to a war film led to more aggression among adult males when it was described as a documentary than when it was labeled a Hollywood production. Subsequent studies showed that a film of a campus fistfight that was introduced as something that actually happened led to greater aggression among college-aged males than did the same fight when it was described as staged (Geen 1975; Thomas and Tell 1974).

Not only adults but also children seem to respond to the realism of violence. In a study of 6- to 10-year-olds, a television program portraying human violence led to more aggressive behavior than did one showing animated violence (Hapkiewicz and Stone 1974). However, it is difficult to draw firm conclusions from this study because the more "realistic" program in this case was the *Three Stooges* and its violent content presumably varied in many important ways from the *Mighty Mouse* cartoon. In a more controlled study by Feshbach (1972), 9- to 11-year-old children were exposed to the same campus riot footage that was described either as part of a news story or as a Hollywood film. Children who perceived the content to be more realistic subsequently behaved more aggressively. Atkin (1983) obtained similar results when 10- to 13-year-olds viewed the same violent scene presented within an actual newscast as compared to viewing the scene within a movie promo.

All of these studies suggest that realistic violence is a more potent elicitor of aggressive behavior than fictional portrayals. Researchers have hypothesized that viewers can more easily identify with perpetrators who are realistic and that such portrayals may more readily reduce inhibitions against aggression because they are so applicable to real-life situations (Atkin 1983; Jo and Berkowitz 1994).

The realism of a portrayal also can influence viewers' fear reactions to violence. In one early study, Lazarus, Opton, Nomikos, and Rankin (1965) found that adults were less physiologically aroused to a movie showing gory accidents when the events had been introduced as fake compared to no such introduction. Subsequent studies have demonstrated that adults are far more emotionally aroused by violent scenes that are perceived to have actually happened than if the same scenes are believed to be fictional (Geen 1975; Geen and Rakosky 1973).

Children also can be frightened by realistic depictions. In one experiment, children who thought that a threatening creature depicted in a movie actually existed in their city were more frightened by the scene than were those who did not believe the creature was a realistic threat (Cantor and Hoffner 1990). Additionally, several surveys have shown that programs that depict events that could possibly happen in real life are more frightening to older children than are programs featuring clearly fantastic events (Cantor and Sparks 1984; Sparks 1986).

To summarize, the research reviewed here suggests that more realistic portrayals of violence can foster the learning of aggressive attitudes and behaviors among children as well as adults. Realistic depictions of brutality also can elevate viewers' fear responses. Based on this contextual factor, one might expect that cartoon or fantasy violence on television is relatively harmless. After all, such depictions obviously are not very authentic. However, research on very young children cautions against such a conclusion. In fact, what seems unrealistic to adults and older children may appear to be quite real to a younger child. We will shortly turn our focus to the topic of developmental differences in how children understand television. Some of our contextual factors take on special consideration when the audience is composed primarily of younger children.

Rewards and Punishments

A critical feature of any violent portrayal concerns whether the aggressive behavior is reinforced or rewarded. Violent characters on television can be rewarded in several ways—they may obtain money or property, they may acquire power, or they may win the admiration of others. They may even exhibit self-reinforcement by feeling proud or exhilarated after an aggressive act. Several previous content analyses of television suggest that much of the violence in entertainment programming involves characters who are rewarded or successful (Potter and Ware 1987; Williams, Zabrack, and Joy 1982).

According to social learning theory, observers are more likely to learn a behavior that is rewarded than one that is punished (Bandura 1986). In a series of famous Bobo doll studies (e.g., Bandura 1965; Bandura, Ross, and Ross 1961, 1963b), Bandura consistently found that children exposed to an aggressive film model who was rewarded were significantly more likely to behave aggressively than were children exposed to an aggressive model who was punished. In most of this research, toys, cookies, and/or adult approval were used as rewards in the films, whereas the removal of toys, spanking, and/or adult disapproval were used as punishments. Other studies have documented similar effects for rewards and punishments on children's imitative behavior (Rosekrans and Hartup 1967; Walters and Parke 1964; Walters, Parke, and Cane 1965).

Media violence need not be explicitly rewarded or punished, however, in order to have an impact on learning. Research indicates children will imitate a model's antisocial behavior so long as there is no explicit punishment delivered to the model, presumably because the lack of punishment actually serves as a sanction for such behavior (Bandura 1965; Walters and Parke 1964). Thus, the absence of punishment for violence seems to be a sufficient condition for fostering imitation, generating essentially the same effect as when violence is rewarded.

Reinforcements not only influence children but also adults. In one experiment, Lando and Donnerstein (1978) found that exposure to violence that was portrayed as "successful" significantly increased aggressive behavior among undergraduates, whereas exposure to unsuccessful violence actually decreased aggression. More recently, Paik and Comstock's (1994) metanalysis provides evidence for the idea that rewarded violence facilitates aggression among both child and adult viewers.

In general, rewarded violence or violence that is not overtly punished fosters the learning of aggressive attitudes and behavior among viewers. In contrast, portrayals of punished violence can serve to inhibit or reduce the learning of aggression. Can such reinforcements affect other audience responses besides aggression? One experimental study mentioned previously examined the impact of rewards and punishments on fear. Bryant, Carveth, and Brown (1981) exposed adults to six weeks of action-adventure programs that depicted either just endings in which violence was punished or unjust endings where violence went unpunished. Subjects who viewed violence that went unpunished were significantly more anxious and more pessimistic about the consequences of real-life violence than were those who saw the just endings. Thus, programs that punish criminals who are violent and that ultimately restore justice can decrease viewer aggression as well as viewer fear.

Consequences of Violence

Another important contextual feature of media violence concerns whether the consequences of aggressive actions are depicted. Gerbner (1992) has criticized television for displaying a predominance of what he calls "happy violence," or portrayals that do not show any pain or tragic consequences to the victims and their loved ones. Indeed, several studies suggest that viewers interpret violent scenes with observable harm and pain as more serious and more violent than scenes showing no such consequences (Gunter 1983, 1985).

Cries of pain and other signs of suffering can affect not only interpretations but also imitation of aggression. Numerous experiments have found that adults who are exposed to overt, intense pain cues from a victim subsequently behave less aggressively than do those who see no such pain cues (Baron 1971a, 1971b; Goransen 1969; Sanders and Baron 1975; Schmutte and Taylor 1980). The assumption is that pain cues inhibit aggression by eliciting sympathy and reminding the viewer of social norms against violence. Children also have been shown to be influenced by the consequences of violence. In one experiment, boys who viewed a violent film clip that showed explicit injuries and blood subsequently were less aggressive than were those who saw a violent clip with no such consequences (Wotring and Greenberg 1973).

It should be noted that a few studies actually have found that pain cues can sometimes enhance or facilitate aggression (Baron 1979; Dubanoski and Kong 1977; Swart and Berkowitz 1976). However, such effects have been restricted to subjects who are highly angered or prone to aggression and are placed in situations where other environmental cues are present to prompt aggressive behavior. Thus, for most viewers the explicit depiction of psychological and physical harm in violent portrayals is likely to inhibit the learning of aggressive attitudes and behaviors.

Humor

Portrayals of violence on television often are cast in a humorous light. Slapstick shows like *The Three Stooges* and cartoons such as *The Road Runner* are obvious examples in which almost every act of violence has a comical tone to it. But even dramatic action-adventure programs can contextualize violence with humor. For example, Dirty Harry challenged criminals to shoot first by saying "Go ahead . . . make my day," and the Terminator offered the infamous "Hasta la vista, baby" before killing an enemy. Indeed, one previous content analysis by Williams, Zabrack, and Joy (1982) found a high incidence of humor in television programs that were violent.

What impact does the addition of humor to a violent scene have on the viewer? Of all the contextual variables that have been examined, we know the least about humor. For one thing, there are many types of humor that can be used in a portrayal. A perpetrator could crack a joke while harming someone, the violent act itself can be shown as farcical, or the target could overreact with pain to a slight injury. Moreover, humor can come in a variety of forms such as sarcasm, a witty remark, a nonverbal gesture, or a funny story. To further complicate the situation, an entire program can be funny or humor can be restricted to violent scenes. Unfortunately, there is no systematic research to date that examines all these various manifestations of humor.

The few studies that have been conducted on humor and aggression offer a mixed set of findings. For instance, Baron and Ball (1974) exposed angered and nonangered subjects either to humorous magazine cartoons or to nonhumorous pictures before allowing them to aggress against a confederate. Results revealed that the humorous material significantly reduced subsequent aggressive behavior among the angered subjects but had no impact on nonangered subjects. In contrast, other studies suggest that humor can sometimes facilitate aggression. Mueller and Donnerstein (1977) found that exposure to highly arousing jokes on an audiotape produced significantly more aggressive behavior among angered subjects than did exposure to milder jokes. A subsequent study revealed similar effects for a humorous movie clip (Mueller and Donnerstein 1983). Taken together, these findings suggest some forms of mild humor are capable of reducing aggression by distracting or creating a positive mood (Berger 1988; Zillmann and Bryant 1991), whereas other more intense forms of humor can instigate aggression because they are arousing.

The key limitation of this research is that it focuses on the impact of humor alone on aggressive behavior, and not the impact of humor in the context of a violent portrayal. What is needed is a controlled study that exposes subjects to the same violent episode with and without humorous overtones. Our literature search revealed no such experiments. However, we found two studies that are closer to the issue at hand because they deal with hostile or aggressive humor rather than more neutral forms of comedy. In one of these studies, undergraduates were first angered or not angered and then listened to a tape recording of either a nonhostile comedian or a hostile comedian (Berkowitz 1970). Results revealed that the hostile humor that included numerous insults to university coeds significantly increased aggressive responses among both angered and nonangered subjects.

In the second study (Baron 1978), subjects were exposed to either 10 still picture cartoons featuring hostile humor, 10 cartoons featuring nonhostile humor, or 10 nonhumorous pictures. Several of the hostile cartoons actually depicted physical violence. For both angered and nonangered subjects, the hostile humor significantly increased electric shocks delivered to a confederate, whereas nonhostile humor decreased such aggression. These two experiments alone provide the strongest evidence that humor combined with violence actually can foster aggression.

Several mechanisms can be used to explain such a facilitative effect of humor on aggression. Humor might elevate a viewer's arousal level over that attained by violence alone, and increased arousal has been shown to facilitate aggression (Zillmann 1979). Humor could serve as a reinforcement or reward for violence, especially if the perpetrator is funny or admired for his or her wit. And humor may diminish the seriousness of the violence and therefore undermine the inhibiting effects of harm and pain cues in a scene (Deckers and Carr 1986). However, we should underscore that our conclusion about the facilitative effect of humor on aggression is tentative until more systematic research on the impact of a violent scene with and without different forms of humor is undertaken.

Some research on audience perceptions of violence suggests that humor also may foster desensitization. Gunter (1985) and Sander (1995) have found that adults actually perceive violent scenes that contain humor to be less aggressive and less brutal than similar scenes without comedic tones. Thus, we tentatively conclude that humor can trivialize violence and its consequences, though clearly further research is needed.

Developmental Differences in the Processing of Television Content

The preceding discussion establishes that both child and adult viewers are influenced by the nine context factors indicated above. Moreover, each factor affects children and adults in the same way or direction. For example, rewarded violence *increases* the likelihood of learning of aggression regardless of the age of the viewer, whereas punished violence *decreases* that risk. Nevertheless, a few special considerations regarding the interpretation of context come into play when considering very young age groups.

Admittedly, many television programs are not designed for young children. In fact, some movies and television series carry parental advisories indicating that the content may be inappropriate for younger age groups. Yet there is no doubt that younger age groups often are in the audience when adult-oriented programs are shown (Condry 1989). Because children view television at all times of the day and because policymakers and parents seem most concerned about the youngest viewers in the audience (Broder 1995; Hundt 1995; Lacayo 1995), we have designed certain aspects of our content analysis to take into account this special age group. In particular, two contextual factors, reality of the violence and the reinforcements associated with violence, pose unique concerns for young viewers.

As children develop, they bring different cognitive skills and different amounts of social experience to the new situations they encounter. Several influential perspectives such as Piaget's (1952, 1960) theory of cognitive development and more recent models of information processing (e.g., Flavell 1985; Siegler 1991) support this idea. Based on their level of development and maturity, younger children can be expected to interpret or make sense of television in a somewhat different way than will their older counterparts. There are no precise age differences associated with these changes because children exhibit substantial variation in how and when they develop various skills. However, most research reveals marked differences between 2- to 6-year-olds and 7- to 12-year-olds both in the strategies that are used to make sense of new information and in the memory limits that constrain the amount of information that can be considered (Kail 1990; Siegler 1991).

For our purposes, we will focus on just two cognitive strategies or skills that are important for television comprehension. The first concerns children's understanding of fantasy and reality. A number of studies have documented developmental differences in the ability to distinguish reality from fantasy or pretending (e.g., Morison and Gardner 1978; Taylor and Howell 1973). For instance, preschoolers have a greater tendency than older children to believe in magical and supernatural creatures (Rosengren, Kalish, Hickling, and Gelman 1994), and they are often swayed by how things appear rather than how things really are (Flavell 1986).

Several researchers have tried to extend these developmental findings to perceptions about television. Studies generally show that children's perceptions about the realism of television portrayals are complex and multidimensional in nature, depending on factors such as the genre or type of program, the production cues, and the social realism or similarity of the content to real life (Potter 1988; Wright, Huston, Reitz, and Piemyat 1994). Regardless of what aspect of reality is measured, however, developmental differences typically are found. In general, younger children judge characters or actions as "real" simply because they have observed their physical presence through television's "magic window" (Hawkins 1977). As children develop, they increasingly consider a wider range of cues, including whether the events and characters *possibly* could occur in real life (Dorr 1983; Wright et al. 1994).

What implications does this have for television violence? Clearly, a fantastic portrayal of violence might be discounted as unrealistic by older children and adults, but perceived as very real by younger children. As an illustration, one study found that preschoolers who were exposed to a violent cartoon model subsequently were just as aggressive as those who watched a human model displaying the same violent acts (Bandura, Ross, and Ross 1963a). Moreover, numerous studies show that young children readily imitate violent cartoon characters such as Batman (Freidrich and Stein 1973; Steuer, Applefield, and Smith 1971) and superheroes with magical powers like the Power Rangers (Boyatzis, Matillo, and Nesbitt 1995).

These findings underscore the importance of *perceived* reality for the viewer. In spite of the fact that realistic depictions of violence pose more risks for all viewers, younger children make these judgments differently than do older children and adults. Thus, we cannot discount cartoon or fantasy violence when considering younger audiences.

The second cognitive skill that is relevant to television viewing is the capacity to draw inferences and connect scenes. Television plots are stories that require the viewer to make causal links between scenes and to fill in gaps in information. Research suggests that older children are better able than younger children to integrate pieces of information from stories and narrations, and then to draw inferences from such information (Schmidt, Schmidt, and Tomalis 1984; Thompson and Myers 1985). Likewise, older children are better able to coherently link scenes together from a television program (Collins 1979, 1983).

This developmental pattern has important implications for the context factor dealing with rewards and punishments. Many action-adventure programs feature criminals or bad guys who get away with violence early on in a program. These characters often are not caught or punished until the end of the program when the plot is resolved. In other words, violence is rewarded in the short run and if it is punished at all, this negative reinforcement is not depicted until much later.

Research suggests that the *timing* of punishments is a critical factor for younger children. In one study (Collins 1973), third, sixth, and tenth graders watched a program in which a crime was either punished immediately after it occurred or punished later, after a four-minute commercial break. The findings revealed that the youngest group was more likely to respond aggressively when the punishment was separated from the violence than when it was temporally contiguous to it. In contrast, the separation manipulation had no impact on the two older groups. Therefore, in order to be an effective deterrent for younger children, punishments must occur in close proximity to the violent action in a program.

To summarize, younger children may respond to two context factors in somewhat different ways than will older children and adults. Younger viewers are more likely to perceive fantasy and animated violence as realistic, thus increasing the risk of imitation and fear when this age group is exposed to such content. They also are less able to link scenes together that are temporally separated. Thus, punishments may not serve as effective inhibitors of imitation and aggression unless such restraints are depicted in the same scene or immediately adjacent to the violence. These special contingencies will be of interest when we consider the 2- to 6-year-old audience and when we examine children's programming in particular.

Summary: Contextual Patterns

The research reviewed above establishes clearly that certain depictions of television violence pose more of a risk for viewers than do others. Specifically, nine different contextual cues or message factors have been documented as important influences on audience reactions. Because the experimental studies to date have only tested these context factors in isolation from one another, we have no solid information about which factors may be most critical or how such factors might interact with one another. For example, it might be that pain and harm cues are more influential when shown within a realistic portrayal of violence than in the context of a fantasy program.

Until more detailed analyses are conducted, we must assume that each factor is somehow important to the overall risk associated with a given portrayal. In that case, a violent program that contains several contextually based risk factors presumably is more problematic than a portrayal featuring only one. The context factors can be examined collectively to reveal certain patterns of portrayals in a program that would affect the potential risk for the audience. A careful review of table 2.1 reveals such patterns. For example, a portrayal that poses the greatest risk for the learning of aggression would feature an attractive perpetrator who is motivated by morally proper reasons; who engages in repeated violence that seems realistic, is rewarded, and employs conventional weapons; and whose violent actions produce no visible harm or pain and are accompanied by humor. In contrast, a portrayal that may actually inhibit or reduce the risk of learning aggression would feature an unattractive perpetrator who is motivated by greed or hatred, who commits violence that produces strong negative consequences for the victims, and who is ultimately punished for this aggression.

Somewhat different risk patterns exist for the other outcomes of concern, desensitization, and fear. A portrayal that poses the greatest risk for desensitization would contain violence that is repeated or extensive and that is depicted as humorous. A portrayal that poses the greatest risk for audience fear would feature violence that is aimed at an attractive or likable target, that seems unjustified, that is extensive and realistic, and that goes unpunished.

Although each context variable is important in its own right, television programming is likely to reveal certain combinations of factors such as those described above. One of the primary goals of the NTVS is to detect whether these patterns exist and if so, to identify where they are most likely to be found. For example, if the themes described above are more commonly found in certain types of programs, then we can draw conclusions about the potential risks and/or benefits associated with different genres of television. Such themes or templates also may be more pervasive on certain types of channels or in certain time slots during the day. If so, parents and educators can use such findings to make more informed decisions about what children should and should not view. Such findings also can help us to teach children to be more critical viewers of television content.

REFERENCES

American Psychological Association. 1993. *Violence and Youth: Psychology's Response.* Washington, DC: American Psychological Association.
Atkin, C. 1983. "Effects of Realistic TV Violence vs. Fictional Violence on Aggression." *Journalism Quarterly* 60:615–21.
Bandura, A. 1965. "Influence of Models' Reinforcement Contingencies on the Acquisition of Imitative Responses." *Journal of Personality and Social Psychology* 1(6): 589–95.
———. 1971. *Social Learning Theory.* New York: General Learning Press.
———. 1986. *Social Foundations of Thought and Action: A Social Cognitive Theory.* Englewood Cliffs, NJ: Prentice-Hall.
———. 1994. "Social Cognitive Theory of Mass Communication." In *Media Effects,* ed. J. Bryant and D. Zillmann, 61–90. Hillsdale, NJ: Lawrence Erlbaum.
Bandura, A., D. Ross, and S. A. Ross. 1961. "Transmission of Aggression through Imitation of Aggressive Models." *Journal of Abnormal and Social Psychology* 63:575–82.

———. 1963a. "Imitation of Film-Mediated Aggressive Models." *Journal of Abnormal and Social Psychology* 66(1): 3–11.

———. 1963b. "Vicarious Reinforcement and Imitative Learning." *Journal of Abnormal and Social Psychology* 67(6): 601–7.

Baron, R. A. 1971a. "Aggression as a Function of Magnitude of Victim's Pain Cues, Level of Prior Anger Arousal, and Aggressor-Victim Similarity." *Journal of Personality and Social Psychology* 18(1): 48–54.

———. 1971b. "Magnitude of Victim's Pain Cues and Level of Prior Anger Arousal as Determinants of Adult Aggressive Behavior." *Journal of Personality and Social Psychology* 17(3): 236–43.

———. 1978. "The Influence of Hostile and Nonhostile Humor upon Physical Aggression." *Personality and Social Psychology Bulletin* 4(1): 77–80.

———. 1979. "Effects of Victim's Pain Cues, Victim's Race, and Level of Prior Instigation upon Physical Aggression." *Journal of Applied Social Psychology* 9(2): 103–14.

Baron, R. A., and R. L. Ball. 1974. "The Aggression-Inhibiting Influence of Nonhostile Humor." *Journal of Experimental Social Psychology* 10:23–33.

Berger, A. A. 1988. "Humor and Behavior: Therapeutic Aspects of Comedic Techniques and Other Considerations." In *Information and Behavior,* ed. B. D. Ruben, vol. 2, 226–47. New Brunswick, NJ: Transaction Books.

Berkowitz, L. 1970. "Aggressive Humor as a Stimulus to Aggressive Responses." *Journal of Personality and Social Psychology* 16(4): 710–17.

———. 1973. "Words and Symbols as Stimuli to Aggressive Responses." In *Control of Aggression: Implications from Basic Research,* ed. J. Knutson. Chicago: Aldine-Atherton.

———. 1984. "Some Effects of Thoughts on Anti- and Prosocial Influences of Media Events: A Cognitive-Neoassociation Analysis." *Psychological Bulletin* 95(3): 410–27.

———. 1990. "On the Formation and Regulation of Anger and Aggression: A Cognitive Neoassociationistic Analysis." *American Psychologist* 45(4): 494–503.

Berkowitz, L., and J. T. Alioto. 1973. "The Meaning of an Observed Event as a Determinant of Its Aggressive Consequences." *Journal of Personality and Social Psychology* 28(2): 206–17.

Berkowitz, L., and R. G. Geen. 1966. "Film Violence and the Cue Properties of Available Targets." *Journal of Personality and Social Psychology* 3(5): 525–30.

———. 1967. "Stimulus Qualities of the Target of Aggression: A Further Study." *Journal of Personality and Social Psychology* 5(3): 364–68.

Berkowitz, L., and A. LePage. 1967. "Weapons as Aggression-Eliciting Stimuli." *Journal of Personality and Social Psychology* 7(2): 202–7.

Berkowitz, L., and P. C. Powers. 1979. "Effects of Timing and Justification of Witnessed Aggression on the Observers' Punitiveness." *Journal of Research in Personality* 13:71–80.

Berkowitz, L., and E. Rawlings. 1963. "Effects of Film Violence on Inhibitions against Subsequent Aggression." *Journal of Abnormal and Social Psychology* 66(5): 405–12.

Berkowitz, L., and K. H. Rogers. 1986. "A Priming Effect Analysis of Media Influences." In *Perspectives on Media Effects,* ed. J. Bryant and D. Zillmann, 57–82. Hillsdale, NJ: Erlbaum.

Berndt, T. J., and E. G. Berndt. 1975. "Children's Use of Motives and Intentionality in Person Perception and Moral Judgment." *Child Development* 46:904–20.

Boyatzis, C. J., G. M. Matillo, and K. M. Nesbitt. 1995. "Effects of 'The Mighty Morphin Power Rangers' on Children's Aggression with Peers." *Child Study Journal* 25:45–56.

Broder, J. M. 1995. "Dole Indicts Hollywood for Debasing Culture." *The Los Angeles Times* June 1: A1, A15.

Bryant, J., R. A. Carveth, and D. Brown. 1981. "Television Viewing and Anxiety: An Experimental Examination." *Journal of Communication* 31(1): 106–19.

Cantor, J. 1994. "Fright Reactions to Mass Media." In *Media Effects,* ed. J. Bryant and D. Zillmann, 213–45. Hillsdale, NJ: Lawrence Erlbaum Associates.

Cantor, J., and C. Hoffner. 1990. "Forewarning of a Threat and Prior Knowledge of Outcome." *Human Communication Research* 16(3): 323–54.

Cantor, J., and G. G. Sparks. 1984. "Children's Fear Responses to Mass Media: Testing Some Piagetian Predictions." *Journal of Communication* 34(2): 90–103.

Cantor, J., and B. J. Wilson. 1988. "Helping Children Cope with Frightening Media Presentations." *Current Psychology: Research and Reviews* 7:58–75.

Carlson, M., A. Marcus-Newhall, and N. Miller. 1990. "Effects of Situational Aggression Cues: A Quantitative Review." *Journal of Personality and Social Psychology* 58(4): 622–33.

Carver, C. S., R. J. Ganellen, W. J. Froming, and W. Chambers. 1983. "Modeling: An Analysis in Terms of Category Accessibility." *Journal of Experimental Social Psychology* 19:403–21.

Centers for Disease Control. 1991. *Position papers from the Third National Injury Conference: Setting the National Agenda for Injury Control in the 1990s.* Washington, DC: Department of Health and Human Services.

Cline, V. B., R. G. Croft, and S. Courrier. 1973. "Desensitization of Children to Television Violence." *Journal of Personality and Social Psychology* 27(3): 360–5.

Collins, W. A. 1973. "Effect of Temporal Separation between Motivation, Aggression, and Consequences." *Developmental Psychology* 8(2): 215–21.

———. 1979. "Children's Comprehension of Television Content." In *Children Communicating: Media and Development of Thought. Speech. Understanding,* ed. E. Wartella, 21–52. Beverly Hills, CA: Sage.

———. 1983. Interpretation and Inference in Children's Television Viewing. In *Children's Understanding of Television,* ed. J. Bryant and D. R. Anderson, 125–50. New York: Academic Press.

Comisky, P., and J. Bryant. 1982. "Factors Involved in Generating Suspense." *Human Communication Research* 9(1): 49–58.

Comstock, G., and H. Paik. 1991. *Television and the American Child.* New York: Academic Press.

Condry, J. 1989. *The Psychology of Television.* Hillsdale, NJ: Lawrence Erlbaum.

Deckers, L., and D. E. Carr. 1986. "Cartoons Varying in Low-Level Pain Ratings, Not Aggression Ratings, Correlate Positively with Funniness Ratings." *Motivation and Emotion* 10(3): 207–16.

Donnerstein, E., R. Slaby, and L. Eron. 1994. "The Mass Media and Youth Violence." In

Violence and Youth: Psychology's Response, ed. J. Murray, E. Rubinstein, and G. Comstock, vol. 2. Washington, DC: American Psychological Association.

Dorr, A. 1983. "No Shortcuts to Judging Reality." In *Children's Understanding of Television*, ed. J. Bryant and D. R. Anderson, 199–220. New York: Academic Press.

Dubanoski, R. A., and C. Kong. 1977. "The Effects of Pain Cues on the Behavior of High and Low Aggressive Boys." *Social Behavior and Personality* 5(2): 273–74.

Feshbach, S. 1972. "Reality and Fantasy in Filmed Violence." In *Television and Social Behavior: Television and Social Learning*, ed. J. P. Murray, E. A. Rubinstein, and G. Comstock, vol. 2, 318–45. Washington, DC: U.S. Government Publication.

Feshbach, N. D., and K. Roe. 1968. "Empathy in Six and Seven Year-olds." *Child Development* 39(1): 133–45.

Flavell, J. H. 1985. *Cognitive Development*, 2d ed. Englewood Cliffs, NJ: Prentice-Hall.

———. 1986. "The Development of Children's Knowledge about the Appearance-Reality Distinction." *American Psychologist* 41(4): 418–25.

Foa, E. B., and M. J. Kozak. 1986. "Emotional Processing of Fear: Exposure to Corrective Information." *Psychological Bulletin* 99:20–35.

Freidrich, L., and A. H. Stein. 1973. "Aggressive and Prosocial Television Programs and the Natural Behavior of Preschool Children." *Monographs of the Society for Research in Child Development* 38 (4, Serial No. 151).

Frodi, A. 1975. "The Effect of Exposure to Weapons on Aggressive Behavior from a Cross-Cultural Perspective." *International Journal of Psychology* 10(4): 283–92.

Geen, R. G. 1975. "The Meaning of Observed Violence: Real vs. Fictional Violence and Consequent Effects on Aggression and Emotional Arousal." *Journal of Research in Personality* 9:270–81.

———. 1981. "Behavioral and Physiological Reactions to Observed Violence: Effects of Prior Exposure to Aggressive Stimuli." *Journal of Personality and Social Psychology* 40(5): 868–75.

Geen, R. G., and L. Berkowitz. 1966. "Name-Mediated Aggressive Cue Properties." *Journal of Personality and Social Psychology* 34:456–65.

Geen, R. G., and J. J. Rakosky. 1973. "Interpretations of Observed Violence and Their Effects on GSR." *Journal of Experimental Research in Personality* 6:289–92.

Geen, R. G., and D. Stonner. 1973. "Context Effects in Observed Violence." *Journal of Personality and Social Psychology* 25(1): 145–50.

———. 1974. "The Meaning of Observed Violence: Effects on Arousal and Aggressive Behavior." *Journal of Research in Personality* 8:55–63.

Gerbner, G. 1969. "Dimensions of Violence in Television Drama." In *Violence in the Media* (Staff Report to the National Commission on the Causes and Prevention of Violence), ed. R. K. Baker and S. J. Ball, 311–40. Washington, DC: U.S. Government Printing Office.

———. 1992. *Testimony at Hearings on Violence on Television before the House Judiciary Committee, Subcommittee on Crime and Criminal Justice*, New York (field hearing), December.

Gerbner, G., and L. Gross. 1976. "Living with Television: The Violence Profile." *Journal of Communication* 26(2): 172–99.

Gerbner, G., L. Gross, M. Morgan, and N. Signorielli. 1986. "Living with Television: The

Dynamics of the Cultivation Process." In *Perspectives on Media Effects*, ed. J. Bryant and D. Zillmann, 17–40. Hillsdale, NJ: Lawrence Erlbaum.

———. 1994. "Growing up with Television: The Cultivation Perspective." In *Media Effects*, ed. J. Bryant and D. Zillmann, 17–41. Hillsdale, NJ: Lawrence Erlbaum.

Gerbner, G., L. Gross, N. Signorielli, and M. Morgan. 1986. *Television's Mean World: Violence Profile No. 14–15.* Unpublished manuscript, University of Pennsylvania at Annenberg School of Communication.

Goransen, R. E. 1969. "Observed Violence and Aggressive Behavior: The Effects of Negative Outcomes to Observed Violence." *Dissertation Abstracts International* 31 (01), DAI-B (University Microfilms No. AAC77 08286).

Gray, T. G., and M. Barry. 1994. *The Kindest Cut?: A Preliminary Examination of the British Film Board's Policy of Censoring Graphic Violence.* Poster session presented at the annual conference of the Speech Communication Association, New Orleans, LA, November.

Gunter, B. 1983. "Do Aggressive People Prefer Violent Television?" *Bulletin of the British Psychological Society* 36:166–68.

———. 1985. *Dimensions of Television Violence.* Aldershots, England: Gower.

———. 1994. "The Question of Media Violence." In *Media Effects,* ed. J. Bryant and D. Zillmann, 163–211. Hillsdale, NJ: Lawrence Erlbaum.

Hapkiewicz, W. G., and R. D. Stone. 1974. "The Effect of Realistic versus Imaginary Aggressive Models on Children's Interpersonal Play." *Child Study Journal* 4(2): 47–58.

Harris, R. J. 1994. "The Impact of Sexually Explicit Media." In *Media Effects,* ed. J. Bryant and D. Zillmann, 247–72. Hillsdale, NJ: Lawrence Erlbaum.

Hawkins, R. P. 1977. "The Dimensional Structure of Children's Perceptions of Television Reality." *Communication Research* 4(3): 299–320.

Hicks, D. J. 1965. "Imitation and Retention of Film-Mediated Aggressive Peer and Adult Models." *Journal of Personality and Social Psychology* 2(1): 97–100.

Hirsch, P. M. 1980. "The 'Scary World' of the Nonviewer and Other Anomalies: A Reanalysis of Gerbner et al.'s Findings of Cultivation Analysis, Part I." *Communication Research* 7(4): 403–56.

———. 1981a. "Distinguishing Good Speculation from Bad Theory: Rejoinder to Gerbner et al." *Communication Research* 8(1): 73–95.

———. 1981b. "On Not Learning from One's Own Mistakes: A Reanalysis of Gerbner et al.'s Findings on Cultivation Analysis, Part II." *Communication Research* 8(1): 3–37.

Hoffner, C., and J. Cantor. 1985. "Developmental Differences in Responses to a Television Character's Appearance and Behavior." *Developmental Psychology* 21(6): 1065–74.

———. 1991. "Perceiving and Responding to Mass Media Characters." In *Responding to the Screen,* ed. J. Bryant and D. Zillmann, 63–101. Hillsdale, NJ: Lawrence Erlbaum.

Hoyt, J. L. 1970. "Effect of Media Violence 'Justification' on Aggression." *Journal of Broadcasting* 14(4): 455–64.

Huesmann, L. R. 1986. "Psychological Processes Promoting the Relation between Exposure to Media Violence and Aggressive Behavior by the Viewer." *Journal of Social Issues* 42(3): 125–40.

Huesmann, L. R., and L. D. Eron, eds. 1986. *Television and the Aggressive Child: A Cross-National Comparison.* Hillsdale, NJ: Lawrence Erlbaum.

Huesmann, L. R., L. D. Eron, M. M. Lefkowitz, and L. O. Walder. 1984. "The Stability of Aggression Over Time and Generations." *Developmental Psychology* 20(6): 1120–34.

Huesmann, L. R., K. Lagerspetz, and L. D. Eron. 1984. "Intervening Variables in the TV Violence-Aggression Relation: Evidence from Two Countries." *Developmental Psychology* 20(6): 1120–34.

Hundt, R. 1995. "An Open Letter from FCC Chairman Reed Hundt." *Broadcasting and Cable* June 5: 7.

Huston, A. C., E. Donnerstein, H. Fairchild, N. D. Feshbach, P. A. Katz, J. P. Murray, E. A. Rubinstein, B. L. Wilcox, and D. Zuckerman. 1992. *Big World, Small Screen: The Role of Television in American Society.* Lincoln: University of Nebraska Press.

Jo, E., and L. Berkowitz. 1994. "A Priming Effect Analysis of Media Influences: An Update." In *Media Effects,* ed. J. Bryant and D. Zillmann, 43–60. Hillsdale, NJ: Lawrence Erlbaum.

Jose, P. E., and W. F. Brewer. 1984. "Development of Story Liking: Character Identification, Suspense, and Outcome Resolution." *Developmental Psychology* 20(5): 911–24.

Josephson, W. L. 1987. "Television Violence and Children's Aggression: Testing and Priming, Social Script, and Disinhibition Predictions." *Journal of Personality and Social Psychology* 53(5): 882–90.

Kail, R. 1990. *The Development of Memory in Children.* New York: Freeman.

Lacayo, R. 1995. "Are Music and Movies Killing America's Soul?" *Time* June 12: 24–30.

Lando, H. A., and E. I. Donnerstein. 1978. "The Effects of a Model's Success or Failure on Subsequent Aggressive Behavior." *Journal of Research in Personality* 12:225–34.

Lazarus, R. S., and E. Alfert. 1964. "Short-Circuiting of Threat by Experimentally Altering Cognitive Appraisal." *Journal of Abnormal and Social Psychology* 69(2): 195–205.

Lazarus, R. S., E. M. Opton, M. S. Nomikos, and N. O. Rankin. 1965. "The Principle of Short-Circuiting of Threat: Further Evidence." *Journal of Personality* 33:622–35.

Lazarus, R. S., M. Speisman, A. M. Mordkoff, and L. A. Davison. 1962. "A Laboratory Study of Psychological Stress Produced by a Motion Picture Film." *Psychological Monographs: General and Applied* 76. (34) Whole No. 553.

Lefkowitz, M. M., L. D. Eron, L. Q. Walder, and L. R. Huesmann. 1977. *Growing Up to be Violent: A Longitudinal Study of the Development of Aggression.* New York: Pergamon Press.

Leyens, J. P., and R. D. Parke. 1974. "Aggressive Slides Can Induce a Weapons Effect." *European Journal of Social Psychology* 5(2): 229–36.

Leyens, J. P., and S. Picus. 1973. "Identification with the Winner of a Fight and Name Mediation: Their Differential Effects upon Subsequent Aggressive Behavior." *British Journal of Social and Clinical Psychology* 12:374–77.

Liebert, R. M., and R. A. Baron. 1972. "Short-term Effects of Televised Aggression on Children's Aggressive Behavior." In *Television and Social Behavior: Television and Social Learning,* ed. J. P. Murray, E. A. Rubinstein, and G. A. Comstock, vol. 2, 181–201. Washington, DC: Government Printing Office.

Linz, D., E. Donnerstein, and S. Penrod. 1984. "The Effects of Multiple Exposures to Filmed Violence against Women." *Journal of Communication* 34(3): 130–47.

———. 1987. "Sexual Violence in the Mass Media: Social Psychological Implications." In *Review of Personality and Social Psychology,* ed. P. Shaver and C. Hendrick, vol. 7, 95–123. Beverly Hills, CA: Sage Publications.

————. 1988. "Effects of Long-Term Exposure to Violent and Sexually Degrading Depictions of Women." *Journal of Personality and Social Psychology* 55(5): 758–68.

Liss, M. B., L. C. Reinhardt, and S. Fredriksen. 1983. "TV Heroes: The Impact of Rhetoric and Deeds." *Journal of Applied Developmental Psychology* 4:175–87.

Malamuth, N., and J. V. P. Check. 1981. "The Effects of Mass Media Exposure on Acceptance of Violence against Women: A Field Experiment." *Journal of Research in Personality* 15(4): 436–46.

Mathai, J. 1983. "An Acute Anxiety State in an Adolescent Precipitated by Viewing a Horror Movie." *Journal of Adolescence* 6:197–200.

Meyer, T. P. 1972. "Effects of Viewing Justified and Unjustified Real Film Violence on Aggressive Behavior." *Journal of Personality and Social Psychology* 23(1): 21–29.

Morison, P., and H. Gardner. 1978. "Dragons and Dinosaurs: The Child's Capacity to Differentiate Fantasy from Reality." *Child Development* 49:642–48.

Mueller, C. W., and E. Donnerstein. 1977. "The Effects of Humor-Induced Arousal upon Aggressive Behavior." *Journal of Research in Personality* 11:73–82.

————. 1983. "Film-Induced Arousal and Aggressive Behavior." *Journal of Social Psychology* 119:61–67.

Mullin, C. R., and D. Linz. 1995. "Desensitization and Resensitization to Violence against Women: Effects of Exposure to Sexually Violent Films on Judgments of Domestic Violence Victims." *Journal of Personality and Social Psychology* 69(3): 449–59.

National Academy of Science. 1993. *Understanding and Preventing Violence.* Washington, DC: National Academy Press.

National Cable Television Association. 1993. *Industry Policy Statement Regarding Violence.* Washington, DC: NCTA.

National Institute of Mental Health. 1982. *Television and Behavior: Ten Years of Scientific Progress and Implications for the Eighties (Vol. I). Summary Report.* Washington, DC: U.S. Government Printing Office.

National Television Violence Study, Volume 1. 1997. Thousand Oaks, CA: Sage.

Neisser, U. 1967. *Cognitive Psychology.* New York: Appleton-Century-Crofts.

Network Television Association. 1992. *Standards for Depiction of Violence in Television Programs.* New York: NTA.

Newcomb, H. 1978. "Assessing the Violence Profile of Gerbner and Gross: A Humanistic Critique and Suggestion." *Communication Research* 5(3): 264–82.

Ogles, R. M., and C. Hoffner. 1987. "Film Violence and Perceptions of Crime: The Cultivation Effect." In *Communication Yearbook,* ed. M. L. McLaughlin, vol. 10, 384–94. Newbury Park, CA: Sage.

Page, D., and E. O'Neal. 1977. "'Weapons Effect' without Demand Characteristics." *Psychological Reports* 41:29–30.

Paik, H., and G. Comstock. 1994. "The Effects of Television Violence on Antisocial Behavior: A Meta-analysis." *Communication Research* 21(4): 516–46.

Parke, R. D., L. Berkowitz, J. P. Leyens, S. G. West, and R. J. Sebastian. 1977. "Some Effects of Violent and Nonviolent Movies on the Behavior of Juvenile Delinquents." In *Advances in Experimental Social Psychology,* ed. L. Berkowitz, vol. 10, 135–72. New York: Academic Press.

Perry, D. G., and L. C. Perry. 1976. "Identification with Film Characters, Covert Aggressive Verbalization, and Reactions to Film Violence." *Journal of Research in Personality* 10:399–409.

Piaget, J. 1952. *The Origins of Intelligence in Children*. New York: International Universities Press.

————. 1960. *The Child's Conception of the World*. London: Routledge.

Plagens, P., M. Miller, D. Foote, and E. Yoffe. 1991. "Violence in Our Culture." *Newsweek* April 1: 46–52.

Potter, W. J. 1986. "Perceived Reality and the Cultivation Hypothesis." *Journal of Broadcasting and Electronic Media* 30(2): 159–74.

————. 1988. "Perceived Reality in Television Effects Research." *Journal of Broadcasting and Electronic Media* 32(1): 23–41.

————. 1993. "Cultivation Theory and Research: A Conceptual Critique." *Human Communication Research* 19:564–601.

Potter, W. J., and W. Ware. 1987. "An Analysis of the Contexts of Antisocial Acts on Prime-time Television." *Communication Research* 14(6): 664–86.

Rosekrans, M. A., and W. W. Hartup. 1967. "Imitative Influences of Consistent and Inconsistent Response Consequences to a Model on Aggressive Behavior in Children." *Journal of Personality and Social Psychology* 7(4): 429–34.

Rosengren, K. S., C. W. Kalish, A. K. Hickling, and S. A. Gelman. 1994. "Exploring the Relation between Preschool Children's Magical Beliefs and Causal Thinking." *British Journal of Developmental Psychology* 12:69–82.

Rubin, A. M., E. M. Perse, and D. S. Taylor. 1988. "A Methodological Examination of Cultivation." *Communication Research* 15:107–34.

Sander, I. 1995. *How Violent is TV-Violence? An Empirical Investigation of Factors Influencing Viewers' Perceptions of TV-Violence*. Paper presented at the International Communication Association conference in Albuquerque, NM.

Sanders, G. S., and R. S. Baron. 1975. "Pain Cues and Uncertainty as Determinants of Aggression in a Situation Involving Repeated Instigation." *Journal of Personality and Social Psychology* 32(3): 495–502.

Schmidt, C. R., S. R. Schmidt, and S. M. Tomalis. 1984. "Children's Constructive Processing and Monitoring of Stories Containing Anomalous Information." *Child Development* 55:2056–71.

Schmutte, G. T., and S. P. Taylor. 1980. "Physical Aggression as a Function of Alcohol and Pain Feedback." *The Journal of Social Psychology* 110:235–44.

Shapiro, M. A. 1991. "Memory and Decision Processes in the Construction of Social Reality." *Communication Research* 18:3–24.

Siegler, R. S. 1991. *Children's Thinking*, 2d ed. Englewood Cliffs, NJ: Prentice-Hall.

Sparks, G. G. 1986. "Developmental Differences in Children's Reports of Fear Induced by the Mass Media." *Child Study Journal* 16:55–66.

Speisman, J. C., R. S. Lazarus, A. Mordkoff, and L. Davison. 1964. "Experimental Reduction of Stress Based on Ego-Defense Theory." *Journal of Abnormal and Social Psychology* 68(4): 367–80.

Steuer, F. B., J. M. Applefield, and R. Smith. 1971. "Televised Aggression and the Interpersonal Aggression of Preschool Children." *Journal of Experimental Child Psychology* 11:442–47.

Surgeon General's Scientific Advisory Committee on Television and Social Behavior. 1972. *Television and Growing Up: The Impact of Televised Violence.* Washington, DC: U.S. Government Printing Office.

Swart, C., and L. Berkowitz. 1976. "Effects of a Stimulus Associated with a Victim's Pain on Later Aggression." *Journal of Personality and Social Psychology* 33(5): 623–31.

Tan, A. S. 1986. "Social Learning of Aggression from Television." In *Perspectives on Media Effects,* ed. J. Bryant and D. Zillmann, 41–55. Hillsdale, NJ: Lawrence Erlbaum.

Tannenbaum, P. H., and E. P. Gaer. 1965. "Mood Change as a Function of Stress of Protagonist and Degree of Identification in a Film-Viewing Situation." *Journal of Personality and Social Psychology* 2(4): 612–16.

Taylor, B. J., and R. J. Howell. 1973. "The Ability of Three, Four, and Five-year-old Children to Distinguish Fantasy from Reality." *Journal of Genetic Psychology* 122:315–18.

Thomas, M. H. 1982. "Physiological Arousal, Exposure to a Relatively Lengthy Aggressive Film, and Aggressive Behavior." *Journal of Research in Personality* 16:72–81.

Thomas, M. H., R. W. Horton, E. C. Lippencott, and R. S. Drabman. 1977. "Desensitization to Portrayals of Real-Life Aggression as a Function of Exposure to Television Violence." *Journal of Personality and Social Psychology* 35:450–58.

Thomas, M. H., and P. M. Tell. 1974. "Effects of Viewing Real versus Fantasy Violence upon Interpersonal Aggression." *Journal of Research in Personality* 8:153–60.

Thompson, J. G., and N. A. Myers. 1985. "Inferences and Recall at Ages Four and Seven." *Child Development* 56:1134–44.

Turner, C. W., and L. Berkowitz. 1972. "Identification with Film Aggressor (Covert Role Taking) and Reactions to Film Violence." *Journal of Personality and Social Psychology* 21(2): 256–64.

Turner, C. W., J. F. Layton, and L. S. Simons. 1975. "Naturalistic Studies of Aggressive Behavior: Aggressive Stimuli, Victim Visibility, and Horn Honking." *Journal of Personality and Social Psychology* 31(6): 1098–1107.

Valenti, J. 1987. *The Voluntary Movie Rating System.* New York: Motion Picture Association of America.

Walters, R. H., and R. D. Parke. 1964. "Influence of Response Consequences to a Social Model on Resistance to Deviation." *Journal of Experimental Child Psychology* 1:269–80.

Walters, R. H., R. D. Parke, and V. A. Cane. 1965. "Timing of Punishment and the Observation of Consequences to Others as Determinants of Response Inhibition." *Journal of Experimental Child Psychology* 2:10–30.

Williams, T. M., M. L. Zabrack, and L. A. Joy. 1982. "The Portrayal of Aggression on North American Television." *Journal of Applied Social Psychology* 12(5): 360–80.

Wilson, B. J. 1995. "Les Recherches sur Médias et Violence: Aggressivité, Désensibilisation, Peur" [Effects of Media Violence: Aggression, Desensitization, and Fear]. *Cahiers de la Sécurité Intérieure* 20(2): 21–37.

Wilson, B. J., and J. Cantor. 1985. "Developmental Differences in Empathy with a Television Protagonist's Fear." *Journal of Experimental Child Psychology* 39:284–99.

Wilson, B. J., D. Linz, and B. Randall. 1990. "Applying Social Science Research to Film Ratings: A Shift from Offensiveness to Harmful Effects." *Journal of Broadcasting and Electronic Media* 34(4): 443–68.

Wilson, B. J., and S. L. Smith. 1995. *Children's Comprehension of and Fright Reactions to*

Television News. Panel presentation at the annual conference of the International Communication Association, Albuquerque, NM.

Worchel, S. 1972. "The Effect of Films on the Importance of Behavioral Freedom." *Journal of Personality* 40:417–35.

Wotring, C. E., and B. S. Greenberg. 1973. "Experiments in Televised Violence and Verbal Aggression: Two Exploratory Studies." *Journal of Communication* 23:446–60.

Wright, J. C., A. C. Huston, A. L. Reitz, and S. Piemyat. 1994. "Young Children's Perceptions of Television Reality: Determinants and Developmental Differences." *Developmental Psychology* 30(2): 229–39.

Zillmann, D. 1979. *Hostility and Aggression.* Hillsdale, NJ: Lawrence Erlbaum.

———. 1980. "Anatomy of Suspense." In *The Entertainment Functions of Television,* ed. P. H. Tannenbaum, 133–63. Hillsdale, NJ: Lawrence Erlbaum.

———. 1991. "Empathy: Affect from Bearing Witness to the Emotions of Others." In *Responding to the Screen,* ed. J. Bryant and D. Zillmann, 135–67. Hillsdale, NJ: Lawrence Erlbaum.

Zillmann, D., and J. Bryant. 1991. "Responding to Comedy: The Sense and Nonsense in Humor." In *Responding to the Screen,* ed. J. Bryant and D. Zillmann, 261–79. Hillsdale, NJ: Lawrence Erlbaum.

Zillmann, D., and J. R. Cantor. 1977. "Affective Responses to the Emotions of a Protagonist." *Journal of Experimental Social Psychology* 13:155–65.

Chapter 3

Content Analysis of Entertainment Television: New Methodological Developments

James Potter, Daniel Linz, Barbara J. Wilson, Dale Kunkel, Edward Donnerstein, Stacy L. Smith, Eva Blumenthal, and Tim Gray

Introduction

The debate over the television program rating system in 1996 featured many claims about the difficulty of defining violence and the subjectivity involved in categorizing the relative harms of different types of violent portrayals. In this chapter, we demonstrate that the research on media effects can be used to fashion a clear definition of television violence linked to the harms indicated by extensive media research. We use this definition to develop a content coding framework based on the context of how violence is used in a program. A framework is developed that allows an analyst to use different units of observation (e.g., program level, interaction level) to describe violent contexts. We examine the advantages of using a large representative sample to conduct the content analysis and discuss in detail in an appendix the measures of coder reliability developed and employed in the analysis. Chapter 4 discusses at length the results from applying the coding framework to an extensive programming sample from 1994 to 1995.

Researchers have analyzed violence on television for as long as the medium has existed (cf. Clark and Blankenberg 1972; Gerbner, Gross, Signorielli, Morgan, and Jackson-Beeck 1979; Greenberg, Edison, Korzenny, Fernandez-Collado, and Atkin 1980; Head 1954; Lichter and Amundson 1992, 1994; Potter and Ware 1987; Schramm, Lyle, and Parker 1961; Smythe 1954; Williams, Zabrack, and Joy 1982). Most of these studies have examined all types of television content, although some have focused more narrowly on children's programming (Poulos, Harvey, and Liebert 1976) or music videos, a genre with strong appeal to youths (Baxter, Reimer, Landini, Leslie, and Singletary 1985; Brown and Campbell 1986; Sherman and Dominick 1986; Sommers-Flanagan, Sommers-Flanagan, and Davis 1993). The monitoring of violence also has been undertaken by citizen activists ("NCTV Says" 1983) and by the television industry itself (Columbia Broadcasting System 1980).

In this first section of this chapter, we review the approaches that have been employed previously to examine the topic of televised violence. Our goal here is to describe the range of findings in this research area and to illustrate how the differences in findings can be traced to methodological decisions made by the various researchers. These methodological decisions reflect differences in defining violence, selecting the units for analyzing violence, and selecting the sample of television programming to be studied. To the extent that these decisions vary across studies, there inevitably will be corresponding differences in the findings produced by the research.

For example, if one study defines violence to include comic or slapstick actions, its count of violence will yield a higher figure than would a comparable study that excluded such actions in its definition. A study that focuses on individual violent acts as the unit of analysis will likely result in a higher count of violence than a study that uses much larger units of analysis such as the scene. And a study that includes certain genres known for very high rates of violence, such as action-adventure movies and cartoons, will produce a higher rate of violence than a study that uses a more narrow sample that excludes such genres. Therefore, the results of a given content analysis are strongly influenced by the definition of violence, the units of analysis, and the sample.

We begin this section by describing the range of previous findings regarding the amount of violence on television. We then present an analysis of various studies to illustrate how methodological decisions have influenced the nature of the results. Next, we overview how context has been addressed in past assessments of television violence. Finally, we provide an overview of the major methodological decisions made in planning the National Television Violence Study (NTVS) to show how we have built on the strengths of the previous research while at the same time avoiding many of the limitations of those studies.

Range of Findings

Since the late 1960s, George Gerbner and his colleagues have conducted the most consistent and widely cited assessments of the amount of violence on American television (e.g., Gerbner, Gross, Morgan, and Signorielli 1980). On average they have found that violence occurs at a rate of 5.4 acts per hour (Signorielli 1990). Studies in both the United States and Britain (Cumberbatch, Lee, Hardy, and Jones 1987) that used Gerbner's definition of violence have consistently found 4 to 6 violent acts per hour of prime-time programming, with substantially more on American children's cartoons.

Higher rates of violence are reported in many other content analyses. For example, a study by the National Coalition on Television Violence ("NCTV Says" 1983) found 9.7 violent acts per hour of U.S. programming. Williams, Zabrack, and Joy (1982) found 18.5 aggressive acts per hour of U.S. and Canadian programming. Potter and his colleagues (1995) found an average of 36.6 acts of aggression per hour. Greenberg and his colleagues (1980) reported a rate of 38 acts of antisocial behavior per hour.

What can account for such a wide range of findings? In the following sections, we will show that the differences in the reported rates are influenced strongly by the differences in definitions of violence, the selection of a unit of analysis, and the sample of television programs.

Definition of Violence

There is no single commonly accepted definition of violence in the research literature. Violence is treated as a construct. That is, different researchers have different ways to assemble elements into their definitions. For example, Gerbner's definition of television violence focused on the act or threat of physical violence. He defined violence as "the overt expression of physical force (with or without a weapon) against self or other, compelling action against one's will on pain of being hurt or killed, or actually hurting or killing" (see Gerbner, Gross, Morgan, and Signorielli 1980). This definition is limited to overt physical acts and has produced findings of about 5 to 6 acts per hour over many years.

Williams, Zabrack, and Joy (1982, 366) used a wider concept of aggression defined as "behavior that inflicts harm, either physically or psychologically, including explicit or implicit threats and nonverbal behavior." Using this broader definition, which includes verbal aggression, they found 18.5 aggressive acts per hour in a mix of U.S. and Canadian programming.

Potter and his colleagues (1995) used a still broader definition: "any action that serves to diminish something in a physical, psychological, social, or emotional manner." The victim of aggression could be a person or a nonhuman entity (e.g., animal, object, or society), and, likewise, the perpetrator could fall within any one of these types. They found an average of 36.6 acts per hour, of which 13.2 were physical in nature.

Greenberg and his colleagues (1980) also used a broad conception in studying violence, including verbal acts of aggression and antisocial behaviors such as deceit. Their study reported 38 acts per hour, 12 of which were physical forms. Like the Williams et al. (1982) and the Potter et al. (1995) studies, the Greenberg definition allows for the inclusion of verbal aggression as well as physical violence.

As these examples demonstrate, the broader the definition, the greater the number of violent behaviors that will be indicated by research. The key elements that broaden a definition are the inclusion of verbal as well as physical violence, the inclusion of accidents as well as intentional acts, and the inclusion of threats as well as acts that involve actual harm.

Selecting Units of Analysis

Most of the findings noted above focus on the number of acts of violence. In these studies, a violent act typically begins with the presence of some action that meets the definition of violence and ends when that discrete action is completed. For example, if a cowboy pulls his gun and kills the sheriff, the act begins with the pulling of the gun and it ends when the sheriff falls down dead. Whether this lasts one second or one minute, it is still one act.

In contrast to coding discrete acts as they occur, some researchers divide a program into narrative scenes. If a scene contains violence it is coded as "yes," and if it does not, it is coded as "no." This is what Lichter and Amundson (1994) did in their one-day study of violence commissioned by *TV Guide*. When they report that violence occurred at the rate of 10.7 scenes per hour during evening prime time in 1992, they are not reporting average numbers of acts. If a scene contained 1, 5, 10, or any number of violent acts, the scene would simply be coded as violent, and their count would increase by only one scene, thereby sacrificing a great deal of precision.

The selection of a unit of analysis substantially influences the findings of any content analysis study. For example, consider a 5-minute scene depicting a barroom brawl where 100 punches are thrown before the mass of combatants tumbles outside on the street where one person draws a gun and shoots another. If we select a very narrow unit of analysis, then each punch might be counted along with the shooting, with each given equal weight. If instead we choose a very broad unit of analysis such as a scene, then all these acts would be collapsed together and simply be counted as one unit—a single violent scene. We could select a mid-level unit of analysis, but then we would face the challenge of constructing rules for chunking some behaviors together while separating others into distinct units. The decisions about unitizing have a direct influence on the numbers that are tallied in reporting the amount of violence observed on television.

Sampling

Although most previous content analyses examined a sample of one week of television programming, there is still wide variation in the nature of the samples gathered. For example, Gerbner's basic approach was to rely upon a single intact week of network programming. All programs on each network were sampled during a consecutive seven-day period, with the time slots limited to prime-time and Saturday morning hours. One possible concern with this approach is that the week selected may not be representative of the overall television season. Signorielli, Gross, and Morgan (1982) acknowledge this concern and seek to overcome it by reporting that no significant differences were found for most measures when comparing one week of their data to seven weeks of data gathered in 1976.

Greenberg et al. (1980) examined a composite week of prime-time programming, spreading the taping process out over a four-week period. This approach reduces the risk of gathering an unrepresentative sample due to a limited time frame in which the material is gathered. Like Gerbner, however, Greenberg collected essentially the same overall amount of content—approximately 60 to 80 hours of programming for each year's entire analysis. Approximately 22 hours were devoted to each of the three existing broadcast networks that were studied. The time periods sampled were the same as those used by Gerbner: prime-time and Saturday morning hours.

Potter et al. (1995) also used a composite week of television programming, but they sampled four networks (ABC, NBC, CBS, and Fox) from 6 P.M. to midnight, for a total of 168 hours of programming. Their sample, which was collected over a three-month period, was larger than that of Gerbner or Greenberg because of the addition of a fourth network (Fox) and the addition of early fringe (6 P.M. to 8 P.M.) and late fringe (11 P.M. to midnight) hours. But Potter et al. did not include any Saturday morning programs, thus omitting a heavy concentration of cartoons that typically contain a substantial amount of violence.

Lichter and Amundson (1994) used a sample that was broader in its inclusion of 10 channels: the broadcast networks ABC, CBS, NBC, Fox, and PBS; an independent broadcast station; and cable-delivered channels WTBS, USA, MTV, and HBO. It also included more parts of the day in its span from 6 A.M. to midnight. However, it was severely limited in its reliance on a single day of programming taped simultaneously on all 10 channels to represent an entire year.

Larger samples are generally superior to smaller ones, because the inclusion of more programs across more day-parts and days is more likely to be representative of the total population of television programming. This is especially clear when we understand that the patterns of violence are relatively stable year to year, but not necessarily day-part to day-part or day to day. To illustrate the importance of this point, we will reexamine the findings from three studies that were conducted across multiple years.

Gerbner's findings are relatively stable from 1967 to 1985, with between 65 percent and 80 percent of prime-time programs containing some violence, and between 89 percent and 98 percent of all Saturday morning children's shows also containing violence over a 20-year period (Signorielli 1990). Greenberg et al.'s

(1980) findings also show stable rates of violence across time, averaging 14.5 acts per hour in 1975–76; 15.2 acts per hour in 1976–77; and 14.1 per hour in 1977–78. Consistent with Gerbner, Greenberg et al. reported that Saturday morning children's programming was substantially more violent than prime-time content. Across the three-year study, acts of physical aggression took place at a rate of 22.9 per hour (1975–76); 25.2 per hour (1976–77); and 21.2 per hour (1977–78) during Saturday morning children's programs.

In contrast, Lichter and Amundson (1994) reported a very large fluctuation of violence, but they examined only a single day to represent each of their two years. Their overall number of violent scenes was 31 percent higher in 1994 than 1992, with some time periods experiencing increases of more than 200 percent. If accurate and representative, such evidence would point to huge, unexplained shifts in the level of televised violence across these two years. In fact, this instability is most likely a function of the small size of the sample that was used to represent each of the two years studied. Had they chosen a different day to represent each of those two years, the resulting pattern might well have indicated a dramatic drop in violence. This sampling base is not adequate to establish stability in the levels of violence that naturally vary somewhat from day to day. In conclusion, broader-based samples with more days, more day-parts, and more channels are more representative of a year's television programming.

Contextual Variables

Although most content analyses of violence focus on the frequency of acts, some have also gathered information on the manner in which violence is presented. The variables that capture this type of information have been regarded as "contextual" variables. Since his earliest content analyses, Gerbner has gathered information about the demographic characteristics (e.g., gender, ethnic background, age group) of both the perpetrators and victims of violence. Over time, content analysts have become more and more interested in these contextual characteristics and have added new variables to the list. For example, when Dominick (1973) counted criminal acts on prime time, he also gathered information on the motives for the acts and how those acts were resolved. Williams, Zabrack, and Joy (1982) assessed the harmfulness of violence to the victim. Potter and Ware (1987) examined four contextual variables: motivation, reward, justification, and portrayal of the characters (hero, villain, or neutral). More recently, Potter et al. (1995) analyzed 21 contextual variables including reward, intentionality, motivation, remorse, consequences, humor, presentational style, and demographic profiles of the perpetrators and victims. Mustonen and Pulkkinen (1993) developed 37 contextual variables. Many of these were the same concepts as used in the Potter et al. study (although operationalized differently), but there were also some additional variables such as graphicness, intensity, duration, and attractiveness.

Contextual variables have been useful in moving the content analysis findings beyond a simple counting of violent acts. However, to date, researchers have selected particular contextual variables for inclusion in their study primarily on the basis of face validity. That is, a variable is deemed important if it appears to be relevant as a factor influencing how viewers make sense of a violent act. There is a need to move beyond the criterion of simple face validity in selecting the attributes examined when studying television violence. Researchers need to construct a unified set of variables that meet a higher criterion of predictive validity. In short, it is important to design a content analysis of violence that will include all the contextual characteristics that have been demonstrated, through experimental research, to influence viewers' reactions to violent portrayals.

The *National Television Violence Study* (1997) strives to meet that challenge. In the remainder of this chapter, we outline the basic framework for the present research, providing a useful overview of our methods for the nontechnical reader. Then, in a subsequent section, we provide a complete explication of our research methods that will be of greatest interest to those more skilled in the practice of research.

Overview of the Present Research

Violence can be depicted in a variety of ways, and we have presented substantial evidence that differences in the context of a portrayal hold important implications for its impact on viewers. These differences in portrayals and their related implications for influencing the audience represent the heart of our interest in undertaking a long-term commitment to the study of televised violence. The goal of our project is to distinguish portrayals of violence most likely to contribute to effects generally considered as antisocial or harmful from portrayals that may be less problematic, or in some cases even beneficial. As noted in chapter 2, the areas of effects upon which we will concentrate are the learning of aggressive attitudes and behaviors; desensitization; and fear. To accomplish our goal, we have crafted a content analysis framework that we believe is uniquely sensitive to the context in which depictions of televised violence occur.

Definition of Violence

The most critical aspect for any study of television violence is the definition that is employed to identify acts classified as "violent." Our fundamental definition of violence places emphasis on three key elements: intention to harm, the physical nature of harm, and the involvement of animate beings. Violence is defined as any overt depiction of a credible threat of physical force or the actual use of such force intended to physically harm an animate being or group of beings. Violence also includes certain depictions of physically harmful consequences against an animate being or group that occur as a result of unseen violent means. Thus, there are three primary types of violent depictions: credible threats, behavioral acts, and harmful consequences.

This definition insures that depictions classified as violent represent actual physical aggression directed against living beings. Such physical action lies at the heart of any conception of violence, and limiting our definition to this type of portrayal (as opposed to including, for example, verbal aggression that might intimidate) renders it a conservative measure of violence on television.

Units of Analysis

In order to capture thorough information about the context of each violent act, it is essential that acts not be viewed in isolation; rather, each act should be considered as part of an ongoing exchange between characters, and each exchange must also be situated within the larger setting of the program as a whole. The richest meaning of any portrayal is found in larger units or chunks, rather than in individual acts. We plan to tap into these larger units of meaning through several different and novel techniques.

First, although we count as violence any act that fits the definition indicated above, we classify acts collectively as part of a larger, superordinate unit of analysis known as a violent incident. A violent incident involves an interaction between a perpetrator (P), an act (A), and a target (T), yielding the convenient acronym PAT as the label for this summary unit. We track and report collectively all violence within the same PAT framework, and we refer to this as the *PAT level* of analysis. For each PAT incident, we ascertain an array of contextual information particular to that exchange that helps us to estimate the likely impact of the depiction.

Second, we gather and report additional descriptive information about the context of violent depictions at the *scene level*. A violent scene encompasses an interrelated series of violent incidents that occur without a meaningful break in the flow of actual or imminent violence. Analysis at this level affords the opportunity to examine relationships between discrete violent acts.

Finally, we also examine violent content at the *program level*. It is important to consider the larger meaning or message that is conveyed by a program, and to do so accurately requires assessment at this level. Some critics have argued that previous studies have failed to differentiate the violence in an artistic or historical program from the violence contained in an entertaining action-adventure program. Both types of programs may contain numerous acts of violence when the focus is at the micro level of analysis. However, the overall narrative of a historical or educational program may be to condemn the evilness of violence, whereas the action-adventure show may seem to glorify violence. For example, the broadcast network program *Kids Killing Kids* first presented situations resulting in youth violence, but then replayed each scene a second time, illustrating nonviolent alternatives for conflict resolution. An analysis of content of *Kids Killing Kids* at the micro level would reveal that it ranks very high in terms of frequency of violent acts. Yet the overall message of the movie, when viewed at the program level, is an antiviolence one.

By analyzing violence at all three of these levels—the interaction or PAT level, the scene level, and the program level—we hope to provide the most rich and meaningful data regarding the nature and extent of violent portrayals yet presented by the scientific community. These units of analysis represent a novel framework devised specifically for this project. Both this overall framework for analysis as well as the individual context measures that are assessed at each of the appropriate levels were refined over roughly a six-month period during which the principal investigators evaluated their validity and reliability. The measures that have survived this process are theoretically grounded, consistent with all existing scientific research assessing the effects of televised violence, and, as we will demonstrate, can be applied consistently by different coders who are assigned to evaluate different types of television programming content.

Measures

Chapter 2 has foregrounded most areas in which we have crafted measures that will be used to describe the most important aspects of violent depictions. These measures include assessment of the type of violent depiction (credible threats, behavioral acts, and harmful consequences); the means by which violence is accomplished (e.g., type of weapon); the extent and graphicness of the violent portrayal; characteristics of the perpetrator and target; the reason for the violence; the consequences of the violence (e.g., pain, harm); the rewards or punishments associated with violence; the degree of realism of the violence; and the use of humor in depictions of violence. In addition, a judgment regarding the overall narrative purpose of each program is applied to help further contextualize any violent depictions. Details regarding the range of values for each measure and the procedures for judging specific content are included in the subsequent section of this chapter.

Coding of Content

Each program included in the sample was evaluated by one of 55 undergraduate research assistants who were trained as coders. Prior to the beginning of the coding process in which judgments are recorded for each of the content measures included in the overall study, coders received approximately 40 hours of classroom training and 20 hours of laboratory practice in recording their observations properly. Only coders who demonstrated strong proficiency with our measures at the completion of training were allowed to continue with the project.

Once the actual process of evaluating videotapes began, coders were assigned randomly to code taped programs. They performed their work in small, individual rooms in a laboratory at the University of California, Santa Barbara. The consistency of judgments across coders was monitored on a biweekly basis throughout all periods of data collection, and the results of these reliability tests are reported in a later section of this chapter. This monitoring insured that the quality of the judgments that were recorded for each tape were consistently high.

Sample

There are two major features that set our sample apart from other content analyses. First, it is significantly larger than most previous studies of television violence. The typical sample size in the studies cited previously in this chapter is in the range of 80 to 120 hours per year examined. In contrast, this project sampled nearly 2500 hours of material. The sample includes programming from 6 A.M. until 11 P.M. across a total of 23 different channels (affiliates of the four leading commercial broadcast networks; a public broadcasting affiliate; three independent commercial broadcast stations; 12 basic cable channels; and three premium cable channels).

Second, rather than sampling intact days or weeks of programming, we selected each individual *program* randomly from a population of 20 weeks of programming spanning from October 1994 to June 1995. Therefore, our sample technically involves literally thousands of sampling units (programs) rather than the more traditional seven units (days). When a sample relies on large units like entire days, there is a greater risk of an anomalous event occurring (e.g., a breaking news story) that could make that block of seven units of programming unrepresentative. In contrast, an anomalous event occurring in one of several thousand units would have much less impact on the overall representativeness of the sample.

Our sample includes most forms of programming on television. However, we did not analyze all shows for violence. Excluded were the genres of religious programming, game shows, instructional shows, home shopping, sports, and newscasts. Consequently, the cable program services CNN and ESPN were excluded entirely from the study. All of these exclusions were stipulated in the research contract with the study's funder, the National Cable Television Association.

Summary

This section has presented a brief review of the previous content analyses of televised violence in order to illuminate the key decisions in the design of those studies. Then we provided a summary of the key aspects in the design of our study. Now we want to highlight the key innovations of our research. These innovations are in the areas of definition of violence, units of analysis, sampling, reliability, and the consideration of context.

Our definition of violence moves beyond a narrow focus on the behavioral act, including credible threats and depictions of harmful consequences of unseen violence. As for units of analysis, we provide for a simultaneous, multiple level (PAT, sequence, and program) examination. Our sample of programs is far more broad than any other scientific content analysis. Our reliability design is particularly complex because of our use of so many coders and the elaborate nature of our measures. And finally, our focus on contextual variables is grounded strongly in the effects literature, so we can be confident of the importance of the content attributes we have selected for study. In the following section, we detail the intricacies of our methods and measures in a thorough fashion that will be of greatest interest to those in the research community who wish to scrutinize our procedures. We begin with information about the sample, then turn to the content measures, and finally to the coding and reliability of our data.

Sample of Programs

We believe that the sample for this study represents a significant improvement over the methodologies employed by past research. Our approach includes a broad range of programming, including most major sources of cable and broadcast television. The sheer size of the sample is approximately 25 to 30 times larger than most previous studies, with a total of approximately 2,500 hours of content. But most importantly, we employ a scientific model for selecting the material included in the sample, thus maximizing the generalizability of our findings to the overall television environment.

The population of interest here is theoretically all programs on television. As a practical matter, however, it is rarely possible for any researcher to truly examine an entire population. Instead, a sample is drawn that is meant to represent the overall population. Some samples accomplish this goal better than others.

Basic Parameters of the Sample

The sampling frame for the present investigation is defined by four parameters: channels, program types, sampling times (i.e., times of day), and sampling periods (i.e., times of year).

Channel.   Twenty-three channels were included in the sample. The channels consist of the following different types: commercial broadcast networks, commercial broadcast independents, the public broadcasting network, basic cable, and premium cable. More specifically, the channels listed in table 3.1 were

TABLE 3.1.   List of Channels in Sample

Commercial Broadcast	Independent Broadcast	Public Broadcast	Basic Cable	Premium Cable
ABC	KCAL	KCET	A&E	Cinemax
CBS	KCOP		AMC	HBO
Fox	KTLA		BET	Showtime
NBC			Cartoon Network	
			Disney	
			Family Channel	
			Lifetime	
			Nickelodeon	
			TNT	
			USA	
			VH-1	
			MTV	

included in each group. All monitoring for each channel was conducted in the Los Angeles market. For the commercial broadcast networks, their Los Angeles affiliates were sampled. These include KABC, KCBS, KTTV for Fox, and KNBC. We did not differentiate between material aired on these stations that originated from the network as opposed to nonnetwork material presented at the discretion of the local affiliate. Thus, what we really have sampled is network affiliate programming, which includes mostly network content but also some syndicated material that would air during fringe hours.

If we had focused solely on network content, we would have excluded many hours of programming that are watched by large numbers of people. We suspect that there is not much variation from one network affiliate to another in terms of how these fringe hours are filled (i.e., mostly syndicated content). Furthermore, for the average viewer it is not always easy or meaningful to differentiate between network and local affiliate programming when both are delivered on the same channel. Therefore, we have chosen to include all network affiliate content in the study and to classify it as network programming. This provides the most comprehensive assessment because it allows us to analyze all television programming that is delivered to the public.

Similarly, we recognize that our sample of PBS programming from the local affiliate in Los Angeles, KCET, will include some small amount of content that is not network-originated. It would be difficult to monitor any PBS affiliate without encountering this concern. In essence, the issue here is the same as with the commercial network affiliates, and we have resolved it in the same fashion. We have monitored all programming on the affiliate and will report it as public broadcasting content.

For the independent stations, the three major outlets in the market were sampled. Because the independents' share of the Los Angeles market is dominated by these three stations, and because almost all nationally syndicated programming airs in the market, we are reasonably confident that our sample includes virtually all of the first-run syndicated content available nationwide. During the 1994–95 television season, two new network services were unveiled: Warner and Paramount. Each of these services began to deliver a "part-time" slate of programs, and this content was aired in the Los Angeles market on two of the independent stations we sampled. Because of the modest scope of the programming efforts and the lack of any established "identity" for these networks that would trigger any particular audience expectations, we have chosen to treat these programs the same as any other syndicated content aired on independent stations. Thus, this material is included in the overall findings for the independent stations category.

The cable channels included in the sample were chosen because of their significant audience reach. Program services that are typically marketed as part of a cable subscriber package without any additional per-channel cost are classified as "basic cable" services. Services that require an additional per-channel fee are classified as premium cable channels. During the period when this study was being conducted, The Disney Channel began to alter its marketing from a premium to a basic cable service. Though not yet implemented in all markets, this shift is well under way. Consequently, we have chosen to include Disney during this transition year in the basic service category where it will ultimately reside.

Program type.   Religious programs, game shows, "infomercials" or home shopping material, instructional programs, sports, and news were excluded from analysis in the study. To maintain the integrity of the sample design and its representativeness of the overall television environment, these programs were included in the sample grid whenever they were selected by the random draw that created our composite week of programming (that process is detailed below). However, none of these program types were examined for violence. Their exclusion was established by the original contract for this research.

Time of day.   All programs listed in *TV Guide* from 6:00 A.M. until 10:59 P.M. were eligible for inclusion in the sample (a total of 17 hours per day).

Sampling period.   A set of 20 weeks beginning October 8, 1994, and ending June 9, 1995, was chosen as the sampling period (see table 3.2 for a list of the specific sample weeks). The time periods around certain holidays (Thanksgiving, Christmas, and Easter) were excluded from the sampling frame. Holiday specials and nonregular programming presumed to be highly variable from year to year were therefore eliminated. The sampling period was of sufficient length to allow for the inclusion of five network "sweep" weeks. Summer weeks were not included in the sample period in order to avoid the over-inclusion of programs due to repeated scheduling.

TABLE 3.2.   Year 1 Sample Weeks

Week Number	Dates
1	October 8–14
2	October 15–21
3	October 22–28
4	October 29–November 4
5	November 5–11
6	December 3–9
7	January 14–20
8	January 21–27
9	January 28–February 3
10	February 4–10
11	February 11–17
12	March 4–10
13	March 11–17
14	March 18–24
15	April 22–28
16	April 29–May 5
17	May 6–12
18	May 20–26
19	May 27–June 2
20	June 3–9

Given the large number of channels, the broad span of weeks, and the 17 hours per channel per day that define the sample of programs, the present study is much more comprehensive than the sample examined in other studies. For comparative purposes it is useful to note that the most widely cited content analysis conducted previously, that of Gerbner and his colleagues, included only one week of prime-time and Saturday morning programs per year.

Obtaining a Representative Sample of the Program Population

Rather than being selected on the basis of convenience as in most other content analysis studies, the programs chosen in the present study were selected with a modified version of the equal probability of selection method (EPSEM). With this method of selection every program has an equal chance, or opportunity, to appear in the sample. This method insures that a subset of the population of television programs that is *representative* of the entire population of programs is obtained for analysis.

A sample is representative of the population from which it is selected if the aggregate characteristics of the sample closely approximate those same aggregate characteristics in the population. Usually social scientists select groups of people for study. For a sample of individuals to be representative of a larger population of people it must contain essentially the same variations and in the same relative proportions as also exist in the overall population. If the population contains a certain proportion of women and a certain proportion of men, then a representative sample would consist of that same proportion of men and women. Similarly, if the population of interest was composed of two children for every eight adults, a representative sample would contain a similar ratio of children and adults.

This logic can be applied equally well to the population of television programs. For example, if the population of television programs contains a given proportion of situation comedies, then a representative sample of programs would also contain approximately that same proportion. Although no sample is ever perfectly representative of the population from which it is drawn, a basic principle of probability sampling is that a sample will be more representative of the population from which it was selected if all members of the population have an equal chance of being selected.

Equal probability samples are more representative because they avoid the biases of convenience samples. For example, the riskiest strategy a researcher wishing to study a population of U.S. residents could pursue would be to walk around his or her neighborhood and interview the first 100 people that could be found. This kind of method is sometimes used by untrained researchers, but it has serious problems. Obviously, the 100 people interviewed by happenstance may share very few characteristics of U.S. residents in general.

The same risks are encountered in selecting television programs for study. Simply selecting programs that are convenient for study (e.g., examining only the first couple of programs in a season, or choosing to examine a single day of programming) risks selecting programs that are not "typical" of the larger population from which they have been chosen. Examining programs only in the beginning of the season is risky because programming strategies may shift during certain times of the year, such as during ratings "sweeps" periods. Selecting a single day for monitoring raises a significant risk that one particularly violent movie or other program would be shown that day and have a major impact on the overall findings. In fact, the possibilities for inadvertent sampling bias are endless and not always obvious. The only technique that guards against bias is the equal probability selection method.

The strength of the method employed in this study is that the sample is representative because every program has an approximately equal chance of being included. This method of selection offers an additional benefit. Because they are chosen randomly, each program can be said to be "independent" of every other program in the sample. This independence among sampling units permits us to make the strongest possible statistical comparisons between groups of programs that might be distinguished by time of day or type of channel, for example.

Program selection.   Two half-hour time slots (defined by hour of day and day of week) were randomly selected for each channel during each week that the sampling occurred. Once a time slot was selected, the *TV Guide* was consulted and the program corresponding to that time slot was entered into a scheduling grid several days before the target week programming began. Programs were retained in the sample in their entirety regardless of the number of time slots they occupied. For example, if the time slot 1:30 P.M., Tuesday, was randomly selected and an hour-long program that began at 1:00 P.M. was identified in the *TV Guide,* that program was selected for inclusion in the sample and permitted to occupy two half-hour time slots (1 P.M.–2 P.M.). Our procedure thus can be said to be a modified version of an EPSEM because the sample is actually self-weighted by length of program. An hour-long program has twice the probability of being included in the final sample as a half-hour program.

TABLE 3.3.   Breakdown of Programs and Exclusions in Sample

Channel	No. of Programs	Not Coded	% Not Coded	Taping Errors	% Taping Errors	Program Overlap	% Program Overlap
ABC	137	40	29	3	2	6	4
CBS	143	54	38	6	4	17	12
NBC	129	48	37	3	2	13	10
Fox	163	26	16	14	9	12	7
PBS	163	12	7	4	2	12	7
KCAL	162	55	34	3	2	9	6
KCOP	147	28	19	3	2	7	5
KTLA	104	41	39	8	8	22	21
A&E	95	0	0	3	3	4	4
AMC	82	0	0	2	2	47	57
BET	133	29	22	5	4	3	2
CAR	171	0	0	9	5	10	6
DIS	166	0	0	8	5	14	8
FAM	174	58	33	5	3	15	9
LIF	145	51	36	7	5	16	11
MTV	153	13	8	4	3	22	14
NIK	229	2	1	9	4	9	4
TNT	94	2	2	7	7	21	22
USA	143	33	23	3	2	27	19
VH1	181	0	0	11	6	30	17
HBO	104	0	0	1	1	42	40
MAX	81	0	0	3	4	48	59
SHO	86	0	0	9	10	43	50
Total	3185	492	15	130	4	449	14

This taping schedule was transmitted to an independent television taping contractor, Killingsworth Inc. of Long Beach, California, where the programs were taped. Once taped, the content was shipped to the University of California, Santa Barbara, where it was checked for completeness, picture, and sound quality. Programs found to be incomplete or for which sound or picture quality were inadequate were dropped from the sample and the time slot was resampled. Table 3.3 shows the total number of programs sampled by channel.

Preemptions.   Only scheduled programming was included in the sample. Programs that were preempted by news bulletins or special reports that exceeded five minutes in length per half-hour of programming were excluded from the sample. The largest number of preemptions were due to the O. J. Simpson trial, which was heavily covered by Los Angeles area independent broadcasters.

Program overlap.   Sampling by half-hour unit resulted in some program overlap due to the availability of half-hour time slots that were "sandwiched" between programs already in the sample. These programs were taped in their entirety and included in the sample. Table 3.3 lists the number and percentage of program overlap by channel. Premium channels with a high proportion of movie programming accounted for the highest overlap. Overall, 14 percent of the programs included in the sample overlap with other programs.

Programs exceeding the 6:00 A.M.–11:00 P.M. time-of-day frame.   Programs that began before 6:00 A.M. or continued beyond 11:00 P.M. were taped in their entirety when they were selected by the sampling process. For example, a program that was selected for sampling for the 10:00 P.M. block that ran 90 minutes would be included even though its final half-hour aired after 11:00 P.M.

Summary Description of the Sample

A composite week of programming.   The sampling procedure described above resulted in a seven-day composite week of programming. Virtually all shows in the regular program schedule for each channel appear in the final composite week. As noted above, the random selection method insures that this composite is theoretically more representative of a "typical" week of cable television programming than an arbitrary selected actual week of programming. Further, the number of independently sampled programs is large enough to make scientifically valid comparisons between violent content in various categories of programming and across times of day.

Total program count.   The taped sample includes a total of 3,185 programs. A complete grid of all programs selected for inclusion in the sample appeared in the *NTVS Sample of Programs for Content Analysis* (1996b). A total of 130 programs (4 percent) were removed from the sample due to taping errors or other technical problems. Missing half-hour program blocks occur most frequently for Showtime (10 percent) and Fox (9 percent).

Sample exclusions.   Of the total 3,185 programs, 492 (15 percent) are religious programs, game shows, sports, "infomercials," instructional shows, and breaking news, and thus were not included in the coding analyses.

Overall Sample Summary

The sample for the present study has several strengths that distinguish it from previous content analyses. Because the method of selection is based on probability and because the parameters of the sample (17 hours per day, 20 weeks, 23 channels) are so broad, a composite week has been assembled that can be said to be more representative of a typical week of television programming than past research efforts. A sample of programming selected in this fashion permits a more accurate estimation of the amount and type of violent programming in a given year. This method is also particularly valuable for insuring accuracy in comparing levels over time. With this method, we are able to track increases or decreases in violence accurately from year to year.

Content Measures

We now turn to the measures that are applied in our analysis of the content collected by our sampling strategy. In this section we deal with three main topics. The first topic, that of defining violence, isolates the depictions that will be the focus of further analysis. The second topic, units of analysis, establishes the framework within which we operate in structuring our assessment of violent depictions. The third topic, contextual measures, details the specific judgments that are recorded for each case of violence that we observe.

Definition of Violence

Our fundamental definition of violence places emphasis on a number of elements, including intention to harm, the physical nature of harm, and the involvement of animate beings. We use the following definition in this study: *Violence* is defined as any overt depiction of a credible threat of physical force or the actual use of such force intended to physically harm an animate being or group of beings. Violence also includes certain depictions of physically harmful consequences against an animate being or group that occur as a result of unseen violent means.

Thus, there are three primary types of violent depictions: credible threats, behavioral acts, and harmful consequences. The key concepts embodied in this definition warrant some explanation and rationale.

Intention to harm.   Intentionality is obviously a private, internal psychological state that is not open to direct observation. Nonetheless, it is the focus of how most humans seek to make sense of their world; that is, they attribute intentionality to the actions of others. If viewers could not attribute intentions to the actions of television characters they observed, the content would hold little interest for them. Consequently, program creators seek to convey motives and intentions to the audience in order for a story to make sense. We believe character intent related to behaviors that threaten or harm others can be inferred from the context of the portrayal and classified reliably.

The concept of intention is an essential aspect of our definition. If intentions were not addressed, many harmful behaviors not reasonably considered as aggressive might otherwise be classified as violent. All accidental harm would be included, as might the actions of surgeons and dentists, neither of which has been associated with harmful psychological effects on the audience. Conversely, it is important that we not exclude acts that attempt to cause harm but which prove unsuccessful. Such acts are clearly aggressive. They could be learned and could contribute to fear responses in the audience as well as increased socialization to aggression. Only through a consideration of intent can such actions be properly classified as falling within our definition of violence.

Physical harm.   One might reasonably assert that verbal assaults that intimidate or physical acts that are meant to cause psychological or emotional harm (e.g., embarrassment, humiliation) should be considered as violence. Certainly such actions are aggressive and may in some cases be associated with antisocial impacts on the audience.

We have chosen, however, to draw the line for our definition of violence at a point which is supported most strongly and unequivocally by the existing base of research evidence, rather than to grapple for the edge of that boundary. Physical harm or the threat thereof is at the root of all conceptions of violence and of most operationalizations of the concept in past research (Baron and Richardson 1994; Reiss and Roth 1993). By employing this approach, we can be confident that our definition of violence is a conservative one, and that our findings will not artificially inflate any estimates of the overall amount of violence on television.

Given that physical harm represents a key dimension in our basic definition of violence, it is important to recognize two key extensions of this concept. One is that credible threats of physical harm must be considered as violent because, just as with a harmful act, they too may contribute to fear responses in the audience (Cantor 1991) as well as increased priming of aggressive thoughts and behaviors (Berkowitz 1984; Berkowitz and Rogers 1986). A second application is that violent actions that are not portrayed overtly but can be inferred clearly from the depiction of the harmful consequences (e.g., police respond to the scene of a shooting and find a victim bleeding to death) also should be considered as violence because of their likelihood of contributing to antisocial effects such as fear (Wilson and Cantor 1985; Wilson 1995).

It is important to note that although our definition of violence will include a range of acts including credible threats, behavioral acts, and depictions of harmful consequences of unseen violence, we do not mean to assert that there is equivalence in terms of harmfulness across this range of depictions. For example, consider a portrayal in which violence occurs offscreen, with only the result of that violence (such as a bloody nose or lip from a blow to the face) depicted instead of the actual act itself. This depiction would be captured by our measures as an example of harmful consequences, yet would likely pose less concern, at least from a social learning or modeling standpoint, than would an overt depiction of the implied behavioral act.

Animate beings as perpetrator and target.   Harm can be caused to individuals by many forces other than the actions of living beings. For example, a person could be injured by an act of nature such as a tornado or a lightning bolt. Although these actions might contribute to fear on the part of some viewers, in particular young children, they would not raise concerns in terms of socialization to or modeling of aggression. Consistent with our previous point that intention to harm is a fundamental aspect in our definition of violence, we believe that at least one animate being capable of possessing intentions must be involved as a perpetrator in order to have an instance of violence.

Similarly, an animate being must be a target in order to meet our definition of violence. Individuals often hit or kick inanimate objects in aggressive fashion. Sometimes this reflects spontaneous anger and, other times, a premeditated intention to damage a target's possessions. In either case, intent to physically harm something living is missing, and thus we would not consider these examples of violence as we have defined it. Again we must note that some such examples of violence against property would certainly be associated with antisocial influences on the audience. Nonetheless, some examples of property damage, such as putting a sledgehammer to an old car at the county fair, could be entirely benign when considered in context. Most importantly, the research evidence documenting the antisocial effects of violence against living beings is compelling, while no comparable body of direct evidence exists regarding the impacts of violence against inanimate objects. Given our desire to measure violence in conservative fashion, we have stipulated that an animate being must be targeted for harm in order for violence to occur.

Of course, the television world is inhabited by a wide range of creatures not all of whom naturally occur on Earth. These include everything from Smurfs to Teenage Mutant Ninja Turtles to Biker Mice from Mars, to name a few children's program characters; beings from other planets such as Superman or Alf; fictional monsters such as King Kong or Godzilla; or even fantasy characters such as anthropomorphized flowers or trees that walk and talk. We will consider animate beings to include humans (either real or animated), animals, supernatural creatures, and anthropomorphized characters of all kinds. Although any of these will count as animate, we do not mean to imply they are all necessarily equivalent. In our assessment of the context in which violence occurs, information about the type of characters involved as well as specific attributes associated with particular characters will be important considerations.

Three forms of violence.   A violent action is any depiction that qualifies as violence according to our basic definition. We have classified violent actions into three primary types: credible threats of violence, behavioral acts, and depictions of harmful consequences of violence.

First, a credible threat is an overt behavior that threatens the use of violence. The behavior may be either verbal or nonverbal. A credible threat occurs when a perpetrator evidences a serious intent to harm a target by either directly communicating the threat verbally or by displaying violent means in a threatening manner. For example, a directly communicated credible threat is when someone says menacingly, "I'll slash your throat." A common example of a threat using a display of violent means is when someone aims a gun at another.

Second, a behavioral act is an overt action using violent physical force against another. These types of acts may employ weapons, ordinary objects, or the perpetrator's own natural means. Common examples of behavioral acts using weapons include stabbings, shootings, and the use of explosives. Ordinary objects used to commit behavioral acts could include beer bottles, chairs, or lead pipes; the common characteristic is that the object is not normally associated with use as a weapon. Finally, punches, kicks, and bites are examples of behavioral acts using natural means.

Third, harmful consequences are depictions of the victims of violence when the violence is clearly implied but not portrayed overtly as it occurs. An example of this type of violence is when two detectives arrive on a scene to find a murder victim lying in a pool of blood. Depictions of harmful consequences are coded only when a program does not include any portion of the violent act, but rather depicts only its physical aftermath. If in the above example the program had shown the victim actually being shot and then later it showed the detectives arriving and encountering the body, we would count the original act as a violent behavioral act, but would not count the harmful consequences as a separate act of violence. In this way, we avoid "double-counting" of any violent actions. Harmful consequences count as violence only when the behavioral act is implied and never shown.

Units of Analysis

The judgments and observations we have recorded for each instance of violence are organized into three distinct levels, or units of analysis. These three levels include: (1) the violent interaction, or PAT level; (2) the scene level; and (3) the program level. The PAT level is the most microscopic of the three.

PAT level.   All violent incidents can be said to represent an interaction between a perpetrator (P) who performs a type of act (A) directed at a target (T). For example, a hijacker with a bomb strapped to his back who threatens a plane-load of passengers would be categorized at the PAT level in the following manner: P = hijacker, A = credible threat, T = passengers on the plane. A CIA agent who shoots a handgun at a group of terrorists would be unitized as: P = CIA agent, A = behavioral act, T = terrorists.

When a violent action occurs, it is coded first as a PAT case or observation. The information recorded for that case encompasses all of the violent actions directed by a particular perpetrator at a particular target within the same scene, so long as the type of act remains the same. Recall that type of act refers to credible threat, behavioral act, and depiction of harmful consequences. Brief threats that are followed immediately by a violent behavioral act are not considered as independent actions, but rather are recorded as a violent behavioral act and thus constitute a single PAT. However, a threat that was followed through with a violent behavior at a later point in time would represent two separate PATs—one for the threat and one for the behavioral act. Even though the P and T remained constant, the change in A (type of act) requires a new PAT. Generally speaking, a different PAT case results whenever there is a significant change in any one of the three elements of the violent interaction: the perpetrator, the act, or the target.

Obviously, not all violent interactions display the same characteristics or contextual features. For our purposes, it is vital to evaluate all violent interactions at their most microscopic level because we need to take into account numerous aspects of the context of each portrayal in order to estimate its potential for influencing the audience. Consider the following example: a law enforcement officer is assaulted by a fleeing felon, who tries to stab the officer in order to escape from the scene of the crime. The officer responds by shooting the suspect in order to save her own life. In this exchange, there are two very different motives for violence. There may also be other important differences, such as the nature of the characters committing the violence, the way in which the violent actions are depicted on-screen, and the consequences of each person's actions. To capture these important differences, we must be able to evaluate the nature of each character's involvement in violence, including what actions they have performed, their reasons for violence, and so on. To accomplish this, we must view each PAT interaction as a separate case.

One PAT would be recorded with the criminal as the P and the officer as the T, with a separate PAT representing the officer as the P and the criminal as the T when the officer responded to the initial assault with more violence. In this example, there is a different reason for violence by the officer than by the criminal. If the entire interaction between the two was recorded as a single unit, that information would be lost or diminished. The obvious qualitative differences inherent within different interactions led to the construction of the PAT unit.

Because perpetrators and targets may come in single, multiple, or implied forms, precise operational rules were crafted in order to maintain the integrity of the PAT unit across a wide range of situations. For example, when a group of people such as a military squad operate collectively to accomplish a common goal, their actions are considered as representing a single P. Similarly, it is important to distinguish interactions such as a credible threat from an implied perpetrator (i.e., an anonymous ransom note) from a visual depiction of a graphic and imitatable behavioral act performed by a heroic character. The details of these and other rules for coding observations are contained in the complete version of the codebook (*National Television Violence Study* 1996a).

Scene level. The second and intermediate level of analysis is called a scene. A violent scene is defined as a related series of violent behaviors, actions, or depictions of harmful consequences of violence that occur without a significant break in the flow of actual or imminent violence. In other words, the actions maintain a narrative flow in which a sequence of actions are connected or related to one another. Therefore, violent sequences typically occur in the same general setting among the same characters or types of characters. One or many PAT interactions may occur within a given scene.

A great deal of rich contextual information that may not necessarily be present at the microscopic PAT level, such as the presence of rewards or punishments for violence, can be captured at this intermediate level of analysis. Also measured at this level is the explicitness or graphicness of the violent depictions.

A violent scene begins whenever any action that fulfills the definition of violence is observed. A scene ends whenever a significant break occurs within the scene. A significant break occurs when the imminent threat of violence ceases to exist or when there is an interruption in the time, place, or setting that would reflect what is commonly referred to as a scene change. Again, specific operational rules have been crafted to facilitate consistency in judgments across coders. For example, films often include "cutaways," or shifts back and forth between events occurring simultaneously at two separate locations. When this occurs, scene shifts or cutaways that continue for a period of 30 seconds or more are considered significant breaks.

Program level. The macroordinate unit of analysis is an entire program. While it is important to evaluate violent interactions at both the PAT and scene level in order to capture vital contextual differences between different interactions, it is also important to evaluate content at the broader level of overall themes or messages represented in a show. We believe the judgments at this level very nearly approximate some of the overall messages that average adult viewers would obtain after watching an entire program. For example, an evil character may be punished for violence only at the end of a program, but not at the time the violence was committed. The PAT and scene measures would not capture this punishment because they are focused on the character's actions (PAT level) and the related developments that occur within the scene in which those actions are depicted (scene level). A measure of punishments for violence at the program level is needed to complement our analysis at the more microscopic PAT and scene level.

Most programs consist of one thematic story or unfolding narrative whose beginning, middle, and end are presented across a scheduled block of time. These programs typically begin and end their time slots with production credits and/or conventions (e.g., teasers, previews, promos). Examples of these types of programs are situation comedies, dramas, daytime soap operas, and movies.

Some other types of programs, however, feature two or more self-contained stories whose unfolding narratives are presented independently of one another. Each of these segments represents only a portion of the overall time devoted to a scheduled program, yet each is an independent "story." The plotline, characters, and/or geographical locations in each segment tend to vary from one story to the next. A good example of this would be a magazine format show such as the long-running Sunday night program *60 Minutes*. We refer to such content as a *segmented program*.

Segmented programs begin and end their time slots with standard production credits and/or conventions (e.g., teasers, previews, promos). However, each independent story nested within the program is introduced and separated in some way from the other stories by some form of production credits. Examples of these types of programs are music videos, news magazines, certain reality-based programs, and some cartoon shows. For material classified as a segmented program, the program level variables are assessed for each segment within that particular program in order to capture the differences that may exist between discrete segments in a program.

Contextual Measures

In order to measure the contextual factors delineated in chapter 2, two types of variables were created: violence-related and character-related variables. In the section that follows, each violence-related contextual measure will be defined and explicated at the level of analysis in which it was assessed. Then, each of the character-related contextual variables designed to capture the qualities of the perpetrators and targets involved in violence will be conceptually and operationally defined.

PAT level context variables.   The first contextual factor assessed at the PAT level was the perpetrator's primary *reason* or motive for engaging in violence. This variable was assessed at the most micro level of analysis because a perpetrator's reason for acting violently may vary as a function of the target she or he is confronting. There were six possible values for this measure: protection of life, retaliation, anger, personal gain, mental instability, and other.

As we indicated in chapter 2, violence that is "justified" may pose a greater risk to viewers than "unjustified" aggressive actions. In an effort to assess "justified violence," four categories of reasons will be collapsed at the level of analysis. Violence that is accomplished in an effort to "protect life" or to "retaliate" for a previous act of violence is usually socially sanctioned in a typical plot. As such, these two reasons will form the variable "justified" violence. Alternatively, aggressive actions that seem to be motivated by "personal gain" or "mental instability" are more likely to appear "unjustified." Consequently, these two reasons will be collapsed in an effort to examine "unjustified" violence.

The second contextual variable assessed the means used in each violent interaction. *Means* was defined as any object, weapon, or device that perpetrators used to threaten and/or harm targets. There were six categories of means: natural means (using a character's normal physical capabilities such as striking with a fist), unconventional weapons (striking with a chair or bottle), conventional weapons—nonfirearms (police baton, knife), handheld firearms (gun, pistol), heavy weaponry (submarines, tanks), and bombs (timer, remote, hand grenades). For any given violent interaction, each different type of means used by a perpetrator against a particular target was captured.

In addition to assessing the type(s), the *extent* of each means used also was recorded. Extent was measured within each means category for a given interaction. There were 5 values for the extent variable: one (single example of act), some (between 2 and 9 examples of the act), many (between 10 and 20 examples of the act), and extreme (over 20 examples of the act).

The next three contextual factors measured the immediate consequences of each violent interaction. Conceptually, *consequences* referred to the amount of physical harm and pain that a target incurred as a result of violence. Two types of harm were measured for each violent interaction: depicted harm and likely harm. Subsequent comparison of these two measures allows us to draw inferences about the relative degree of realism associated with specific portrayals.

The evaluation of *depicted harm* was based on two specific factors: the amount of physical injury done to a target's body, and the target's ability to function after experiencing violence. In some cases of unrealistic depictions, such as in cartoons, these two elements are often in conflict. That is, a character may be flattened like a pancake by a steamroller, but then pop right up and walk away unfazed. In such cases, the depicted harm would be judged as minimal because the target continued to function seemingly without harm even though suffering temporary disconfiguration of the body. There were four possible values for depicted harm: none, mild, moderate, or extreme.

A measure of *likely harm*, on the other hand, assessed the level of physical injury and incapacitation that would likely occur if the same violent means were targeted toward a human in real life. To judge this, an inference had to be drawn about the potential seriousness of the means used. The values for likely harm were the same as those for depicted harm.

In addition to depicted and likely harm, the amount of *depicted pain* a target experienced as a result of violence was also assessed. Conceptually, pain was defined as the audible (i.e., screams, moans, yells, gasps) or visible (i.e., facial expressions, physical reactions such as clutching of a wound/injury) expression of physical suffering that occurred as a result of violence. There were four possible values for pain: none, mild, moderate, and extreme. The measure was not applied in cases where there was no opportunity to observe a target's pain or suffering either during or immediately after experiencing violence.

Finally, violent behaviors were assessed for instances of sexual assault. Sexual assault was defined as violence that occurred in conjunction with intimate physical contact involving sexual and/or erotic overtones; or other erotic touching or physical contact intended to arouse or sexually gratify the perpetrator against a target's will. If any of these elements were present either immediately before, during, or after a violent act, then the act was coded as including sexual assault.

Scene level context variables.   At the scene level, several violence-related contextual variables were assessed. These variables were judged after the coder had viewed the entire scene and the one that immediately followed it. Oftentimes, relevant contextual information such as reinforcements given or taken for violence are not depicted in the actual violent scene but in the immediately adjacent scene. For this reason, coders were instructed to always watch the scene that immediately followed the scene prior to making their contextual judgments at this level of analysis. If a violent scene was followed by a commercial break, by definition, no subsequent scene existed and the coder was instructed to simply assess the following variables at the end of the scene.

The first contextual factor at the scene level assessed the *rewards* that were associated with a perpetrator's violent action. A reward was defined as any verbal or nonverbal reinforcement that was given to or taken by a perpetrator for acting violently. The presence or absence of three types of rewards were assessed at this level: self-praise, praise from others, or material rewards.

Similarly, *punishments* associated with violent actions were also measured at the scene level. Conceptually, a punishment was defined as any verbal or nonverbal sign of disapproval or disappointment that was expressed toward a perpetrator for acting violently. The presence or absence of four specific types of punishments were assessed at the scene level: self-condemnation, condemnation from others, nonviolent condemnation, and violent condemnation.

The next contextual factor assessed at the scene level was *graphicness*. Three types of graphicness were assessed. The first factor assessed the explicitness of the violent behavioral act and the second measured the explicitness of the means-to-target impact. Explicitness was defined as the focus, concentration, or level of detail with which violence was presented. The camera focus for each of these variables was coded as either shown up-close, shown long-shot, or not shown at all.

In addition to assessing explicitness, the amount of *blood and gore* displayed within each scene was also measured. This variable evaluated the degree or quantity of blood, gore, and/or dismemberment that was depicted within a violent scene. There were four levels of graphicness: none, mild, moderate, and extreme.

The last contextual factor assessed at this level was humor. As indicated in chapter 2, very little research has been conducted on the effects of humor presented within the context of violence. Due to the paucity of research in this area, we adopted a very broad conceptualization of this variable. Humor was defined as those verbal or nonverbal words, actions, and/or behaviors that a character engaged in that were intended to amuse either the self, another character or characters, and/or the viewer. Humor, regardless of the type, was simply coded as either present or absent within each violent scene.

Program level context variables.   At the program level, several global or macro level contextual variables were measured. These variables were ascertained by the coder only at the end of each program viewed. The first variable was designed to assess the program's purpose for including violence within its unfolding narrative. More specifically, this variable measured whether or not the program contained an "antiviolence theme."

A program was judged to possess an antiviolence theme if it illustrated that using violence is morally and/or socially wrong. Operationally, an antiviolence theme was coded as present if any of the following conditions were met within the context of the unfolding narrative: (1) alternatives to violent actions were presented and/or discussed throughout the program; (2) main characters repeatedly discussed the negative consequences of violence; (3) the physical pain and emotional suffering that results from violence were clearly emphasized; or (4) punishments for violence clearly and consistently outweighed rewards. If a program did not fit one of these criteria, then it was coded as having no antiviolence theme.

The next two contextual variables assessed the degree of realism surrounding the presentation of violence and its negative effects. The purpose of these program-level contextual variables was to identify and discriminate those programs that present violence in a realistic context from those that present violence in a fantastic context.

Operationally, each program was evaluated for its *level of realism*. The coder assessed whether the content represented: (1) actual reality (i.e., programs that show footage of actual, real life events); (2) re-creation of reality (i.e., reenacted events that are presented similarly to how they actually occurred); (3) fiction (i.e., creative constructions not based upon actual events, yet depicting actions and events that could possibly occur; and (4) fantasy (i.e., programs containing characters that could not possibly exist or events that could not possibly happen in the real world as we know it).

The second measure of realism assessed the *presentational style* of each program. This variable indicates whether a program was presented via animation, live action, or a mix of both formats.

Although research evidence indicates that more realistic portrayals of violence put most viewers at a greater risk in terms of learning aggressive acts, research also suggests that realistically depicting the negative consequences that result from engaging in violence inhibits viewers from learning and/or modeling aggressive actions. In an effort to assess how each program presented the long-term pain and suffering that results from violence, the next contextual factor, *harm/pain*, was assessed at the end of each program viewed. This program-level variable was defined much more broadly to include not only physical harm, but also emotional, financial, and psychological suffering that is experienced as a result of violence.

Those programs that presented pain/harm as a result of violence in the same scene or in the immediately adjacent scene were coded as presenting the consequences of violence in a "short-term" fashion. Those programs that depicted pain/harm later in the program were coded as presenting the consequences of violence in a "long-term/extended fashion." Those programs that did not present any pain/harm within the context of the plot were coded as presenting "no harm" as a result of violence.

The next program-level contextual factor assessed the overall *pattern of punishments* that were delivered to all good, bad, and good-and-bad (to be defined below) characters involved in violence. The focus of this variable was to ascertain the patterns with which different types of characters (i.e., all of the good characters or all of the bad characters) received punishment for acting violently in a program. All good, bad, and both-good-and-bad characters that engaged in violence were coded as being punished in one of the following patterns: punished throughout an entire program, punished at the end only, never or rarely punished, or not punished by any one of the above patterns.

Character context variables.   In addition to assessing the nature and consequences surrounding violent acts, several character-related context variables were crafted in an effort to gain rich, descriptive data about the perpetrators and targets involved in violence. All characters, whether they instigated violence or received it, were coded for both demographic and attributive qualities. In terms of demographics, a character was assessed for its type (i.e., human, animal, supernatural creature, anthropomorphized animal, anthropomorphized supernatural being), form (single, multiple, implied), size if a multiple unit (2; 3–9; 10–99; 100–999; 1,000 or more), sex (male, female, can't tell), age (child, teen, adult, elderly, can't tell) and apparent ethnicity (i.e., white, Hispanic, black, Native American, Asian/Pacific Islander, or Middle Eastern).

In addition to these demographic data, characters were assessed in terms of specific attributive qualities. The following contextual features were crafted in an effort to measure the "attractiveness" of the characters who engaged in violence. First, a character's "goodness" or "badness" was evaluated. Good characters were defined as those who acted benevolently, helped others, and/or were motivated to consider the needs of others before themselves. Bad characters, on the other hand, were those who acted primarily in their own self-interest, accommodated their own needs, and had very little regard for others. Those characters who were both good and bad were those that displayed a balance of both characteristics in a program. And finally, those characters who were either (1) not featured long enough to ascertain their orientation toward others or (2) their orientation could not be determined from the context of the plot, were coded as "neutral."

Each character was also assessed for hero status. As indicated in chapter 2, heroes are characters that children and adults are most likely to identify with and potentially imitate. In order to clearly differentiate heroes from good characters, we crafted a very narrow definition of this variable. A character was only coded as a hero if all of the following criteria were met: (1) the character appeared as one of the primary characters in the program's plotline, (2) the character's role in the program was to protect others from becoming victims of violence, and (3) the character engaged in helping other characters above and beyond the call of duty. All characters who did not meet this definition were coded as a "nonhero."

Coding and Reliability

The coding of data for this project was performed by undergraduate students at the University of California, Santa Barbara. Individuals were recruited in the Department of Communication and screened to obtain those with the strongest academic records. To perform coding work, individuals had to master all aspects of our codebook, which explicates all of our variables and measures in detail at both the conceptual and operational levels. This training was accomplished through a number of complementary processes. We began with approximately 40 hours of instruction for all coders in a class setting. We then added small group training sessions. Throughout the entire training process, coders regularly practiced applying our measures by individually coding programs in our lab. Feedback on these practice sessions was provided individually, in small groups, and to the entire class of coders as appropriate to the training task.

With the content analysis methodology, researchers must demonstrate that their coders have made decisions consistently. In other words, if several coders are asked to view the same program, they should apply the definitions and measures of violence in the same way, and their resulting judgments regarding the presence or absence of violence should show high agreement. Thus, the designing of a good test of intercoder reliability is an important part of making a case for the quality of data. The result of such a test is a series of reliability coefficients ranging between a possible 1.0 for perfect intercoder agreement to .00 indicating no consistency.

Our testing for the reliability of coders was conducted in two phases. In the first phase, we monitored the decision making of the coders in order to determine when they were fully trained and able to begin coding of actual data to be used in the analyses. Here the focus was on the coders themselves and their aptitude in internalizing all the coding rules. The second phase consisted of two different prongs. The first was an examination of the patterns in the coded data themselves so as to determine the degree of reliability, and hence the quality, of the data. For this analysis, we shifted the focus from individual coders to individual decision points in the process of coding. The second prong involved an assessment focused again on the coders' performance so as to spot fatigue or other problems that might diminish the quality of the data. Both of these different aspects of the second phase were conducted concurrently throughout the duration of the coding process. The same raw data were employed for both of the prongs, but they were analyzed in different ways. The details of these procedures are described in appendix 3.1. Overall, the results of the reliability testing indicate that coders were generally consistent in their coding decisions.

Summary

The goal of this chapter was to delineate several of the innovative methodological developments and contributions of the NTVS's content analysis of 1994–95 entertainment programming. To this end, we spent a considerable amount of time reviewing past approaches to assessing violent television content and many of the limitations of those investigations. We then highlighted several of the approaches that we utilized in our own content analysis of American television. Namely, we delineated our unique and representative sampling strategy, use of multiple units of analysis, conceptual and operational definitions of our empirically grounded contextual measures, and the new process and statistical formula by which intercoder reliability was ascertained. In the next chapter, we present the results of applying this methodology to programming from the 1994–95 television season.

APPENDIX 3.1

Coding and Reliability

Initial Diagnostic Testing

By March 1995, the NTVS coding scheme was sufficiently developed to warrant initial testing. At this time, we began a series of diagnostic coding exercises.

Purpose.   The initial diagnostic testing provided a check on the training. It consisted of a series of coding exercises that were designed to (1) determine the extent to which coders were consistent in applying the coding rules as written, and (2) identify those coders who had missed key elements in the training. In the development of the coding scheme, we were guided by the principle of providing coding rules at a sufficient level of detail along with concrete examples so that all coders would be able to make consensus decisions about any violent content they might encounter. How well were we achieving this goal? In order to answer this question, we needed to conduct diagnostic testing.

Also, we were concerned that all 40 coders might not have internalized the training to an equally high degree. So we needed to identify those coders who were having problems applying the coding rules so that they could receive some additional training.

Of course the two purposes of the diagnostic testing are interrelated. For example, if we found that all coders were having trouble with a particular coding decision, then we would need to determine if the problem could be traced to the way the coding rule was written or if the problem was traceable instead to training. However, if instead we found that the majority of the coders were applying a particular rule consistently, then we could conclude that those few coders who were not part of the majority needed remedial training. If a large number of coders applied a coding rule consistently one way while another large number of coders applied it consistently another way, we concluded that the rule was ambiguous and required rewriting.

Procedures.   Each diagnostic test followed six steps. First, a program was selected to serve as a good coding challenge for a particular aspect of the coding scheme being tested. Second, all coders were assigned to code the program individually. Third, the coding data were collected and arranged into 40-column matrices comparing the decisions by all coders. For PAT-level codes, a matrix was constructed for each PAT-level variable. Each of these matrices was 40 columns wide, and the number of lines corresponded to the largest number of interactions any coder identified. We could then compare the extent to which each coder recognized the same number of violent interactions.

A coder who missed coding a violent interaction was able to be easily identified because they missed a PAT line in the matrix. A set of matrices was also constructed for each variable at the scene level. These scene-level matrices were 40 columns wide, and the number of lines corresponded to the number of scenes the coders identified within a program. The program-level codes were all entered into a single program-level matrix for a show. The program-level matrix was 40 columns wide, and the number of lines corresponded to the number of variables coded at the program level. Thus, at the end of this third step in the procedure, we had a set of matrices for the PAT-level codes, a set of matrices for the scene-level codes, and a single program-level matrix.

Fourth, the appropriate coding values were entered in the matrices. For example, on the scene-level reward matrix, a "1" was entered into a cell for every coder who decided that the scene did not depict the violence as being rewarded and therefore coded "no" for the reward variable. Coders who decided that the violence in a scene was rewarded had a "2" entered in the appropriate matrix. Then for each line in a matrix, we determined the mode, which is the most prevalent code used by the 40 coders. The modal frequency was then divided by 40 to arrive at the percentage of agreement of codes on that one line. For example, if a given scene (one line of data in the scene matrix) displayed 36 codes of "1" and the remaining 4 codes as "2," then the mode is clearly "1," which occurs 36 times. This means that 90 percent of the coders agreed on this code for this scene. Finally, by summing all the modal frequencies for each line on the matrix and dividing by the total number of coding decisions exhibited in the matrix, we arrive at the total percentage of agreement for that variable. This procedure was repeated for each PAT- and scene-level matrix. For the program-level matrix, the total percentages of agreement were computed for each line, because each line contained the total data for each program-level variable.

Fifth, for each variable, the percentages of agreement were reported to the planning group. We used the convention in the content analysis literature of regarding .70 as a minimum acceptable percentage of agreement, and if we found a percentage that was lower than .70, it was a signal of a coding problem. With all problems, we solicited feedback from the coders to try to ascertain the root of the problem as being either: (a) unclear directions in the codebook, (b) incomplete training of all coders, or (c) inconsistent training where some coders understood the decision while others did not. The group members studied the patterns in the matrices of the problem variables and brainstormed about possible solutions to the inconsistencies. Many of these discussions resulted in revisions to the preliminary coding rules. In certain instances we found that a few coders were consistently making wrong coding decisions, and these coders were targeted for further training. In some instances, the members of the planning group did not feel confident in identifying a problem, so they waited for the results of the next step before deciding how to improve the consistency of coding decisions.

Sixth, the coders were debriefed. Discussions were stimulated among coders, either in the full group or in subsets, focusing on the coding decisions that were diagnosed as being a problem. Often the program that was coded was rescreened so that coders could talk through their decision-making processes. These discussions served two purposes. One purpose was to give members of the planning team feedback about the coding process so that they could pinpoint causes of inconsistent decision making. The other purpose was to highlight points where decision making was done consistently so as to reinforce those good decisions and to show the inconsistent coders how their decisions should have been made.

The series of diagnostic tests. In early March, we began running the first series of diagnostic testing. This first series included 8 rounds as follows:

Round 1.1:   A 12-minute segment of the cartoon *Tom and Jerry* was selected for coding for the first diagnostic test. The coders limited their analysis to PAT-level variables.

Round 1.2:   Coders analyzed PAT variables in an episode of *Hawkeye*.

Round 1.3:   Coders analyzed PAT-, scene-, and program- (character codes only) level codes in episodes of four programs: *Remington Steele, Tales from the Crypt, MacGyver,* and *Looney Tunes.*

Round 1.4:   Coders tested four program-level variables (narrative purpose, realism, harm/pain, and reward/punishment) for episodes of three programs: *Tales from the Crypt, The Rifleman,* and *Power Rangers.* The discussions from these results served to make changes in the codes for harm/pain as well as reward/punishment.

Round 1.5:   Coders tested program-level codes on episodes of *Starsky and Hutch* and *Magnum, P.I.* The reward/punishment code continued to be a problem and additional changes were made with it.

Rounds 1.6 and 1.7:   Coders looked at an episode of *Silk Stalkings* for PAT-level analysis. A few problems in dealing with multiple perpetrators and targets were discovered, so additional rules were written to help coders distinguish when multiple characters were acting in concert or independently. Coders received additional training. The following week these new rules and retraining were tested on the same program.

Round 1.8:   Coders analyzed an episode of *Magnum, P.I.* and a segment of the *Looney Tunes* cartoon. All variables at the PAT, scene, and program levels were coded.

In June, we began diagnostic testing on a second group of coders who joined the project. This second group required only three rounds of testing, because by this point our training procedures were more efficient and the codebook was complete. We had corrected most of the problems encountered during the first round of training. The three rounds of testing with the second group of coders overlapped with rounds 1.7 and 1.8 of the original coders. This was done so that the data from the two groups of coders could be compared. The second group of coders performed almost as well as the first group, indicating that the codebook and training procedures were working well.

Round 2.1:   Coders analyzed an episode of *Starsky and Hutch.*
Round 2.2:   Coders analyzed an episode of *Silk Stalkings.* This was the same episode that the first group had coded in Rounds 1.6 and 1.7. This group of second-round coders exhibited far fewer problems with multiple perpetrators and multiple targets than the first-round coders had in round 1.6.
Round 2.3:   Coders looked at an episode of *Magnum, P.I.* and coded at all three levels. They also coded a segment of the *Looney Tunes* cartoon.

In July, the training phase was completed, and the actual coding of programs began. At this point, we had achieved acceptable levels of reliability consistently exceeding .70 on most variables.

The coding process was conducted by randomly assigning individual coders to programs. Coders viewed each show alone in a video lab and were instructed to code all content as it unfolded in the narrative. They were also told that they could watch any given scene as many times as necessary to make the required coding judgments needed. Data for each program were obtained from the observations of a single coder. For this reason, it is essential to demonstrate that the coding process maintained a strong and consistent level of performance over time in order to insure the quality of the data. The next section describes how we monitored the reliability in coding of the data upon which the findings of this study are based.

Checking the Quality of Data

Procedure.   The coding process required roughly 20 weeks (not counting holidays and break periods) to complete. During each week when coding was conducted, half of the active coders independently evaluated the same program. Their coding judgments were then compared for reliability assessment purposes. Thus, the decision-making of each coder was checked once during each two-week period.

The programs selected for reliability assessments were randomly chosen within each genre. All genres were examined at least twice. Two examples of each genre were tested in back-to-back weeks so that each coder's performance would be evaluated across the complete range of program content. Appendix table 3.1 presents the list of randomly selected programs used for the reliability tests.

The sections that follow lay out the conceptual basis and operational as-

TABLE A3.1. Programs Randomly Selected for the Continuing Reliability Tests

Genre	Program Name
Children's series	Top Cat
Children's series	Captain Planet
Drama series	Rockford Files
Drama series	Lou Grant
Movie	God Is My Co-Pilot
Movie	Coma
Drama series	Sherlock Holmes
Drama series	Wild, Wild West
Drama series	Days of Our Lives
Drama series	Young and the Restless
Comedy series	Designing Women
Comedy series	Fresh Prince
Reality-based	Cops
Reality-based	Highway Patrol
Music video	Yo! MTV Raps
Music video	VH-1 Video

pects of our reliability assessments. After the appropriate details are explicated, the findings of our assessments are presented.

Conceptualization of reliability. Because the coding scheme developed in this project is very complex, coders had to make many different types of decisions when examining a show. It is best to categorize these decisions as existing at two distinct levels. The first level focuses on unitizing, that is, the identification of PATs and scenes. The second level is concerned with the degree of consistency among coders in choosing the same value for a given variable. In total we have 38 variables. Below, we explain the purpose and procedures for evaluating reliability at both of these levels.

Unitizing. This is a critical part of the coding process. In this study, unitizing refers to the process of identifying each PAT and each scene. If coders agree at the beginning and ending point of each PAT and each scene, then they are consistently identifying our units of analysis.

The fundamental building block of the coding scheme is the PAT—a single interaction involving violence. Every time a coder perceived an act of violence, s/he created a line of data that included the string of values on the variables that had to be coded at this level. In evaluating the unitizing process, we are not focusing on the string of numbers selected; instead we are focusing on the number of PAT lines a coder creates—that is, the number of violent interactions the coder perceives to exist in the program.

If all coders have the same number of PAT lines on their coding form for a show and if those PAT lines refer to the same acts, then there is perfect agreement. To reiterate, both conditions must be met for perfect agreement. If coders differ on the number of PAT lines, then there is not perfect agreement. If coders all have the same number of PAT lines, but if there is disagreement about what those PATs are, then there is not perfect agreement.

For each show coded, the determination of PAT-level reliability began with the construction of a matrix. This matrix was composed of one column for every coder and one line for every PAT identified by those coders. For purposes of illustration, let us say that there are 12 coders, so the PAT reliability matrix would have 12 columns. If the first coder perceived 8 PAT lines, then the matrix would start with 8 lines, and the resulting matrix would have 96 cells (12 x 8 = 96). An "X" to indicate agreement would be placed in each of the 8 cells in the first coder's column, because this coder perceived each of those 8 acts of violence. If the remaining 11 coders each perceived the *same* 8 acts of violence, they would each have 8 X's in their columns. This matrix would then have 96 X's— one in every possible cell. Such a pattern indicates total agreement among all coders on all acts of violence. What if the PAT reliability matrix did not display a full set of X's? This would indicate some disagreement. The fewer X's, the greater the disagreement.

How can we report a useful indicator of the degree of agreement? It is not sufficient to sum all the X's and divide by the number of cells in the matrix, because the X's indicate position, not agreement. For example, let us say we have 9 coders, each of whom sees only one PAT line in a program, and they all agree that it is the same PAT. However, let us say that a tenth coder sees 3 PATs, one of which is the same as the other 9 coders have seen. In this case, there are 10 X's on the first line to indicate that all 10 coders saw the first PAT, but on each of the next two lines of the matrix, there is an X only in the column of coder 10. Thus the matrix has 30 cells and 12 X's for a simple agreement ratio of 40 percent. Clearly this figure underestimates the situation where we have complete agreement among 9 out of 10 coders.

What we have done to avoid this problem is to report three descriptors: the Agreement Mode, the range of PATs, and a Close Interval around the Agreement Mode (CIAM). An example will illustrate what we mean by the "Agreement Mode." If we have 10 coders and one reported 7 PAT lines, 7 reported 8 PAT lines, one reported 9 PAT lines, and one reported 11 PAT lines, the mode would be 8 PAT lines because that is the number reported by the greatest number of coders. Thus 70 percent of the coders are at this mode. If all 7 coders had the same 8 PAT lines, then the agreement mode is 8.

In many cases, not all coders were at the Agreement Mode, so we also report the range of PAT lines exhibited by the set of coders. The smaller the range, the tighter the pattern of agreement. But sometimes the range can be misleading as an indicator of how much variation there is in a distribution. For example, let us say that we have 10 coders: 3 have 4 PAT lines, 5 have 5 PAT lines, 1 has 6 PAT lines, and 1 has 12 PAT lines. The range here is from 4 to 12 PAT lines, which appears to signal a wide range of disagreement. However, 90 percent of the coders are within one PAT line of the mode. So we also compute a Close Interval around the Agreement Mode (CIAM). We operationalized "close to the agreement mode" as those judgments that were within one PAT line on either side of the agreement mode. For example, if the agreement mode were 4, we would include in the CIAM each of the following: (a) other coders who also saw 4 PATs but disagreed on one of the PATs, (b) other coders who saw only 3 PATs but each of those 3 match PATs in the set of the 4 PATs that determine the Agreement Mode, and (c) other coders who had 5 PATs where 4 of those 5 PATs were identical to the 4 that determine the Agreement Mode. When the Agreement Mode is greater than 5, we establish the width of the CIAM as 20 percent on either side of the mode. For example, if the Agreement Mode is 10, we include coders who exhibit no more than 2 disagreements with the coders at the Agreement Mode.

The procedure explained above for determining the Agreement Mode and the CIAM for PAT lines is the same with scenes. For each show coded, a scene-level matrix was constructed, where there was a column for each coder and a line for each scene identified. We then computed and reported an Agreement Mode, a range, and a CIAM for scenes for each program.

Selecting values on the coding variables.   Now we turn our attention to the consistency among coders in choosing a value on each coding variable. Our coding scheme contains a total of 38 variables: 12 at the program level, 13 for each scene within each program, and 13 for each PAT within each scene. At the program level, the coder judged the overall narrative purpose (from among 2 values), realism of the program (4), harm/pain (3), style of presentation (3), punishment of bad characters (5), punishment of good characters (5), and punishment of mixed (good and bad) characters (5). Also, each character who was involved (either as a perpetrator or victim) in violence was coded for type (7 values), sex (4), ethnicity (9), good/bad (6), and hero status (4).

At the scene level, the coder judged whether there was a reward of self-praise (from among 2 values), praise from other (2), and material praise (2); whether there was punishment of self-condemnation (2), condemnation from another (2), nonviolent action (2), and violent actions (2); whether there was explicitness of the action itself (4) and means-to-target impact (4); degree of graphicness (5), and humor (2). Also, the characters were coded for age (6) and physical strength (6).

At the PAT level, each act was coded for type (from among 4 values), means used (8), extent of means (5), harm depicted (7), harm likely (7), pain (7), visual depiction (2), and sexual assault (2). The perpetrator was coded for type (4), size if multiple (6), and reason for committing the violence (6). Finally, each target was coded for type (3) and size if multiple (6).

The reliability for coding variables was assessed in the following manner. At the program level, the modal value was identified for each variable. The number of coders at the modal value was divided by the total number of coders, thus computing a percentage of agreement.

At the scene and PAT levels, each line of the matrix was examined for its modal value. All coders at the modal value were counted and this number was written in the margin. These margin numbers were summed down all the rows of a matrix. This sum was divided by all the decisions reflected in the matrix, and the resulting fraction was the percentage of agreement among coders on that variable.

The computation of the reliability coefficient for scene and PAT level is more complicated than the computation for the program-level codes because of the unitizing issues described above. At the PAT-level analysis, the first step starts with the PAT-level matrix of coders. This becomes a template of cells. This template is used to build 13 PAT matrices, one for each variable coded at the PAT level. For each line in each matrix, the modal value is identified; thus the reliability testing is based on a norm determined by the coders, not a prescribed criterion value. The number of coders selecting the modal value is entered in the margin of the matrix. These margin numbers (one for each PAT line) are summed and then divided by the number of cells in the matrix. This proportion is the percentage of agreement. These percentages of agreement were then converted into reliability coefficients by using a PRE (proportional reduction of error) procedure.

The term "percentage of agreement" is used several times in the above section. This is simply the number of times coders actually agreed divided by the number of times they could have possibly agreed. The larger the number, the better the agreement.

Although percentage of agreement is often a useful indicator of consistency, it is an incomplete measure, particularly for complex judgments. With complex measures, some context is needed to better interpret the meaning of the statistic. Below, we describe two ways of providing this context: employing a proportional reduction of error technique and providing an inferential context for interpreting our reliability calculations.

Proportional reduction of error.   A percentage of agreement reflects a combination of two elements: real agreement (uniformity in decision making due to training) and error agreement (selection of the same codes by chance alone). If two coders looked at the same show and had to decide whether there was violence in a scene, the probability that they would agree by chance alone is 50 percent. If we cannot correct for chance agreement, then the percentages of agreement are inflated by error.

How do we correct for chance agreement? We modified the Scott's pi formula to account for multiple coders performing the same task. We took the percentages of agreement and converted them into reliability coefficients by using a proportional reduction of error (PRE) procedure using the following formula:

$$\text{Reliability coefficient} = \frac{A - P}{1 - P}$$

Where
A = percentage of agreement
P = proportion of agreement due to chance

This formula is essentially pi as developed by Scott (1955). However, Scott's pi is limited to pairs of coders and does not allow for a test of multiple coders on the same task. Therefore, the formula needed to be adapted, specifically the proportion of agreement due to chance or P. To compute such a probability, we developed the following formula from probability theory using binomial decisions.

$$P = \frac{N!}{M!(N - M)!}(p^M)(q^{N-M})$$

where
N = the number of coders in a test
M = the number of coders who agree
p = probability of choosing the option on which there is agreement
q = probability of not choosing the option on which there is agreement

The sum of p and q is 1. For example, if coders are given a choice between two options, then p is .5 and q is also .5. If coders are given a choice among three options, then p is .33 and q is .67 (the probability of choosing either of the two options not chosen by the plurality of coders). The formula for P computes the probability of agreement among N coders. Once this probability of agreement by chance alone is determined, it is entered in the previous formula so that its effect is proportionally reduced from the percentage of agreement.

Inferential context.   A second context for interpreting the consistency is to use inferential procedures to compute a confidence level for reliability coefficients. In the content analysis literature, authors will arbitrarily select a certain value (usually about .70) as being a minimum acceptable reliability coefficient, then demonstrate that their coefficients surpass this minimum. While this strategy at first may appear to demonstrate acceptable strength, it really has no intrinsic meaning; it acquires meaning only as a convention when most scholars agree to use it.

We wanted to develop a better strategy for several reasons. First, a 70 percent agreement is much easier to achieve when using two coders than when using a much larger group as we planned to do. And second, we wanted to avoid arbitrary cutoff points and instead put the interpretation of our coefficients on a firmer foundation. Therefore we chose to use an inferential procedure to determine the probability that each of our reliability coefficients could have occurred by chance alone.

For each coding decision, we computed a z score using the following formula:

$$Z = \frac{X - \mu}{\sigma} \qquad \mu = pn$$

$$\sigma = \sqrt{pqn}$$

where

p = the probability of a single coder selecting the modal value

q = the probability of a single coder not selecting p

n = number of coders in test

X = upper real limit of number of coders at mode

Then we looked up z in a Unit Normal Table. This indicates the probability of obtaining the observed level of agreement by chance alone. For example, let us say we ran a test with 12 coders who had to choose among 4 options and that 7 of those coders all chose the same option. Using the above procedure, we would find that the chance of getting 58.3 percent agreement (7 out of 12 agreeing on the same option out of four) would be less than one in a thousand or $p < .001$. With only 2 options available, we would need an agreement of 10 out of 12 (83.3 percent) in order to have this same high level of confidence ($p < .001$) that this pattern could not have occurred by chance alone.

In summary, three procedures were used for reliability testing. First, agreement on the unitizing for PATs was assessed for each show. Second, agreement on the unitizing for scenes was assessed for each show. And third, the selection of codes (at program, scene, and PAT levels) was assessed. We realize the importance of going beyond reporting simple percentages of agreement, because they can be misleading. In our procedures we do both of the following: (1) convert percentages of agreement into reliability coefficients by removing the error portion of the agreement, and (2) report the confidence level we have that each reliability coefficient could have occurred by chance alone.

Results of reliability testing.   The results of the reliability testing indicate that coders were generally consistent in their decisions. Their consistency in unitizing was quite good given the complexity of the task and the number of coders involved (see appendix table 3.2). There was always a range in the number of sequences, but in over half of the tests, 100 percent of coders fell within the 20 percent interval around the mode. Likewise with PATs, there was always a range in

TABLE A3.2. Reliability Coefficients for PAT and Scene Range and Mode

Title	PAT Range	PAT Mode/ %	PAT Mode +/− 20%	Sequence Range	Sequence Mode/%	Sequence Mode +/− 20%
Top Cat (N = 14)	7–12	9/-	57	4–5	5/64	100
Captain Planet (N = 12)	7–12	18/-	55	4–11	7/50	50
Rockford Files (N = 15)	5–10	6/40	73	4–6	4/87	93
Lou Grant (N = 9)	1–4	3/33	89	1–3	3/44	89
God Is My Co-Pilot (N = 9)	13–19	17/11	78	4–5	4/44	100
Coma (N = 11)	5–8	6/27	91	3–5	4/55	100
Sherlock Holmes (N = 9)	6–9	7/11	67	3–4	4/78	100
Wild, Wild West (N = 9)	18–24	24/-	75	7–10	9/44	89
Days of Our Lives (N = 7)	1–7	3/-	43	1–3	3/43	71
The Young and the Restless (N = 12)	2–3	2/50	100	1–2	2/92	100
Designing Women (N = 9)	2–4	2/56	89	1–2	1/89	100
Fresh Prince (N = 11)	2–4	3/55	100	1–3	2/55	100
Cops (N = 16)	1–4	2/69	88	1–2	1/75	100
Highway Patrol (N =10)	3–7	3/40	70	2–5	2/80	100
Yo! MTV Raps (N = 10)	2–11	4/20	40	2–9	4/30	50
VH-1 Videos (N = 10)	4–13	11/10	50	4–8	5/10	60

the number of violent interactions, but coders usually clustered tightly around the mode. Across all of the programs examined for reliability, most coders were able to agree on the number of PATs (83 percent median agreement) and scenes (100 percent median agreement) within the 20 percent interval around the mode.

As for the consistency of coding the variables within units, we first computed a level of confidence for each of our 608 reliability coefficients (38 variables on each of 16 programs in the reliability test). Out of those 608 coefficients, only 33 (5.4 percent) were too small to attain statistical significance ($p < .05$). This proportion is almost exactly what we should expect by chance alone.

The reliability on each of the 38 variables was quite high as indicated by the median level of agreement that ranged from a low of .63 to a high of 1.0 (see appendix tables 3.3–3.5). Half of these medians are above .94, which is very good for a task of this magnitude and with so many coders. On only 5 of the 38 variables was the median reliability lower than .80. Four of these were program-level codes of harm/pain (median of .70), punishment of bad characters (.64), punishment of good characters (.63), and the judgment about whether a character was good or bad (.75). The other relatively low reliability was on the variable for perpetrator reason (.75), which was coded at the PAT level.

TABLE A3.3. Reliability Coefficients for PAT Context Variables

Title	Type of Act	Means Used	Extent of Means Used	Harm Depicted	Harm Likely	Pain	Visual Depicted
Top Cat ($N = 14$)	.99	.94	.91	.81	.78	.84	.99
Captain Planet ($N = 12$)	1.0	.88	.86	.87	.85	.88	.97
Rockford Files ($N = 15$)	1.0	.90	.85	.73	.83	.72	.98
Lou Grant ($N = 9$)	1.0	.81	1.0	.92	.88	.92	.96
God Is My Co-Pilot ($N = 9$)	1.0	.89	.73	.84	.88	.66	.99
Coma ($N = 11$)	1.0	.89	.65	.84	.84	.72	1.0
Sherlock Holmes ($N = 9$)	1.0	.92	.80	.76	.75	.71	.97
Wild, Wild West ($N = 9$)	1.0	.96	.89	.85	.74	.80	1.0
Days of Our Lives ($N = 7$)	1.0	.90	.85	.90	.70	.95	1.0
The Young and the Restless ($N = 12$)	1.0	.79	.88	.79	.79	.79	1.0
Designing Women ($N = 9$)	1.0	.71	.70	.51*	.62	.62	.80
Fresh Prince ($N = 11$)	1.0	.93	.96	.93	.89	.89	.89
Cops ($N = 16$)	1.0	.97	.91	.91	.88	.82	.94
Highway Patrol ($N = 10$)	1.0	1.0	.92	.95	.95	.95	1.0
Yo! MTV Raps ($N = 10$)	1.0	.96	.98	.82	.84	.82	.98
VH-1 Videos ($N = 10$)	1.0	.99	.96	.79	.77	.80	.98
Overall range ($N = 173$)	.99–1.0	.71–1.0	.65–1.0	.51–.95	.62–.95	.62–.95	.81–1.0
Overall median ($N = 173$)	1.0	.90	.88	.84	.83	.81	.98

Title	Sexual Assault	Perpetrator Type	Perpetrator Size (if multiple)	Perpetrator Reason	Target Type	Target Size (if multiple)
Top Cat ($N = 14$)	1.0	.96	.87	.75	.99	.89
Captain Planet ($N = 12$)	1.0	.99	.88	.84	.95	.85
Rockford Files ($N = 15$)	1.0	.99	.98	.70	.96	.96
Lou Grant ($N = 9$)	1.0	1.0	.92	.81	1.0	.96
God Is My Co-Pilot ($N = 9$)	1.0	.98	.82	.62	.98	.83
Coma ($N = 11$)	1.0	.97	.97	.75	1.0	1.0
Sherlock Holmes ($N = 9$)	1.0	.98	.95	.61	1.0	.97
Wild, Wild West ($N = 9$)	.99	.97	.95	.80	.98	.97
Days of Our Lives ($N = 7$)	.95	1.0	.85	.65	1.0	.85
The Young and the Restless ($N = 12$)	1.0	1.0	.92	1.0	1.0	.92

(continued)

TABLE A3.3.—Continued

Title	Sexual Assault	Perpetrator Type	Perpetrator Size (if multiple)	Perpetrator Reason	Target Type	Target Size (if multiple)
Designing Women (N = 9)	1.0	.90	1.0	.81	1.0	1.0
Fresh Prince (N = 11)	.96	.86	.96	.96	.93	.93
Cops (N = 16)	1.0	.94	.94	.73	.91	.97
Highway Patrol (N = 10)	1.0	1.0	1.0	.89	1.0	.92
Yo! MTV Raps (N = 10)	1.0	.95	.95	.63	.96	.93
VH-1 Videos (N = 10)	1.0	.96	.96	.68	.93	.93
Overall range (N = 173)	.95	.86–1.0	.86–1.0	.61–1.0	.91	.83–1.0
Overall median (N = 173)	1.0	.97	.97	.75	.98	.93

$^*p > .05$; all other coefficients, $p < .05$.

Check for Fatigue in Coder Performance

Consistency over time in coding practices is essential for establishing the reliability of the data. Therefore, as noted above, we conducted a continual check to spot instances of coder fatigue as soon as possible and to make any necessary corrections. Using the same reliability data as that reported in the preceding section, but analyzing it from a different perspective, we were able to assess the performance of individual coders relative to the performance of the overall group.

For each reliability test, three indexes of quality were constructed: one for program coding, one for scene coding, and one for PAT coding. Each time a coder was in the modal group on a coding decision, he or she earned a point. If coders were close to the mode, they could earn partial points (see appendix table 3.6). Thus, coders who amassed the greatest number of points on an index were ranked the highest on consistency and were regarded as the best coders. Coders who had low index scores were regarded as the least consistent compared to other coders.

For the tests in which the range between the best coders and the least consistent coders was small and the overall reliability coefficients remained high, we were assured that coder fatigue had not occurred. When that gap widened, however, we had to make a subjective judgment about the performance of individual coders who fell at the bottom of our index. Our first method of dealing with inconsistent coders was to retrain them in the areas where they were diagnosed as having difficulty making proper judgments. In most cases this worked well, and the subsequent coding work was found to be consistent. When this was the case, we retained the individual as a coder on the project.

In the two instances when a coder could not be retrained successfully to

TABLE A3.4. Reliability Coefficients for Scene Character and Context Variables

Title	Character Age	Character Physical Strength	Rewards: Self-Praise	Rewards: Praise from Other	Rewards: Material Praise	Punishments: Self-Condemnation	Punishments: Condemnation from Other
Top Cat (N = 14)	.86	.88	.88	.95	.95	.98	.92
Captain Planet (N = 12)	.89	.91	.77	.63	.89	1.0	.96
Rockford Files (N = 15)	.93	.98	.93	1.0	.85	1.0	.97
Lou Grant (N = 9)	1.0	.79	.85	.95	1.0	.95	.69*
God Is My Co-Pilot (N = 9)	.92	.97	.87	.82	.93	1.0	.73*
Coma (N = 11)	.91	.98	.89	1.0	1.0	.91	.88
Sherlock Holmes (N = 9)	.97	.91	.94	.80	1.0	1.0	.84
Wild, Wild West (N = 9)	.98	.92	.85	.94	.97	1.0	.85
Days of Our Lives (N = 7)	1.0	1.0	.78*	.93	1.0	.93	.63*
The Young and the Restless (N = 12)	1.0	1.0	.91	1.0	1.0	1.0	1.0
Designing Women (N = 9)	.95	.86	1.0	1.0	1.0	.76*	1.0
Fresh Prince (N = 11)	.86	.84	1.0	1.0	.82	1.0	.94
Cops (N = 16)	1.0	.95	.95	.95	.95	.95	.90
Highway Patrol (N = 10)	1.0	1.0	1.0	1.0	.77	1.0	.95
Yo! MTV Raps (N = 10)	.98	.98	1.0	1.0	.94	.98	.92
VH-1 Videos (N = 10)	1.0	.96	.97	.97	1.0	1.0	.98
Overall range (N = 173)	.86–1.0	.79–1.0	.77–1.0	.63–1.0	.77–1.0	.76–1.0	.63–1.0
Overall median (N = 173)	.97	.95	.93	.95	.96	1.0	.92

	Punishments: Nonviolent Action	Punishments: Violent Action	Explicitness: Violent Action	Explicitness: Focus on Impact	Graphicness	Humor
Top Cat (N = 14)	.98	.94	.86	.82	.89	.91
Captain Planet (N = 12)	.85	.93	.89	.91	1.0	.96
Rockford Files (N = 15)	.98	.98	.97	.85	.97	.72
Lou Grant (N = 9)	.80	.95	.90	.86	.81	.74*
God Is My Co-Pilot (N = 9)	.93	.76*	.54*	.78	.75	.93
Coma (N = 11)	.87	1.0	.89	.84	.93	.98
Sherlock Holmes (N = 9)	.84	.97	.97	.97	.80	.84
Wild, Wild West (N = 9)	1.0	.77*	.95	.94	.99	.88
Days of Our Lives (N = 7)	.63*	1.0	.87	.87	.87	.87
The Young and the Restless (N = 12)	1.0	1.0	.83	.64	.65	1.0
Designing Women (N = 9)	.76*	.88	.89	.89	.89	1.0
Fresh Prince (N = 11)	1.0	1.0	.89	1.0	1.0	1.0
Cops (N = 16)	.80	1.0	.85	.85	.85	1.0
Highway Patrol (N =10)	.55*	.77	1.0	.86	.86	1.0
Yo! MTV Raps (N = 10)	.73*	.96	.92	.88	.94	1.0
VH-1 Videos (N = 10)	.98	.95	.76	.85	.88	.80
Overall range (N = 173)	.55–1.0	.77–1.0	.54–1.0	.64–1.0	.65–1.0	.72–1.0
Overall median (N = 173)	.86	.96	.89	.86	.88	.95

*p > .05; Unstarred coefficients, p < .05

TABLE A3.5. Reliability Coefficients for Program Character and Context Variables

Title	Narrative Purpose	Realism	Harm/Pain	Style	Punishments: Bad	Punishments: Good
Top Cat ($N = 14$)	1.0	.86	.64	1.0	.79	.71
Captain Planet ($N = 12$)	1.0	1.0	.92	1.0	.56	1.0
Rockford Files ($N = 15$)	1.0	1.0	.80	1.0	.87	.59
Lou Grant ($N = 9$)	.41*	1.0	.54	1.0	.66	.78
God Is My Co-Pilot ($N = 9$)	1.0	.78	.67	1.0	.51*	.89
Coma ($N = 11$)	1.0	1.0	.73	1.0	.51*	.82
Sherlock Holmes ($N = 9$)	1.0	1.0	.54	1.0	.66	.66
Wild, Wild West ($N = 9$)	.89	.54	.54	.89	.13*	.54*
Days of Our Lives ($N = 7$)	1.0	.54	.54	1.0	1.0	.51*
The Young and the Restless ($N = 12$)	1.0	1.0	1.0	1.0	.44*	.44*
Designing Women ($N = 9$)	1.0	1.0	.36*	1.0	.66	.51*
Fresh Prince ($N = 11$)	.71*	1.0	.91	1.0	.91	.35*
Cops ($N = 16$)	.81	.94	.69	1.0	.69	.75
Highway Patrol ($N = 10$)	.55*	.66	1.0	1.0	.47*	1.0
Yo! MTV Raps ($N = 10$)	1.0	.94	.82	1.0	.62	.53*
VH-1 Videos ($N = 10$)	.96	.85	.73	1.0	.40	.76*
Overall range ($N = 173$)	.41–1.0	.54–1.0	.36–1.0	.89–1.0	.13–1.0	.35–1.0
Overall median ($N = 173$)	1.0	.97	.70	1.0	.64	.63

Title	Punishments: Good/Bad	Character Type	Character Sex	Character Ethnicity	Character Good/Bad	Character Hero Status
Top Cat ($N = 14$)	.19*	.99	1.0	.91	.73	1.0
Captain Planet ($N = 12$)	.56	.76	.96	.84	.80	.90
Rockford Files ($N = 15$)	.80	1.0	1.0	.99	.90	1.0
Lou Grant ($N = 9$)	.30*	1.0	1.0	1.0	.49	1.0
God Is My Co-Pilot ($N = 9$)	1.0	1.0	.93	.98	.76	.90
Coma ($N = 11$)	.91	1.0	1.0	1.0	.83	.92
Sherlock Holmes ($N = 9$)	1.0	.96	.96	.96	.72	.94
Wild, Wild West ($N = 9$)	1.0	.93	.98	.99	.78	.92
Days of Our Lives ($N = 7$)	.70	.79	1.0	1.0	.86	1.0
The Young and the Restless ($N = 12$)	.75	1.0	.91	1.0	.57	1.0
Designing Women ($N = 9$)	.51*	1.0	1.0	1.0	.44	1.0
Fresh Prince ($N = 11$)	.82	1.0	.97	.97	.75	.86
Cops ($N = 16$)	.88	1.0	1.0	.93	.78	.98
Highway Patrol ($N = 10$)	.89	1.0	.97	1.0	.94	.81

(continued)

Title	Punishments: Good/Bad	Character Type	Character Sex	Character Ethnicity	Character Good/Bad	Character Hero Status
Yo! MTV Raps ($N = 10$)	.75	1.0	.96	.94	.63	1.0
VH-1 Videos ($N = 10$)	.88	1.0	.91	.91	.53	.93
Overall range ($N = 173$)	.19–1.0	.76–1.0	.91–1.0	.84–1.0	.44–.94	.81–1.0
Overall median ($N = 173$)	.81	1.0	.97	.96	.75	.93

*$p > .05$; unstarred coefficients, $p < .05$

TABLE A3.6. Computation of Coder Index

Program Level-Context		Scene Level-Characters		PAT Level-Context	
M	Narative purpose (2)	M	Perpetrator age (6)	M	Type of act (4)
M	Realism (4)	M	Perpetrator physical strength (6)	M+	Means used (8)
M+	Harm/pain (3)	M	Target age (6)	M+	Extent of means (5)
M	Style of presentation (3)		Scene Level-Context	M+	Harm depicted (7)
M	Punishments: bad characters (5)	M	Reward: self-praise (2)	M+	Harm likely (7)
M	Punishments: good characters (5)	M	Reward: Praise from other (2)	M+	Pain (7)
M	Punishments: good and bad characters	M	Reward: materal praise (2)	M	Visual depiction (2)
	Program Level-Characters	M	Punishment: self-condemnation (2)	M	Sexual assault (2)
	Character type (7)				PAT Level-Characters
M	Character sex (4)	M	Punishment: condemnation from another (2)	M	Perpetrator type (4)
M	Character ethnicity (9)			M+	Perpetrator size, if multiple (6)
	Character good/bad (6)	M	Punishment: non-violent action (2)	M?	Perpetrator reason for committing the violence (6)
	Character hero status (4)	M	Punishment: violent actions (2)	M	Target type (3)
		M+	Explicitness: action itself (4)	M+	Target size, if multiple (6)
		M+	Explicitness: means-to-target impact (4)		
		M+	Degree of graphicness (5)		
		M	Humor (2)		

Note:

M = Modal response earns 1 point; non-modal responses earn no points.

M+ = Modal response earns 1 point. Also, divide the list of possible values on the variable into two categories (a) none (codes that indicate the absence of the characteristic named by the variable) and (b) some (a list of codes that indicate the presence of the characteristic to varying degrees). Then consider the following rules:

Rule 1: If the modal response is a "none" code, then all nonmodal responses earn no points.

Rule 2: If the modal response is a value from "some" distribution, then selection of a coding value directly contiguous to the modal response earns 1/2 point unless the contiguous response has crossed the line into a "none" code, in which case it earns no points.

produce consistent coding, she or he was removed from coding responsibilities and assigned another task. In this situation, data generated by a problem coder was discarded back to the time of the previous test of reliability for which that coder had demonstrated satisfactory performance.

REFERENCES

Baron, R. A., and D. R. Richardson. 1994. *Human Aggression.* 2d ed. New York: Plenum.
Baxter, R. L., C. D. Reimer, A. Landini, L. Leslie, and M. W. Singletary. 1985. "A Content Analysis of Music Videos." *Journal of Broadcasting and Electronic Media* 29:333–40.
Berkowitz, L. 1984. "Some Effects of Thoughts on Anti and Prosocial Influences of Media Events: A Cognitive-Neoassociation Analysis." *Psychological Bulletin* 95(3): 410–27.
Berkowitz, L., and K. H. Rogers. 1986. "A Priming Effect Analysis of Media Influences." In *Perspectives on Media Effects,* ed. J. Bryant and D. Zillmann, 57–82. Hillsdale, NJ: Erlbaum.
Brown, J. D., and K. Campbell. 1986. "Race and Gender in Music Videos: The Same Beat but a Different Drummer." *Journal of Communication* 36(1): 94–106.
Cantor, J. 1991. "Fight Responses to Mass Media." In *Responding to the Screen,* ed. J. Bryant and D. Zillmann, 169–98. Hillsdale, NJ: Lawrence Erlbaum.
Clark, D. G., and W. B. Blankenberg. 1972. "Trends in Violent Content in Selected Mass Media." In *Television and Social Behavior: Media and Content Control,* ed. G. A. Comstock and E. A. Rubinstein, vol. 1, 188–243. Washington, DC: U.S. Government Publication.
Columbia Broadcasting System. 1980. *Network Prime Time Violence Tabulations for 1978–1979 Season.* New York: Columbia Broadcasting System.
Cumberbatch, G., M. Lee, G. Hardy, and I. Jones. 1987. *The Portrayal of Violence on British Television.* London: British Broadcasting Corporation.
Dominick, J. 1973. "Crime and Law Enforcement on Prime-Time Television." *Public Opinion Quarterly* 37(2): 241–50.
Gerbner, G., L. Gross, M. Morgan, and N. Signorielli. 1980. "The 'Mainstreaming' of America: Violence Profile no. 11." *Journal of Communication* 30(3): 10–29.
Gerbner, G., L. Gross, N. Signorielli, M. Morgan, and M. Jackson-Beeck. 1979. "The Demonstration of Power: Violence Profile No. 10." *Journal of Communication* 29(3): 177–96.
Greenberg, B. S., N. Edison, F. Korzenny, C. Fernandez-Collado, and C. K. Atkin. 1980. "Antisocial and Prosocial Behaviors on Television." In *Life on Television: Content Analyses of U.S. TV Drama,* ed. B. S. Greenberg, 99–128. Norwood, NJ: Ablex Publishing.
Head, S. 1954. "Content Analysis of Television Drama Programs." *Quarterly of Film, Radio and TV* 9:175–94.
Lichter, S. R., and D. Amundson. 1992. *A Day of Television Violence.* Washington, DC: Center for Media and Public Affairs.
———. 1994. *A Day of TV Violence 1992 vs. 1994.* Washington, DC: Center for Media and Public Affairs.

Mustonen, A., and L. Pulkkinen. 1993. "Aggression in Television Programs in Finland." *Aggressive Behavior* 19:175–83.

National Television Violence Study, Volume 1. 1997. Thousand Oaks, CA: Sage.

National Television Violence Study. 1996a. *Content Analysis Codebook.* Studio City, CA: Mediascope.

———. 1996b. *Sample of Programs for Content Analysis 1994–95.* Studio City, CA: Mediascope.

"NCTV Says Violence on TV Up 16%." 1983. *Broadcasting Magazine,* March 22: 63.

Potter, W. J., M. Vaughan, R. Warren, K. Howley, A. Land, and J. Hagemeyer. 1995. "How Real Is the Portrayal of Aggression in Television Entertainment Programming?" *Journal of Broadcasting and Electronic Media* 39(4): 496–516.

Potter, W. J., and W. Ware. 1987. "An Analysis of the Contexts of Antisocial Acts on Prime-Time Television." *Communication Research* 14(6): 664–86.

Poulos, R. W., S. E. Harvey, and R. M. Liebert. 1976. "Saturday Morning Television: A Profile of the 1974–75 Children's Season." *Psychological Reports* 39:1047–57.

Reiss, A. J., and J. A. Roth, eds. 1993. *Understanding and Preventing Violence.* Washington, DC: National Academy Press.

Schramm, W., J. Lyle, and E. B. Parker. 1961. *Television in the Lives of Our Children.* Stanford, CA: Stanford University Press.

Scott, W. A. 1955. "Reliability of Content Analysis: The Case of Nominal Scale Coding." *Public Opinion Quarterly* 19:321–25.

Sherman, B. L., and J. R. Dominick. 1986. "Violence and Sex in Music Videos: TV and Rock 'n' Roll." *Journal of Communication* 36(1): 79–93.

Signorielli, N. 1990. "Television's Mean and Dangerous World: A Continuation of the Cultural Indicators Perspective." In *Cultivation Analysis: New Directions in Media Effects Research,* ed. N. Signorielli and M. Morgan, 85–106. Newbury Park, CA: Sage.

Signorielli, N., L. Gross, and M. Morgan. 1982. "Violence in Television Programs: Ten Years Later." In *Television and Social Behavior: Ten Years of Scientific Progress and Implications for the Eighties,* ed. D. Pearl Bouthilet and J. Lazar, 158–73. Rockville, MD: National Institute of Mental Health.

Smythe, D. 1954. "Reality as Presented on Television." *Public Opinion Quarterly* 18:143–56.

Sommers-Flanagan, R., J. Sommers-Flanagan, and B. Davis. 1993. "What's Happening on Music Television? A Gender Role Content Analysis." *Sex Roles* 28:745–53.

Williams, T. M., M. L. Zabrack, and L. A. Joy. 1982. "The Portrayal of Aggression on North American Television." *Journal of Allied Social Psychology* 12(5): 360–80.

Wilson, B. J. 1995. "Les Recherches sur Médias et Violence: Aggressivité, Désensibilisation, Peur" [Effects of Media Violence: Aggression, Desensitization, and Fear]. *Cahiers de la Sécurité Intérieure* 20(2): 21–37.

Wilson, B. J., and J. Cantor. 1985. "Developmental Differences in Empathy with a Television Protagonist's Fear." *Journal of Experimental Child Psychology* 39:284–99.

Chapter 4

Content Analysis of Entertainment Television: The 1994–95 Results

Barbara J. Wilson, Stacy L. Smith, James Potter,
Daniel Linz, Edward Donnerstein, Dale Kunkel,
Eva Blumenthal, and Tim Gray

Introduction

In this chapter, we apply the framework discussed in chapters 2 and 3 to analyze a sample of entertainment programming from 1994–95. The results from our content analysis demonstrate the context of how violence is used in television programming and how this context varies across genres of programming and channel types. When these results were first released in 1996 in the *National Television Violence Study,* media coverage generally focused on a single number in the content analysis, that is, 57 percent of all programs in the sample contained violence. Yet the results from this chapter reveal the importance of going beyond a single number to characterize television violence. The figures presented here demonstrate that violence is frequently used in contexts that are most likely to stimulate learning and imitation. Nearly half of all violent actions on television fail to show a victim's pain/harm and are portrayed as justified. The majority of violent actions are not followed in the same scene by any sort of punishment. In programs that contain violence, a third contain nine or more violent interactions. A high number of violent interactions is more prevalent on premium channels and independent stations and more likely in movies and reality-based programs.

Our results demonstrate that the context of violence does vary across genre, channel type, and time of day. These differences in context should concern parents trying to shield their children from damaging content, groups such as the American Medical Association and the National PTA that have an interest in children's welfare, and industry participants worried about the possible impacts of program content. The age-based program ratings adopted in the *TV Parental Guidelines* do not provide parents with detailed information on violent program content, so that parents may not gain much information on the context of violence from the current ratings system. In the next chapter we explicitly consider what the implications are of our content analysis for parents, industry members, and policymakers.

This chapter is organized into five sections. In the first section we provide an introduction to the overall analysis, which focuses on programs randomly selected from 23 broadcast and cable channels during 1994–95. All programs were selected between the hours of 6 A.M. and 11:00 P.M. over a 20-week period to create a composite week of content for each channel. As described in chapter 3, this yielded a sample of approximately 119 hours of programming per channel. In the second and third sections of the chapter, we analyze the prevalence and distribution of violence on American television and delineate the context of its use. The fourth section focuses on programs with an antiviolence theme, while the fifth section summarizes the main findings of the chapter.

Before proceeding, however, we must highlight briefly two caveats that frame our results. First, we did not code and assess every program in our sample. Several types of programs were not stipulated in our contact with National Cable Television Association (NCTA) (e.g., religious programming, game shows). Although these programs represent only 15 percent of the shows in our sample, readers should be aware that this small percentage is not part of our final sample of *coded and analyzed* programs (see chapter 3, and *National Television Violence Study, Volume 1* 1997).

Second, we want to underscore the importance of interpreting our findings accurately. The results should always be framed in terms of the correct unit of analysis. That is, the results delineated below will pertain to the percentage of either programs, scenes, or violent interactions that contain a particular contextual feature or attribute. For example, graphicness was coded at the scene level. Thus, all results regarding this variable refer to the *percentage of violent scenes* that feature graphic violence. We encourage the reader to consider carefully each finding in terms of its correct unit of analysis (i.e., program, scene, interaction) when reading and interpreting our results.

Plan of Analysis

Our plan of analysis is structured into three areas of focus: presence of violence, context of the violence, and presence of antiviolence themes. In examining the presence of violence on television, we highlight both its prevalence and its distribution. Prevalence addresses the question, What percentage of programs contain violence? In contrast, the concept of distribution refers to the range in the frequency of violence across programs. Although many programs may contain violence (prevalence), a program that features only one violent interaction is very different from a program that contains 10 interactions.

After we present the general patterns of prevalence and distribution from the entire sample of coded programs, we assess whether those patterns hold across different locations in the composite week of programming. We created four "locator variables" that partition the total sample into meaningful subgroups. The locator variables allow us to determine if the violence is more likely to occur during particular spots in the programming schedule. Our locator variables are: channel type, program genre, day-part, and type of day (i.e., weekday or weekend).

As for channel type, the 23 channels in the sample were arranged into five groups as follows: (1) *broadcast networks,* which include ABC, CBS, Fox, and NBC; (2) *public broadcast,* which includes PBS; (3) *independent broadcast,* which includes KTLA, KCOP, and KCAL; (4) *basic cable,* which includes Arts and Entertainment, American Movie Classics, Black Entertainment Television, Cartoon Network, The Family Channel, Lifetime, Music TV, Nickelodeon, Turner Network Television, USA Network, Video Hits 1, and The Disney Channel; and (5) *premium cable,* which includes Cinemax, Home Box Office, and Showtime.

As for the genre locator variable, we classified all the different types of programs in our sample into six groups: drama series, comedy series, movies, music videos, reality-based programs, and children's series. The locator variable dealing with day-part was constructed by dividing the 17-hour sampling frame (6 A.M. to 11 P.M.) into five time periods: *early morning* (6 A.M. to 9 P.M.), *midday* (9 A.M. to 3 P.M.), *late afternoon* (3 P.M. to 6 P.M.), *early evening* (6 P.M. to 8 P.M.), and *prime time* (8 P.M. to 11 P.M.). The type of day locator variable was constructed by dividing the seven days of the week into two groups: weekday and weekend.

In all analyses involving locator variables, we essentially are searching for differences. For example, does the prevalence or distribution of violence differ significantly across the five types of channels or across the six genres of programming? To answer such a question, we looked for two types of significance: statistical and substantive. Statistical significance refers to how much confidence we have that the patterns we observe in the sample accurately reflect the patterns in the entire population of all television programming. To assess statistical significance, we computed a chi-square statistic for the pattern of data across each locator variable. Each chi-square has an accompanying probability value (p), which indicates the level of confidence we have that the pattern is not due to chance or error. For example, if the p value is $p < .001$ it means that there is less than one chance in 1,000 that this pattern is a result of error. Virtually all analyses of differences in this report are statistically significant at $p < .05$.

However, not all of the differences that are statistically significant are necessarily meaningful. For instance, if a table reveals that 55 percent of all programs contain violence whereas only 50 percent of comedy series contain violence, should we conclude that this difference of 5 percent is meaningful? Our answer is no, because we view 5 percent as being too small for us to regard as a notable difference. To assess substantive significance (our second type of significance), we examined the magnitude of difference in percentages. Unless we observe a difference of at least 10 percent between the overall pattern across all programming (i.e., industry average) and the pattern found for a specific subgroup of programming, we are not prepared to argue that there is a substantive difference. Differences of 10 percent to 19 percent are regarded as moderate differences, whereas differences of 20 percent or more are regarded as substantial. Although these cutpoints are somewhat arbitrary, we use them because they are a helpful tool in summarizing important differences that might exist in the programming schedule.

Our second task in the analysis plan is to describe the context in which the violence is portrayed (as discussed in chapter 2). Our contextual analysis is organized around a set of specific contextual factors: the nature of the perpetrator of violence, the nature of the target, the reason for the violence, means used (weapons), extent of violence, graphicness, realism, reward/punishment, consequences, and humor. For each contextual variable, we present the overall pattern across all programming, and then we present any important differences that emerge as a function of the four locator variables.

The final task in our analysis plan is to assess antiviolence themes in television programming. In particular, we are concerned with how many programs feature such a theme and how such themes may be used. This analysis differs somewhat from the quantitative focus that characterizes the sections pertaining to the presence and context of violence. Our analysis of antiviolence themes focuses instead on detailed descriptions of sample programs that feature an antiviolence theme. Our goal is to illustrate how writers and producers in the television industry can creatively portray violence in order to emphasize its negative consequences for society.

Presence of Violence

In this section, we deal with general patterns of prevalence and distribution of violence across all programming. Then we turn to an analysis of differences in these patterns by locator variables. The section concludes with an examination of the topics of sexual violence and violence advisories.

Prevalence of Violence

The issue of prevalence addresses the question, What percentage of the coded television programs contain violence? If a program contained one or more acts of violence, we regarded it as a violent program for purposes of our prevalence analysis. By this criterion, 57 percent of all programs in our sample were classified as violent; the remaining 43 percent of programs contained no portrayals that qualified as violence given our definition.

Recall that our definition of violence from chapter 3 has three main components: (1) behavioral acts, (2) credible threats, and (3) harmful consequences of unseen violence. Although most accidents were not coded because they lacked the most important element of our definition (intent to harm), accidental violence was included in situations where a character experienced unintentional harm as a result of ongoing violence.

A total of more than 18,000 violent interactions were observed in our sample of programming. What is the most prevalent form of violence in these interactions? Two-thirds of the violent incidents (66 percent) on television feature a perpetrator committing an actual behavioral act of violence. Far fewer of the violent interactions involve credible threats (29 percent), where the perpetrator demonstrates a clear intent to physically harm the target and has the means ready to do so, but for some reason does not follow through immediately. Much more rare are interactions involving harmful consequences of unseen violence (3 percent), or instances where an injured victim is depicted but the violence itself is not shown on screen. Also quite rare are accidents (2 percent), where targets are unintentionally harmed in the course of ongoing violence.

Distribution of Violence

The issue of distribution addresses the question, What is the range of violent interactions across programs? Our goal in answering this question is to be able to contrast those programs that display only one or two violent interactions with those that feature many violent incidents.[1] Violent programs differ quite a bit in terms of the number of violent interactions they contain. The frequency of violent interactions per program ranges from 1 to 88. However, most of the programs cluster at the lower end of the frequency distribution, with 15 percent of programs containing only one violent interaction, 12 percent containing two, and 10 percent containing three. This means that slightly more than one-third of all violent programs contain between one and three violent interactions. Another one-third contain between four and eight violent interactions, and the remaining one-third feature nine or more violent interactions.

We must emphasize that a violent interaction does not necessarily mean that a single act of violence occurs. Instead, it means that a particular perpetrator committed some amount of violence against a particular target. If, for example, a criminal fires a gun six times in rapid succession at a hero, coders recorded this as a single violent interaction rather than six independent acts of violence. The information about multiple gunshots is captured by a variable called "extent" (discussed below in the context section of this chapter). Thus, when we report that one-third of the programs feature nine or more violent interactions, we mean that these shows contain nine or more separate violent incidents involving different perpetrator and target combinations. This statistic tells us nothing about the number of individual behavioral acts *within* each incident, so it is not comparable to other studies that report on the rate of violent acts per hour or per program.

Analysis by Locator Variables

Now we turn our attention to *where* violence is located in the programming schedule. For both prevalence and distribution, there are significant differences across channel types and program genres. Differences also exist, but to a lesser extent, across day-parts and types of day.

Channel type. In terms of prevalence, programming on premium cable (85 percent) is more likely to contain violence than the industry average (57 percent). In contrast, programming on the broadcast networks (44 percent) is less likely to contain violence, and the percent of violent programs on public broadcast (18 percent) is even lower. Programs on basic cable (59 percent) and independent broadcasters (55 percent) did not differ from the industry norm. From this point on, all the differences we highlight in the results section have met the statistical criterion of $p < .05$ according to a chi-square test of frequencies, as well as a more conservative criterion of substantive significance.

As for distribution, public broadcast exhibits the smallest range of violent interactions per program (from 1 to 29), followed by the broadcast networks (1 to 35), basic cable (1 to 64), independent broadcast (1 to 69), and premium cable (1 to 88). Recall that in our sample of violent programs, about one-third of the programs have one to three violent interactions ("low"), one-third have four to eight interactions ("medium"), and one-third have nine or more ("high"). When we break down programs by channel type and compare across these three groupings, we find some interesting patterns (see fig. 4.1). Premium cable and independent broadcast both have a very large percentage of programs containing a *high* number of violent interactions. In contrast, programming on the broadcast networks is more likely to feature a low number of violent interactions.

Program genre. The prevalence findings also vary significantly by program genre. A higher percentage of movies and drama series contain violence compared to the industry average, whereas fewer comedy series, reality-based shows, and music videos contain violence (see fig. 4.2). It is not surprising that the movie genre would display the greatest prevalence given that premium cable, which is dominated by films, also has the highest prevalence among the channel types. Somewhat unexpectedly, reality-based programs are less likely to

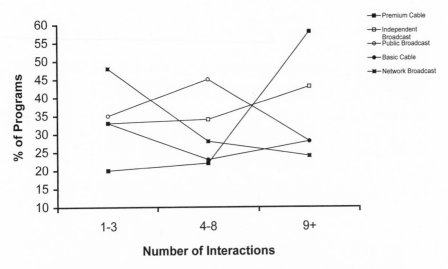

Fig. 4.1. Percentage of programs with PATs at three frequency levels, by channel

be violent, although we must underscore that this genre not only includes programs like *Cops* and *American Justice,* but also talk shows and documentaries that may be less likely to feature aggression. Music videos often are criticized for being violent, but our data show that only a third of them contain violence. Per-

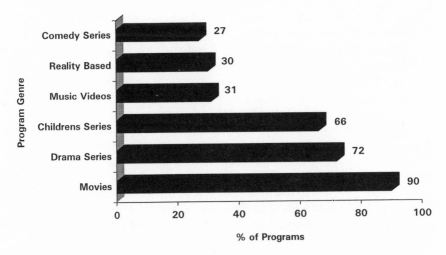

Fig. 4.2. Percentage of programs with violence, by genre

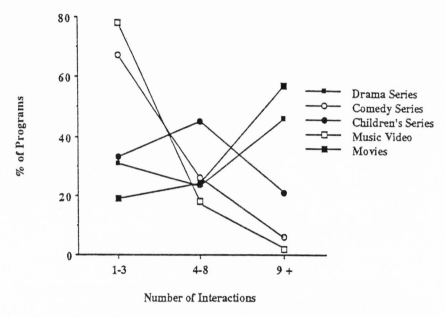

Fig. 4.3.   Percentage of programs with PATs at three frequency levels, by genre

haps the most violent examples of this genre capture critics' attention and the numerous nonviolent, performance videos get underrepresented.

The pattern on distribution of violence generally parallels the pattern on prevalence. Concerning the ranges, movies exhibit the widest range of violent interactions (1 to 88 per program), followed by dramatic series (1 to 41) and children's series (1 to 40). Comedy series and reality-based programs feature a smaller range of violent interactions (1 to 26 for each). The lowest range is found for music videos (1 to 18). When we compare the genres across levels of frequency, we see that most music videos and comedy series feature a "low" number of violent interactions (see fig. 4.3). In contrast, nearly two-thirds of reality-based programs and movies contain a "high" number of violent interactions.

Day-part and type of day.   In general, programs shown on the weekends have a slightly higher prevalence (62 percent) compared to programs shown on weekdays (55 percent). An examination of the prevalence of violent programs across day-part reveals that almost all percentages are very close to the overall average of 57 percent. There are only two minor deviations from this norm. In the early morning time slot (6:00–9:00 A.M.) during weekdays, only 45 percent of all programs contain violence, whereas in the late afternoon (3:00–6:00 P.M.) on weekends, 68 percent of programs are violent.

Summary of Prevalence and Distribution

The majority (57 percent) of programs in a composite week of television contain some violence. Furthermore, most of the violent incidents on television involve behavioral acts of aggression rather than credible threats or implied violence. The highest percentages of violent programs are found on premium cable and within the genre of movies specifically; this is also where the highest frequencies of violent interactions are displayed. In contrast, the lowest percentage of violent programming is found on the broadcast networks and especially on public broadcast. Violence is less likely in comedy series, music videos, and reality-based programs. These channel types and genres also are characterized by relatively few violent interactions per program.

Prevalence of Sexual Violence

The probability of encountering a sexual assault within a violent incident is very low. On average, less than 1 percent of violent interactions in our sample involve a sexual assault. There are too few examples of these depictions to identify any variation by channel type, genre, day-part, and type of day.

Prevalence of Advisories

Very few of all coded programs in our sample contain any type of advisory or content code (see chapter 7 for discussion of advisories). We followed up on this analysis by examining *only* those programs that were coded as violent. Specifically, our findings reveal that among those programs featuring any violence, only 15 percent are preceded by an advisory or content code. In other words, viewers are rarely advised about programs that contain violence.

However, the presence of advisories or content codes differs substantially across channel type and genre. That is, three-fourths of the violent programs on premium cable are preceded by some type of viewer advisory. In striking contrast, very few of the violent programs on the network stations (3 percent), independent broadcasters (5 percent), public broadcast (11 percent) or basic cable (1 percent) are preceded by a violence advisory or content code. With respect to genre, violent movies (47 percent) are substantially more likely to contain an advisory or content code than the overall average (15 percent). Violent children's series (0 percent), violent drama series (2 percent), and violent comedy series (4 percent), however, are less likely. Reality-based programs are not different from the industry norm in terms of the presence of advisories or content codes, though very few of them contain such warnings.

The presence of advisories or content codes does not differ much in terms of day-part and type of day, with one exception. Violent programs featured during prime time (8–11 P.M.) on the weekend (26 percent) are more likely than the industry average (16 percent) to be preceded by some type of advisory or content code.

Contextual Factors

The heart of this study is to assess the nature or context of violent portrayals. The preceding section describes what proportion of programs contain violence as well as how many violent interactions occur in different types of content. However, such figures tell us nothing about *how* that violence is portrayed. In this section of the chapter, we turn our attention to the analyses that provide us with that information. More specifically, we review the results of the analyses of each of the contextual factors and how those factors vary by channel, genre, daypart, and type of day.

Nature of the Perpetrator

The nature of the perpetrator of violence is an important consideration in terms of imitation and learning. Research indicates that perpetrators who are attractive or who are demographically similar to the viewer are potent role models in entertainment programming (Bandura 1986, 1994; Jose and Brewer 1984). Violent interactions that feature these types of models are more likely to increase learning of aggression.

Coders identified a perpetrator for *each* violent interaction in a program. Summing across all the violent interactions provides a profile of the characters that is weighted according to the number of interactions in which they are involved. For example, if a program features two characters, a male who is the aggressor in eight violent interactions and a female who is the aggressor in two violent interactions, we would report that 80 percent of the perpetrators are male and 20 percent are female. This weighting is appropriate because our focus is a behavioral one. Thus, we are interested in describing the attributes (such as character demographics) associated with violent interactions, rather than focusing on characters independent of the extent of their behaviors.

Perpetrators could be classified as single individuals, groups of individuals, or implied (unidentified) individuals. Across more than 18,000 violent interactions, two-thirds of the perpetrators are single individuals (67 percent) and therefore are relatively easy to code in terms of demographics and attributes. Most of the remaining perpetrators (30 percent) are groups of individuals. We represent each group as "one" perpetrator in our data because, by our definition, groups act collectively against a target. Like individuals, each group is assigned a value on the demographics and the character attribute variables. When individuals in a group are not homogeneous on a particular characteristic (e.g., some men and some women), coders identified the perpetrator as "mixed" on that variable. Only 3 percent of the perpetrators of violence are implied or unknown. Percentages reported below do not always add up to 100 percent because demographic and attributive qualities of implied or unknown perpetrators are oftentimes difficult and/or impossible to ascertain.

Type of character. Coders classified each perpetrator according to one of five character types: human, animal, anthropomorphized animal, supernatural creature, or anthropomorphized supernatural creature. The findings indicate that almost three-fourths of perpetrators of violence are human characters (71 percent). Two other categories account for nearly all the remaining perpetrators: anthropomorphized animals (12 percent) and anthropomorphized supernatural creatures (10 percent). Supernatural creatures (3 percent) and animals (1 percent) are rarely involved as perpetrators of violence. Thus, most of the initiators of aggression on television are humans or humanlike characters. According to the social science research (see chapter 2), these characters should be easier for viewers to identify with than those who do not resemble humans.

In addition to the overall patterns across all programming, we assessed each character variable by program genre and by channel type. We did not, however, look at character variables in terms of day-part and type of day because preliminary analyses suggested no meaningful differences here. For every program genre except children's series, nearly all perpetrators of violence are humans. In contrast, almost half of the perpetrators in children's series are anthropomorphized (48 percent) and only 40 percent are humans. This pattern is reflective of the high proportion of cartoons that constitute children's programming.

In terms of channel type, nearly all the perpetrators featured on public broadcast (96 percent) are humans. Premium cable (86 percent) also displays a higher proportion of human perpetrators than the overall industry average (71 percent). In comparison, independent broadcast (57 percent) is *less* likely to feature human perpetrators, and *more* likely to show anthropomorphized creatures (34 percent) as aggressors. Such a finding is indicative of a higher concentration of cartoons on this channel type.

Sex. More than three-fourths of the perpetrators in violent interactions are male (78 percent), whereas only 9 percent are female. This robust pattern does not differ across genre or channel type.

Age. Coders judged the approximate age of each perpetrator as one of the following: child (0–12 years), teen (13–20 years), adult (21–64 years), or elderly (65 years or older). The results reveal that 76 percent of the perpetrators in violent interactions are adults. Teens make up the next largest category, though only 5 percent of perpetrators fall into this age group. Very few perpetrators of violence on television are children (2 percent) or elderly (1 percent).

Age of perpetrator does not differ across the five channel types. Differences emerge as a function of genre, however. Drama series contain a higher proportion of adult perpetrators (90 percent) than the overall industry norm (76 percent). In contrast, children's series feature a lower proportion of adult perpetrators (60 percent). Nevertheless, the lower percentage of adults does *not* translate into more child or teen perpetrators in such programming, as might be expected. Instead, many of the perpetrators in children's series cannot be classified in terms of age, presumably because their supernatural or anthropomorphized qualities make chronological age difficult to ascertain.

Apparent ethnicity. The perpetrator's apparent ethnicity was coded for human characters only as: White, Hispanic, Black, Asian, Native American, or Middle Eastern. Approximately three-fourths of the perpetrators of violence on television are White (76 percent). Only 5 percent of the perpetrators are Black, 3 percent are Native American, 3 percent are Asian, 2 percent are Hispanic, and 1 percent are Middle Eastern.

Character ethnicity varies by program genre. Music videos and reality-based programs are substantially less likely to feature White perpetrators compared to the industry average (see fig. 4.4) and *more* likely to show Black perpetrators. This latter finding is most pronounced for music videos, where over one-third of the perpetrators are Black (38 percent) compared to a 5 percent industry norm. In terms of channel type, the only difference that emerges is that broadcast networks are *less* likely to feature White perpetrators (65 percent) than the overall average (76 percent). This pattern is accounted for by the fact that slightly more Black perpetrators show up on the broadcast networks (13 percent), although according to our criterion this latter difference is not substantively significant (i.e., at least 10 percent different from the margin).

Hero. Most perpetrators do *not* qualify as heroes (93 percent) according to our data. Given our rather strict definition, only 6 percent of all perpetrators on television are primary characters who go above and beyond the call of duty to protect others. No differences are found in this pattern by genre or channel type.

Good/bad. Coders judged each perpetrator as good, bad, *both* good and bad (blended), or neutral (neither good nor bad). A bad character was defined as an animate being who is motivated primarily by self-interest, whereas a good character was defined as one who is motivated by a concern for others. Our findings reveal that 45 percent of the perpetrators of violence on television are bad characters, 24 percent are good, 13 percent are both good and bad, and only 14 percent are purely neutral. Taken together, then, approximately 37 percent of the perpetrators of violence have some good qualities with which a viewer might identify (percent of good plus percent of blended).

This overall pattern characterizes perpetrators across all five channel types. The only difference pertains to one of the program genres—music videos. In music videos, a higher proportion of the perpetrators are neutral (33 percent),

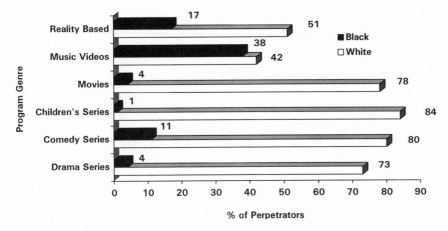

Fig. 4.4.   White and Black perpetrators, by genre

whereas a lower proportion are good (13 percent) or bad (31 percent) compared to the overall average. Clearly, the brief duration of most videos makes it more difficult to ascertain the motives of characters, making the neutral category a more viable option.

Summary of perpetrators.   The typical perpetrator of violence on television is a human character who is adult, White, and male. Most often, the perpetrator is not a hero, and in fact is likely to be a "bad" rather than a "good" character. However, more than one-third of all perpetrators have some good qualities that could make them attractive and therefore potent role models for viewers.

The profile of the typical perpetrator varies some by genre. Children's series are more likely to feature anthropomorphized or humanlike perpetrators and less likely to feature actual humans as aggressors compared to other genres. But this pattern is not surprising given the preponderance of cartoons within this genre. Music videos and reality-based programs also show some differences in the nature of the perpetrator. In particular, both genres feature a higher proportion of Black perpetrators and a lower proportion of White perpetrators compared to the overall pattern. In fact, music videos contain almost equal proportions of Black and White perpetrators. Music videos also are less likely than other genres to feature "bad" or "good" characters as perpetrators, and more likely to portray perpetrators as "neutral."

Fewer differences are present for channel type.   Public broadcast and premium cable are more likely than the norm to feature human perpetrators, whereas independent broadcast is less likely to show humans as perpetrators, primarily because of the number of cartoons on this channel type. The only other finding of substance is that the broadcast networks are less likely to feature White perpetrators compared to the overall industry norm.

Nature of the Target

The target is the character or characters to whom violence is directed. The nature of the target of violence is an important consideration in terms of audience fear. Research indicates that viewers feel concern for and share emotional experiences with characters who they perceive as attractive and similar to themselves (Zillmann 1980, 1991). As a result, when an attractive or well-liked character is threatened or attacked in a violent scene, viewers are likely to experience anxiety or fear (Zillmann and Cantor 1977; Comisky and Bryant 1982).

Coders identified a target for each violent interaction in a program. As was done with perpetrators, summing across all the violent interactions provides a profile of the characters that is weighted according to the number of interactions in which they are victims. Across more than 18,000 violent interactions, almost 69 percent of targets are single individuals and only 29 percent are groups of individuals. As with the perpetrator data, each group of targets is assessed as a single unit on the demographic and character attribute variables. If individuals in a group are not homogenous on a particular characteristic (e.g., ethnicity), then coders identified the target as "mixed" on that variable. The remaining 2 percent of the targets of violence are implied or unidentifiable.

Type of character.   The vast majority of targets in violent interactions are human characters (70 percent). Two other categories account for most of the other targets: anthropomorphized animals (14 percent) and anthropomorphized supernatural creatures (9 percent). Supernatural creatures (2 percent) and animals (2 percent) rarely are involved as targets of violence. It should be noted that this pattern is almost identical to that of the perpetrators. Overall then, most of the victims of aggression on television are humans or humanlike characters who presumably are easier for viewers to identify with than nonhumans.

When examining genre, 90 percent or more of all targets are human in drama series, movies, comedy series, reality-based programs, and music videos. In striking contrast, children's series feature a substantially lower proportion of human targets (36 percent) and a higher proportion of anthropomorphized characters (51 percent) as targets. Again, this difference is consistent with the fact that much of children's programming is comprised of cartoons.

In terms of channel type, nearly all the targets shown on public broadcast are humans (99 percent). Likewise, premium cable features a higher proportion of humans (88 percent) as targets compared to the overall average (70 percent). Yet the broadcast networks and independent broadcasters contain a smaller proportion of human targets (59 percent and 59 percent respectively), and a greater proportion of anthropomorphized targets (33 percent and 32 percent respectively). Again, this pattern is indicative of more cartoons on these types of channels.

Sex. Just as with perpetrators, the vast majority of targets of violence are male (75 percent). In spite of public concern that women may be singled out as victims on television, only 9 percent of the targets in our sample are female. This pattern generally does not differ across channel type or across genre, with one exception. In reality-based programs, a lower proportion of targets are male (59 percent), and a slightly higher percentage are female (14 percent) compared to the overall pattern (9 percent). However, the latter difference is not substantively significant according to our minimum criterion of 10 percent difference from the overall industry average.

Age. As with perpetrators, most of the targets of violence are adults (72 percent). The next most common victim is a teenager, but this age group makes up only 7 percent of all targets. Very few of the victims of violence on television are children (3 percent) or elderly (1 percent).

The age of the target does not vary by channel type. In terms of genre, drama series are more likely than the norm to feature adult victims (89 percent), and children's series are less likely (54 percent). The latter finding is due to a higher proportion of targets who cannot be classified by age, again because many of the characters in children's series are anthropomorphized.

Apparent ethnicity. Similar to perpetrators, more than three-fourths of the targets of violence on television are White (77 percent). Only 6 percent of the targets are Black, and the remaining groups each account for 3 percent or less of the victims. In spite of the overall predominance of White victims, ethnicity does vary by program genre. Music videos and reality-based programs are substantially *less* likely to feature White victims compared to the industry average (see fig. 4.5), and music videos are substantially *more* likely to display Black victims. In fact, targets are almost equally split between Black and White characters when looking at music videos. Target ethnicity does not vary by channel type.

Hero. Targets of violence typically are not heroes. Only 6 percent of victims meet our strict definition of what constitutes this type of character (i.e., primary character who goes above and beyond the call of duty to protect others in a program). This finding does not differ across genre or channel type.

Good/bad. Our findings suggest that almost one-third of targets can be described as good characters (31 percent). A total of 31 percent of the targets are bad, 12 percent can be classified as both good and bad, and 21 percent are best described as neutral. Taken together, then, almost half of the victims of violence on television (42 percent) possess some good qualities that might encourage a viewer to identify with them.

There are no differences in this variable as a function of channel type. In

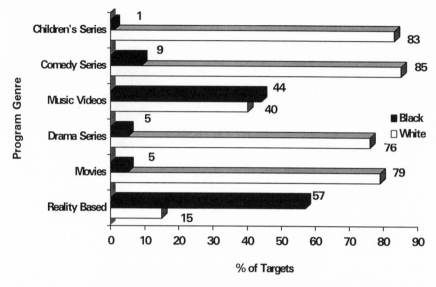

Fig. 4.5.   Percentage of White and Black targets, by genre

terms of genre, targets in comedy series are more likely to be neutral when compared to the overall average. Furthermore, targets in music videos are substantially more likely to be neutral and less likely to be good. This latter finding presumably is a function of the difficulty in fully developing the motives or nature of characters in such brief programming.

Summary of targets.   The profile of the typical target of television violence is nearly identical to that of the average perpetrator. Most targets are humans, and most are adult White males. Thus, the prototypical scenario for violence on television is an adult White male attacking another adult White male. The fact that so many of the profile variables look identical for both perpetrators and targets suggests that most of the characters involved in violence are not only aggressing but also are being aggressed against.

Like perpetrators, very few targets are heroes. However, almost half of the targets of violence on television possess some good qualities that might encourage viewer identification. Indeed, targets are slightly more likely to be good characters than are perpetrators. As indicated above, research indicates that viewers are more likely to experience fear when violence is directed toward an attractive or well-liked victim (Zillmann and Cantor 1977; Comisky and Bryant 1982). Our findings suggest that a majority of violent interactions involve good characters as targets and thus have the potential to cause anxiety in viewers.

There are some differences in the nature of the target across genre. Children's series are more likely to feature anthropomorphized or humanlike victims and less likely to feature actual humans as the target of violence compared to other genres. Even so, research reviewed in chapter 2 suggests that younger children are quite responsive to animated and unrealistic characters, so we cannot conclude that such depictions are somehow less problematic in terms of viewer fear. Music videos and reality-based programs also show some differences in the nature of the target. Both genres feature a lower proportion of White victims, and music videos in particular display a higher proportion of Black victims compared to the overall pattern. Lastly, music videos as well as comedy series are more likely than other genres to feature "neutral" victims who cannot be classified as either good or bad. In terms of channel type, public broadcast and premium cable are more likely to feature human targets compared to the overall average, whereas the broadcast networks and independent broadcasters are more likely to contain anthropomorphized victims. Clearly, these patterns are roughly parallel to the perpetrator findings.

Reasons for Violence

For every violent interaction, coders assessed the reason or motive for the perpetrator's aggression against a particular target. Reasons were coded into one of six categories: protection of life, anger, retaliation, personal gain, mental instability, or other. The "other" category was used whenever the perpetrator's motive did not fit into one of the five specific options, or whenever the program did not provide enough information to determine the perpetrator's reason (e.g., the perpetrator was not shown).

The findings reveal that violence on television is generally motivated by one of three reasons—personal gain, anger, or protection of life. Specifically, 30 percent of the violence is committed by perpetrators for personal gain, such as obtaining material goods (e.g., money, power, or affection). Another 24 percent of the violence is committed because the perpetrator feels anger over something the target did or said. And 26 percent of the violence is committed by a perpetrator in order to protect the self or another character. In contrast, very little of the violence on television is motivated by mental instability (5 percent) or retaliation for an act of previous violence in an earlier scene of the program (2 percent). The remaining 14 percent of violent interactions fell into the "other" category because they could not be clearly classified into one of the five reasons outlined above.

Reasons for violence do not vary much across the locator variables. Compared to other channel types, the violence on public broadcast is less likely to be motivated by personal gain or protection, and more likely to be motivated by some "other" or unknown reason. However, there is so little violence on PBS that this differential pattern should be interpreted with caution.

There also are some differences in the reasons across the program genres.

Compared to the overall industry norm, violence in comedy series is more likely to be committed because of anger. In comparison, violence in music videos is less likely to be motivated by protection of life, and more likely to occur for some "other" reason. The fact that much of the violence in music videos was classified as "other" is not entirely surprising. Because of the brief nature and production format of most videos (e.g., quick cuts to numerous images), a perpetrator's reason for acting violently may be difficult to ascertain. Reasons for violence do not fluctuate across day-parts or type of day.

Research suggests that violence portrayed as justified or somehow morally sanctioned poses a greater risk for viewers than does violence that appears unjustified (Berkowitz and Geen 1967; Berkowitz and Powers 1979; Geen and Stonner 1973, 1974). We collapsed categories of reasons in order to make this comparison. Violence that is committed to protect life or to retaliate for a previous act of aggression is likely to appear as justified within the context of a typical plot. In contrast, violence that is enacted for personal gain or because of mental instability is likely to seem unjustified. Anger, the only remaining reason, is more difficult to classify because some violence motivated by anger may appear justified (e.g., perpetrator shoves a target who is burning down his house), whereas some may not (e.g., perpetrator shoots a target because of a sarcastic remark). Thus, we excluded all interactions motivated by anger in the analysis of justification.

When reasons are collapsed as indicated (excluding the category "other"), nearly half of the violent interactions portray violence as justified (44 percent) and half portray it as unjustified (56 percent). There are no differences across channel type in the depiction of justified violence. In terms of genre, music videos are *less* likely than other types of content to portray violence as justified, consistent with the finding above that protection of life is less likely to be a motive for violence in this genre. There are no differences in justified violence across day-part or type of day.

To summarize, almost one-third of the violence on television is committed for instrumental purposes and almost one-fourth is motivated by anger. The only other reason that accounts for a substantial amount of violence (one-fourth) is to protect life. When reasons are classified in terms of justification, almost half of the violent interactions appear justified and half seem unjustified. This pattern is fairly consistent across channels, genre, day-part, and type of day.

Means/Presence of Weapons

For each violent interaction, the means or method that a perpetrator used to engage in violence was coded. Means were classified into one of seven categories: natural means, unconventional weapon, handheld firearm, conventional handheld weapon other than firearm, heavy weaponry, bombs, or means unknown.

Coders recorded all the different means that a perpetrator uses against the same target. However, in nearly all of the violent interactions in our sample (89 percent), the perpetrator uses only one form of means against a target. Thus, the findings only report the primary means employed in each violent interaction.

The most prevalent method perpetrators use to enact violence on television is natural means. Indeed, 40 percent of all violent interactions involve perpetrators using their own bodies to commit violence, such as hitting, punching, or kicking the target. When weapons are used, handheld firearms (i.e., guns) are the most common. In fact, guns are used in 25 percent of all violent interactions. The next most common form of weapon used is unconventional objects that are not traditionally associated with violence (e.g., rope, chair). Perpetrators use unconventional weapons in 20 percent of violent interactions. In contrast, bombs (2 percent), heavy weaponry like tanks and missiles (3 percent), and conventional handheld weapons other than guns (8 percent) are rarely used. And finally, only 2 percent of the interactions featured perpetrators using means or weapons to inflict violence that were unidentifiable or unknown.

Because the two most prevalent means (natural means and guns) are of most interest theoretically, we will now focus on them more specifically. Violence by natural means warrants special attention because conceivably it is more imitable by a viewer given that it does not require a special object or weapon. Guns have special significance because of the potential priming effect associated with such conventional weapons (Berkowitz and LePage 1967; Carlson, Marcus-Newhall, and Miller 1990).

Do these two types of means differ across the locator variables? Our data indicate that there are no differences in the use of natural means or the use of guns across channel type. There are, however, some significant differences in use of these two means across program genres. Compared to all types of content, natural means are used *more* often in music videos and *less* often in reality-based programs (see fig. 4.6). Guns, on the other hand, are used *more* often in reality-based programs and drama series, and *less* often in children's series. Therefore, music videos pose the highest risk for imitating behaviors like hitting and kicking, whereas reality-based programs and drama series present the highest risk of weapon priming. There are no differences in the use of natural means or guns across day-part and type of day.

Extent of Violence

For each violent interaction in a program, the amount or extent of repeated violence was examined. This measure applies to behavioral acts only and is not applicable to credible threats or harmful consequences. For extent, coders were trained to count the number of times a behavioral act was repeated by a perpetrator against the same target within the same scene. The range of times was

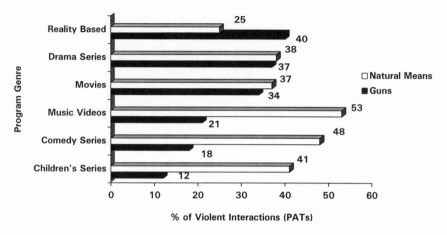

Fig. 4.6.   Use of guns and natural means, by genre type

coded as follows: one, some (2 to 9 times), many (10 to 20 times), or extreme (21 or more times). For example, a perpetrator might punch a target 15 times and this would be coded as a single violent interaction involving "natural means" (punch with fist) with an extent of "many" (hitting 15 times). In cases where behavioral acts are interconnected and thus impossible to count individually, like a wrestling match or automatic gunfire, coders judged extent based on the amount of time the behavior lasted, using the same four categories (see chapter 3).

Coders were trained to assess extent for each means or method of violence employed in a particular interaction. However, as mentioned above, most of the violent interactions involve only one type of means (89 percent). Thus, the analysis of extent focuses only the primary means. Our data indicate that 43 percent of the violent interactions involve only one act of aggression. Put another way, nearly 60 percent of the violent interactions on television involve repeated or extended behavioral violence. In particular, 42 percent of the violent interactions feature "some" violence, 9 percent involve "many" acts of violence, and 7 percent involve "extreme" amounts of violence.

In terms of the locator variables, there are no differences in the extent or repetition of violence across the five channel types. In contrast, extent of violence differs as a function of program genre. In particular, reality-based programs are more likely to contain repeated violence than are the other types of content (see fig. 4.7). It is important to point out that children's series do not differ from other genres in terms of the extent of violence shown. There are no significant differences in the extent of violence by day-part or type of day.

Overall, a majority of violent interactions on television feature repeated or

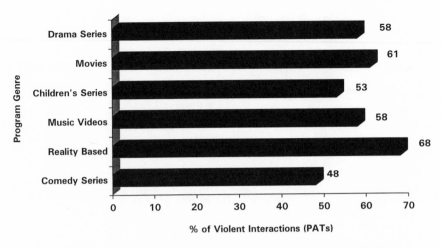

Fig. 4.7.   Percentage of interactions with repeated behavioral violence, by genre

extensive aggression, though very few could be classified as extreme. Furthermore, reality-based programs are more likely than other genres to feature extended behavioral violence.

Graphicness of Violence

Graphicness of violence was measured in terms of the explicitness of the violence and in terms of the amount of blood and gore shown. *Explicitness* refers
to the focus or concentration on the details of violence. *Blood and gore* refers to
the amount of bloodshed and carnage shown. Both types of measures were assessed at the level of each violent scene. Given its definition, explicitness is applicable only to behavioral violence, and not to credible threats or harmful consequences of unseen violence. Two types of explicitness were assessed: (1)
explicitness of the violent behavioral act itself (i.e., the level of detailed focus on
the perpetrator using the means or weapon), and (2) explicitness of means-to-
target impact (i.e., the level of detailed focus on the means or weapon impact-
ing and damaging the target's body). Both types of explicitness were coded into
one of three categories: close-up focus, long-shot focus, or not shown at all. Our
findings reveal that very little of the violence on television is explicit. In particular, only 3 percent of all violent scenes contain a close-up focus on behavioral
acts of violence, and only 2 percent of violent scenes feature a close-up focus on
the impact of violence on a target's body (see fig. 4.8).

There were no differences among the locator variables on explicitness. The

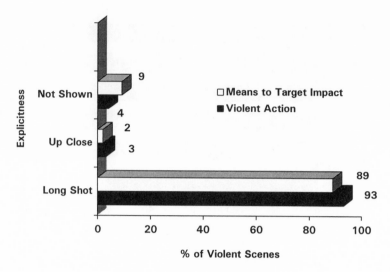

Fig. 4.8.   Explicitness of violent scenes

other measure of graphicness deals with the amount of blood and gore shown. Amount of graphicness was classified into one of four categories: none, mild, moderate, or extreme. Our findings reveal that the vast majority of violent scenes on television depict no blood and gore (85 percent); and very few of the scenes contain a "mild" amount of blood and gore (6 percent) or a "moderate" amount (6 percent). Almost none of the scenes depict an "extreme" amount of blood and gore (3 percent).

Some variability exists, however, in where this bloodshed and carnage is found. For the analyses involving locator variables, the categories of "mild," "moderate," and "extreme" were combined because of their low frequencies. The analyses, then, look at the percent of scenes that contain *any* blood and gore versus *none*. Approximately 15 percent of all violent scenes contain some blood and gore. In terms of channel, viewers are more likely to encounter blood and gore in violent scenes featured on premium cable (28 percent). All other types of channels do not differ from the industry average (15 percent) on this measure.

As for genre, only two types of programs vary from the industry average (15 percent). That is, movies (28 percent) are more likely than the industry norm to contain blood and gore within violent scenes. In contrast, bloodshed is virtually nonexistent in children's series (1 percent). Finally, blood and gore are more likely to be found in prime-time hours than in any other time slot during the week (see fig. 4.9). There are no differences in the depiction of bloodshed across day-parts during the weekend.

To summarize, the most robust finding here is that only a small percent-

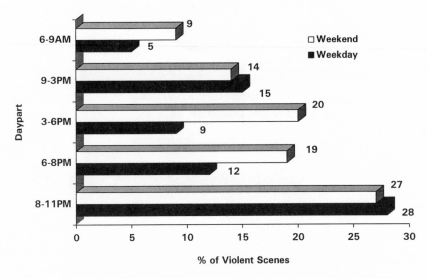

Fig. 4.9.   Percentage of violent scenes with blood and gore, by day-part

age of violent scenes on television can be described as graphic. There are very few close-ups of violent behaviors or of victims as they are injured. In addition, not much bloodshed and carnage are depicted. But this is not to say that all programming shares equally in this relatively positive pattern. When blood and gore are portrayed, they are most likely to be found on premium cable, on movies, and in prime-time hours during the weekdays.

Realism

Research indicates that viewers who perceive television violence as realistic are more likely to be influenced by it (see chap. 2). But what is real? Answering such a question requires that we consider several features of realism as well as the developmental level or age of the viewer. Consequently, we cannot simply label a particular portrayal as real or unreal, but we can array certain features of a program on a continuum where we can safely argue that some depictions reflect reality more than do others.

One feature of realism that we coded was the degree of authenticity of the characters and events on television. For each program, coders judged whether the characters and events represented actual reality, re-created reality, fiction, or fantasy. Our findings reveal that almost half of the violent programs in our sample can be classified as fantasy (49 percent). Most of the remaining programs fall into the fictional category (43 percent). Only 4 percent of violent programs involve actual reality and only 4 percent depict re-creations of reality. For purposes of

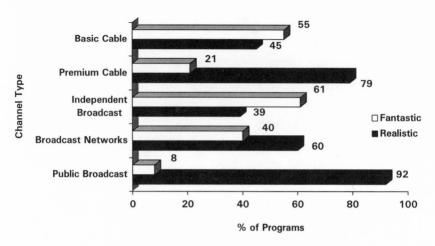

Fig. 4.10. Authenticity of violent programs, by channel

subsequent analyses, we collapsed the latter three categories into a "realistic" grouping that represents all programs based on events that could possibly occur in the real world (51 percent total).

When we analyze authenticity by channel type, we see that public broadcast and premium cable feature substantially more programs involving realistic violence than the industry average (see fig. 4.10). In contrast, independent broadcast is more likely to feature fantasy violence compared to the industry norm.

The analysis by genre reveals some differential patterns in terms of authenticity (see fig. 4.11). As might be expected, all reality-based programs are classified as involving realistic characters and events. Music videos, drama series, movies, and comedy series also are more likely to feature realistic events when compared to the industry average. In contrast, nearly all of the violent programs in children's series feature fantastic or impossible events and characters. Moreover, of all the programs featuring fantasy in our sample, 89 percent of them are in the single genre of children's series. In other words, fantasy violence is almost exclusively found in programs targeted to young viewers.

Consistent with this pattern, fantasy programs are also limited to a particular time of day. For both weekday and weekend, violent programs that feature fantasy or impossible events are most likely to be found in the early morning time slot. Again, this scheduling difference is presumably due to the concentration of children's series during the early morning hours. In general, the percentage of fantasy programs drops after the early morning time slot and is at its lowest during prime time, where most violent programs tend to feature fictional events.

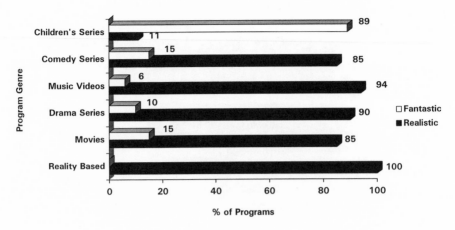

Fig. 4.11. Authenticity of violent programs, by genre

Now we turn our attention to another feature of realism, the style of presentation. This variable refers to the production format that might influence how reality is assessed by viewers. Some producers use human actors in live-action scenes, whereas others use animated characters and settings. Still others use a combination of live action and animation. If characters and events are animated, it is more likely that viewers will regard them as being unrealistic. There are exceptions, however. As noted in the chapter 2, younger children respond to many animated characters as if they were real. Also, some animated characters like Bart Simpson may seem more realistic even to adult viewers compared to a nonanimated character like the Terminator. Still, we contend that characters and events that are animated generally seem less real than human characters and live action. Coders rated the style of each violent program using three values: live action, animated action, or both live and animated action.

Violent programs are almost evenly split between live action (51 percent) and animated action (46 percent). Only 3 percent contain both live action and animation. This pattern differs a bit when we look at channel type. Compared to the industry average, broadcast networks are more likely to feature violence in live action (64 percent), and public broadcast (88 percent) and premium cable (89 percent) almost exclusively present violent programs in live action.

When we look at genre, nearly all the violence on children's series is animated (91 percent). Furthermore, nearly all (97 percent) of the animated programs containing violence are in the single category of children's series. The remaining genres all are substantially more likely to feature live action violence compared to the industry average, which is lower simply because of children's series.

As for day-part, programs with animated violence are more prevalent in

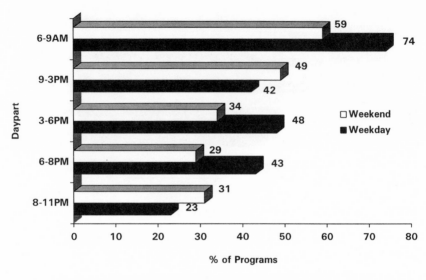

Fig. 4.12.   Percentage of programs with animated violence, by day-part

the early morning time slot on both weekdays and the weekend (see fig. 4.12). Animated violence drops off throughout the day, although it drops more gradually on the weekends than on weekdays. By prime time, the pattern shifts dramatically to a higher percentage of live action violence.

In summary, our two ways of assessing realism (degree of authenticity and style of presentation) result in very similar patterns. Overall, very few violent programs in our sample involve real or re-created events. Instead, most of the violent programs fall into one of two categories: fictional or fantasy. In terms of style of presentation, programs divide almost equally between live action and animated violence. However, the location of these depictions is very much tied to certain genres. Five of the six genres feature realistic violence that is conveyed in live action. Alternatively, children's programs contain mostly fantasy violence shown in an animated style. This animated fantasy violence is mostly concentrated in the early morning hours before children go to school (6–9 A.M.) and then declines throughout the day.

It may be tempting to conclude that children's series are less problematic than other genres because their portrayals are so unrealistic. However, very young children have difficulty distinguishing fantasy from reality on television and often readily imitate animated characters who bear little resemblance to humans (as discussed in chapter 2). Thus, we cannot exonerate this genre of programming when we consider the developmental capabilities of many of its viewers. It also may be tempting to conclude that much of the violence targeted to adult viewers poses little risk because it is not based on real-life events. Two caveats should be pointed out here. First, we did not assess any hard news programming (per our contract) so our findings surely underrepresent the amount of real-life violence on television. Second, even fictional violence, which is the norm in adult programming, can seem realistic to a viewer because the events and characters are feasible in real life.

Rewards and Punishments

Rewards and punishments for violence were coded at the end of each violent scene as well as at the end of each program. The scene coding allows us to examine reinforcements for violence that are delivered during or immediately after aggression occurs. The program coding allows us to assess the pattern of reinforcements across the entire program.

In the majority of violent scenes (58 percent), aggression is neither rewarded nor punished when it occurs. A much smaller proportion of scenes shows violence as being explicitly punished (19 percent) or rewarded (15 percent), and even fewer depict violence as *both* rewarded and punished (8 percent). As demonstrated in chapter 2, violence that goes unpunished poses the greatest risk for viewers in terms of learning aggressive attitudes and behaviors (see Wilson et al. 1996). Taken together, our findings indicate that almost three-fourths of the violent scenes on television (73 percent) portray no punishments for violence within the immediate context of when it occurs. This robust pattern holds across all types of genres, including children's series. The pattern also holds across different types of channels, and across day-parts and type of day.

What types of rewards and punishments typically are depicted? We classified rewards as involving self-praise that a perpetrator expresses after acting violently, praise from other characters, and material goods that are received as a consequence of violence (e.g., money, jewelry). A given violent scene could feature one or all of these types of rewards. Although rewards do not occur very often in the immediate context of violence, the most common forms involve self-praise and praise from other. In particular, the perpetrator expresses personal satisfaction for violence in 14 percent of all violent scenes, whereas other characters express approval in 10 percent of all scenes. Only 6 percent of all scenes depict material rewards for violence.

Punishments were classified as involving self-condemnation that a perpetrator expresses for acting violently, condemnation from others, nonviolent action to stop or penalize violence, and violent action by a third party to terminate further violence. A given scene could feature one or more of these types of punishments. Although punishments do not occur very often in the immediate context of violence, the most common forms involve condemnation expressed by characters other than the perpetrator (16 percent of all scenes) and violent action taken by a third party to stop violence (12 percent of all scenes). Only 9 percent of the violent scenes feature a nonviolent action to penalize violence, and virtually none of the scenes (3 percent) show a perpetrator feeling remorse over violence.

At the program level, reinforcements were examined as well. However, here we focused only on the presence or absence of punishment because of its importance for inhibiting viewers' learning of aggression. Coders assessed the overall pattern of punishments delivered to good perpetrators, to bad perpetrators, and to perpetrators who are both good and bad. It should be noted that reliabilities for these measures are somewhat lower than for other program-level variables so the data should be interpreted with some caution.

Our findings reveal that in a majority of programs (62 percent), bad characters are punished for violence. However, such punishments typically are delivered at the end of the program (40 percent). Only 23 percent of programs depict bad characters as punished throughout the narrative. The remaining 37 percent of the programs feature bad characters who engage in violence and are "never or rarely" punished for their behavior. This pattern of punishments for bad characters generally holds across channel type, day-part, and type of day.

Several differences emerge, however, when looking at the patterns of punishments by genre. Specifically, drama series (74 percent) are *more* likely to show the bad characters being disciplined or chastised, whereas comedy series (35 percent), music videos (45 percent), and reality-based (51 percent) programs are *less* likely to depict bad characters as punished.

The findings above indicate that in most television programming, bad characters are eventually punished. Yet the picture looks quite different for good characters. Good characters who engage in violence are punished in only 15 percent of all programs. In other words, in the vast majority of programs good characters never feel remorse, nor are they reprimanded or hindered by others when they engage in violence. This robust pattern is stable across the five channel types and six genres of programming. It also is found consistently across all day-parts during the weekday and weekend.

Slightly fewer programs feature characters who are both good and bad. Such characters more commonly are found in movies than in the other program genres. The pattern of punishments for these characters is similar to the pattern for purely good characters. Blended characters (both good and bad) who engage in violence are punished in only 33 percent of the programs. This pattern is fairly consistent across the locator variables, especially given the low frequency of such characters in violent programming.

In sum, the vast majority of violence on television is *not* punished at the time it occurs or immediately after within a scene. Punishments more typically occur later in the program, particularly toward the end of the plot. But this pattern is true only for bad characters. Good characters who engage in violence are rarely punished at all on television, and characters who are both good and bad typically are not punished either. Thus, the characters that children are most likely to identify with are rarely discouraged or punished for acting aggressively. These patterns are fairly consistent across all locator variables, with a few exceptions pertaining to genre. Most importantly, drama series are more likely to feature bad characters being punished for violence, whereas comedy series, reality-based programs, and music videos are less likely to portray bad characters as punished.

Consequences of Violence

Consequences refer to the harm and pain that result from violent actions. We coded the consequences of violence at both the interaction and the program level. Coding at the interaction level allows us to examine the *immediate* consequences of violence at the time that it occurs. Coding at the program level enables us to assess the aftermath of violence in terms of *long-term* pain and suffering.

For each violent interaction, we coded harm and pain separately. Because our definition of violence is grounded in physical as opposed to psychological damage, we coded harm and pain for behavioral acts and harmful consequences only. For harm, we assessed: (1) the amount of physical injury that is actually *depicted* on screen, and (2) the amount of *likely* injury that would have occurred if the violence had been enacted against a human in real life. Both of these measures of harm had four possible values: none, mild, moderate, or extreme. Coders also noted when the target literally is not shown in the program such that depicted harm could not be ascertained.

Our findings indicate that across all violent interactions, 44 percent depict *no* physical injury to the target. In an additional 3 percent of the violent interactions, the target is not even shown on screen (camera moves away or the scene changes abruptly). Thus, almost half of violent incidents (47 percent) on television contain no observable indications of harm to the victim. This finding is particularly important given that the research suggests that harm and pain cues inhibit viewers' learning of aggression (Baron 1971a, 1971b; Goransen 1969; Sanders and Baron 1975; Schmutte and Taylor 1980). To round out these findings, approximately 22 percent of the violent interactions show mild harm to the target, 12 percent show moderate harm, and 18 percent depict harm as extreme.

Some differences in depicted harm emerge across the locator variables. In terms of channel type, broadcast networks (57 percent) are more likely to show *no* harm to victims compared to the industry average (47 percent). For genre, children's series (62 percent) are significantly more likely to portray *no* observable harm to victims of violence. On the other hand, movies (35 percent) are less likely to circumvent harm cues. No differences in depicted harm occur across day-part and type of day.

In addition to depicted harm, we also measured likely harm in order to locate those interactions that portrayed less harm to the target than they should have, given the seriousness of the violence. To accomplish this, we developed a new variable called *unrealistic harm,* defined as any instance in which the degree of depicted harm (none, mild, moderate, extreme) is less than the degree of likely harm in real life (mild, moderate, extreme). An example would be a farcical depiction of a target who is hit over the head with a sledgehammer and walks away with only a small lump on the forehead. This type of injury would be coded as "mild" for depicted harm but "extreme" for likely harm in real life. Such a violent interaction would be characterized as showing unrealistic harm. This constructed variable allows us more accuracy in gauging the degree of authenticity of the harm depicted on television.

Overall, only 35 percent of all violent interactions portray unrealistic harm on television. In other words, almost two-thirds of the violent incidents feature a realistic portrayal of the degree of injury to the victim. The portrayal of unrealistic harm differs, however, across channel type. Compared to the overall pattern, public broadcast (15 percent) and premium cable (23 percent) are *less* likely to feature unrealistic harm. The pattern for unrealistic harm also differs with respect to program genre. That is, reality-based programs (18 percent), movies (20 percent), and drama series (21 percent) all contain the lowest proportion of interactions featuring unrealistic harm. Arguably, the most important finding is that children's series (56 percent) contain the highest percentage of unrealistic depictions of harm. In fact, more than half of the violent interactions in children's series portray an unrealistic amount of injury to the victim. There are no differences in the occurrence of unrealistic harm across day-part or type of day.

Like harm, depicted pain was coded at the level of each violent interaction. The amount of depicted pain ranged from none (no verbal or nonverbal expressions of pain, anguish, or suffering) to extreme (expression of intense, enduring, and protracted pain and suffering). Our findings reveal that across all violent interactions, 50 percent depict the target experiencing no pain. In an additional 8 percent of the interactions, the target is not even shown on screen so pain cues could not be assessed (i.e., camera moved away or the scene changed). Therefore, a total of 58 percent of all violent interactions show no observable pain to the victim. Rounding out the findings, mild pain is depicted in 30 percent of the violent interactions, moderate pain is depicted in 7 percent, and extreme pain is shown in 6 percent of the violent interactions.

These overall depictions of pain are consistent across day-parts and type of day. Yet some interesting differences emerge when we examine program genres. Although a clear majority of violent interactions depict no pain, music videos (76 percent), reality-based programs (70 percent), and children's series (68 percent) are even *more* likely to show no observable pain cues to the victim.

In fact, over three-fourths of violent interactions in music videos and nearly 70 percent of the interactions in reality-based programs and children's series show no pain cues to the target. Depicted pain also differs as a function of channel type. Public broadcast is slightly more likely to show no pain than the industry norm.

In addition to coding harm and pain for each violent interaction, the consequences of violence were coded at the program level. This measure provided an overall judgment about harm and pain combined. It asked coders to consider not only the physical harm and pain experienced as a result of violence, but also the emotional, psychological, and financial costs to the participants, their families, and the community at large. Coders assessed the extent of harm and pain depicted across the entire program, indicating whether such consequences generally were: (1) *not shown* at all, (2) *short-term* or immediate in nature (limited to within the violent scene or immediately thereafter), or (3) *long-term* in nature (displayed throughout the program).

Our findings indicate that almost one-third of all programs (32 percent) can be characterized as showing no negative consequences of violence. Slightly more than half of the programs depict short-term negative consequences of violence (52 percent), and only 16 percent depict more long-term pain and suffering associated with violence.

The pattern of negative consequences does not differ by day-part or type of day, but there are some differences for the other two locator variables. As for channel type, premium cable features more programs that depict the long-term negative consequences of violence (34 percent) and fewer programs that show no consequences at all (14 percent) compared to the industry average.

In terms of genre, music videos are substantially more likely to show *no* negative outcomes of violence compared to the industry average. On the other hand, drama series and especially movies are more likely to portray the long-term repercussions of violence than the industry norm (see fig. 4.13). Perhaps the most notable finding is that children's series are *less* likely to portray the extended negative consequences of violence.

In summary, most violent interactions on television contain no observable harm or pain cues to the victim. This pattern is especially true of children's series, in which much of the harm that is depicted is unrealistic when compared to what would happen in real life if such aggressive actions were to occur. On the overall program level, about one-third of the programs do not portray any physical, emotional, psychological, or financial consequences of violence. When such consequences are shown, they are for the most part depicted as short-term in nature. Of all the channel types, premium cable is the most likely to portray the negative outcomes of violence. Of all genres, movies and drama series are the most likely to feature the serious repercussions of violence, whereas children's series are the least likely to show such consequences.

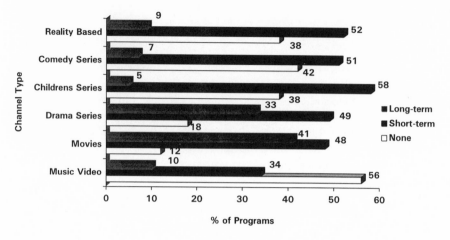

Fig. 4.13.   Pattern of negative consequences, by genre

Humor

The presence or absence of humor was assessed within each violent scene. Our findings reveal that humor frequently accompanies violence on television. Indeed, humor is present in 39 percent of all violent scenes. This relatively high rate is fairly consistent across channel types, with one exception. In public broadcast, only 8 percent of violent scenes are contextualized with humor.

When we compare the use of humor across different genres, we see some considerable differences. As might be expected, humor accompanies violence substantially more often in children's series (67 percent) and comedy series (65 percent), and substantially less often in music videos (7 percent), reality-based programs (12 percent), and drama series (13 percent). Humor also is less likely to be present in violence scenes featured in movies (25 percent), though this difference is not as great.

The day-part and type of day analyses also reveal some differences, although not as dramatic as the genre analysis. Humor is featured in violent scenes more often during early morning hours, and less often during prime time hours (see fig. 4.14), and this pattern holds for weekday as well as weekend. These differences presumably are due in part to the distribution of program types within these day-parts; children's series commonly are found in the early morning hours, whereas drama series and reality-based programs are often shown during prime time.

In sum, many of the violent scenes on television are portrayed in some form of comedic context that may serve to undermine the seriousness of ag-

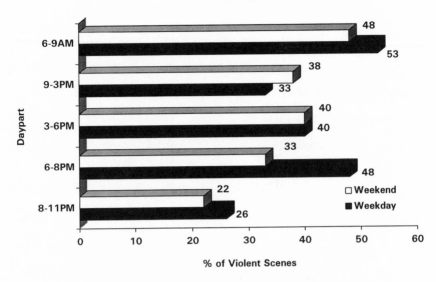

Fig. 4.14. Percentage of violent scenes containing humor, by day-part

gression. Humorous violence is most often found in children's series and in comedy series, and generally during early morning (6 A.M. to 9 A.M.) programming.

Programming with an Antiviolence Theme

Programs were coded as having an antiviolence theme if the overall message was that violence is destructive or wrong. This concept was operationalized using four different criteria. In order to be categorized as an antiviolence theme at least one of the following patterns had to be a strong focus of the narrative: (1) alternatives to violence are discussed or presented, (2) the main characters show reluctance or remorse for committing acts of violence, (3) pain and suffering are depicted throughout, and some attention is devoted to how the victims' family and/or the community is affected, or (4) on balance, there are many more punishments for violence throughout the program than there are rewards.

Of all programs containing some violence, only 4 percent strongly feature an antiviolence theme. Table 4.1 contains examples of various types of programs that emerge in our sample as having an antiviolence theme.

Our analyses by locator variables reveal that the presence of an antiviolence theme does not vary across the different program genres. Nor does the presence of an antiviolence theme differ across day-part or type of day. Nevertheless, there is a difference as a function of channel type. Compared to the industry norm, public broadcast (20 percent) is more likely to feature programs with an

TABLE 4.1. Examples of Programs in Sample Containing an Antiviolence Theme, by Genre

Genre	Title of Program	Channel	Time
Children's series	Beetlejuice	Nickelodeon	4:00–5:00 P.M.
	G-Force	Cartoon Network	3:00–3:30 P.M.
	Ghostwriter	PBS	4:00–4:30 P.M.
	Mighty Max	KCAL	7:30–8:00 P.M.
	Rin Tin Tin K-9 Cop	Family Channel	6:00–6:30 P.M.
Comedy series	Doogie Howser, M.D.	KTLA	5:00–5:30 P.M.
	Roseanne	KCOP	6:00–6:30 P.M.
	Fresh Prince of Bel-Air	NBC	8:00–8:30 P.M.
Drama series	Beverly Hills, 90210	Fox	8:00–9:00 P.M.
	Kung Fu	TNT	4:00–5:00 P.M.
	Mystery	PBS	9:00–10:00 P.M.
	Star Trek: Deep Space Nine	KCOP	9:00–10:00 P.M.
Movies	Avalon	Showtime	5:00–7:30 P.M.
	Pollyanna	Disney Channel	7:00–9:30 P.M.
	Project X	Cinemax	12:00–2:00 P.M.
	Romeo & Juliet	AMC	6:00–8:30 P.M.
	Snowy River	Family Channel	6:00–7:00 A.M.
	Twins	KTLA	8:00–10:00 P.M.
Reality-based	American Justice	A&E	6:00–7:00 P.M.
	Cops	Fox	6:30–7:30 P.M.
	Rescue 911	Family Channel	9:00–10:00 P.M.
	Jenny Jones	KCOP	11:00–12:00 P.M.
	To the Contrary	PBS	1:00–1:30 P.M.
Music videos	Don't Tell Me	MTV	7:30–9:00 A.M.
	I Miss You	MTV	10:00–12:00 P.M.
	I Remember	MTV	7:30–9:00 A.M.
	If Anything Ever Happened	BET	6:00–8:00 P.M.
	Zombie	MTV	7:30–9:00 A.M.

antiviolence theme. Yet very few programs contain violence on this channel so such a difference should be interpreted with caution.

Below we present a brief description of several of the programs in our sample that carry an antiviolence theme. We present these to illustrate how violence can be used in a prosocial manner in entertainment programming. Such descriptions should be informative to parents and educators who want to be able to distinguish violent programs that pose risks for children from those that might be prosocial or educational. In addition, these descriptions should be informative for writers and producers who are seeking creative ways to portray conflict in a socially responsible manner.

Children's Series

Beetlejuice is a half-hour cartoon that features a ghostlike character named Beetlejuice who loves to play jokes and has supernatural powers. His best friend is a young girl named Lydia who delights in his games and magic. This particular episode aired on Nickelodeon at 4:30 P.M. and focuses on Halloween. Beetlejuice and Lydia discover that a neighborhood witch has taken Lydia's cat, so the two are forced to crash a witches' Halloween party to retrieve the animal. Beetlejuice and Lydia disguise themselves as witches and join in the festivities while trying to find the cat. When the witches discover the disguise, they threaten to harm Beetlejuice and Lydia with their magical powers. Just as the witches are ready to attack, Lydia reminds them of how Beetlejuice managed to spark up their party and make it more fun. Beetlejuice then challenges the witches: "Don't use your magic on evil, use magic for fun!" The witches realize that Beetlejuice has been a good addition to their party and they decide not to hurt him or Lydia. Instead, the witches proceed to use their magic to play party games.

Of the four ways that could be used to emphasize antiviolence, this program is a good example of the first—the presentation and discussion of alternatives to violence. In this case, both of the main characters, Beetlejuice and Lydia, persuade the angry witches to use their powers to have fun instead of to hurt others. The witches turn from nasty, evil creatures to fun-loving party goers after they accept this nonviolent alternative. Interestingly, this cartoon contains 12 violent interactions, most of which occur before Beetlejuice and Lydia are able to convince the witches to change their behavior.

Drama Series

Star Trek: Deep Space Nine is a science fiction series based on the original *Star Trek* program. This particular episode aired at 9:00 P.M. on KCOP, one of the independent channels in our sample. The episode involves Quark's discovery of a humanoid baby on a nearby space wreckage. The baby is brought on board and rapidly develops into an adult. Dr. Bashir's scientific testing reveals that the creature is not a humanoid at all, but rather a Jem'Hadar that is genetically programmed to kill. During the remainder of the episode, Odo tries to teach the creature to be nonviolent. Whenever the Jem'Hadar displays aggressive tendencies, Odo talks to it about channeling those impulses and about alternative ways to release frustration. For example, Odo tries to get the creature to smile and to work out with a computer punching machine when he feels aggressive. Odo manages to keep the creature from hurting anyone on the spaceship, but it eventually escapes to search for its own people.

Like the program described above, the antiviolence theme in this episode is conveyed primarily through talk and discussion about nonviolent alternatives. In fact, there are very few behavioral acts of violence in this episode, though the creature manages to threaten others. Odo, a primary character in the series, is shown in several different scenes trying to teach nonviolence and peace to an aggressively predisposed Jem'Hadar. Taken together, the cartoon example presented above and the drama series described here demonstrate that genres typically containing violence can be entertaining while still featuring conflict in a prosocial manner.

Comedy Series

Fresh Prince of Bel Air is a situation comedy featuring an African-American teenager (Will) who moved from the inner city to Bel Air, California to live with his wealthy aunt and uncle. The series is shown at 8:00 P.M. on NBC. In this episode, Will and his cousin Carlton are robbed at gunpoint at an automated teller machine. The robber shoots at the two cousins and hits Will. The remainder of the program focuses on the difficulties that the family experiences because of this violent crime. Will is dangerously close to being paralyzed and is in the hospital for the latter half of the show. The family waits in agony until they find out that he will recover. In the meantime, Carlton is traumatized by the violent experience and decides in anger to start carrying a gun. In the final scene, Will lays in his hospital bed and begs Carlton to give up the gun, saying "that's not your way . . . that's them." Carlton finally gives him the gun and the program closes as Will empties the bullets from the gun and breaks down in tears.

Of the four possible ways to convey antiviolence, the first and third are used in this episode. The serious consequences of violence are repeatedly depicted. The victim (Will) is shown in physical pain, has a nightmare about the crime, and is in the hospital for the entire episode. His family is emotionally upset and Will's girlfriend sleeps on the chair near his bed, because she refuses to leave the hospital. Though Will still cracks an occasional joke, he points out that humor helps him deal with the trauma. In contrast, Carlton finds no humor in the situation and reprimands Will several times for his jokes. All in all, this is a very serious episode in spite of the fact that it is a situation comedy. In addition to showing pain and harm, alternatives to violence are emphasized in this episode when Will pleads emotionally with Carlton to not become violent like the criminal who robbed them. For example, he tells Carlton that carrying a gun is not a solution to the problem.

Two other points are worth mentioning. This program contains only two violent interactions in spite of the fact that the entire plot focuses on violence. Moreover, the robber is never visually shown to the viewers, but rather is kept offscreen. Thus, there is no explicit visual depiction of the violent act. The other point is that NBC aired an antiviolence public service announcement during one of the commercial breaks in this episode. Though this project does not include an analysis of commercial material, it is worth mentioning this instance because of the reinforcement value of showing an antiviolence PSA within an antiviolence program. The PSA features Eriq La Salle, an actor from *ER*, saying "Everyone has a right to get angry but you don't have a right to fight. Walk away. Chill. You win."

Music Video

The music video *You Gotta Be* by Ahmad aired on BET at 12:30 p.m. in our sample. This rap video tells the story of a young man who tries to resist his own gang's criminal behavior. After he is threatened by his fellow gang members, he reluctantly goes to a mini-mart with them and tries to rob the store. In the process, he is shot by the store clerk. The video then shows the man lying on the floor of the store as medics frantically work to save his life. In the next scene, he sings as he lays in his open casket. Meanwhile, his gang is arrested by the police and sent to prison. The gang members are then shown being assaulted in the prison by older inmates.

This four-minute video uses the second and fourth ways of emphasizing nonviolence: the perpetrator shows reluctance while engaging in violence, and the violence is punished throughout the scenario. In this video, the young man is threatened into going along with his gang. As he rides in the car, he expresses anguish and concern. In addition, all of the perpetrators are seriously punished for their actions. The main character is killed and dramatically speaks from his coffin. The other gang members are immediately arrested and sent to prison. The lyrics remind the audience that all of this happened "cuz you gotta be rough . . . gotta be tough."

Made-for-Television Movie

A Cry for Help was shown on the Lifetime channel at 5:00 p.m. It is based on the true story of Tracy Thurman, who was tragically beaten by her husband. The movie was preceded by an advisory stating that it contains graphic scenes that may be "too intense for some viewers." The movie opens dramatically with Tracy's husband attacking her with a knife. Then the movie jumps back in time and tells how this couple met, fell in love, and married. The relationship is characterized from the beginning by threats and physical abuse. Though Tracy leaves her husband early on, the police do not treat her complaints very seriously and often do little to protect her against her husband. After Tracy's husband stalks her for months, he attacks her viciously, slashing her face and jumping on her neck as a policeman helplessly stands by. After the attack, the husband is sent to prison and Tracy then sues the police department. She wins the suit, and the case results in the passage of the "Thurman Law" in Connecticut, stipulating that police must treat domestic partners no differently than any other accused perpetrators of violence.

Unlike most of the other examples, this movie contains extensive and repeated violence. In fact, 12 different violent interactions were coded, and they all involved extensive violence. However, the movie also features a strong antiviolence theme. This theme is conveyed primarily through dramatic portrayals of the pain, fear, and suffering of the victims. Most notably, Tracy is terrorized throughout the movie by her husband, and even their baby son seems traumatized by his presence. In addition, close-ups of her painful bruises and black eyes are shown after each beating. In the husband's final attack, Tracy is seriously hurt, and her recovery in the hospital is depicted in graphic detail. At first she is paralyzed from the neck down. When she finally regains movement in her body, she limps when she walks and has no use of one arm. Moreover, an ugly scar runs down her face and neck. She spends so much time in the hospital that her son hardly recognizes her when she comes home. The violence also affects Tracy's friends and family, who agonize over the abuse and are frightened themselves of the violent husband.

In addition to painful consequences, an antiviolence theme is conveyed through the punishment of violence. Throughout the program, the husband is portrayed as a sick and possessive individual. Though the police do little at first, Tracy's friends publicly condemn the husband as does Tracy's attorney. In the end, the husband is sentenced to 20 years in prison for the attack. Furthermore, a second trial results in public condemnation of the police department for overlooking domestic abuse. The final scene provides a transition back to "real life" by reminding viewers that a new law was passed in Connecticut to ensure that domestic partners are arrested immediately for such abuse.

Theater-Released Movie

South Central was released in the theaters in 1992 and subsequently was aired by one of the premium channels in our sample. The movie aired on HBO, at 8:00 P.M. HBO clearly labeled the film as having received an R rating from the MPAA. In addition, HBO gave the film its own ratings indicating that it contained "violence, adult content, and graphic language." The movie tells the story of Bobby, an African American from South Central Los Angeles, who is a gang member. The movie opens as Bobby is released from the county jail and goes home to meet his newborn son. He resumes his gang activity soon thereafter, but because of his new responsibility as a father, he experiences reluctance and regret in his role as a gang member. After being threatened by a rival gang, Bobby gets involved in a violent shoot-out and is sent back to prison for killing a man. Over his years in prison, he agonizes about his young son who is becoming involved with gangs. Bobby finally gets out of prison after educating himself and vowing to give up violence. He then finds his son, promises to be a better father, and successfully urges his son to give up the gang affiliation.

Like *A Cry for Help*, this movie contains numerous violent events (19 violent interactions) but still conveys an overall antiviolence theme. In fact, the plot features all four of the ways that antiviolence can be shown. First, alternatives to violence are emphasized. In prison, Bobby meets a fellow inmate who teaches him to control his anger and to read the works of nonviolent heroes. The inmate convinces Bobby that the only way to get out of prison and help his son is to eliminate violence from his life. Second, Bobby shows remorse when he engages in gang violence and seems to be struggling to avoid it in the early part of the movie. He even tries to stay away from his fellow gang members. Third, the painful consequences of violence are emphasized throughout. Bobby's girlfriend is unable financially or emotionally to raise her child alone while Bobby is in prison. She becomes addicted to drugs, and her 10-year-old son's involvement with the gang intensifies. While trying to steal a car radio, the son is shot in the back and almost dies. The movie portrays the son's slow and painful recovery in the hospital including several scenes of difficult physical therapy and repeated views of the large scar on his back. Fourth, the story line continually stresses immediate and harsh punishment for violence. Bobby is shown being released from county jail in the beginning of the movie and spends the latter half of it in prison. Prison life is portrayed as rough and full of violence. The movie is a good example of a multipronged effort at depicting the realistic and negative consequences of gang violence in society.

Summary of Results

Three questions guided our analysis in this chapter: (1) How much violence is on television and where is it located? (2) What is the nature or context of violence on television? (3) How often is violence used in an educational or prosocial manner to promote an antiviolence message? In this summary section, we will focus on the most robust findings rather than detailing all the patterns across all the locator variables.

Presence of Violence
1. 57 percent of coded programs contain some violence.
    Premium cable is more likely to contain violence, whereas the broadcast networks and particularly public broadcasting are less likely. Movies and drama series are more likely to contain violence, whereas

comedy series, reality-based programs, and music videos are less likely.
2. About two-thirds of the violence involves behavioral acts of aggression.
Only one-third involves credible threats.
Very little involves harmful consequences of unseen violence.

Distribution of Violence
1. About one-third of violent programs contain nine or more violent interactions. The highest frequencies of violent interactions are found on:
Premium cable and independent broadcast
Movies and reality-based programs.

Context of Violent Portrayals
1. Perpetrators of violence are:
Overwhelmingly human, adult in age, White, and male
More often characterized as bad rather than good
Typically *not* heroes.
2. Targets of violence are similar to perpetrators.
3. Most violence is committed for one of three reasons:
Personal gain
Anger
Protection.
4. Nearly half of the violence on television is portrayed as justified.
5. Guns on television:
Are used in about one-quarter of all violent interactions
Are used most often in reality-based programs and drama series.
6. How extensive is violence?
The majority of violent interactions involve *repeated* behavioral acts of aggression.
16 percent of violent interactions include 10 or more acts of aggression against a victim.
7. How graphic is violence?
Most violence is *not* shown in close-up shots.
Blood and gore are rarely shown on television.
Blood and gore are most often seen on premium cable and in movies.
8. How realistic is violence?
Very little of television violence is based on actual events in the real world, but most events seem fairly realistic in that they *could* happen in real life.
Fantasy or unrealistic violence is rare except in children's series.

9. Rewards and punishments:

The vast majority of violence is *not* punished at the time that it occurs within a scene.

Punishments more typically occur toward the end of the program, but only for bad characters.

Good characters who engage in violence are rarely punished at all.

Characters who engage in violence almost never show remorse.

10. Consequences of violence:

Roughly half of the violent interactions on television contain no observable harm or pain to the victim.

Children's series contain the highest percentage of unrealistic depictions of harm.

Almost one-third of violent programs portray *no* negative consequences of violence.

Very few programs depict the long-term negative repercussions of violence.

11. Humor:

39 percent of all violent scenes contain humor.

Humor is more often linked to violence in children's series and comedy series.

12. Only 4 percent of all programs with violence feature a strong antiviolence theme.

Overall, our findings indicate that violence is more likely to be found on premium cable and within the genres of movies and drama series. However, the context of violence or the way in which it is portrayed do not differ substantially across channels or genres. Violence typically involves behavioral acts that are perpetrated by White males against other White males. Acts of aggression often are repeated and frequently involve guns. Violence is typically sanitized on television. It is rarely punished in the immediate context in which it occurs, and it rarely results in observable harm to the victims. In fact, violence is often funny on television. In other words, the serious consequences of violence are frequently ignored. In the next chapter, we discuss the policy implications of these results.

NOTE

1. Some programs in our sample are segmented. That is, they contain independent stories or narrative units within a larger framework (e.g., *Looney Tunes*, *60 Minutes*). For all distribution and contextual analyses reported, we use the program segment as our base of comparison. Although most programs are composed of a single segment (e.g.,

movies, drama series, situation comedies), the overall N in our analyses is slightly larger when treating segmented programs as individual units.

REFERENCES

Bandura, A. 1986. *Social Foundations of Thought and Action: A Social Cognitive Theory.* Englewood Cliffs, NJ: Prentice-Hall.

———. 1994. "Social Cognitive Theory of Mass Communication." In *Media Effects,* ed. J. Bryant and D. Zillmann, 61–90. Hillsdale, NJ: Erlbaum.

Baron, R. A. 1971a. "Aggression as a Function of Magnitude of Victim's Pain Cues, Level of Prior Anger Arousal, and Aggressor-Victim Similarity." *Journal of Personality and Social Psychology* 18(1): 48–54.

———. 1971b. "Magnitude of Victim's Pain Cues and Level of Prior Anger Arousal as Determinants of Adult Aggressive Behavior." *Journal of Personality and Social Psychology* 17(3): 236–43.

Berkowitz, L., and R. G. Geen. 1966. "Film Violence and the Cue Properties of Available Targets." *Journal of Personality and Social Psychology* 3(5): 525–30.

———. 1967. "Stimulus Qualities of the Target of Aggression: A Further Study." *Journal of Personality and Social Psychology* 5(3): 364–68.

Berkowitz, L., and A. LePage. 1967. "Weapons as Aggression-Eliciting Stimuli." *Journal of Personality and Social Psychology* 7(2): 202–7.

Berkowitz, L., and P. C. Powers. 1979. "Effects of Timing and Justification of Witnessed Aggression on the Observers' Punitiveness." *Journal of Research in Personality* 13:71–80.

Carlson, M., A. Marcus-Newhall, and N. Miller. 1990. "Effects of Situational Aggression Cues: A Quantitative Review." *Journal of Personality and Social Psychology* 58(4): 622–33.

Comisky, P., and J. Bryant. 1982. "Factors Involved in Generating Suspense." *Human Communication Research* 9(1): 49–58.

Geen, R .G., and D. Stonner. 1973. "Context Effects in Observed Violence." *Journal of Personality and Social Psychology* 25(1): 145–50.

———. 1974. "The Meaning of Observed Violence: Effects on Arousal and Aggressive Behavior." *Journal of Research In Personality* 8:55–63.

Goransen, R. E. 1969. "Observed Violence and Aggressive Behavior: The Effects of Negative Outcomes to Observed Violence." *Dissertation Abstracts International* 31(01), DAI-B (University Microfilms No. AAC77 08286).

Jose, P. E., and W. F. Brewer. 1984. "Development of Story Liking: Character Identification, Suspense, and Outcome Resolution." *Developmental Psychology* 20(5): 911–24.

National Television Violence Study, Volume 1. 1997. Thousand Oaks, CA: Sage.

Sanders, G. S., and R. S. Baron. 1975. "Pain Cues and Uncertainty as Determinants of Aggression in a Situation Involving Repeated Instigation." *Journal of Personality and Social Psychology* 32(3): 495–502.

Schmutte, G. T., and S. P. Taylor. 1980. "Physical Aggression as a Function of Alcohol and Pain Feedback." *Journal of Social Psychology* 110:235–44.

Zillmann, D. 1980. "Anatomy of Suspense." In *The Entertainment Functions of Television*, ed. P. H. Tannenbaum, 133–63. Hillsdale, NJ: Lawrence Erlbaum.

———. 1982. "Television Viewing and Arousal." In *Television and Behavior: Ten Years of Scientific Progress and Implications for the Eighties*, ed. D. Pearl, L. Bouthilet, and J. Lazar, vol. 2, 53–67. Washington, DC: U.S. Government Printing Office.

———. 1991. "Empathy: Affect from Bearing Witness to the Emotions of Others." In *Responding to the Screen*, ed. J. Bryant and D. Zillmann, 135–67. Hillsdale, NJ: Lawrence Erlbaum.

Zillmann, D., and J. R. Cantor. 1977. "Affective Responses to the Emotions of a Protagonist." *Journal of Experimental Social Psychology* 13:155–65.

⊙ Chapter 5

Content Analysis of Entertainment Television: Implications for Public Policy

Dale Kunkel, Barbara J. Wilson, James Potter, Daniel Linz, Edward Donnerstein, Stacy L. Smith, and Eva Blumenthal

Introduction

The recent political debate surrounding the topic of television violence is quite distinct from controversies of the past. It is clear that the public, most government officials, and many segments of the media industry now accept that television violence contributes to real-world violent behavior, as well as other causes of concern such as increased fear and desensitization. The debate that continues in this realm is not about whether harmful effects of viewing televised violence exist; rather, the controversy has shifted to the question of what to do about the problem. Both means and goals are implicated in the debate. Should violence be reduced, restricted, or labeled, among other options, and if so how and by whom? What is the proper role of government, the media industry, and parents in addressing the issue of television violence?

The findings from the *National Television Violence Study* (*NTVS*) (1997), along with the extensive body of research evidence upon which the content analysis is based, provide a foundation for some general prescriptions that address the current situation. In this chapter, we analyze the implications for public policy of the research discussed in chapters 2 through 4. For the television industry, we call not simply for reductions in violence, but particular sensitivity to avoiding contextual elements that increase the risks of harmful effects. We urge the industry to place greater emphasis on the use of antiviolence themes that may have a prosocial effect when violence is to be included within a program. We also suggest more effective use of program advisories for identifying violent content. These efforts, coupled with continued monitoring by policymakers and more careful supervision of children's viewing by parents, offer realistic potential to reduce the harmful effects of television violence on society.

Background

Concern about televised violence is an enduring issue with a long history. The roots of the concern precede the medium's existence, tracing back historically to early studies of motion pictures' influence on the audience (e.g., Charters 1933). By the time television had penetrated most American households in the 1950s, Congress had already begun to hold hearings addressing the issue (U.S. Senate Subcommittee to Investigate Juvenile Delinquency 1954), although little scientific evidence was available at the time to help inform the discussion. Since then, a tremendous amount of research has emerged assessing the influence of television violence on viewers. As research evidence accrued throughout the next several decades, an increasing consensus emerged in the scientific community regarding the antisocial effects of most media violence.

Today, there is no longer a scientific debate about whether or not television violence poses a risk of negative effects for its audience. The extent of agreement about this position is reflected in many recent major reports and policy documents that have reviewed all of the available research evidence. As we noted in chapter 2, such prestigious professional organizations as the American Psychological Association, American Medical Association, National Academy of Science, and Centers for Disease Control and Prevention have all concluded that television violence contributes to learning aggressive attitudes and behaviors, to emotional desensitization, and to fear about becoming a victim of violence in viewers.

The consensus reflected in these reports represents the premise outlined in chapter 2—that most violent media content poses a substantial risk of harm to many in the audience, particularly children. However, as we have demonstrated, certain types of violent portrayals may pose a much greater risk of negative psychological effects than others, and indeed it is true that some violent depictions may actually have prosocial effects such as reducing the likelihood of subsequent aggressive behavior in viewers. A crucial factor in differentiating these outcomes is the nature of the presentation of violent behaviors in television programming. In other words, context matters. The context in which violent depictions are presented holds important implications for the effects of the material on the viewing audience.

The recent political debate in the United States surrounding the topic of television violence is quite distinct from controversies of the past. It is clear that the public, most government officials, and many segments of the media industry now recognize and accept that television violence contributes to real-world violent behavior, as well as other causes of concern such as increased fear and desensitization. The debate that continues to flare is not about whether harmful effects of viewing televised violence exist; rather, the controversy has shifted to the question of what to do about the problem. Both means and goals are implicated in the debate. Should violence be reduced, restricted, or labeled, among other options, and if so, how and by whom? What is the proper role of the government, the media industry, and parents in addressing the issue of television violence?

The axiom indicated above—that context matters—clearly renders more complicated the task of responding to concerns about televised violence. That difficulty, however, does not diminish the importance of addressing the issue.

Recommendations

The findings of our work in the *NTVS*, coupled with the extensive body of research evidence upon which our content analysis is based, provide a foundation for some general prescriptions that could reduce the risk of social harms caused by violence on television. The recommendations offered here address several different audiences: the television industry, public policymakers, and parents, all of whom have an important interest in the topic of television violence.

For the Television Industry

1. Produce more programs that avoid violence; if a program does contain violence, keep the number of violent incidents low.

No one can ignore the issue of the overall amount of violence that exists on television, and the cumulative exposure to violence that average viewers inevitably encounter. Our data indicate that a majority of all programs sampled (57 percent to be precise) contained some violence, and one-third of all violent shows included nine or more violent interactions. No objective standard exists to determine the point at which the collective levels of violence across the television landscape can fairly be labeled as "excessive." Still, our findings make clear that violence is a predominant behavior present across all programming and that violence is extensive within many shows.

We do not advocate that all violence be eliminated from television, nor do we profess to know exactly how much is "too much." We trust that interested observers will monitor changes over time in the levels of violence that are measured by this study and will encourage appropriate efforts to limit the presentation of televised violence. Our recommendation is simply to begin efforts to cut back.

This is indeed a long-term goal. The amount of violence on television has been high since its beginnings almost 50 years ago. A substantial reduction in the amount of violence will not happen in one or two years. Tremendous economic risk is inherent in any alteration of established programming patterns that have proven effective in attracting large audiences, which are the television industry's lifeblood. Realistically, such alterations can only be expected to occur slowly.

It will take time for the television industry to accept that the American viewing public will watch and enjoy programming with lower amounts of violence. In the short term, we suggest that producers working in those genres where violence is particularly high (e.g., movies, drama series, and reality-based shows) begin working to bring their levels of violence closer to the industry averages. This, of course, would begin to reduce that industry average, and over time would contribute to lower norms for the overall level of televised violence.

> 2. Be creative in showing more violent acts being punished; more negative consequences—both short and long term—for violent acts; more alternatives to the use of violence in solving problems; and less justification for violent actions.

This recommendation recognizes that violence is not likely to be declared "off limits." Our focus is on promoting its presentation, when violence is deemed essential, in a manner that should reduce its risk of negative influence on the audience. Much of the portrayal of violence on television is formulaic, a finding that is reflected in the consistency of many of our results on the contextual variables. We encourage producers to move beyond the "old formula" where a bad character stirs things up with repeated acts of violence; where the suffering of victims is seldom shown; and where the bad character continually gets away with the violent action until a good character retaliates with violence of his or her own. All of these factors add to the risk that a given violent portrayal will contribute to antisocial effects on the audience.

> 3. When violence is presented, consider greater emphasis on a strong antiviolence theme.

There are a number of ways to do this. Among the most obvious are: (1) present alternatives to violent actions throughout the program; (2) show main characters repeatedly discussing the negative consequences of violence; (3) emphasize the physical pain and emotional suffering that results from violence; and (4) show that punishments for violence clearly and consistently outweigh rewards.

Our assessment of 1994–95 programming indicated that only 4 percent of all violent programs fit any of these criteria. Violence emphasizing these patterns represents the most socially responsible approach when depicting aggression. It is striking that this type of depiction occurs so infrequently.

4. Make more effective use of program advisories or content codes to identify violent programming.

We recognize that an audience exists for violent programming, and that such
shows will always persist to some degree. Nonetheless, many violent programs
pose a risk to the audience and that risk should be communicated as clearly as
possible, especially to parents. Our data indicate that premium cable channels
consistently provide program advisories, but there are many violent programs on
other types of channels that are not identified for the audience. When we recommend warnings, we do not mean a simple statement that the program contains
violence. Rather, we suggest something more substantial and specific that warns
potential viewers about the context of the violence and its corresponding risks,
rather than a mere indication of the presence or absence of violence in a program.

The findings produced for the NTVS project by the University of Wisconsin site discussed in chapter 7 raise the prospect that some violence advisories
may in fact make the designated programming more appealing for audiences of
young boys. Thus, one may argue that labeling such programming could lead
to a boomerang effect in which problematic material may actually be seen by
more rather than fewer child viewers once it is designated with a warning. While
this possibility deserves careful attention, we believe the evidence here is too
preliminary to warrant avoidance of all labeling strategies. Although the Wisconsin study indicated that 10- to 14-year-old boys were more strongly attracted
to television program listings when the content was labeled with a parental advisory, there are alternative labeling strategies available that can avoid this effect. Moreover, the value of labeling to assist parents who wish to utilize such
information must be weighed carefully in tandem with any considerations
about how such information will be received by children.

On balance, we believe that the risks associated with most violent programs are great enough to warrant the clear communication of this information to parents in a manner that allows them the greatest opportunity to consider it when supervising their child's media exposure. Our data indicate that a
significant amount of television violence is presented without any warning at
times when children are likely to be viewing. Given the compelling evidence of
risk associated with viewing such material, we encourage the industry to pursue further efforts to identify violent programming to the public. We will address the most recent developments regarding the V-chip program labeling categories later in this chapter.

For Public Policymakers

Our study does not argue for or against any specific proposal to address the issue. Rather, it provides information to help policymakers better understand the

problems associated with violence on television. It also establishes a benchmark for comparisons over time in the levels of televised violence.

Because our data are oriented more to specifying the nature and extent of the problem of televised violence than to identifying the most appropriate solution, we cannot endorse any specific plan to address the problem of television violence. Our recommendations to policymakers are therefore at a more fundamental level.

1. Recognize that context is an essential aspect of television violence.

Treating all acts of violence as if they are the same disregards a rich body of scientific knowledge about media effects. An appreciation of key contextual factors is crucial for understanding the impact of televised violence on the audience. Furthermore, an appreciation of these elements may contribute to more effective policies should any regulatory action be pursued. At the base of any policy proposal in this realm is the need to define violence and, assuming that not all violence is to be treated equally, to differentiate types of depictions that pose the greatest cause for concern. This requires the careful consideration of the contextual elements we have identified in the NTVS.

This principle has important applications for virtually any public policy proposal addressing televised violence. For example, if one wished to pursue the "safe harbor" approach of restricting violent portrayals to certain times of day, it would seem important that the content subject to restriction should in fact be material that poses a risk of harm. A fundamental premise of this study is that all acts of violence are not inherently equal in the risk that they pose for harmful effects. Indeed, some presentations of violence (albeit only 4 percent of all programs containing violence) were identified by our program-level measures as being fundamentally prosocial, or antiviolent, in nature. If these programs were subjected to a "safe harbor" restriction on permissible times for broadcast, it might be more difficult to establish that the regulation fulfilled the "least restrictive means" test in any legal assessment of the policy's constitutionality.

The bottom line here is that treating all violence the same—as if context did *not* matter—oversimplifies the issue. As public policymakers pursue initiatives to address concern about violent portrayals, it is important that they recognize that context is an essential aspect of television violence.

2. Continue to monitor the nature and extent of violence on television.

Evidence of the harmful effects associated with televised violence is well established and well documented in the complete report of our study (NTVS 1997). The stakes are high in terms of the social implications in this realm not so much because of the strength of the effects of viewing violence but more because of the fact that almost everyone watches, most people watch a lot, and most of television contains violence. The effects are pervasive and cumulative. The importance of the issue warrants continued attention to help sensitize the television industry as well as to help alert and inform the public.

One of the most valuable aspects of the NTVS project is that the content analysis we have produced yields precise findings that can be compared over time to track any variation that may occur in the nature and extent of televised violence. There have been many past instances when industry officials have committed to or claimed reductions in the levels of violence. This project introduces a new dimension of accountability for evaluating such claims.

The results from our second-year report will reveal any meaningful changes that have occurred in the patterns of violence on television. Because the programming analyzed each year for this study is an extraordinarily large and scientifically representative sample of the overall television environment, one can be confident that any changes observed over time are indicative of actual shifts in programming practices, rather than the artifact of an inadequate sample or research design, a limitation that has afflicted many previous studies in this area (see chapter 3). The NTVS project, which has been funded by the National Cable Television Association, was contracted to produce reports for three years of television programming (1994–95, 1995–96, 1996–97). It is possible that the project may be extended over time, contingent upon future funding from either industry sources or other entities interested in supporting this work.

For Parents

The ultimate consumers of the information in our report are the nation's television viewers. Of particular interest are parents of young children, who often express helplessness in the face of fifty or more channels of programming across seven days a week. Our study was designed in part to help families make more informed decisions about television violence, and toward this end we have several recommendations for parents.

    1. Be aware of the three potential risks associated with viewing television violence.

Evidence of the potential harmful effects associated with viewing violence on television is well established and fully documented in the *NTVS* work. Most attention has been devoted to the impact of television violence on the learning of aggressive attitudes and behaviors. Though not all children will imitate media violence, certain children who are exposed to repeated depictions of a particular nature are at risk for such learning. Arguably more pervasive and often underemphasized are the other two risks associated with television violence: fear and desensitization. A clear understanding of these three effects will help parents better appreciate the role of television in children's socialization.

2. Consider the context of violent depictions in making viewing decisions for children.

As demonstrated in chapter 4, not all violent portrayals are the same. Some depictions pose greater risks for children than do others; some may even be educational and pose very little risk at all. When considering a particular program, think about whether violence is rewarded or punished, whether heroes or role models engage in violence, whether violence appears to be justified or morally sanctioned, whether the serious negative consequences of violence are portrayed, and whether humor is used in a way that trivializes violent behavior.

3. Consider a child's developmental level when making viewing decisions.

Throughout our work, we underscore the importance of the child's developmental level or cognitive ability in making sense of television. Very young children do not typically distinguish reality from fantasy on television. Thus, for preschoolers and younger elementary school children, animated violence, cartoon violence, and fantasy violence cannot be dismissed or exonerated merely because it is unrealistic. Indeed, many younger children identify strongly with superheroes and fantastic cartoon characters who regularly engage in violence. Furthermore, younger children have difficulty connecting nonadjacent scenes together and drawing causal inferences about the plot. Therefore, punishments, pain cues, or serious consequences of violence that are shown later in a program, well after the violent act occurs, may not be comprehended fully by a young child. For younger viewers, then, it is particularly important that contextual features like punishment and pain be shown *within* the violent scene.

4. Recognize that different program genres and channel types pose different risks for children.

Our findings suggest that children's series may be particularly problematic, especially for younger viewers. Such programming is characterized by unrealistic depictions of harm, frequent use of humor in the context of violence, and little attention to the long-term negative consequences of violence. Although it is tempting for adults to dismiss cartoons as fantasy, these contextual features enhance the risk of imitation of aggression for younger viewers. In addition to genre differences, the type of channel has important ramifications for violence. Premium cable contains more violence than the industry norm, but it also depicts the serious consequences of violence more often. In contrast, public broadcasting contains less violence overall. These differences should be taken into account when planning a family's media environment and viewing habits.

    5. Watch television with your child and encourage critical evaluation of the content.

Of all the recommendations we could make, perhaps the most important is to watch television with your child. The only way to ensure that a child appreciates the contextual aspects of violence is to teach a child while viewing. Parents can help a child to understand that violence in the real world may result in more serious injury and may have more long-term repercussions than what is shown on television. Parents also can help children to recognize that nonviolent strategies exist for solving problems in society.

Advent of the V-Chip

Since the initial release of the *NTVS* report in early 1996, perhaps the most striking development in the long controversy surrounding television violence has occurred—the advent of the V-chip. In approving the Telecommunications Act of 1996, Congress stipulated that the television industry establish its own rating system for identifying "sexual, violent, or other indecent material" [47 U.S.C. 551 (e)(1)(a)] and that it be linked technologically to a lockout device installed in all new television sets, allowing parents to electronically filter the material their children may watch. In the absence of such efforts, the FCC would have been empowered to devise such a system on its own, although the industry would not have been required to use it. In February 1996, shortly after the law was enacted, leading industry executives met with President Clinton and agreed to implement rather than oppose the V-chip technology.

    Long-time MPAA president Jack Valenti led the industrywide effort to create a rating system for use with the V-chip technology. That program rating system was unveiled in late December 1996 and implemented almost immediately on the major broadcast networks. By early 1997, most cable networks were using it as well, even before the FCC had formally considered the system's merits or established the technical specifications needed to employ the V-chip's electronic blocking capabilities. Under the statute that led to the V-chip, the FCC must review the industry's rating system and deem it "acceptable" in order to avoid triggering further government action.

    The industry's initial system of categories for rating television programs is grounded in an age-based advisory framework virtually identical to that employed in the MPAA's film ratings system. That system, introduced in 1968, was also devised by Jack Valenti. The MPAA ratings have been criticized for largely ignoring scientific evidence about the impact of media on children while placing emphasis on parents' judgments of the "offensiveness" of the content (Wilson, Linz, and Randall 1990). The hallmark of the MPAA approach is to provide a single prescriptive judgment about the appropriateness of the content for children of a particular age range, without giving any specific descriptive content information.

In their present (i.e., spring 1997) form, the V-chip ratings do not indicate whether or not a given program contains violence; rather, the system judges programs for their overall "suitability," intermingling three distinct areas of content concern: violence, sexual material, and coarse language. Depictions involving any of these areas may result in a program being rated as inappropriate for certain audiences, although it is impossible to tell which one is implicated in a given rating. In other words, the rating system does not make clear which programs contain violence, which contain sexual material, and which contain adult language.

All decisions about each show's rating are made by the television industry in a highly decentralized process. Most programs are rated by their parent broadcast network or cable channel. In addition, some broadcast material that is not network-based (such as syndicated programming) will be rated by the producer, although the final decision about ratings for all programs on broadcast television will rest with the local licensee. In contrast, cable networks make the final determination for their content. The local cable system operator has neither authority nor responsibility for rating programs on any of the channels—cable or broadcast-based—that are delivered to subscribers.

The *TV Parental Guidelines* system, as the V-chip ratings are known, is shown in table 5.1. It employs the following criteria for identifying violence in general audience programming: TV-G programs contain "little or no violence," TV-PG includes "limited violence," TV-14 "more intense violence," and TV-MA "graphic violence." As initially implemented, there are no examples or explanations to assist telecasters in interpreting and applying these criteria.

Applying Contextual Considerations to V-Chip Ratings

The V-chip rating system initially introduced by the television industry provides virtually no consideration of context—at least not insofar as context has been defined by the scientific research evidence that forms the foundation of the NTVS project. In the absence of any clarification about the meaning of terms such as "limited violence" or "more intense violence," these categories will most likely reflect the program raters' judgments about the potential risks of different approaches to the depiction of violence, rather than the application of any scientific knowledge in this area.

As we have noted throughout chapters 2, 3, and 4, research demonstrates that not all violence is the same in terms of its impact on the audience. Context

TABLE 5.1.   TV Parental Guidelines, Spring 1997

These categories are for programs designed for children:

TV-Y. All Children.   *This program is designed to be appropriate for all children.*
Whether animated or live-action, the themes and elements in this program are specifically designed for a very young audience, including children from ages 2–6. This program is not expected
to frighten younger children.

TV-Y7. Directed to Older Children.   *This program is designed for children age 7 and above.*
It may be more appropriate for children who have acquired the developmental skills needed to
distinguish between make-believe and reality. Themes and elements in this program may include
mild physical or comedic violence, or may frighten children under the age of 7. Therefore, parents may wish to consider the suitability of this program for their very young children.

These categories are for programs designed for the entire audience:

TV-G. General Audience.   *Most parents would find this program suitable for all ages.*
Although this rating does not signify a program specifically designed for children, most parents
may let younger children watch this program unattended. It contains little or no violence, no
strong language, and little or no sexual dialogue or situations.

TV-PG. Parental Guidance Suggested.   *This program may contain some material that some parents
would find unsuitable for younger children.*
Many parents may want to watch it with their younger children. The theme itself may call for
parental guidance. The program may contain infrequent coarse language, limited violence, some
suggestive sexual dialogue and situations.

TV-14. Parents Strongly Cautioned.   *This program may contain some material that some parents
would find unsuitable for children under 14 years of age.*
Parents are strongly urged to exercise greater care in monitoring this program and are cautioned
against letting children under the age of 14 watch unattended. This program may contain sophisticated themes, sexual content, strong language, and more intense violence.

TV-MA. Mature Audience Only.   *This program is specifically designed to be viewed by adults and
therefore may be unsuitable for children under 17.*
This program may contain mature themes, profane language, graphic violence, and explicit sexual content.

matters in terms of risk for the audience of any negative psychological effects.
Indeed, most of the content measures examined in the NTVS were created
specifically because the contextual information assessed helps to identify the degree of risk from exposure. For example, violence that goes unpunished has a
greater probability of increasing viewers' aggressive behavior than violence that
leads to negative outcomes. Other content attributes such as the degree of realism of the act, the attractiveness of the perpetrator, and the depiction of any
harms from violence, among many other variables, represent important elements that contribute to a better understanding of the likely effects of violent
depictions.

By employing the content considerations encompassed in the NTVS in any
ratings scheme, it would be possible to construct an index that would reflect a
collective assessment of the degree of risk associated with a given violent pro-

gram. The greater the presence of contextual elements that contribute to negative psychological effects that are present in a program, the greater its "risk" score. Scores could then be classified within a manageable number of levels (for example, the Canadian system now being tested employs five) that could be used as the basis for electronic screening, with the appropriate level for each child left up to the discretion of the parent.

Another important consideration in this realm is that age-related differences in children's cognitive abilities are important mediators of children's reactions to media violence. For example, very young children lack the ability to link violent acts early in a program with the ultimate punishment for those acts that is depicted at the end of the show (see Collins 1973, 1979, 1983). Thus, the risk of a child viewer learning aggressiveness from some programs may be greater for younger than older children.

The NTVS has addressed this situation by gathering measures of punishment associated with violent acts *both* within the scene in which violence occurs (most salient for a young child viewer) as well as by the end of the program (the more relevant consideration for older audiences). This example underscores the need to consider carefully how children are likely to understand and respond to violent content, a topic that has received a great deal of empirical attention and support.

For a ratings system to be most effective, then, it must be able to assess and label the "risk" violent content poses for child viewers at different ages or stages of development. Most research recognizes that pronounced differences exist between preschool, early elementary, older elementary, and teenaged children's cognitive abilities (see chapter 2 and Wilson et al. 1990). Unfortunately, the current rating system does not incorporate any of these age-related factors in identifying violent material that poses particular need for parental advisories. The lack of adequate consideration of important age-based issues in the new ratings system is underscored most clearly in the program categories that are applied to shows intended solely for children. Only two rating categories are available as options. Shows may be rated TV-Y, which indicates they are appropriate for all children, even the youngest ones, or TV-Y7, which indicates the content is "designed for children age 7 and older" and "may contain mild physical or comedic violence."

Given that these are the only two categories available for rating children's programming, it is implicit that the television industry believes (a) that children's programs never contain violence that exceeds "mild physical or comedic" levels; and (b) that even the most violent of all children's programs (i.e., those rated Y7) must be appropriate for all those above 6 years of age. Our content analysis data indicate clearly that many children's programs present extensive violent depictions that raise serious concerns for adversely affecting the child audience. The current ratings framework provides no possibility of properly identifying children's programs that pose a serious risk of antisocial effects, and thus should be considered inappropriate for children in the 7- to 10-year-old range.

In sum, we have argued in this final section of the chapter that there are two important considerations for creating a system for rating violent content: (1) the context within which aggression is portrayed, and (2) the age of the viewer who is interpreting the portrayal. More specifically, an effective ratings system needs to be sensitive enough that it is capable of identifying the "high-risk" factors associated with depictions of televised violence; and once identified, such content must be labeled in appropriate categories that convey clearly to parents the true degree of risk associated with their child's viewing of such content. It is apparent that the new V-chip rating system has extremely limited capabilities in both of these areas, and thus its utility for families will be severely constrained.

The Future of the National Television Violence Study

In the research described in chapters 2 through 4 and in the *NTVS* report (1997), we have assessed violent depictions at multiple levels, taking into account the differing message characteristics that have been established by previous research as influential in shaping the effects of television violence. Our goal in conducting the NTVS was to provide the most thorough and elaborate description of the contextual elements associated with television violence yet produced by the scientific community. In this chapter, we have discussed the implications of our initial findings for public policy, media industry practice, and parental supervision from analysis of programming from the 1994–95 television season. In years two and three of the NTVS work, we will assess the extent of any changes over time that may occur in the presentation of televised violence. The importance of this issue for society warrants continued careful scrutiny not just by researchers but also by policymakers, parents, and media practitioners.

REFERENCES

Charters, W. W. 1933. *Motion Pictures and Youth: A Summary.* New York: Macmillan Company.
Collins, W. A. 1973. "Effect of Temporal Separation between Motivation, Aggression, and Consequences." *Developmental Psychology* 8(2): 215–21.
———. 1979. "Children's Comprehension of Television Content." In *Children Communicating: Media and Development of Thought, Speech, Understanding,* ed. E. Wartella, 21–52. Beverly Hills, CA: Sage.
———. 1983. "Interpretation and Inference in Children's Television Viewing." In *Children's Understanding of Television,* ed. J. Bryant and D. R. Anderson, 125–50. New York: Academic Press.

National Television Violence Study, Volume 1. 1997. Thousand Oaks, CA: Sage.

Telecommunications Act of 1996. 47 U.S.C. 551. *Parental Choice in Television Programming.*

U.S. Senate Subcommittee to Investigate Juvenile Delinquency. 1954. *Juvenile Delinquency: Television Programs.* Hearings, June 5, October 19–20. Washington, DC: U.S. Government Printing Office.

Wilson, B. J., D. Linz, and B. Randall. 1990. "Applying Social Science Research to Film Ratings: A Shift from Offensiveness to Harmful Effects." *Journal of Broadcasting and Electronic Media* 34:443–68.

Chapter 6

Television Visual Violence in Reality Programs: Differences across Genres

Dominic Lasorsa, Wayne Danielson, Ellen Wartella,
D. Charles Whitney, Marlies Klijn, Rafael Lopez,
and Adriana Olivarez

Introduction

Television violence has become a growing concern of most Americans (Gallup 1993), and that concern has not escaped the attention of political leaders (Windhausen 1994). In 1994, the nation's leading broadcasters and cable operators agreed to sponsor major studies to address these concerns. The broadcasters (Network Broadcasters Association) funded a three-year study being conducted by the Center for Communication Policy at the University of California at Los Angeles. The cable operators (National Cable Television Association) sponsored a comparable three-year study being conducted by the National Television Violence Study (NTVS), a consortium of researchers at the University of California at Santa Barbara, the University of North Carolina at Chapel Hill, the University of Texas at Austin, and the University of Wisconsin at Madison.[1]

At the University of Texas, researchers have been analyzing television's so-called reality programming. Reality programs are nonfictional programs in which the portrayal is presumed to present current or historical events or circumstances. A reality program presents itself as being a realistic account. While reality programs have been on television almost from its beginnings (Allen Funt's *Candid Camera*, Art Linkletter's *People Are Funny*, Edward R. Murrow's *Person to Person*), in recent years there has been a significant increase in such nonfictional programming.

Making a clear distinction between fictional and reality programming, however, is not always easy. One of our first major tasks was to decide which programs to include in the analysis. Once we decided what programming to analyze, we attempted to categorize it by easily recognizable program types, or genres. We then examined differences in television reality programming violence across these genres. This chapter reports the results of these analyses. Examining the use of violence in reality programming is particularly important since some reality programs may be treated as news under the *TV Parental Guidelines,* which means they will not carry a viewer rating.

Why analyze television's reality programming by genres? A primary goal of the NTVS project is to provide television users with information about violence on television that they will find useful in making decisions about what to watch and how to watch it. One of the major ways people make such decisions is by genre. If television genres differ not only in the amount of violence they contain but in the nature of that violence, then it should be helpful to inform viewers not only of the overall amount of violence they can expect to find in a particular television genre but also the context of that violence.

The NTVS essentially split the television world into fictional programming, which was analyzed at the University of California at Santa Barbara (UCSB), and reality programming, analyzed at the University of Texas. While most American television programming can be categorized easily as one or the other, some negotiation was required. For example, is *America's Funniest Home Videos* a fictional program or a reality program? The NTVS researchers decided to include it as a reality program. Excluded, on the other hand, were "docu-dramas" featuring invented or composite characters or dialogue which it can be reasonably inferred did not occur, and other programs in which the entertainment intent of the program outweighs intent to represent actual events or circumstances. Any such program or programming type that was excluded from the analysis of reality programs was included in the analysis of fictional programs conducted at UCSB, with one exception. Certain types of programs were excluded entirely from the study from the beginning, regardless of whether they were fictional or reality programs. Some programming types were eliminated because they represent a program type already known to contain practically no violence as defined by the project. Quiz shows and religious services, for example, were not analyzed for this reason. Other programming types were excluded from analysis because they have unique properties that require special consideration in the analysis of violent content. Sporting events, for example, were not analyzed for this reason. Also excluded were regularly scheduled bona fide newscasts, such as *ABC World News Tonight* and the *CBS Evening News,* as well as the national and local news "drop-ins" on morning news programs such as NBC's *Today* show. The rest of *Today,* however, was studied. The decision not to analyze bona fide newscasts and news drop-ins was part of the original research contract. All other types of news and public affairs programming were analyzed.

Also not analyzed were infomercials and commercials within and between programs.

Once it was decided which types of programming to exclude from the analysis, an attempt was made to categorize all other reality programs into a handful of easily recognizable genres. We identified six genres of reality programming:

1. *Documentaries.* While "docu-dramas" are considered to be fictional programs, documentaries, on the other hand, represent a major genre of reality programming. Documentaries are re-creations of historical events. While they may differ in their overall entertainment value, all documentaries make the claim of presenting only factual information. A&E's *Biography* and PBS's *Frontline* are examples of documentary series included in this genre. As a genre, documentaries are relatively easy to recognize, despite the fact that their content varies widely. In the 1994–95 season, television presented documentaries about such diverse subjects as Arthur Ashe, baseball, the Civil War, and Dracula.

2. *Entertainment news and review shows.* A second major reality program genre consists of entertainment news and review shows. These programs often contain film clips of theatrical films, as well as television dramas, which often contain violence themselves. Celebrity interview shows, such as the Barbara Walters specials, also appear in this genre. The syndicated *Entertainment Tonight* and *Siskel & Ebert* are examples of programs in this genre.

3. *News and public affairs shows.* A third genre consists of news and public affairs shows. While this genre normally would include regular newscasts such as the *CBS Evening News* and the local and national news "drop-ins" in news magazine programs, recall that this type of news programming was excluded from this study. All other types of news programming, however, were included. NBC's *Dateline* and PBS's *Wall Street Week* are examples of programs in this genre.

4. *Police shows.* A fourth genre of reality programming consists of police shows, such as the syndicated *Top Cops* and *Real Stories of the Highway Patrol.* These dramalike programs are easy to identify because of their recognizable subject matter. They often contain re-creations of actual police actions.

5. *Tabloid news shows.* A fifth group of programs consists of tabloid news shows. Programs in this genre often resemble bona fide regular newscasts in format but what distinguishes them is their content, which generally highlights and may even exaggerate the sensational aspects of stories. Programs in this genre include the syndicated *American Journal* and *Hard Copy.*

6. *Talk shows.* Finally, a sixth genre of reality programs consists of talk shows. These programs usually have a host and guests who converse with each other and a studio audience consisting of members of the general public. Programs in this genre include the syndicated *Oprah Winfrey Show* and *Geraldo.*

7. *Other reality shows.* Some reality programs do not fall readily into an easily recognizable genre. Because it is something of a catchall category of reality programming, this group contains the most diversity in content, ranging from medical emergency shows (*Rescue 911*), cinema-verité shows (MTV's *Real World*), comedy-verité (*America's Funniest Home Videos*), and programs focusing on the paranormal (Fox's *Sightings*). Given our definition of genre, we do not list this group of programs as a genre per se but we do include it in our analyses of all reality programs.[2]

It should be noted that this analysis defines television violence as the term has traditionally been used in social science research, that is, it is limited to visually depicted violent acts, credible threats of such acts, and consequences of such acts. The University of Texas research team also examined talk about violence, which we defined as the verbal recounting of threats, acts, and/or harmful consequences of violence. In a talk show, for example, there may be little visual violence but much talk about violence. In this chapter, we are not analyzing talk about violence but only television violence as the term is commonly used. Therefore, when we speak here of "violence" we mean what we refer to in our first-year report as "visual violence."[3]

Literature

Guiding the NTVS project from its inception has been the consideration that we should study the context of television violence that the social science research literature has indicated may be harmful to those exposed to it. Over the years, a number of major studies of television violence have contributed to this knowledge, among them the reports of the U.S. Surgeon General in 1972, the National Institutes of Health in 1982, the U.S. Centers for Disease Control in 1991, the National Academy of Sciences in 1993, and the American Psychological Association in 1993. From this work, the NTVS distilled three major effects that might occur as a result of viewing certain types of television violence, and it used them to guide the analysis of the violent content of television: imitation, fear, and desensitization.[4]

In some cases, the research literature is remarkably clear about the relationship between a contextual factor and one of the three major outcomes studied. For example, unjustified violence is known to decrease significantly the possibility of modeling aggressive behavior while it is known to increase the possibility of fear. Table 2.1 in chapter 2 lists the contextual factors that have been studied over the years and what is known about their effects on real violence (aggression), fear, and desensitization. As can be seen from table 2.1, considerably more is known about the learning of aggression from television violence than is known about desensitization. Nonetheless, all of these findings helped greatly in guiding the analysis. By looking at the context of television violence across reality program genres we are able to understand better which genres are likely to contain not just much violence but violence that is particularly problematic. That ultimately is the goal of this analysis.

Of the contextual factors identified in table 2.1, we were able to study seven here. Some factors, such as the attractiveness of perpetrators and targets, we found to be too difficult to measure reliably in reality programs. The seven contextual factors of violence studied here include rewarded violence, punished violence, realistic violence, extreme violence, graphic violence, pain and harmful consequences of violence, and humor in violence. As noted in table 2.1, most of the contextual factors are expected to increase effects, but a few are expected to decrease effects. Of the factors studied here, the two expected to decrease effects are punished violence and pain and harm cues. Both aggression and fear are expected to decrease when violence is either punished or accompanied with pain and/or harm cues.[5]

Method

A random sample of American television programs shown during the 1994–95 television season was drawn for 23 channels, including network, independent, basic cable, and premium cable channels. Programs were recorded during the period October 8, 1994, through June 9, 1995. For each channel a "composite day" was created such that for each half-hour time slot in the 6 A.M. to 11 P.M. programming day a program was selected as representative of programs on that channel at that time on that day. This has resulted in what is probably the largest sample ever taken of an American television season, consisting of 3,185 programs.

Unlike fictional television programs, which generally share a single theme, reality programs often are segmented. A segment was defined as a coherent part of a broadcast, a partitioned narrative within a program that exhibits unity within itself and separation, by topic and/or central focal character, from other segments within a program. One segment on *60 Minutes* usually stands independent of the next. Therefore, besides being analyzed as individual programs, reality programs also were analyzed at the segment level. Segments were coded for the presence and duration of sequences of violence. They also were examined for whether the violence is rewarded or punished, whether harm and pain are depicted and whether the violence occurs in realistic or fantastic situations. Finally, sequences of violence within segments were examined for their portrayal of moderate to extremely violent acts, their portrayal of graphic violence, and their use of humor.

The following is a description of how each of the seven contextual factors studied here was measured.

1. *Realistic violence.*   Program segments found to contain violence were coded as actual reality only, re-creation of reality, fictional, or fantasy. Actual re-

ality refers to coverage of real events in which the segment attempts to convey events as they actually occurred. No actors are used (e.g., *48 Hours*). Re-creations are reenactments of real events, although some events or dialogue may be fictionalized (e.g., *Rescue 911*). Fictional segments are not based on real events but the events could happen in reality (e.g., *Roseanne*), whereas fantasy segments contain characters or settings that could not exist in reality (e.g., *The Making of Bram Stoker's Dracula*). Violence in fantasy segments was considered unrealistic whereas violence in any of the other three types of segments was considered realistic.

2. *Harm and painful consequences.* Segments containing harm and/or pain cues resulting from violence were differentiated from those segments in which the violence is not followed by any harm and/or pain cues.

3. *Rewarded violence.* Segments in which the violence is rewarded were differentiated from those in which the violence is not followed by any kind of positive reinforcement delivered in return for violence. A reward was not considered the absence of punishment. Rewards also might occur later in the program, not immediately following the violence.

4. *Punished violence.* Segments in which the violence is punished were differentiated from those in which the violence is not followed by any kind of negative consequence for the perpetrator of the violence. As with rewards, punishments may be immediate or delayed.

5. *Extreme violence.* We separated what chapter 2 refers to in table 2.1 as "extensive/graphic violence" into two separate variables, "extreme violence" and "graphic violence." Extreme violence refers to how extensive the physical injury in a violence sequence is. There may be no pain or injury (a credible threat or an unsuccessful attempt); minor pain or injury (bloody nose, minor cuts, scrapes, burns that do not require medical attention); moderate pain or injury (bullet and stab wounds to nonvital organs, broken bones, and other signs of substantial injury that require medical attention); severe pain or injury (injury to the point of physical incapacitation such as bullet and stab wounds to vital organs); death and suicide. Programs containing violent sequences with no or only minor pain or injury were differentiated from those containing major pain or injury. This is a matter of how serious the pain or injury resulting from the violence is.

6. *Graphic violence.* While violence that ends in death is more extreme than violence that ends with only bruises, even violence that ends in little pain or injury may be presented in an editing style that makes the violence seem more vivid, more gruesome, more dramatic—more graphic—than it otherwise would. To get at how graphic the violence is, we combined two measures. First, we asked coders to estimate how graphically the consequences of the violence are depicted. Sometimes, no consequences of the violence are shown. Sometimes, viewers see small flesh wounds, surface cuts, minor tissue damage, which

is somewhat graphic. Sometimes, viewers see blood splattered on people and objects, excessive wounds, severed body parts, which is very graphic. We also considered here the degree of intensity of the act. This, too, refers to how the violent act is shown, not the nature of the act itself. A sequence of violence ending in a face slap, while less extreme than one that ends in murder, might be presented more intensely than the latter if it is done in close-up, with emotional music, in slow motion, and accompanied with prolonged screaming. Camera focus, duration, use of music, and any other editing devices that draw attention to the violence are considered here. Graphic consequences and intensity were then considered together to arrive at an overall measure of graphic violence. Thus, a sequence ending in extreme violence (e.g., murder) may be less graphic than one ending in a face slap if the latter contains vivid images of blood, body parts, or other gore, *or* if the latter contains close-ups, slow motion, emotional music, or other heightening through editing techniques. Programs containing sequences of violence with either moderate to extreme intensity or somewhat to very graphic depictions were differentiated from those containing mild intensity or no graphic consequences.

7. *Humor.*   Finally, sequences were coded as containing humor related to the violence, or not.

The reliability of the measures used in this study was estimated by calculating the percentages of agreement among coders for program, segment, sequence, and character coding. Overall, for a total of 1,314 variables coded in the reliability test, the percentages of intercoder agreement ranged from 86 to 94 percent, indicating relatively high reliability for the coding measures.[6]

Results

As might be expected, many of the programs sampled in the composite week of programming were entertainment and fictional ones, characteristic of much of American television. Still, the amount of reality-based programming is not small, and it appears to be growing. Of the 3,185 programs in the 23-channel programming week, 20 percent (629) were reality-based.

Many of these reality programs, however, were not studied. Recall that network and local newscasts, sporting events, hobby, cooking and other instructional programming, religious services, travelogues, and infomercials were not included in this study. Some of these genres have unique characteristics that require special analysis, and others are known already to contain practically none of the television violence we are studying here. Of the 629 reality programs sampled, 62 percent were studied. These include the major reality-based television genres that contain violence as defined here.

Of the 393 reality programs studied, nearly half were talk shows (26 percent) or news and public affairs programs (23 percent). Of the rest, 16 percent were documentaries, 15 percent were entertainment news and review shows, 5 percent were tabloid news shows, and 5 percent were police shows. Ten percent of the programs did not fit readily into a reality program genre ("other reality programs").

As expected, we found that the sheer amount of television violence is not spread equally across television's reality program genres. While just about four out of every ten reality programs were found to contain at least some violence, some genres contained significantly more violence than others.

As table 6.1 shows, the distribution of violence across reality programming genres is not equal. Three programming genres—police shows, tabloid news shows, and documentaries—tend to contain much violence. The other three genres—talk, entertainment news, and news and public affairs programs—tend to contain little violence. As can be seen, every police program in the sample was found to contain some violence. In contrast, very little violence is found in talk shows. (Recall that we are speaking here only of visual violence. Talk shows actually contain much talk about violence.)[7]

Another striking difference revealed in table 6.1 is the large amount of violence found in tabloid news shows, compared to more traditional news and public affairs programs. While nearly nine of every ten tabloid news programs contain at least some violence, only about one in four news and public affairs programs contains violence.

One thing we have learned from the long history of television violence research, however, is that not all television violence is created equal. We can further help viewers by telling them which genres contain particularly harmful depictions of violence. When we go beyond the sheer amount of violence and begin to examine the nature of that violence, we find that reality program genres differ not only in the quantity of violence they contain but in the quality of that violence, as well.

Table 6.2 gives a profile of violence across the six program genres analyzed. The first column in table 6.2 gives the overall percentages for all reality programs

TABLE 6.1. Overall Visual Violence in Six Reality Program Genres

Genre	% of Programs with Violence
Police ($n = 19$)	100
Tabloid News ($n = 21$)	86
Documentaries ($n = 62$)	72
Other reality programs ($n = 41$)	46
News and public affairs ($n = 91$)	26
Entertainment news ($n = 56$)	21
Talk ($n = 103$)	15
Average—all programs ($N = 393$)	39

TABLE 6.2. Profile of Visual Violence across Six Reality Program Genres

	Overall %	Police		Entertainment News		News		Tabloid News		Documentary		Talk		Other	
		N	%	N	%	N	%	N	%	N	%	N	%	N	%
% of programs with visual violence (N = 393)	39	19	100	56	21	91	26	21	86	62	72	103	15	41	46
% of segments with visual violence (N = 1686)	17	84	63	358	8	535	8	151	27	160	38	238	9	160	25
Of segments with visual violence . . . (N = 277)															
% of segments where violence is rewarded	9	48	21	29	0	39	8	40	5	61	12	21	0	39	3
% of segments where violence is punished	34	48	63	29	7	39	46	40	25	61	25	21	29	39	33
% of segments where harm and pain are depicted	61	48	62	29	55	39	74	40	55	61	66	21	52	39	54
% of segments where violence occurs in realistic situations	86	48	100	29	38	39	90	40	80	61	87	21	95	39	97
% of sequences with visual violence (N = 1534)	54	241	77	99	77	223	35	107	66	476	59	196	17	192	52
Of visual violence sequences . . . (N = 820)															
% of sequences that portray extreme violence	50	183	61	75	61	77	40	66	54	280	45	35	43	104	43
% of sequences that portray graphic violence	40	183	24	75	13	77	57	66	36	280	50	35	49	104	47
% of sequences that portray humor related to violence	3	185	0	76	11	78	3	71	6	281	4	34	6	100	0

TABLE 6.3. Profile Comparison of Visual Violence across Six Reality Program Genres

	Overall %	Police	Entertainment News	News	Tabloid News	Documentary	Talk	Other
% of programs with violence	39	− −	+	+	− −	− −	+ +	*
% of segments with violence	17	− −	*	*	−	− −	*	*
Of those segments with violence . . .								
% of segments where violence is rewarded	9	−	*	*	*	*	*	*
% of segments where violence is punished	34	+ +	− −	+	*	*	*	*
% of segments where harm and pain are depicted	61	*	*	+	*	*	*	*
% of segments where realistic violence occurs	86	−	+ +	*	*	*	*	−
Of those violent sequences . . .								
% that portray extreme violence	50	−	−	+	*	*	*	*
% that portray graphic violence	40	+	+ +	−	*	−	*	*
% that portray humor related to violence	3	*	*	*	*	*	*	*

++ = Substantially better than reality programming average (over or below 20 percent points from the average).
+ = Moderately better than reality programming average (betweeen ± 10 and ±19 points from the average).
* = Reality programming average (up to ±9 percent points from the average).
− = Moderately worse than reality programming average (between ±10 and ±19 points from the average).
− − = Substantially worse than reality programming average (over or below 20 percent points from the average).

Note: For most contextual factors, less is better and more is worse. Police shows have more rewarded violence than other reality program genres, according to table 6.2. Rewarded violence increases the chances of aggression and fear, according to table 2.1. Therefore, police shows are identified here as doing moderately worse than other genres in terms of presenting rewarded violence. *For two contextual factors, however, more is better and less is worse. These are italicized above for easy reference.*

taken together. The remaining columns are broken down by individual genres. For each genre the overall number of programs containing violence is recorded, and that is expressed also as a percent of the total. In addition, a number of contextual factors about the violence are also listed and compared. These include rewarded violence; punished violence; whether harm and pain cues are depicted; how realistic the violence is; how extreme the violence is; how graphic the violence is, and whether humor is included in the violence. Because of the complexity of the information contained in table 6.2, a simplified version of these data is presented in table 6.3. Table 6.3 highlights the reality program genres that tend to present violence in particularly problematic contexts.

What do tables 6.2 and 6.3 tell us about differences in the nature of the violence observed across genres? Overall, they tell us that context matters.

If we were to be concerned only about the amount of television violence in a genre then we might conclude that entertainment news and review shows are a safe bet, but here is a good example where the quality of the violence may be as telling—or more telling—than its quantity. While these shows contained the second-lowest amount of violence, behind talk shows, the violence they do contain tends to go unpunished and to portray extreme violence. This may be due primarily to the frequent use of decontextualized film and news clips on such programs. The producers of this genre of reality programming have considerable control over the images they project. Even though entertainment news and reviews programs contain little overall violence, perhaps the makers of such programs might give more attention to the particular scenes of violence they do show.

Police shows tend to show considerably more violence than all other reality genres, and that, coupled with the nature of that violence, may make them particularly problematic. The reality-based police program tends to portray extreme violence. It also tends to depict more violence as rewarded than do other genres. On the other hand, the police show also tends to depict violence as punished, a characteristic it shares with news shows. News shows, however, do not tend to show extreme violence or violence as rewarded. Furthermore, unlike police shows, news shows tend to do a better job also of depicting the harm and pain associated with violence. Finally, police-show violence is problematic in another important way. It is almost always realistic.

Besides police shows, two other genres contain relatively high levels of violence—tabloid news shows and documentaries—but here again the importance of context reveals itself. Documentaries do tend to portray graphic violence, but otherwise the violence in tabloid news shows and documentaries is not particularly problematic, relative to other reality program genres and, in particular, police shows. Given the overall amount of violence in these genres, however, they still may be of concern to those wanting to limit their diet of television violence.

Besides entertainment news and review programs, two other genres of reality programming contain relatively little violence—news shows and talk shows. Overall, the violence on news shows is considerably less problematic than the violence in other genres. Besides containing relatively little violence, news shows do a relatively good job of portraying unpunished violence, harm and pain, and extreme violence. As with documentaries, however, news shows do tend to contain high levels of graphic violence.

Finally, the violence on talk shows is both infrequent and relatively benign, relative to other reality genres. While there are more talk shows on American television than any other type of reality program, one does not see much visual violence on them, and what violence one does see is not especially troublesome in nature, generally. Recall, however, that we are speaking here only of violence as it has been measured traditionally—what we call "visual violence." As noted earlier, content in which violence is not depicted visually but is described orally—"talk about violence"—is a staple of talk shows.

Summary

The differences in the amount of violence across reality programming genres are so strong that it is perhaps not too far-fetched to say that violence is a defining characteristic of reality program genres. While other considerations such as time slots and personal tastes certainly may affect one's choice of programming fare, these data suggest that viewers can screen their viewing for violence by selectively choosing genres of programs to watch (or not watch).

The *TV Parental Guidelines* explicitly exempt news programs from rating, so viewers may not be alerted to the potential for violent content in some reality programs. Our advice, then, is to urge viewers who are concerned about the harmful effects of television violence to limit viewing to particular genres. Police shows, in particular, tend to show problematic violence. Documentaries and tabloid news shows also contain lots of violence but little problematic violence. News shows and talk shows contain little violence overall and little violence that is particularly troublesome. Entertainment news and review programs, on the other hand, do not contain much violence either but what violence they do contain often is problematic.

The analysis, of course, need not end here. Genres do not share only content characteristics. They tend to occupy certain time blocks and to appeal to certain audiences. It should be of concern, for instance, that some of the genres that contain the most problematic violence are shown typically at times when children are likely to be watching.

There is another area of television violence not studied here—talk violence—that may also deserve the attention of television users, political leaders, and industry operators. We have found that 18 percent of reality programs contain no visual violence, but they do contain talk about violence. Similar to the analysis of visual violence performed here, we intend to investigate differences in talk violence across the six reality programming genres and to compare that to visual violence patterns in the same genres. Given what we found here regarding visual violence, reality program genres may well differ not only in the overall quantity of "talk violence" but also in its quality. Just as we hope that the information provided here may help television viewers make more informed viewing decisions, we hope that additional information about talk violence in reality programs may help television users, as well.

NOTES

The NTVS Research Team at the University of Texas comprises (in alphabetical order) faculty members Wayne Danielson, professor of journalism and computer sciences; Dominic Lasorsa, associate professor of journalism; Ellen Wartella, dean of the College of Communication, and Charles Whitney, professor of journalism and radio-television-film; and graduate research assistants Marlies Klijn, Rafael Lopez, and Adriana Olivarez. The researchers gratefully acknowledge the assistance of former graduate research assistants Shannon Campbell and Saam Haddad, and our project coders Patrick Aziz, Meredith Butler, Alison Cabral, Ben Chorush, Sylvana Fierro, Shane Miller, Neil Pollner, Diane Quest, Arlene Rivero, Pamela Rivero, Felipe Stevenson, Liza Trevino, Alice Tsai, and Lisa Wyatt. NTVS is a project sponsored by the National Cable Television Association to study television violence in the United States over three years. The findings reported here are based on the analysis of the first year's TV programming, 1994–95.

1. Both studies recently released the results of their analyses of the first year's programming (Cole 1995; Biocca, Brown, Cantor, Donnerstein, Kunkel, Lasorsa, Linz, Potter, Wartella, Whitney, and Wilson 1996). This chapter focuses on major results of the work done at the University of Texas at Austin during the first year of the NTVS project (Whitney, Danielson, Lasorsa, Wartella, Campbell, Haddad, Klijn, Lopez, and Olivarez 1996). For information about the work done at the other NTVS research sites, see Biocca, Brown, Shen, Bernhardt, Batista, Kemp, Makris, West, Lee, Straker, Hsiao, and Carbone 1996; Cantor and Harrison 1996, and Kunkel, Wilson, Linz, Potter, Donnerstein, Smith, Blumenthal, and Gray 1996.

2. For a listing of all reality programs in the first-year sample by genre, see Whitney, Danielson, Lasorsa, Wartella, Campbell, Haddad, Klijn, Lopez, and Olivarez 1996.

3. Because we are not analyzing talk about violence here, we have not used the distinguishing label "visual" in this analysis.

4. For evidence on the possible imitation effect, see Andison 1977; Comstock, Chaffee, Katzman, McCombs, and Roberts 1978; Friedrich-Cofer and Huston 1986; Comstock and Paik 1991; Donnerstein and Linz 1995; and on the possible fear effect, see Gerbner and Gross 1976; Gerbner, Gross, Morgan, and Signorielli 1980. Focus on the possible desensitization effect is discussed in Leifer and Roberts 1972; Collins 1973; Linne 1973; Drabman and Thomas 1974; Linz, Donnerstein, and Adams 1989.

5. For more information about these contextual factors and their expected out-

comes, see Biocca, Brown, Cantor, Donnerstein, Kunkel, Lasorsa, Linz, Potter, Wartella, Whitney, and Wilson 1996.

6. For additional information about reliability, see Whitney, Danielson, Lasorsa, Wartella, Campbell, Haddad, Klijn, Lopez, and Olivarez 1996.

7. For more information about "talk violence," see Whitney, Danielson, Lasorsa, Wartella, Campbell, Haddad, Klijn, Lopez, and Olivarez 1996.

REFERENCES

American Psychological Association. 1993. *Violence and Youth: Psychology's Response.* Washington, DC: American Psychological Association.
Andison, F .S. 1977. "TV Violence and Viewer Aggression: A Cumulation of Study Results, 1956–1977." *Public Opinion Quarterly* 41:314–31.
Biocca, F., J. Brown, J. Cantor, W. Danielson, E. Donnerstein, D. Kunkel, D. Lasorsa, D. Linz, J. Potter, E. Wartella, C. Whitney, and B. Wilson. 1996. *National Television Violence Study Scientific Papers: 1994–1995.* Los Angeles: Mediascope.
Biocca, F., J. Brown, F. Shen, J. Bernhardt, L. Batista, K. Kemp, G. Makris, M. West, J. Lee, H. Straker, H. Hsia, and E. Carbone. 1996. "Assessment of Television's Antiviolence Messages: University of North Carolina, Chapel Hill Study." In *National Television Violence Study Scientific Papers: 1994–1995.* Los Angeles: Mediascope.
Cantor, J., and K. Harrison. 1996. "Ratings and Advisories for Television Programming: University of Wisconsin, Madison Study." In *National Television Violence Study Scientific Papers: 1994–1995.* Los Angeles: Mediascope.
Cole, J. 1995. *The UCLA Television Violence Monitoring Report.* Los Angeles: UCLA Center for Communication Policy.
Collins, W. A. 1973. "Effect of Temporal Separation between Motivation, Aggression, and Consequences: A Developmental Study." *Developmental Psychology* 8:215–21.
Comstock, G., S. Chaffee, N. Katzman, M. McCombs, and D. Roberts. 1978. *Television and Human Behavior.* New York: Columbia University Press.
Comstock, G., and H. Paik. 1991. *Television and the American Child.* San Diego, CA: Academic Press.
Daly, M., and M. Wilson. 1994. "Evolutionary Psychology of Male Violence." In *Male Violence,* ed. J. Archer, 253–88. London: Routledge.
Donnerstein, E., and D. Linz. 1995. "The Media." In *Crime,* ed. J. Q. Wilson and J. Petersilia, 237–64. San Francisco, CA: Institute for Contemporary Studies.
Drabman, R. S., and M. H. Thomas. 1974 "Does Media Violence Increase Children's Toleration of Real-Life Aggression?" *Developmental Psychology* 10:418–21.
Friedrich-Cofer, L., and A. C. Huston. 1986. "Television Violence and Aggression: The Debate Continues." *Psychological Bulletin* 100:364–71.
Gallup, G. 1993. "Public Says: Too Much Violence on TV." *Gallup Poll Monthly,* August: 18–20.
Gerbner, G., and L. Gross. 1976. "Living with Television: The Violence Profile." *Journal of Communication* 26(2): 173–99.
Gerbner, G., L. Gross, M. Morgan, and N. Signorielli. 1980. "The 'Mainstreaming' of America: Violence Profile No. 11." *Journal of Communication* 30(3): 10–29.

Jo, E., and L. Berkowitz. 1994. "A Priming Effect Analysis of Media Influences: An Update." In *Media Effects: Advances in Theory and Research,* ed. J. Bryant and D. Zillmann, 43–60. Hillsdale, NJ: Lawrence Erlbaum.

Klein, J. D., J. D. Brown, K. W. Childers, J. Oliveri, C. Porter, and C. Dykers. 1993. "Adolescents' Risky Behavior and Mass Media Use." *Pediatrics* 92(1): 1–13.

Kunkel, D., B. Wilson, D. Linz, J. Potter, E. Donnerstein, S. Smith, E. Blumenthal, and T. Gray. 1996. "Violence in Television Programming Overall: University of California, Santa Barbara Study." In *National Television Violence Study Scientific Papers: 1994–1995.* Los Angeles: Mediascope.

Leifer, A. D., and D. F. Roberts. 1972. "Children's Responses to Television Violence." In *Television and Social Behavior, Volume 2,* ed. J. P. Murray, E. A. Rubenstein, and G. A. Comstock, 43–180. Washington, DC: Government Printing Office.

Lewis, M., C. Yeager, F. Lovely, A. S. Stein, and C. Chobham-Portorreal. 1994. "A Clinical Follow-up of Delinquent Males: Ignored Vulnerabilities, Unmet Needs, and the Perpetuation of Violence." *Journal of the American Academy of Adolescent Psychiatry* 33(4): 518–35.

Linne, O. 1973. *Reactions of Children to Violence on TV.* Stockholm: Swedish Broadcasting Corp.

Linz, D., E. Donnerstein, and S. M. Adams. 1989. "Physiological Desensitization and Judgments about Female Victims of Violence." *Human Communication Research* 15:509–22.

Malamuth, N., and J. Check. 1981. "The Effects of Mass Media Exposure on Acceptance of Violence against Women: A Field Experiment." *Journal of Research on Personality* 15:436–46.

Reiss, A. J., and J. A. Roth. 1993. "Patterns of Violence in American Society." In *Understanding and Preventing Violence,* ed. A. J. Reiss and J. A. Roth, 42–97. Washington, DC: National Academy Press.

Sutton, S. R. 1982. "Fear-Arousing Communications: A Critical Examination of Theory and Research." In *Social Psychology and Behavioral Medicine,* ed. J. R. Eiser. New York: Wiley.

Tyler, T. R. 1980. "The Impact of Directly and Indirectly Experienced Events: The Origin of Crime-Related Judgments and Behaviors." *Journal of Personality and Social Psychology* 39:13–28.

Whitney, C., W. Danielson, D. Lasorsa, E. Wartella, S. Campbell, S. Haddad, M. Klijn, R. Lopez, and A. Olivarez. 1996. "Television Violence in 'Reality' Programming: University of Texas, Austin Study." In *National Television Violence Study Scientific Papers: 1994–1995.* Los Angeles: Mediascope.

Windhausen, J. 1994. "Congressional Interest in the Problem of Television and Violence." *Hofstra Law Review* 22:783–91.

● Chapter 7

Ratings and Advisories: Implications for the New Ratings System for Television

Joanne Cantor, Kristen Harrison, and Marina Krcmar

Introduction

This chapter discusses the research on ratings and advisories from the National Television Violence Study that are most relevant to the development and evaluation of the new ratings system for television. The ratings system implemented in January 1997 has provoked a great deal of criticism because, like its similar predecessor the Motion Picture Association of America (MPAA) ratings, it does not indicate the specific content of a program, but merely provides parental guidance regarding the age of the viewer who should see it. Although the research reported here was completed before the television industry had designed its new system, the results are highly relevant because they demonstrate the effects of the similar MPAA ratings on children's viewing choices and show the types of content that the MPAA ratings have been associated with on television.

The research presented here shows that parental discretion warnings and the more restrictive MPAA ratings stimulate some children's interest in viewing programs. Specifically, in an experiment in which children between the ages of 5 and 14 were given choices of programs to view, the label "parental discretion advised" had a strong and positive effect on boys' interest in the programs, and the effect was strongest for older boys (ages 10–14). The MPAA ratings G, PG, PG-13, and R also strongly affected children's desire to see a movie. Older boys were especially interested in the target movie when it was rated PG-13 or R and completely avoided it when it was rated G. For older girls and younger boys, interest in the movie peaked when it was rated PG-13. In contrast, another type of label worked more or less as intended: "Viewer discretion advised" did not increase boys' interest, and it decreased girls' (and particularly younger girls') desire to view programs.

Further analyses suggest that the increased interest in restricted programs is more strongly linked to children's desire to reject control over their viewing (the "forbidden fruit hypothesis") than to their seeking out of violent content (the "information hypothesis"). In line with this interpretation, the label "contains some violent content; parental discretion advised" was no more attractive than "parental discretion advised" by itself. Moreover, "viewer discretion advised" produced higher expectations of violent content than "parental discretion advised," yet only the parental advisory proved attractive to children.

In analyses not included in the original *National Television Violence Study* (*NTVS*) report, we also looked at the Year 1 random sample of television programming in terms of the correspondence between MPAA ratings and the premium channel content codes used on HBO, Showtime, and Cinemax. These content codes indicate the type and level of sex, violence, and coarse language a program contains. Problems with the MPAA ratings were noted in the fact that there was considerable overlap in the content of movies rated PG and PG-13, and so each of these ratings signals a variety of different combinations of content that might be objectionable to different groups of parents.

Based on these findings, we conclude that the new ratings system is especially problematic because it provides little information about specific content at the same time that it is likely to stimulate some children's interest in more restricted fare. A system based on information about specific content rather than who should or should not see a program would better serve the interests of parents and others who are concerned about the welfare of children.

Background

As part of the NTVS, funded by the National Cable Television Association, researchers at the University of Wisconsin-Madison explored the use and effects of ratings and advisories (Cantor and Harrison 1997). With the passage of the Telecommunications Act of 1996, the questions posed here have come to the center of public attention. The act mandated that within two years of passage, new televisions be manufactured with a "V-chip," which will permit the blocking of objectionable content, and that television programs be rated or labeled to provide information that will be readable by the V-chip. Shortly after passage of the act, entertainment industry executives agreed to develop a ratings system that would be in effect by January 1997. The new system was released to the public on December 19, 1996, and presented to the Federal Communications Commission on January 17, 1997.

The new system, referred to as the *TV Parental Guidelines,* is different in some ways from the MPAA ratings. A separate, two-level ratings system is used for programs that are considered to be designed for children (TV-Y: All Children; and TV-Y7: Directed to Older Children). Other programs are designated with one of four ratings: TV-G: General Audience . . . most parents would find this program suitable for all ages; TV-PG: Parental Guidance Suggested . . . some parents would find unsuitable for younger children; TV-14: Parents Strongly Cautioned . . . many parents would find unsuitable for children under 14; and TV-MA: Mature Audiences Only . . . may be unsuitable for children under 17. The important similarity between the new ratings and the MPAA ratings is that they both give parental guidelines for viewing by different age groups and they both do not tell specifically what type of potentially inappropriate content is in a program.

Television networks and cable channels began using the new ratings in January 1997. They promised to conduct focus groups and commission quantitative studies to determine "whether the Guidelines are in fact providing useful information to parents" and agreed "to consider any needed changes to them" (Ratings Implementation Group 1997).

Previous Research on Ratings and Advisories

The idea of providing warnings or ratings for television programs has been in the public consciousness for a long time, and support for the idea has mushroomed in the past few years. In 1973, for example, a nationwide *TV Guide* survey reported that 55 percent of those questioned were in favor of a ratings system for television programming (Wurtzel and Surlin 1978). By 1995, a *New York Times* poll reported that 84 percent of adults and 91 percent of parents thought that television programs should have ratings (Federman 1996).

Before the NTVS, there was surprisingly little research regarding the impact or effectiveness of ratings and advisories. The few studies that had been conducted are described here. A major issue has been whether advisories and ratings have their intended effect, that is, to prevent people from seeing content that they wish to avoid, and to help parents protect their children from being exposed to problematic content. There has been concern that these labels might have a boomerang effect, that is, they might make the content seem more interesting and exciting and attract a larger audience.

A study by Wurtzel and Surlin (1978) reported a random survey of attitudes toward viewer advisories among adults in Athens, Georgia, in 1976. In their study, only 24 percent of respondents stated that television advisories had influenced them in deciding whether to watch a show. Interestingly, 39 percent of those who had been influenced reported that the advisory resulted in their not watching the show, but 24 percent said that the advisory made them watch the show with increased interest. Furthermore, Wurtzel and Surlin found that more than half of the respondents with children (54 percent) stated that the warnings had influenced their decisions about their child's viewing. The overwhelming majority (81 percent) of the parents who had been influenced said they had not let their children watch the program, and most of the remainder said that although they had let their children watch, they had watched the program with them.

As for the actual effects of violence ratings and advisories, that is, whether they decrease or increase exposure, previous research findings were decidedly mixed. A study published by Herman and Leyens (1977) reported data on Belgian television viewership between 1972 and 1975. This study looked at televised movies only and compared the audience size for movies broadcast with violence advisories to those broadcast with sex advisories and without advisories. Their main finding was that films carrying violence or sex advisories had larger audiences than those without them. Although these data might seem to support the notion that advisories attract viewers, this conclusion cannot be drawn with confidence, because the study did not isolate the effect of content from the effect of advisories. It could very well be that the programs were watched more because they contained violence and sex, not because they were broadcast with an advisory.

A publication by Austin (1980) reported on a laboratory experiment in which high school students were presented with a series of fictitious film titles and plot synopses. For different students, the same film was associated with different MPAA ratings (G, PG, R, or X). According to Austin's report of the findings, the ratings had no significant impact on students' desire to see the films.

A third study of the effect of advisories, an experiment by Christenson (1992), examined the effect of parental advisory labels for popular music albums ("Parental advisory: Explicit lyrics"). In this study, adolescents gave lower evaluations of music from albums displaying advisory labels than of the same music from albums without such labels, and they reported less interest in purchasing the labeled albums.

The conflicting findings of these three studies left us knowing very little about the impact of violence ratings and advisories on adult and child viewers' attraction to or avoidance of television programming. A recent study reported by Hamilton (1994) began to remedy this situation by using regression analysis to determine the factors that made significant contributions to the Nielsen ratings of movies broadcast on network television between 1987 and 1993. In his analysis, Hamilton included a variety of characteristics that are known to have an impact on the rating a program receives, such as its scheduling, the rating of the show preceding it, and the manner in which it was described and categorized in *TV Guide*. Hamilton's major finding was that the presence of a viewer discretion warning was associated with a significant reduction in Nielsen ratings among viewers in the 2- to 11-year-old category. These advisories had no significant impact on the size of the teen or adult audience, however. This study represents the first successful demonstration that viewer discretion advisories can serve one of their major intended purposes, that is, to shield some of the youngest and most impressionable children from exposure to controversial content, without either increasing or reducing the size of the audience in other age groups.

A study such as Hamilton's, involving aggregate data, can tell us only about the end result of a process by which children are exposed to or protected from exposure to movies on television. What we cannot tell from such a study is how the reduction in child audience size was brought about. Did parents make decisions about their child's exposure by themselves, or were children involved in the decision to avoid these movies? It is possible that parents and children made their decisions in concert, but it is also possible that parents made these decisions unilaterally. Some of the questions that remain unaddressed, therefore, are whether or not children knew about the advisories at all; whether, if they did, they understood what they meant; and further, whether the advisories had any effect on the children's desire to see the movies.

Do Ratings and Advisories Affect Children's Viewing Choices?

The main thrust of the research at the Madison site was to investigate the effect of advisories and ratings on children's desire to see programs associated with them. Although it is commonly agreed that ratings and advisories are directed at adults to permit them to protect their children or themselves from objectionable content, it is difficult to ignore the question of how these messages affect children. Children's viewing decisions are often made in the absence of the parent, and anecdotal evidence suggests that children are aware of advisories and ratings. It is therefore important to determine the impact of ratings and advisories on children themselves.

For the first year of the project period, we looked at those ratings and advisories that seemed most prevalent on television. We tested four advisories: "Parental discretion advised," "Contains some violent content; Parental discretion advised," "Viewer discretion advised," and "Contains some violent content; Viewer discretion advised." We also included the four major MPAA ratings that are associated with movies shown on television: G: General audiences; PG: Parental guidance suggested; PG-13: Parents strongly cautioned; and R: Restricted.

The participants were 297 schoolchildren in Madison, Wisconsin, who received parental permission to participate. The students were recruited from 3 schools and 10 afterschool programs. They ranged in age from 5 to 14 years. Many of the analyses compared subjects in two age groups. The "younger" group was composed of children between the ages of five and nine years ($N =$

159; 55 percent male). The "older" group was composed of children between 10 and 14 ($N = 138$; 42 percent male). The overwhelming majority of the children were Caucasian.

Children in first and second grades were interviewed individually by groups of trained interviewers. The older children were tested in groups of four to eight by two research assistants, with the exception of one middle school, whose students were tested simultaneously by two research assistants as one large group. In all cases, children were told not to put their names on any of the booklets and were assured that their answers would be completely anonymous.

After they filled out a background questionnaire (to be described in a later section), children filled out a five-page mock channel guide. They were instructed to choose one program to view from among the three described on each page. They were told that they would be shown a video clip after completing the questionnaire, and that their viewing choices would help the researchers decide which video clip to show.

The first page of listings described three reality-based crime shows with fictitious names, each associated with a short description of the plot of an episode (e.g., "A gun dealer who is selling illegal firearms is taken into custody after a shoot-out"). Children were told that all the programs were real, but that some were not currently being broadcast locally. In every booklet, one of the three programs and its description was followed by an advisory that read "Parental discretion advised" (parental advisory) or "Contains some violent content; parental discretion advised" (parental violence advisory). The program that contained an advisory was randomly varied, as were the advisory version (with or without the mention of violent content) and the order of the show descriptions.

The third page of listings described three crime dramas with fictitious names, also followed by episode descriptions. One of these descriptions was followed by an advisory that read "Viewer discretion advised" (viewer advisory) or "Contains some violent content; viewer discretion advised" (viewer violence advisory). Again, the show description containing the advisory was randomly varied, as were the advisory version and the order of presentation of the show descriptions.

The fifth page of listings described three feature-length movies whose names and plot descriptions contained both real and fictional elements. The titles were *Hidden Island, Cold River,* and *The Moon-Spinners.* The descriptions for *Hidden Island* and *Cold River* were always followed by the MPAA rating PG: Parental guidance suggested. The MPAA rating for *The Moon-Spinners* was randomly varied to read one of four ways: G: General audiences; PG: Parental guidance suggested; PG-13: Parents strongly cautioned; or R: Restricted. As on the first and third pages, the order of presentation of the movie descriptions was randomly varied.

Pages 2 and 4 of the booklet contained the names of real programs, and no advisories and ratings were mentioned. The program choices on these pages were not analyzed.

Children's Viewing Selections

Parental discretion advisories.   To determine whether the presence of the advisories "Parental discretion advised" or "Contains some violent content; parental discretion advised" influenced children's choices of reality-action programs, the percentage of children choosing the program with an advisory was compared to what would be expected by chance (33 percent). Analyses were performed to determine the patterns of interest in programs with parental advisories in the four age-by-sex groupings, that is, younger girls, younger boys, older girls, and older boys. These patterns are displayed in figure 7.1. The data revealed that younger and older girls were highly similar, with 27 percent and 28 percent, respectively, choosing a program with a parental advisory. These responses were not significantly different from what would be expected by chance. In contrast, boys showed more interest in programs with parental advisories. Although more than one-third of both younger and older boys chose such shows, the preference of older boys was much stronger. Thirty-nine percent of the younger boys, but 51 percent of the older boys, chose a program with a parental advisory. Binomial tests revealed the percentage for the older boys to be significantly different from chance ($p < .01$). When the data were analyzed by gender of participant, collapsing age, it was found that the percentage for all boys was significantly higher than chance levels ($p = .01$) as well.

The two versions of the parental advisory (mentioning violence vs. not mentioning violence) were also analyzed separately. These analyses showed that the two types of parental advisories exerted highly similar effects, with 35 percent of subjects choosing a program with the parental advisory and 36 percent choosing a program when it had the parental violence advisory. The only real difference between the effects of the two forms of the parental advisory was that the difference between boys and girls was larger for the parental violence advisory (47 percent vs. 25 percent, respectively) than for the parental advisory that did not mention violence (40 percent vs. 30 percent). The former comparison was significant ($\chi^2(2, N = 143) = 6.47, p < .01$).

Viewer discretion advisories.   Next, the "viewer discretion advised" warnings from the third page of the television booklet were analyzed in the same fashion. As can be seen from figure 7.2, overall, 27 percent of the children chose a drama associated with one of the two forms of viewer discretion advisories, and this percent was lower than would be expected by chance, approaching significance ($p = .07$).

The data within the four age-by-sex groupings are also shown in figure 7.2.

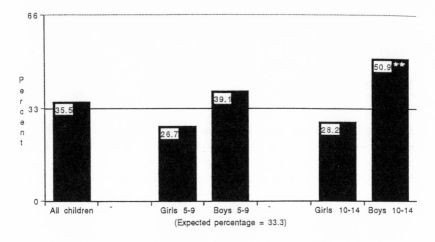

Fig. 7.1.   Percentage of children choosing program with "parental" advisory
($^{**}p < .01$)

As the figure shows, younger girls chose programs with a viewer discretion advisory at the lowest rate (21 percent), and this rate was significantly different from chance ($p < .05$). Moreover, when the patterns for both genders were looked at, collapsing age, the proportion of girls choosing a program with a viewer advisory (24 percent) was significantly lower than chance expectations ($p < .05$). In contrast, viewer discretion advisories did not significantly affect boys' interest in the programs.

When the two forms of the viewer advisory were compared, there was no significant difference between advisories with and without the mention of violence.

MPAA ratings.   The data from children's choices of movie as a function of its MPAA rating revealed that the pattern of choices for girls differed significantly from that for boys, and the pattern for older children differed significantly from that for younger children ($p < .01$ for both). Figures 7.3a through 7.3d show the patterns of choice within the four age-by-gender groupings. These figures show that for younger girls, there was a decreasing tendency to choose the movie as its rating became more restrictive. For younger boys and older girls, interest in the movie peaked at PG-13 and fell off dramatically with the R rating. In sharp contrast, for older boys, interest in the movie was strongest in the two more restrictive rating categories. It seems particularly remarkable that in this group, not one of the boys who were told the movie was rated G chose it, but 53 percent of those who were told it was rated PG-13 and 50 percent of those who were told it was rated R wanted to see it (for this group, $\chi^2(3, N = 56) = 9.02, p < .05$, Cramer's $V = .40$).

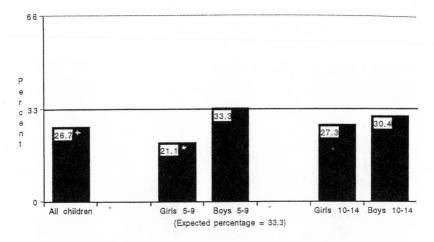

Fig. 7.2.   Percentage of children choosing program with "viewer" advisory ($^*p <$ .05; $^+p < .07$)

What Explains Children's Choices?

The results of the main experimental project indicate unequivocally that ratings and advisories can have a significant impact on children's choices of programs and movies on television. Precisely what that impact is depends on a number of things, including aspects of the advisory or rating and the age and sex of the child making the choices.

The well-known admonition "parental discretion advised" had a strong and positive effect on boys' interest in viewing reality-action programs, and the effect was strongest for boys in the older group. This same advisory had no impact on girls' tendency to choose such programs. In contrast, another frequently used advisory, "viewer discretion advised," did not increase boys' interest in viewing crime dramas, and it decreased girls' (and especially younger girls') choices of such programs.

The MPAA ratings G, PG, PG-13, and R also strongly affected children's desire to see a movie. Older boys were especially interested in the target movie when it was rated PG-13 or R and completely avoided it when it was rated G. In contrast, younger girls were most interested in the movie when it was rated G. For older girls and younger boys, interest in the movie peaked when it was rated PG-13.

These intriguing and diverse effects warrant explanation, and two possible rationales suggest themselves. One could be called the *forbidden fruit hypothesis,* which involves the psychological notion of "reactance" (Brehm and Brehm 1981). Reactance theory posits that when people perceive that their freedom is

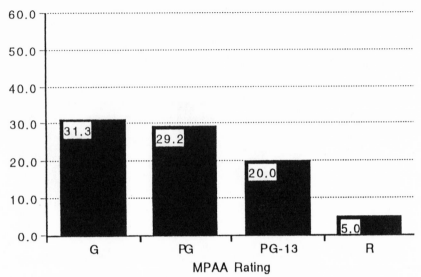

Fig. 7.3a.   Percentage of younger girls (ages 5–9) choosing target movie

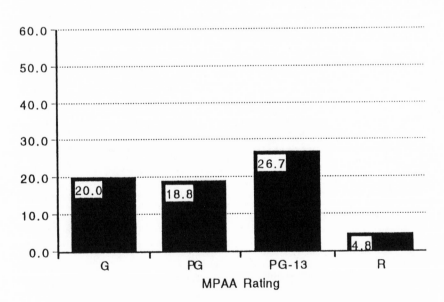

Fig. 7.3b.   Percentage of younger boys (ages 5–9) choosing target movie

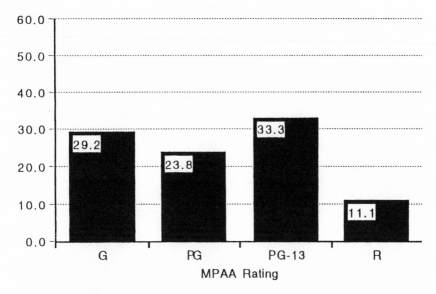

Fig. 7.3c.　Percentage of older girls (ages 10–14) choosing target movie

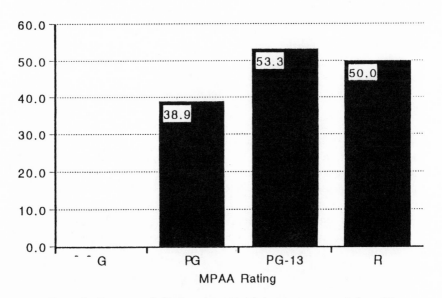

Fig. 7.3d.　Percentage of older boys (ages 10–14) choosing target movie ($p < .05$)

being restricted, they are motivated to restore their freedom by performing the restricted behavior. This process has been invoked by Bushman and Stack (1996) to explain the results they observed when college students showed increased interest in movies with warning labels. It is possible that in our study, those children who showed more interest in programs labeled "parental discretion advised" and movies with the more restrictive MPAA ratings were reacting against these implied threats to their freedom of choice. It may well be, then, that these ratings are perceived as saying "this is not for you," or "this is not for kids," or "you're too young to see this."

The other explanation, which we will refer to as the *information hypothesis*, contends that restrictive ratings and advisories simply provide information about content. According to this reasoning, these labels imply that a violent show has more violence or more intense violence than one without a label. Therefore, those viewers who want to see violence choose fare with such labels to obtain access to the content they desire. It may be, then, that programs advertised with advisories and more restrictive ratings are sought out by some children because they are expected to be more violent.

Children's Interpretations of Advisories and Ratings

Although the design of the first year of research did not permit definitive answers on this issue, our selective exposure experiment did provide some data that are relevant to these explanations. At the end of the session, after viewing and rating scenes from one of the movies that had been described in their channel guide, children filled out a questionnaire assessing their interpretations of the advisories and ratings that had been involved in the selective-exposure questionnaire. Each child's booklet contained one advisory and one MPAA rating. These messages were selected at random for each booklet, and thus the advisory and rating the child responded to were not necessarily the same ones he or she had seen earlier.

Perceived meaning of labels.   For each discretion advisory, children were asked to choose the phrase that came closest to the meaning of the message. They chose between the following four possible meanings: "people shouldn't watch," "kids need a grownup's permission to watch," "parents should be careful in deciding whether to let their kids watch," or "people should be careful in deciding whether to watch." These choices were included predominantly to test comprehension (with the third and fourth choices representing the correct response for the parental and viewer advisories, respectively). However, it is possible to look at children's answers on these measures for clues to the processes underlying their viewing choices.

In terms of the reactance notion, all four advisories imply some restriction on who should see the program. However, one obvious difference between the parental and the viewer advisory is that the parental advisory is a message that bypasses children entirely and urges parents to protect their children. In contrast, the viewer advisory addresses the viewers directly and exhorts them to make their own decisions. Perhaps boys' and particularly older boys' attraction to programs with parental advisories was based in part on their rebellion against a message they perceived as treating them like children.

Figures 7.4a and 7.4b display children's choices of meanings for the parental and viewer advisories, respectively. Although we cannot tie a particular child's choice to his or her perception of the advisory, we did observe that older children made a distinction between the two types of advisory in terms of the degree of parental involvement in the decision. This distinction was not made by the younger children. For example, for "parental discretion advised," 93 percent of the older children chose an option that implied parental control (either "kids need a grownup's permission to watch" or "parents should be careful in deciding whether to let their kids watch"), while 70 percent chose these options for "viewer discretion advised." The difference between these two percentages is predominantly due to a reduction in the number of children who chose "kids need a grownup's permission to watch." Moreover, among older children, more than four times as many chose the implicitly "autonomous" answer ("people should be careful in deciding . . . .") for the viewer advisory than for the parental advisory (22 percent vs. 5 percent). Younger children seem not to have been consciously aware of this difference between the two forms of the advisory. They chose options involving parental guidance equally for "parental" (75 percent) and "viewer" (78 percent) discretion, and they chose the option involving autonomy equally for the two versions ("parental," 10 percent; "viewer," 8 percent).

In responding to the question regarding the meaning of the four MPAA ratings, children could choose among the following five answers: "anyone can watch," "parents should decide whether their kids can watch," "parents should be very careful about letting their kids watch," "kids shouldn't watch without a parent," and "no kids are allowed to watch." Again, although these choices were involved to assess comprehension of the literal meaning of the message, they can be evaluated in terms of their degree of implied restrictiveness. The children's choices, broken down by age group, are displayed in figures 7.5a through 7.5d. In general, the older children showed a basic understanding of the meaning of these ratings, with the highest percentage of children always choosing the option that involved the correct meaning. The most striking aspect of these responses seems to be that 100 percent of the older children chose "anyone can watch" as the meaning of the G rating. Perhaps the knowledge that there were no restrictions at all on G rated movies led older children, and especially older

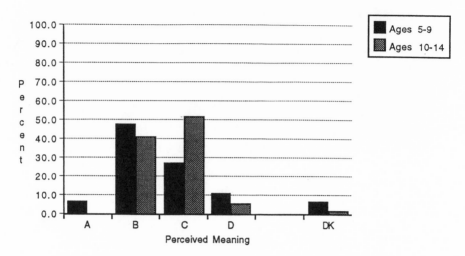

Fig. 7.4a. Children's perceptions of the meaning of "Parental discretion advised."
(Patterns for age groups significantly different at the $p < .05$ level.)

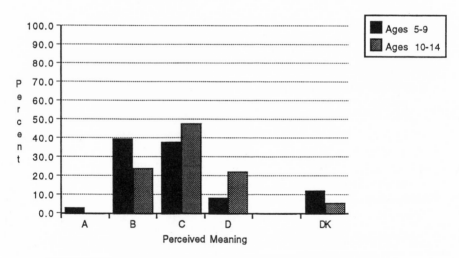

Fig. 7.4b. Children's perceptions of the meaning of "Viewer discretion advised."
(Patterns for age groups significantly different at the $p < .05$ level.)

PERCEIVED MEANING KEY: A -- People shouldn't watch
                           B -- Kids need a grownup's permission to watch
                           C -- Parents should be careful in deciding whether to let their kids watch
                           D -- People should be careful in deciding whether to watch
                           DK -- Don't know

boys, to avoid them. Only 50 percent of the younger children knew that G means "anyone can watch," and this group seems to have been responding almost at random to the choices for the other three ratings.

In general, then, there is some evidence that is consistent with the notion that reactance could have occurred for some of the older children in making their choices. Older children perceived a greater level of parental involvement and a lesser amount of viewer autonomy in the "parental" than the "viewer" advisory. Older children also perceived the G rating to imply no restrictions and saw restrictiveness to increase with the other ratings, particularly with PG-13 and R.

Expectations of content.   For each advisory and each MPAA rating, children were also given a list of thirteen types of content, many of which were violent (e.g., punching, shooting), and were asked to circle all those things that they would expect to see in a program that was preceded by that advisory or rating. By examining these content data, we can observe whether particular advisories and ratings suggested that the content would be more violent, and we can evaluate the degree to which the data are consistent with the information-based rationale for the effects of the advisories on selective exposure.

Analysis of expectations regarding the four forms of the discretion advisory revealed that expectations about two types of violent content were differentially affected by the advisories. The percentage of children expecting punching or kicking in a program increased over the four forms of advisory, from "Parental discretion advised" to "Contains some violent content; viewer discretion advised." This pattern is illustrated in figure 7.6 for expectations of punching ($\chi^2(3, N = 280) = 20.26, p < .01$).

Although it is not surprising that the phrase "contains some violent content" would increase the number of children expecting punching and kicking, it is interesting that the viewer advisories led to higher expectations of these behaviors than the parental advisories. Part of the reason for the different effects of these two types of advisories may be, then, that "viewer discretion advised" suggests more violent content than "parental discretion advised." However, the fact that the advisory that was perceived as more violent was not the one that attracted more children suggests that information about violent content per se is a less potent magnet for children than the exhortation that the child should be prevented from seeing it.

The analyses of the MPAA ratings revealed that these ratings exerted significant effects on expectations for all of the violent content variables. The observed pattern is illustrated in figure 7.7 for punching ($\chi^2(3, N = 280) = 49.05, p < .001$). For all these measures, the percentage of children expecting violent content was lowest for the G rating and increased dramatically up to the PG-13 rating. The percentage declined somewhat for the R rating.

These findings regarding expectations of violent content for the MPAA rat-

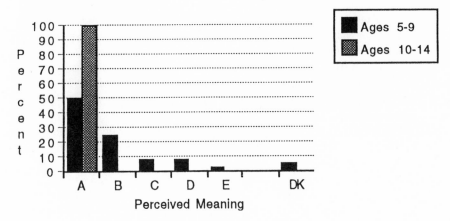

Fig. 7.5a.   Children's perceptions of the meaning of MPAA rating G ($p < .01$ for younger versus older group comparisons)

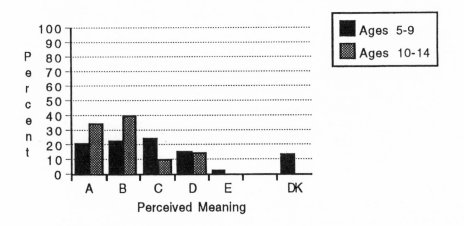

PERCEIVED MEANING KEY:

A -- Anyone can watch

B -- Parents should decide whether their kids can watch

C -- Parents should be very careful about letting their kids watch

D -- Kids shouldn't watch without a parent

E -- No kids are allowed to watch

DK -- Don't know

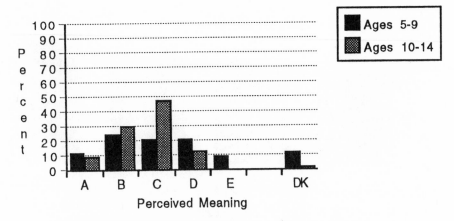

Fig. 7.5c.   Children's perceptions of the meaning of MPAA rating PG-13 ($p < .05$ for younger versus older group comparisons)

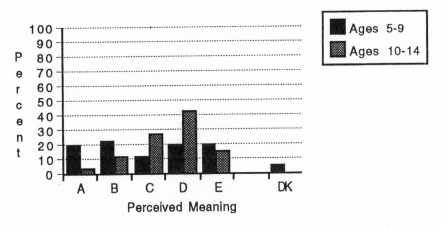

Fig. 7.5d.   Children's perceptions of the meaning of MPAA rating R ($p < .10$ for younger versus older group comparisons)

PERCEIVED MEANING KEY:

A -- Anyone can watch
B -- Parents should decide whether their kids can watch
C -- Parents should be very careful about letting their kids watch
D -- Kids shouldn't watch without a parent
E -- No kids are allowed to watch
DK -- Don't know

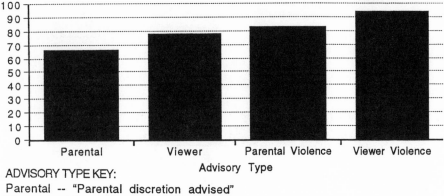

ADVISORY TYPE KEY:
Parental -- "Parental discretion advised"
Viewer -- "Viewer discretion advised"
Parental Violence -- "Contains some violent content; parental discretion advised"
Viewer Violence -- "Contains some violent content; viewer discretion advised"

Fig. 7.6.   Children's expectations of specific violent content in programs with advisories (percent expecting punching, $p < .001$)

ings are consistent with the notion that information about violent content draws children to MPAA-rated movies. The selective-exposure data for boys (combining the two age groups) and for older children (combining the sexes), show a strikingly similar pattern to these content ratings, with interest in the movie lowest for the G rating and peaking at PG-13 (see figs. 7.8a and 7.8b).

The Impact of Background Variables

In making sense of the effects of advisories and ratings on children's choices of programs, it is also of interest to look at the influence of other characteristics of the children making the choices. In our main experiment, we included a background questionnaire containing a series of personality items and parental guidance measures. To observe the relationship between background variables and program choices, we conducted a series of multiple logistic regression analyses, in which the background variables were entered after age and gender, and in which the dependent variable was whether or not the child chose a program with an advisory, or the target movie when it was rated PG-13 or R.

Personality variables.   The personality dimensions of greatest interest

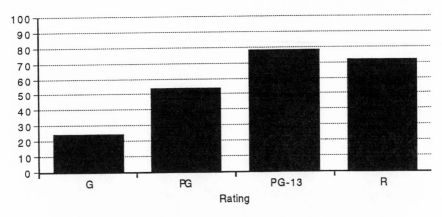

Fig. 7.7.   Children's expectations of specific violent content in movies with MPAA ratings (percent expecting punching, $p < .001$)

were anxiety reactions and aggressiveness. Examples of the items in these dimensions are "seeing scary things on television upsets me" (anxiety) and "I get into fights with other children" (aggression). Response choices were "never," "some of the time," "most of the time," and "all of the time."

Some items related to anxiety and aggression were associated with the tendency to choose restricted content after the contributions of age and gender were accounted for. Of the items related to anxiety, the only one that had a significant relationship to choosing restricted content was "seeing scary things on television upsets me." Children who reported getting upset more often by scary television were less likely to choose a program with an advisory. Specifically, after the contributions of age and sex were accounted for, responses on this item were negatively related to the choice of programs with both parental advisories ($\beta = -.18$, $p < .01$, $R^2_{change} = .03$) and viewer advisories ($\beta = -.18$, $p < .01$, $R^2_{change} = .04$).

This finding is encouraging because it shows that in some instances, children behaved sensibly and in their own best interest. Those children who reported experiencing fright reactions from television were more likely to avoid programs with both parental and viewer advisories. These children had apparently learned from their previous experiences and used these messages as they were intended, to shield themselves from future emotional upsets.

On a less positive note, we also found that children who reported more aggression-related behavior showed more interest in programs with advisories. Specifically, liking "rough and tumble games" was a positive predictor of the tendency to choose a program with a parental discretion advisory ($\beta = .15$, $p < .05$,

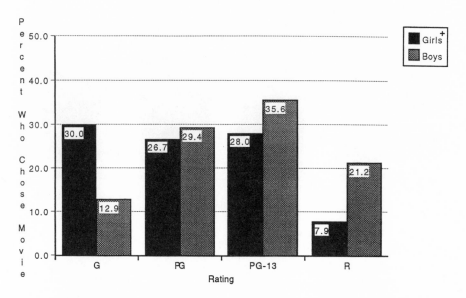

Fig. 7.8a.   Choice of target movie based on MPAA rating, by gender. (For girls, $p <$ .08; for girls versus boys, $p < .01$.)

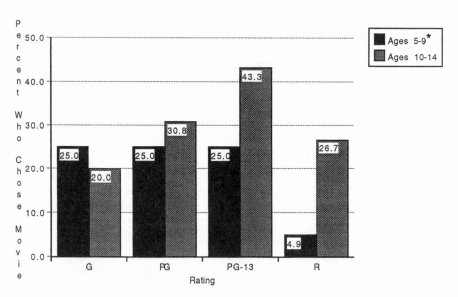

Fig. 7.8b.   Choice of target movie based on MPAA rating, by age. (For ages 5–9, $p <$ .05; for younger versus older groups, $p < .01$.)

R^2_{change} = .02). Similarly, children's responses to the item "I get into fights with other kids" was positively related to choosing a program with a viewer discretion advisory, approaching significance (β =.12, p = .059, R^2_{change} = .03).

The implications of these findings are somewhat disturbing. The more benign item, "I like rough and tumble games," was positively associated with choosing a program with a parental advisory. The more directly aggression-related item, "I get into fights with other kids," was positively related to choosing a program with a viewer advisory, although this relationship only approached significance. If this relationship holds up under replication, it will suggest that advisories may be attracting just those viewers who are of prime concern in our desire to reduce the contribution of violence on television to violence in our society. Research has repeatedly shown that children who are already aggressive are the most likely to become even more violent as a function of exposure to television violence.

Parental involvement. Parental involvement was assessed with items regarding whether the parents set any limits on children's television time or content, and the frequency with which they watched television with their children and discussed programs with them. A scale was constructed from children's responses on these four items. After controlling for age group and gender, parental involvement contributed significantly and negatively to choice of programs with a parental advisory ($\beta = -.15, p = .01, R^2_{change}$ = .02). In other words, children who rated their parents as more involved in their television viewing were less likely than other children to choose a program with a parental discretion advisory. Parental involvement was also negatively related to the choice of the target movie when it was rated PG-13 or R. Thus, children whose parents were more involved in their television viewing were less likely to choose the movie when it had these more restrictive ratings ($\beta = -.17, p < .05, R^2_{change}$ = .03). These findings suggest that parental involvement may become internalized and have beneficial effects even when the child selects programming without adult supervision.

Parents' and Children's Comments about Advisories and Ratings

Another way in which we explored the reasons for the effects of advisories and ratings on children's viewing selections was to conduct a second study, in which we observed parent–child pairs discussing viewing choices involving these labels. In this study, parents and children were given a choice of programs for the child to watch, and their interactions were videotaped as they discussed the choices available to them. We were especially interested in the way parents and children referred to the ratings and advisories in discussing their choices.

The sample included 70 parent–child dyads who were recruited from five parochial schools in the Madison, Wisconsin, area. The dyads were approximately equally divided into a younger group, including children who were attending kindergarten or first grade and ranging in age from 5 to 7, and an older group, including children in fourth or fifth grade and ranging in age from 9 to 11 years. Within each age group, there were equal numbers of girls and boys.

The parent–child pair was given a television program guide booklet, somewhat similar to the one used in the main experiment. The participants were told to select one program out of the three that appeared on each page of the booklet. Further, they were permitted to reject any programs they considered inappropriate. The experimenter left the room while the parent and child made their decisions.

One page of the viewing-choice booklet contained titles of three fictitious reality-action programs, one of which, at random, was associated with the advisory "Contains some violence. Parental discretion advised." Another page contained the fictitious titles of three animated violent movies, one of which, at random, was given the rating of PG-13: Parents strongly cautioned. The other two were assigned the rating, PG: Parental guidance suggested.

As expected, there was a strong tendency to avoid choosing the program with the advisory when parents and children made their decisions in concert. Out of the 70 dyads, only five (7 percent) chose a program with an advisory, and this percentage was dramatically and significantly below chance expectations of 33 percent ($p < .001$). Similarly, there was a significant tendency to avoid movies with PG-13 ratings when pitted against others rated PG. Out of the 70 dyads, ten (14 percent) chose the movie that had the PG-13 rating, and this number was significantly below the 33 percent that would be expected by chance ($p = .001$). Not surprisingly, dyads involving younger children were more likely than those involving older children to reject programs with advisories (χ^2 (2, $N = 36$) = 4.46, $p < .05$) and movies with the PG-13 rating (χ^2 (2, $N = 34$) = 4.02, $p < .05$). The sex of the child, however, did not significantly affect the tendency to reject programs or movies with these labels.

The most interesting aspect of the findings was an analysis of the discussions between the parent and child. Almost half of the parents (47 percent) made comments about the advisory, and all of these comments were unfavorable, indicating that the content was inappropriate or that the child could not see the program. Some of these mentioned the child's age as a reason to avoid the program (e.g., "that means it's for big kids"); some referred to the violence in the advisory (e.g., "says it contains violence and so, no"); some mentioned that it would be frightening ("it means it's scary"). The remaining parents gave nonspecific negative references (e.g., "parental discretion. I'd probably say not").

Half of the parents (50 percent) made comments about the PG-13 rating, and almost all of these were negative. Again, many of these referred to the child's age or to the fact that the movie would be frightening. One of these comments had a positive tone, but it may have been tongue-in-cheek ("I'm strongly cautioned, so that's the one!" [laughing]).

The children did not comment on the advisory or the PG-13 rating nearly as often as their parents, but when they did, their comments were as likely to be favorable as unfavorable. Seven children (10 percent) made negative comments about the advisory (one suggesting the program would be "scary") and eight (11 percent) made positive comments (e.g., after reading the advisory, "that's awesome!" and "they all say that. It's fine. They just all say that"). Older children were much more likely than younger children to make favorable references to the advisory ($\chi^2(1, N = 70) = 4.70, p < .05$).

A similar pattern was observed in children's references to the PG-13 rating. Five children (7 percent) made negative references (e.g., "PG-13. Adios") and eight (11 percent) made positive references (e.g., "PG-13. Choose that one"). One older girl disparaged the movies with the less-restrictive rating, saying, "those two [PG rated movies] are little loser ones. They rated *Home Alone* PG. The cooler the movie, the higher the rating." There were no sex differences in the tendency of children to make positive versus negative comments about the advisory or the PG-13 rating.

The comments observed in this study suggest that parents take advisories and ratings seriously in determining the appropriateness of television fare for their children. At the same time, the children's comments further illuminate the processes by which advisories and restrictive ratings may have attracted some viewers in the main experiment. Although none of the comments specifically differentiate between the forbidden fruit hypothesis and the information-based rationale, these labels somehow made the selections seem "cooler" and more "awesome."

The ability of restrictive ratings, particularly MPAA ratings, to increase the allure of movies was illustrated vividly to us when we recently addressed a church parenting group about children's television viewing. One mother volunteered the following anecdote:

> We recently told our son that he would be getting a new 10-speed bike for his thirteenth birthday. But he told us he wouldn't need a new bike. He declared that he wouldn't have time to ride it after he was 13, since he would be spending all his free time watching PG-13 movies!

This anecdote illustrates the degree to which an age-based ratings system can increase the allure of the restricted behavior. Together with the data provided here, it suggests the perils of using a system that is based on the notion of who is restricted from viewing.

Tentative Conclusions Regarding the Reasons for Children's Choices

The findings regarding children's interpretations of the advisories and ratings in the main experiment, and their comments about these labels in the second experiment, lead to some tentative explanations for their viewing choices. Children's interpretations of the MPAA ratings provided support for both the forbidden fruit effect and the information-based rationale, in that the higher-level ratings were perceived both as more restrictive (at least by the older children) and as containing more violence. However, children's interpretations of the advisories were clearly more consistent with the forbidden fruit effect, since "viewer discretion advised," which was perceived to be more violent, did not provoke increased interest. Moreover, it was perceived by the older children as involving less parental control than "parental discretion advised." Finally, children's positive comments about the parental advisory and the PG-13 rating demonstrate how restrictive labels not only can enhance the attractiveness of the labeled material, but may reduce the appeal of less restricted fare.

The analyses involving background variables suggest that some children who shy away from programs with advisories may be doing so to avoid experiencing emotional distress. They also suggest that some children who seek out programs with advisories may be those who are already violent. Such children may be particularly prone to experiencing reactance when told not to do something, or they may simply be more interested in viewing violence than other children.

As indicated earlier, data regarding the reasons for children's choices are only suggestive because the study was not designed to permit a definitive analysis of the underlying mechanisms. The NTVS research conducted for Year 2 was designed with potential explanations in mind, however. In the Year 2 research, after completing a selective exposure booklet, children filled out a second booklet, evaluating the same programs with the same ratings and advisories that they had just seen. For each program, they rated how violent and how scary they expected it to be, and they indicated the age of viewer that the program seemed to be intended for. Through this design, we will be better able to see how children's perception of the characteristics of a program are related to their eagerness to see it.

How Well Do MPAA Ratings Distinguish the Content of Movies?

There is one further aspect of the research conducted in Year 1 of the National Television Violence Study that seems relevant both to the development of the new ratings system and to the usefulness of ratings for parents. That aspect relates to the degree to which MPAA ratings consistently reflect the amount and type of controversial content present in a movie. MPAA ratings have sometimes been criticized for being summary judgments, and for not communicating the specific content that prompted a particular rating.

One way to determine how well MPAA ratings correspond with various forms of content is to look at the movies that appeared on television in the Year 1 sample of the NTVS research. Although we have not yet related the actual violent content of movies to their MPAA ratings, our approach here was to look at those movies that displayed MPAA ratings and were evaluated according to the content codes currently being employed by the three premium channels in the sample (HBO, Cinemax, and Showtime). These codes include notations for adult content, nudity, violence, and language. The codes are assigned by the channel showing the movie and presumably reflect what personnel employed by the channel perceive to exist in the film.

In the Year 1 sample, we identified 188 movies that displayed an MPAA rating and appeared on one of the three premium channels. Figures 7.9a through 7.9d display how a movie's MPAA rating related to its assignment to content codes by the channel showing it. Only 12 movies in the sample were rated G, and, as can be seen from the figure, only one of these (8 percent) displayed any of the content codes. Specifically, one G rated movie contained "mild violence." Looking at the high end of the MPAA system, in contrast, the 38 R rated movies in the sample contained a great deal of controversial content. Eighty-five percent or more of these movies displayed codes indicating adult content, violence, and language, and 61 percent displayed a nudity code. Further analysis of these codes revealed that 50 percent of the R rated movies contained codes indicating content in all four areas.

Whereas these content codes suggest that the MPAA ratings of G and R were well warranted by the movies' contents (as viewed by the premium channel personnel), the content codes for PG and PG-13 suggest a great deal of overlap between these two rating levels ($N = 68$ and 70, respectively). According to the figure, the levels of PG and PG-13 are somewhat distinguishable in terms of content related to sexuality (47 percent vs. 62 percent, respectively, for adult content), but not in terms of violence or language. The percentage of movies with adult language is actually slightly smaller for PG-13 than for PG (76 percent vs. 80 percent, respectively). Moreover, the same percentage of PG and PG-13 movies contained violence codes (62 percent), with the only difference being a shift of 7 percent of movies from the "mild violence" to the "violence" category when moving from PG to PG-13.

What this means is that for 138, or 73 percent of the movies in the sample, the MPAA ratings of PG and PG-13 signal virtually the same probability of encountering violence and adult language. This suggests that these ratings are perhaps somewhat helpful for parents interested in shielding their child from sex-

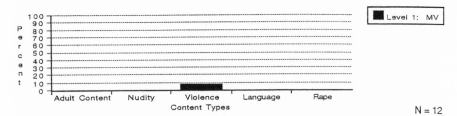

Fig. 7.9a.   Percentage of G rated movies having each content code

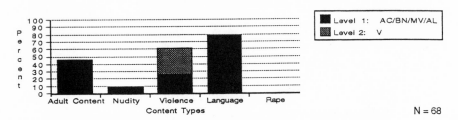

Fig. 7.9b.   Percentage of PG rated movies having each content code

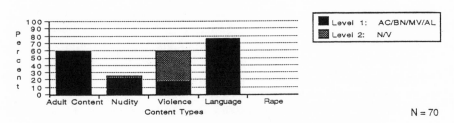

Fig. 7.9c.   Percentage of PG-13 rated movies having each content code

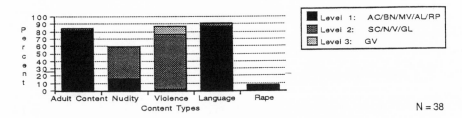

Fig. 7.9d.   Percentage of R rated movies having each content code

KEY: Adult Content Codes: AC = Adult Content, SC = Strong Sexual Content
       Nudity Codes: BN = Brief Nudity, N = Nudity
       Violence Codes: MV = Mild Violence, V = Violence, GV = Graphic Violence
       Language Codes: AL = Adult Language, GL = Graphic Language

Fig. 7.9.   Relationship of MPAA ratings to content codes—year 1 NTVS sample

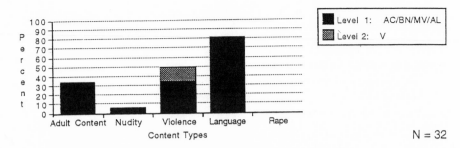

Fig. 7.10a. Percentage of PG rated movies having each content code

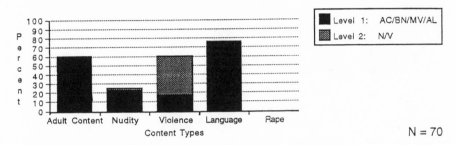

Fig. 7.10b. Percentage of PG-13 rated movies having each content code

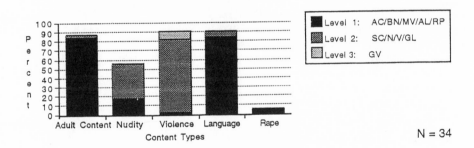

Fig. 7.10c. Percentage of R rated movies having each content code

Fig. 7.10. Relationship of MPAA ratings to content codes—post-1983 NTVS sample. (None of the post-1983 "G" rated movies ($n = 6$) contained any of the above content codes. All "PG-13" rated movies were made in 1984 or later.)

ual content, but not for those interested in protecting their child from violence or offensive language.

It must be taken into account, however, that the PG-13 rating was not introduced until 1984. It is possible, therefore, that the enormous overlap between PG and PG-13 in our sample was due to the presence of a large number of

PG rated movies that were produced before the PG-13 rating was available. In order to test this possibility, we reran the same analyses, limiting the sample to movies that came out in 1984 or later. Figures 7.10a through 7.10c present these analyses.

These analyses revealed that only 6 of the 12 G rated movies in the original sample were from 1984 or after. None of these was associated with any of the content codes for adult content, nudity, violence, or language. Figures 7.10a, 7.10b, and 7.10c show how PG, PG-13, and R rated post-1983 movies in the sample related to their assignment to content codes. The first thing to notice is that elimination of the pre-1984 films reduced the sample of PG rated movies from 68 to 32. Therefore, more than half of the PG rated movies in the original sample were produced before the MPAA system made a distinction between PG and PG-13. By definition, none of the PG-13 movies in the sample were eliminated in this second analysis, because this rating did not exist until 1984. Finally, only 4 of the R rated movies in the sample were released before 1984. This left 34 such movies in the post-1983 sample.

Figures 7.10a and 7.10b reveal that PG and PG-13 movies were somewhat better differentiated in the post-1983 period. Although these two ratings are still not distinguishable in terms of language content (with PG again slightly exceeding PG-13 in adult language), a slightly higher portion of PG-13 than PG movies had violence codes, and PG-13 had a heavier weighting of "V = Violence" relative to "MV = Mild Violence." One important problem that is brought to light by this analysis, however, is that parents need to be informed that the PG rating must be interpreted in conjunction with the date of a movie's release. Any parent who feels comfortable with PG, but not PG-13 rated movies, should be warned that this level of comfort should extend only to movies issued after 1983.

A more basic problem with MPAA ratings is that they do not specify which type of content led to the movie's assignment to a particular rating. A parent who is concerned with violence but not language, for example, cannot tell from the rating itself whether the movie received its rating because of one or both or neither of these types of content.

To determine the frequency with which the various MPAA ratings were associated with language, violence, and sex, alone or in various combinations, we conducted a further analysis. For the sake of simplicity, we combined the "adult content" and "nudity" codes into a single category suggesting sexual content. We then determined, for each MPAA rating, what percentage of the post-1983 movies in the sample contained each of these three types of content and all possible combinations thereof.

Figures 7.11a through 7.11c show these distributions for the movies rated PG, PG-13, and R in the post-1983 sample. As can be seen from figure 7.11a, 22 percent of PG rated movies contained language only, 6 percent contained sex

Fig. 7.11a. Distribution of language, sex, and violence in PG rated movies (*N* = 32)

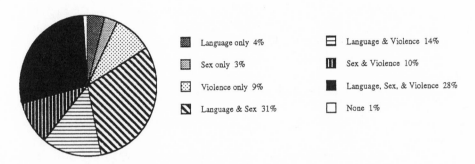

Fig. 7.11b. Distribution of language, sex, and violence in PG-13 rated movies (*N* = 70)

Fig. 7.11c. Distribution of language, sex, and violence in R rated movies (*N* = 34)

Fig. 7.11. Distribution of content codes in MPAA rated movies in post-1983 NTVS sample

only, and 13 percent contained violence only. Another 22 percent contained only language and sex, and 28 percent contained only language and violence. Clearly, there are many possible combinations of potentially problematic material that could be represented by a PG rating. Therefore a mother, for example, who is largely concerned about violence only or sex only, but is unconcerned about language, is not given specific enough information to make a viewing decision for her child. And given the paucity of G rated movies, this puts her in a difficult position regarding the availability of suitable movies on television.

The variety of content combinations represented by the PG-13 rating are shown in figure 7.10b. Only with the R rating, shown in figure 7.10c, is the doubt minimized, since almost 80 percent of these movies contained the three forms of objectionable content: sex, violence, and language.

This analysis highlights the importance of developing a ratings system that would provide specific information about different types of content. National surveys conducted in the fall of 1996 show that parents are aware of the problems associated with age-based ratings and strongly prefer ratings that provide them with specific information about the content of each program (Cantor, Stutman, and Duran 1996; Silver and Geier 1996).

Implications and Recommendations

Advice to Parents

Our findings have some direct implications for parents as they struggle with the problem of protecting their children from exposure to inappropriate television content. One is that the process of parental guidance of children's television viewing is perilous and paradoxical. Conscientious parents, who want to protect their children, need to recognize the potential hazards of imposing restrictions. Saying that something is forbidden may pique the interest of some children. One solution to this problem would be to use the V-chip when it becomes available. This device could potentially block out programs without actively calling the child's attention to the program being censored. This approach will have obvious limitations, however, especially when dealing with children who are highly motivated to circumvent the restrictions, and who may well have more technological savvy than their parents.

Another approach might be to involve the child somehow in the decision-making process, making the restriction seem more like a consensual judgment than an edict delivered from "on high." The fact that "viewer discretion advised," an admonition that leaves it to the viewers themselves, did not serve as a magnet suggests that involving children in decision making might make them feel less controlled by the parent and less motivated to rebel against the restrictions.

The findings with regard to parental involvement in children's viewing seem relevant in this regard as well. It will be recalled that children who rated their parents as more involved in their television viewing were less likely than others to choose programs with advisories and movies with more restrictive ratings. Perhaps this parental involvement makes the purpose behind ratings and advisories more understandable and more acceptable to the child.

Finally, parents need to be reminded that the television industry has said that the new ratings system is subject to modification if parents do not find it useful. It is hoped that parents will make their voices heard and insist that the ratings system that is ultimately adopted provide them with useful information in the manner least likely to attract their children to inappropriate content.

Implications for the New Ratings System

The findings of this research have direct implications for the formulation and evaluation of a ratings system for television content.

1. *Effects on children's interest in programs must be taken into consideration.* This research has clearly demonstrated that ratings and advisories are not for parents only. Ratings and advisories that are available to children have the potential to affect their interest in programs. In some cases, the labels will have their intended effects of discouraging viewing, while in others, they will serve as a magnet for a larger child audience.

2. *Different forms of ratings and advisories have different effects.* Some advisories are more "magnetic" than others. "Parental discretion advised" served as a magnet for boys and especially older boys, but "viewer discretion advised" did not. The MPAA rating of PG-13 attracted viewers in all groups but the younger girls, and R attracted the older boys. Some labels may be more tactful than others. "Parental discretion advised," while appearing euphemistic to an adult, may be received as a challenge or a lure to a teenage boy.

On the other hand, some advisories have their intended effects on some viewers. In our study, "viewer discretion advised" was used sensibly by girls, especially younger girls, and both types of advisories were used by children who had earlier been upset by television, to avoid programming that they had reason to be wary of.

3. *The evidence for the forbidden fruit theory was stronger than that for the information-based rationale.* The reason for the magnetic effect of "parental discretion advised" and not of "viewer discretion advised" was best explained by the reactance notion. Although "parental discretion advised" conveyed perceptions of less violent content than "viewer discretion advised," it made the programming more attractive to boys, presumably because it implied stronger attempts at parental control.

4. *The new ratings system for television seems likely to engender the same "forbidden fruit" effect that the MPAA ratings system produced in our studies.* Like the

MPAA system, the "TV Parental Guidelines" make recommendations that children of different ages be shielded from viewing, and they use phrases such as "parental guidance suggested" and "parents strongly cautioned" that emphasize the parents' role.

5. *MPAA ratings have developed a reputation with children, and it is not unreasonable to expect that this reputation will generalize to the similar new television system.* Many children have come to believe, as one child in our study did, that "the cooler the movie, the higher the rating." Given the attitudes of many children, it is perhaps not surprising that so few G rated movies were found in the NTVS sample. Moreover, a TV-14 or TV-MA rating (the equivalents of the MPAA's PG-13 and R, respectively) might be actively sought out by advertisers, especially those who are seeking an audience of teenage males.

6. *Another problem with MPAA ratings (and TV Parental Guidelines) is that you cannot tell what is in the show from the rating.* These ratings are summary judgments that represent evaluations of a show's content in terms of language, violence, or sex, among other things. So when a parent sees a PG rating for a movie, or a TV-PG rating for a program, he or she does not know if that rating was assigned because of language, violence, sex, or a combination of some or all of these. Our analysis of the NTVS sample of movies revealed that PG and PG-13 movies have considerable overlap in contents. Moreover, the levels PG and PG-13 both contain a variety of combinations of potentially objectionable content that different parents might feel are differentially offensive.

7. *These data strongly support the recommendation that a television ratings system stress content rather than who should or should not see a program.* This recommendation is based on the expectations that content-based ratings will prove to make the labeled programs less attractive than age-based ratings and that they will communicate better with parents. As mentioned earlier, this choice is also consistent with the preferences of parents (Cantor et al. 1996; Silver and Geier 1996).

8. *Another reason why content-based labels are recommended is that they are less prone to the "eye-of-the-beholder" phenomenon.* What is TV-14 to the producer of one program might be TV-PG or TV-MA to another. But producers and viewers should be less likely to disagree on whether or not a murder or a rape, for example, occurred in the program. In one of the national surveys mentioned earlier, parents rated the content based-system employed by HBO, Showtime, and Cinemax as significantly more objective than the age-based MPAA ratings (Cantor et al. 1996).

9. *Most importantly, any ratings system for television must be designed to meet parents' desires and needs.* The sole purpose of the new ratings system is to help parents shield their children from content they do not wish them to be exposed to. There is no point in having a ratings system that does not serve the

purpose for which it was intended. It would be sadly ironic if we ended up with a system that makes parents' jobs even harder than it is now.

REFERENCES

Austin, B. A. 1980. "The Influence of the MPAA's Film-Rating System on Motion Picture Attendance: A Pilot Study." *Journal of Psychology* 106:91–99.

Brehm, J. W., and S. S. Brehm. 1981. *Psychological Reactance.* New York: Wiley.

Bushman, B. J., and A. D. Stack. 1996. "Forbidden Fruit versus Tainted Fruit: Effects of Warning Labels on Attraction to Television Violence." *Journal of Experimental Psychology: Applied* 2:207–26.

Cantor, J., and K. Harrison. 1997. "Ratings and Advisories for Television Programs." In *National Television Violence Study, Volume 1,* 361–410. Thousand Oaks, CA: Sage.

Cantor, J., S. Stutman, and V. Duran. 1996. *What Parents Want in a Television Rating System: Results of a National Survey.* Report released by the National PTA, the Institute for Mental Health Initiatives, and the University of Wisconsin-Madison.

Christenson, P. 1992. "The Effects of Parental Advisory Labels on Adolescent Music Preferences." *Journal of Communication* 42(1): 106–13.

Federman, J. 1996. *Media Ratings: Design, Use and Consequences.* Studio City, CA: Mediascope.

Hamilton, J. T. 1994. *Marketing Violence: The Impact of Labeling Violent Television Content.* Paper presented at the International Conference on Violence in the Media. New York: St. John's University.

Herman, G., and J. P. Leyens. 1977. "Rating Films on TV." *Journal of Communication* 27(4): 48–53.

National Television Violence Study, Volume 1. 1997. Thousand Oaks, CA: Sage.

Ratings Implementation Group. 1997. Letter to William F. Caton, Secretary, Federal Communications Commission, January 17.

Silver, M., and T. Geier. 1996. "Ready for Prime Time?" *U.S. News & World Report,* September 9: 54–61.

Wurtzel, A., and S. Surlin. 1978. "Viewer Attitudes toward Television Advisory Warnings." *Journal of Broadcasting* 22:19–31.

Chapter 8

Does Viewer Discretion Prompt Advertiser Discretion? The Impact of Violence Warnings on the Television Advertising Market

James T. Hamilton

As the industry committee headed by Motion Picture Association of America president Jack Valenti struggled in 1996 to develop a television program ratings system, a public debate ensued over what type of information parents "wanted" to help guide their family viewing decisions. The National PTA, in conjunction with Professor Joanne Cantor, produced a survey indicating that when faced with a choice between "an overall summary rating of a program" or "separate ratings for different types of content, such as violence, sex, and language," 80 percent of the parents surveyed preferred the content-based information to a single summary rating for a program.[1] The industry committee, however, initially developed an age-based system television ratings system that did not specify the presence or intensity of violent or sexual content. Valenti argued that parents actually wanted summary ratings rather than extensive content information because these were "simple to use and easy to understand."[2] Less evident in the public debate but as central to the concern of the industry's committee deliberations were the information demands of another group interested in program ratings: companies that advertise on broadcast and cable television. Content ratings offered the prospect of linking advertisers more directly to content deemed objectionable by consumers. This chapter uses advertiser reactions to an early form of program information, parental discretion advisories, to investigate the impact of program labeling on advertiser behavior.

Television networks sell audiences to advertisers by offering programs to viewers. While ratings data track who watches particular programs, commercials reveal which viewers are targeted by the firms that sponsor programs. This chapter focuses on how the products and firms that advertise on television programs differ between violent and nonviolent programs and vary across different types of violent shows. The analysis also explores how broadcasters and sponsors react to the placement of viewer discretion warnings on programs, which may raise the probability that firms will become involved in controversy because of their sponsorship of violent shows. Two sets of data, a sample of 19,000 commercials from movies on prime-time network broadcast television and 5,700 advertisements from programs on four cable channels, are used to test a model that predicts how firms decide to advertise on violent programming and how companies will react to viewer discretion warnings.

The exact impact of program content warnings on advertiser decisions is an open empirical question. When entertainment executives announced an agreement on February 29, 1996, to rate television programs for violent and sexual content, opinions varied widely on how advertisers would react to the content rating system. Ted Turner, president of Turner Broadcasting Systems, stated that the ratings system would "cost us quite a bit of money because there are going to be a lot of advertisers, when the programs are rated, that consider themselves family-oriented companies that are not going to want to advertise in programs that carry parental guidance warnings." He predicted that "there will be more 'Brady Bunch'-type programming and less what we call cutting edge programming."[3] The president of ABC, Robert Iger, disagreed with the notion that warnings would cause an advertiser exodus, since companies already are sensitive to program content in their advertising decisions.[4]

Some in the entertainment industry felt that the warnings could spur more violent programming. As Dick Wolf, the producer of the crime drama *Law and Order*, put it, "If all these shows have warnings on them, you could have a situation where producers are saying to standards people at the networks, 'I've got a warning. I can say whatever I want. I can kill as many people as I want.'"[5] Advertisers explained that a warning such as an R rating on a program could have an additional impact on the decision whether to sponsor the program. The rating could make it more likely a company would be targeted by interest groups concerned about violence and sexual content. Philip Guarascio, president of marketing and advertising at General Motors, believed that ratings could become red flags that drew interest group attention: "We want to sell our cars and trucks to a broad audience, but you cannot ignore external forces. We're a highly visible company, so we're under a magnifying glass."[6] Predictions about advertiser reactions to ratings thus include a massive migration of sponsors away from controversial programs, an increase in the violence levels on rated programs, and a marginal adjustment in sponsorship decisions to the additional information conveyed by warnings.

This chapter develops a theory of the reaction of broadcasters and advertisers to program warnings and tests explicit hypotheses about these reactions with a unique data set of more than 19,000 commercials from a sample of 251 movies broadcast on prime-time network television from May 1995 through February 1996. The networks placed viewer discretion warnings on 14 percent of the prime-time films broadcast during this time period, which were often stated as, "Due to some violent content, parental discretion is advised." Program warnings on prime-time movies lower viewership by children 2 to 11 by approximately 14 percent.[7] They have no net impact on the viewership of adults, perhaps because viewers drawn to violent programs are likely to know the content without the addition of a warning label. Even if the magnitudes of adult audiences for prime-time movies are not affected by warnings, however, advertisers may react to the labeling of a movie if they believe that this will increase the likelihood of companies being targeted by interest groups or increase the probability their brand images could be damaged by controversy.

Advertiser reactions to program warnings will vary depending on the audience for a broadcast film, the demographic makeup of a company's customer base, and the attitudes of viewers and consumers toward violent television. The prime adult consumers of violent television programming are men 18 to 34, followed by women 18 to 34 and men 35 to 49. These groups are less likely to view violent television as harmful to society or to believe it is a major cause of breakdown in law and order.[8] Companies that appeal primarily to these demographic groups may face little or no backlash from their customers from advertising on violent films. Firms whose consumers include older viewers or whose products are aimed primarily at females (both groups that report higher frustration with violent programming) may face a greater risk of offending their customer base by advertising on labeled programs. If this theory of firm incentives is correct, then warning labels may cause the demographic mix of products to shift on violent films with warnings toward goods that have higher use among young or male consumers.

Viewer demand for a program determines the profit-maximizing number of "nonprogram" (e.g., commercial) minutes per hour on prime-time movies. If a warning label is placed on a film, the supply of commercial minutes will remain the same but the demand for advertising sponsorship may drop because some firms may fear a consumer backlash from advertising on a show with warnings. The consequent drop in price means that networks may run more public service announcements and more promotions for their own programs on movies that carry viewer discretion warnings, since the cost in terms of forgone commercial prices will be lower on these films. Although in the longer run the networks' use of violent versus nonviolent films may also change as returns to programs change, this chapter investigates the short-run changes in the mix of advertisers and use of commercial time caused by program warnings.

The results from analysis of the broadcast network data set of more than 19,000 commercials indicate that warnings on prime-time network movies do change broadcaster and advertiser incentives. Broadcasters run more network promotions and fewer general product advertisements on theatrical films with warnings, consistent with the theory that warnings cause advertiser pullouts that lower prices. Violent theatrical films with warnings are more likely to have products aimed at younger consumers, males, and households without children. Products in industries aimed at these consumers, such as alcoholic beverages or sports and leisure, are more likely to advertise on theatrical movies with warnings. Products from industries where "family" brand images are important, such as food or kitchen products, are less likely to sponsor advertisements on theatrical films with warnings. Advertisers also react to warnings on made-for-television movies, though not as strongly as to warnings placed on violent theatrical films. The results underscore the incentives that determine why broadcasters and advertisers support violent programming and how they react to providing information about television content to viewers.

The second set of results focuses on how the audiences targeted by advertisers on cable vary across different types of violent programming. The cable data set consists of 5,700 commercials aired from noon to midnight on violent movies or series during the week of April 1 through 7, 1995, on TBS, TNT, USA, and WKFT (an independent broadcast station in the Raleigh–Durham television market). This yielded a set of 146 programs, which was supplemented with the addition of all movies (21) that carried viewer discretion warnings on these channels during the remainder of April. Analysis of the products advertised on these cable channels reveals that within the set of "violent" programs there are substantial differences in the audiences targeted by advertisers. Products advertised on crime series were more likely to be aimed at younger viewers than those on mystery series, consistent with the evidence from Nielsen ratings that the mystery genre attracts older viewers.[9] Violent cable series are more likely to have products aimed at women than violent movies, consistent with the indications from syndicated violent series ratings data that young women view series programming in violent genres. Programs on the local independent station, WKFT, were more likely to have products aimed at men, consistent with the finding from the *National Television Violence Study* (*NTVS*) that violent programs on independent stations are more likely to contain a higher number of violent interactions.[10] The differences between products advertised on violent cable movies with warnings and those without warnings are not as stark as those observed on broadcast network television movies. This may be due to the fact that advertising on cable channels or independent stations is not monitored by groups such as the American Family Association (AFA), so firms are less likely to experience a backlash for supporting violent programming on these channels. This underscores the role that anticipated scrutiny plays in the decision by firms to advertise on violent programs.

After a brief review of the literature on program warnings, I develop theories of the reactions of viewers, advertisers, and broadcasters to the use of program warnings. I next describe the data and results from the tests on prime-time network movies, followed by an analysis of the advertisements on violent cable movies and series. These results demonstrate that the advertising audiences for violent programs do vary as predicted by the models developed here and that the reactions of advertisers and broadcasters to the provision of information about program content are consistent with a concern about the potential backlash from publicity about sponsoring violent shows.

Viewer, Advertiser, and Broadcaster Reactions to Program Warnings

Viewer Reactions

In 1993 broadcast networks and cable programmers voluntarily adopted a new policy of providing viewers with information about violent program content. Each network promised to provide parental advisories on a violent show, use audio and visual warnings when the program was broadcast, and include the warning in all promotions for the show. Three studies have since examined the impact of discretion warnings on viewer behavior. In an experimental setting where children were given descriptions of programs to select for viewing, Cantor and Harrison (1996) found that, on net, children's selections of reality-action programs were not influenced by a parental advisory (e.g., "Parental discretion advised"). Boys 10 to 14, however, were more likely to select programs with a parental discretion advisory. If the warning is phrased as "viewer discretion advised," children overall and especially girls 5 to 9 were less likely to select the program. The influence of MPAA ratings similarly varied by age and gender. The authors found that "although younger children and girls showed a tendency to shy away from the movie when it had the restrictive rating 'R,' older boys were attracted to the more restrictive ratings and avoided the 'G' rating."[11] In a separate experiment, Cantor and Krcmar (1996) found that when a parent and child were offered the chance to select programs to watch, the joint decision was nearly always to avoid programs with parental discretion warnings. The authors note that the increased interest by boys in movies and programs with parental discretion warnings and PG-13 or R ratings suggests a need to study further how ratings are used and interpreted by children. In chapter 7, Cantor, Harrison, and Krcmar conclude that program ratings similar to those developed by the MPAA would be problematic because they provide parents with little content information while stimulating children's potential interest in programs.

Bushman and Stack (1996) found experimental evidence that warning labels can increase interest among college students in violent films. Students reported an increased interest in viewing movies labeled with warnings, especially when the U.S. Surgeon General was mentioned in the warning. If the viewer advisory is phrased as informational (e.g., "This film contains some violence") rather than as a warning (e.g., "Viewer discretion is advised"), students were not more attracted to violent films with the informational label. These results, combined with those of Cantor et al., indicate the importance of investigating how ratings are worded and understood by different demographic groups.

Most relevant to the study of advertiser reactions to warnings on prime-time movies are the results presented in Hamilton 1998 that analyze Nielsen ratings data for 2,295 prime-time broadcast network television movies aired from 1987 to 1993, 2 percent of which had viewer discretion warnings. Regression results indicate that, controlling for variables that influence audience size such as movie genre, program starting time, day and month, and network, warnings reduced the viewership by children 2 to 11 by nearly 14 percent. This means that movies that carried a broadcast warning had approximately 222,000 fewer children in their audience. In regression models of ratings among teens and adults, warnings had no independent effect on audience size. These results are consistent with warnings being used by parents to intervene in the viewing decision of young children. Warnings may not affect viewership among adults since those likely to watch violent films may not find any additional information conveyed by the presence of a warning.

Advertiser Reactions

Nearly 70 percent of advertising spots on network prime time are sold in the spring and early summer before the start of the television season. In this "upfront market," which totaled $5.6 billion in 1995, companies buy advertising on particular series and movies scheduled for the new season without knowing the exact content of the given episodes their advertisements will run on.[12] The networks reserve 30 percent of the advertisements for the scatter market, which allows them to provide companies with additional commercial time if ratings were not delivered on earlier shows and allows them to sell advertisements on a spot market closer to the air time of the program. Once a prime-time program or movie is finished advertisers can learn the content of the episode through prescreening by a specialized firm or their advertising agency. Advertisers may then pull out of their sponsorship agreement if they have concerns about content or a warning label.

Research by Montgomery (1989) and Cowan (1979) details how advertisers often recoil from being associated with controversial television programming. For a company, an advertisement on a prime-time network movie represents a significant investment. Reported advertising prices for a 30-second slot on prime-time movies in November 1995 ranged from $90,000 to $150,000 depending on the evening and network.[13] To avoid sponsoring programs that may generate controversy for a particular product, firms often hire a company in New York (AIS) to prescreen prime-time network programs and alert them to content concerns, including violent and sexual content. Even without network warnings, major advertisers are thus apprised of the content of programs such as prime-time movies.

If firms find a program too controversial, they may pull their advertising from the show. Broadcasters may end up selling this advertising time at reduced rates or not selling it at all. The costs of controversy will vary by program and network. Robert Iger, president of Capital Cities/ABC, estimated that the network loses nearly $20 million in advertising revenues each year because of decisions by sponsors to avoid controversial programs.[14] Statistical analysis of advertisement rates for the first season of *NYPD Blue* indicates that relative to the demographics of the audience it was attracting the program was selling at a discount of at least 40 percent.[15] Producer Dick Wolf estimates that NBC lost $800,000 in advertising revenues on a single episode of *Law and Order* that focused on bombings at abortion clinics.[16] Industry estimates of the cost to a network of placing an advisory on prime-time movies run to $1 million in lost advertising per show (Federman 1996).[17]

Broadcaster Reactions

If warnings generate problems for some advertisers, then one would expect that broadcast networks would attempt to avoid placing advisories on shows that contain violence and that cable programmers would be more willing to use advisories since they are less reliant on advertisers for revenue. Recent research bears out both these predictions. For the 1994–95 television season, Cole (*UCLA Television Violence Monitoring Report* 1995) found that of 161 made-for-television movies and miniseries on the four broadcast networks, 23 raised issues of concern with respect to violence. Only 6 carried viewer warnings. Of 118 theatrical films shown on prime-time network television that were examined by the UCLA group, 50 were found to raise concerns about their use of violence. Yet only 28 of these films had viewer discretion warnings. Overall, Cole's work demonstrates that for the 1994–95 television season the networks were placing advisories on less than half of the violent films that outside reviewers found raised issues of concern with their use of violence.

The *NTVS* (1996b) found that in their sample of 2,445 programs examined from broadcast and cable television, 4 percent carried viewer advisories. Nearly half of these advisories came from one premium channel, Showtime. Premium cable channels were much more likely to provide detailed information on content relating to violence and sexual content for the movies they aired than broadcast channels. Since premium channels rely on subscription rather than advertiser support, they do not face the same potential for backlash as broadcasters do in terms of labeling. Of the programs containing violence in this sample, 75 percent of those on premium cable had some type of viewer advisory before the program versus 3 percent for the violent programs aired on broadcast stations affiliated with the networks.[18]

Academic and anecdotal evidence offer a mixed assessment of the impact of viewer advisories. Some viewers, especially children 2 to 11, may be deterred from watching movies with warnings. Some advertisers may choose to avoid labeled programs for fear of being targeted by pressure groups. Faced with advertising losses, the networks place viewer discretion warnings on only some of the films that merit them because of violent content. The following sections develop more precise theories about how advertisers will react to warnings and assess the independent impact of program warnings on who advertises on violent programs and how much paid advertising is aired on these programs.

Theories of Viewer, Advertiser, and Broadcaster Reactions

Viewer Incentives

Warnings on prime-time movies provide information to individuals in their roles as parents, viewers, and consumers. Consider first a parent trying to shield a child from programs with violent content. The benefits of steering a child away from violent programming include a reduction in the probability the child will be stimulated to short-term or longer-run aggression, will be frightened by the content, or will become desensitized by violence. The costs to a parent of monitoring television viewing involve deciding what programs contain violence or other content the parent finds objectionable, determining when these programs air, and taking steps to prevent the child from watching these shows. Program ratings or warnings will increase monitoring by some parents because this information lowers the transaction costs of determining what is violent and when violent programs are aired. The value that parents place on shielding their children from programming will vary, since parents will differ in their opinions about the influence of particular programs. The costs to parents of monitoring will also vary, especially for parents at work while their children are viewing. While parental notices will not reduce violent television consumption for all children, these warnings will reduce viewing by the children of some parents since their costs of monitoring will be lowered. Warnings on prime-time movies may be particularly effective since parents may be more likely to be at home in prime time and thus be able to intervene more readily in viewing decisions.

The independent impact of a warning on viewers' own decisions about whether to watch a program will depend in part on how much information consumers already have about the particular product. A television series may be sampled over a period of weeks so that viewers can assess likely content. Prime-time movies on television may at first glance appear to present a viewer with greater uncertainty about content, since they are not part of a continuing series with an established brand identity. Nearly 35 percent of the movies shown on the four broadcast networks in prime time have previously been released in the theater, so that viewers may be familiar with reviews of the given film or the work of specific actors. Television reviews also provide data on story lines and genre so that viewers will develop assessments of likely content. Viewers most likely to be attracted to violent films, e.g., males and younger viewers, may be more likely to be familiar with the violent movies offered. The sparse amount of information conveyed in the warnings (e.g., "Due to some violent content, parental discretion is advised") may also mean that the information does not change assessments of content a great deal among those likely to view. While warnings may thus convey information to some viewers, those likely to watch violent programs may already know the content of the particular films likely to be shown on prime-time broadcast television.

Psychologists note that labels can change the nature of the good consumed, so that the warning may affect the utility derived from watching a film. Bushman and Stack (1996) describe how the placement of a warning on a film may attract some viewers to the program if they view prohibited actions as more appealing. Other viewers may derive less utility from a program if it is labeled in a way that indicates the program is objectionable. The net impact on viewing would depend on the wording of the warning and the extent that viewers exhibit these "forbidden fruit" and "tainted fruit" reactions.

Television warnings and ratings also provide information to individuals in their roles as consumers and citizens. Groups such as the AFA often target companies that sponsor violent programs for consumer boycotts. The AFA, led by the Rev. Donald Wildmon, mails updates each year to its members that track the top 12 sponsors of violence on prime-time network programming.[19] The group determines these ratings by monitoring a sample of programming and developing an index of a company's sponsorship of sex, violence, and profanity based on the number of commercials on shows with content perceived to be objectionable by the AFA. At times the group targets specific companies (such as Unilever) for boycotts, while at other times the threat of a boycott is used to sway company advertising policies. Some companies studiously attempt to avoid landing on the AFA list, while others take efforts to explain that their place on the ranking is due to support of controversial programming such as *NYPD Blue*.[20]

A person contemplating whether to boycott a product because she objected to the company's sponsorship of violent programming would trade off the benefits of this action with its costs. The net benefits of a boycott to an individual are captured by (Perceived benefits of reduced television violence brought about by a drop in corporate sponsorship) x (Probability a person's action will lead a company to change its advertising policies) + (Ideological satisfaction of participating in a boycott) - (Costs of learning about company sponsorship policies and costs of switching to another product to replace a boycotted item). Since the probability of influencing a company's policy is nearly zero for any individual, the returns to boycotting are negative unless a person derives a feeling of satisfaction from "doing the right thing" by participating in a boycott. This logic of collective action (Olson 1971) explains why most people do not boycott companies even though they feel that there is too much violence on television. Although the majority of viewers in a 1993 Roper poll said they had seen something "personally offensive or morally objectionable" on television within the previous few weeks, only 1 percent said they had stopped buying a product advertised on a program the last time they had been offended. Instead, 45 percent said they simply turned the channel (Roper 1993).

Though consumer boycotts are thus unlikely to attract large numbers of participants, companies may still fear being the targets of such efforts. Even a small percentage of customers participating may translate into lost sales. In addition, a company's brand identity may be damaged by the association with controversy. Consumers' reactions to a product could thus be negatively affected even if they were not consciously attempting to boycott a firm. Advertising on labeled films could thus appear less attractive to particular firms if they felt that the warnings made it more likely that they could be accused of supporting "violent television."

Advertiser Incentives

Firms advertising on prime-time broadcast movies explicitly face a decision of how much advertising time to buy on nonviolent versus violent programs. The prior theatrical runs for a third of prime-time movies and information from prescreening by advertising agencies and the networks provide companies with detailed information on the content of prime-time movies. The sales generated for a firm by advertising on violent programs are a function of how many advertisements the company purchases, what the ratings among different demographic groups are for these shows, and what the demographics of the purchasers of a company's products are.[21] If a program achieves a 5 rating among men 18 to 34, this translates into exposure of 1.6 million men in this demographic to a commercial sponsored by the firm.[22] The more men in this age group who use or potentially might use this product, the more likely these exposures would translate into additional sales. Sales revenues from nonviolent programs are similarly a function of the number of advertisements bought on these shows, the ratings for these programs, and the demographics of a company's customers. Total advertising costs are the sum of the price of the advertisements multiplied by the number of advertisements in each program category.

The potential for a backlash against a company advertising on violent television introduces another element for a firm to consider in advertising decisions. Advertising on a violent program may increase the likelihood a firm will be targeted for a boycott or increase the probability a firm's brand name will be damaged by association with controversy. Either of these effects translates into lower expected sales. The backlash will be higher the more advertisements bought on shows and the higher the ratings (and hence exposures to violence) of the programs. The amount of information available on whether a firm has advertised on violent programs will also influence the expected size of the backlash because it will raise the probability that people are aware of the firm's advertising practices. If the movie carries a warning, this will lower the cost to interest groups or individuals of linking a firm with violent programming and hence raise the potential backlash. The demographics of a firm's customers will also influence the expected loss in sales. If young consumers or males constitute a higher percentage of a firm's customers, the expected backlash from advertising on violent programs will be lower since these consumers are less likely to believe violent television is a serious public policy problem.

The firm's advertising decision can be modeled as follows. The firm chooses the amount of advertising time to purchase on violent programs (Q_v) and nonviolent shows (Q_{nv}), which have ratings R_v and R_{nv} and ad prices P_v and P_{nv}. Sales generated by these advertisements will in part be a function of the demographic characteristics α_i of a company's customers. For example, the higher the percentage of customers in the 18 to 34 age group the more sales generated by advertising on violent shows (since these programs have a higher percentage of 18 to 34 viewers) and the lower the sales generated by nonviolent programs (which have a lower percentage of 18 to 34 viewers). Relevant demographic characteristics for this decision include the age and gender distribution of a company's customers. Sales from advertising on violent programs (*VS*) and nonviolent programs (*NS*) are thus $VS(Q_v, R_v, \alpha_i) + NS(Q_{nv}, R_{nv}, \alpha_i)$. If everyone were fully informed about the advertising practices of a firm, the backlash (*BL*) of lost sales from consumer reaction to the news that a firm advertises on violent programs would be a function of Q_v, R_v, α_i. The likelihood that this backlash will occur depends on the amount of information people have on the firm's advertising on violent programs. If a program carries a viewer discretion warning, for example, this makes targeting by interest groups more likely and thus press coverage more likely. The expected loss in sales is thus a product of the "fully informed" backlash BL and the function $A(I)$, which represents the probability the backlash will occur as a function of information available about the firm's advertising. The firm will maximize profits here by maximizing the expression $VS(Q_v, R_v, \alpha_i) + NS(Q_{nv}, R_{nv}, \alpha_i) - A(I)BL(Q_v, R_v, \alpha_i) - P_vQ_v - P_{nv}Q_{nv}$.

Appendix 8.1 describes the solution to the model and comparative statics results. When the firm is maximizing profits, we find that

$$\frac{VS_{Q_v} - A(I) - BL_{Q_v}}{P_v} = \frac{NS_{Q_{nv}}}{P_{nv}}$$

This means that when profits from advertising are maximized the company will make advertising purchases $\bar{Q}_v$ and $\bar{Q}_{nv}$ so that the return per dollar spent on violent program advertisements equals the return per dollar spent on nonviolent program advertisements. Note that the returns to advertising on violent programs reflect both the increase in sales from additional advertisements and the decrease in sales from the expected backlash of advertising on violent programs. The amount of advertising time $\bar{Q}_v$ and $\bar{Q}_{nv}$ may change as company demographics, information about advertising, ratings, and advertising prices change. The results in the appendix reveal:

1. As the percentage of a firm's customers in the 18 to 34 demographic group or the percentage of customers that are male increases, the firm's purchase of advertising time on violent programs may increase or decrease depending on the relationship between sales increases and expected consumer backlash. Consider the increase in sales from the purchase of an additional advertisement versus the decrease in sales because of a backlash from the purchase of the ad. If the sales effect is larger than the backlash effect as the percentage of 18–34 consumers increases for a company (i.e., $VS_{Q_v\alpha_i} > A(I)BL_{Q_v\alpha_i}$), then the firm will purchase more advertising time on violent programs as α_i increases. If the backlash effect dominates, the firm will purchase less time as α_i increases. In terms of the optimal purchase of advertising time on nonviolent programs, $\bar{Q}_{nv}$ will decrease as the percentage of young consumers increases.

2. The placement of a warning on violent movies increases the information (I) about a company's advertising practices and thus increases the likelihood $A(I)$ that there will be a backlash from advertising on violent programs. As I increases, the amount of time purchased on nonviolent programs is unchanged but the amount of time purchased $(\bar{Q}_v)$ on violent shows decreases. This decrease will be larger for firms with higher values of BL, such as companies with higher proportions of older consumers and higher proportions of female consumers.

3. As ratings for violent programs increase, the amount of advertising on nonviolent programs is unchanged but the amount of advertising time purchased on violent shows will increase or decrease depending again on the relationship between additional sales and the expected backlash. If the increase in ratings increases the marginal impact of an additional advertisement on sales more than an increase in ratings increases the marginal impact of an additional advertisement on the expected backlash (i.e., $VS_{Q \cdot R_v} > A(I)BL_{Q \cdot R_v}$), then the amount of advertising time purchased on violent programs will increase. If the change in the expected backlash outweighs the change in sales, then purchases of advertisements on violent programs would decrease.

4. Increases in the price of advertisements on violent programs (P_v) would decrease purchases of $\bar{Q}_v$ and leave $\bar{Q}_{nv}$ unchanged, while increases in the price of advertisements on nonviolent programs (P_{nv}) will leave $\bar{Q}_v$ unchanged and decrease the purchase of advertisements on nonviolent programs $\bar{Q}_{nv}$.

This model of advertiser reaction suggests a series of hypotheses about the types of products that will be advertised on violent versus nonviolent prime-time broadcast movies and about how the mix of products on violent programs may change as warning labels are placed on violent programs. Specifically:

H$_1$: Products advertised on violent movies will be more likely to be used by younger consumers and male consumers than those on nonviolent movies. Products advertised on nonviolent movies will be more likely to be used by older consumers and female consumers than those on violent movies.

H$_2$: If a viewer warning is placed on a violent film, the mix of products advertised will change. Relative to a violent film without a viewer warning, a violent film with a warning will have a higher proportion of advertisements for products used by younger or male consumers.

H$_3$: Viewer discretion warnings will have a different impact depending on the type of company. Larger companies and those with "family" brand images are likely to face higher scrutiny for advertising on violent shows. Relative to violent programs without warnings, violent films with warnings should have fewer advertisements from larger companies and those with "family" brand identities.

Broadcaster Incentives

Broadcast networks face a trade-off in determining the number of commercial minutes to include during a program. While additional advertisements bring the prospect of additional revenue, the inclusion of more advertising time in a program may lead some viewers to select alternative shows. In this sense, view-

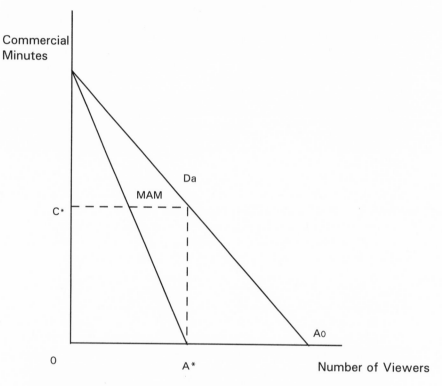

Fig. 8.1. Broadcaster determination of commercial minutes. (Adapted from Owen and Wildman 1992, 126 [fig. 4.15]. Copyright © 1992 by the President and Fellows of Harvard College.)

ing a television commercial represents the "price" individuals pay for viewing broadcast television. Figure 8.1, from Owen and Wildman's *Video Economics* (1992), conveys the decision broadcasters face in determining the amount of commercial time in a show. As Owen and Wildman point out, if the advertising market is perfectly competitive the price per advertisement on a program will be constant. This means that the profit-maximizing amount of advertising will be the product of the number of advertising minutes sold times the number of viewers of these advertisements (i.e., "audience advertising minutes"). If there were no commercials in a program, A_0 viewers would watch the program. As the number of commercial minutes climbs, the number of viewers willing to pay this "price" to watch a show drops. The demand curve D_a conveys the number of viewers willing to watch at a given amount of advertising time. The curve *MAM*, the "marginal audience minutes" curve, represents the change in audience advertising minutes from the addition of another commercial. The broadcaster will add minutes of commercials until MAM equals zero, which is the point at which the gain in total audience advertising minutes from adding another commercial is just offset by the loss in total audience advertising minutes from viewers fleeing the program because of the added commercial. Total audience advertising minutes are maximized at this point. The broadcaster will choose to include C^* commercial minutes in the program, attract A^* viewers, and sell a total of $(C^* \times A^*)$ audience minutes to advertisers.

If this model of advertising holds true, consider how a broadcaster will react to a system of voluntary warning labels on prime-time movies such as that adopted in 1993. If the value of advertising on a show is reduced for some advertisers because of the costs of controversy, the advertisement price a company can charge may drop.[23] The profit-maximizing amount of commercial minutes will remain the same (C^*), since this figure was independent of the price received for advertisements. In addition to running paid advertising from corporate sponsors, networks also run promotions for their own programs. These promos are essentially investments which yield later returns in the form of additional viewers. The networks also run public service announcements, such as the commercials provided in campaigns sponsored by the Advertising Council.[24] As the price received for commercial advertisements drops, the networks will run more commercials promoting their own shows and more public service announcements since the "opportunity cost" of running these advertisements will have dropped. Since warning labels translate into lower advertisement prices and ultimately lower advertising revenues, broadcasters will have an incentive to avoid placing warnings on programs even if they contain violent material that parents might consider objectionable or research might indicate is harmful. In the long run, the change in returns to programming may also affect the decision of which types of programs to air.[25]

This model of broadcaster incentives implies additional testable hypotheses:

H_4: *Films with viewer discretion warnings will have the same number of "nonprogram" minutes per hour as those without warnings.*

H_5: *If the price of advertising drops on movies with warnings, broadcasters may run more promotions for their own shows and more public service announcements on these programs.*

Prime-Time Movie Data

Movies on prime-time broadcast network television were selected to test theories of advertiser reactions to viewer discretion warnings since there was a large enough fraction of films carrying these warnings (14 percent) to generate substantial data on sponsorship decisions. The results of both the UCLA (1995) and

National Television Violence Study (1996b) suggest that violence on broadcast television may be most problematic in prime-time movies. The UCLA study noted that for the 1994–95 season, "A large majority of the violence on broadcast television that raises concerns can be found in theatrical films."[26] As the study's principal investigator Jeffrey Cole put it:

> . . . of the 118 theatrical films we looked at this season, 50, or about 42 percent, would've raised concerns. The ones that raise the most concerns contextually were those action films that tended to have 40 to 60 scenes of violence. And what the networks are able to do is only remove the worst moments of the worst part. They can't do much more. And even though they do take the worst part of the worst moment, to say it better, they still have a film that has, really has nothing but scenes of violence.[27]

The *National Television Violence Study* (1996b) also found in its analysis of movies on cable and broadcast that:

> Movies as a genre have the highest percentage of programs with violence and the highest proportion of programs with numerous violent interactions. Movies portray violence in realistic settings much more than the norm and depict graphic blood and gore moderately above average. The positive features of movies are that long-term consequences are portrayed substantially more often, and that humorous violence and unrealistic harm are avoided.[28]

These findings suggest that studying advertising on movies allows one to analyze who sponsors some of the most violent programming on broadcast network television.

Testing theories about advertiser reaction to viewer discretion warnings on movies requires information on program content, commercials aired, the consumer demographics of advertised products, and the demographics of program audiences. Information on movies aired on the four major networks during prime time from May 1, 1995, through February 29, 1996, was collected from *TV Guide* (e.g., movie air time, genre) and from *What's on Tonite,* an Internet source that had the MPAA ratings for movies and indicators (for theatrical movies) of whether the film contained violence, nudity, adult situations, and adult language. An attempt was made to record all prime-time broadcast network movies from May 1 through December 31, 1995. To expand the comparison sets of films, all movies with warnings or violence indicators were recorded for January 1, 1996, through February 29, 1996. For each recorded movie, research assistants coded the commercial length and product advertised. All nonprogram segments were coded, for example, commercials for products, television show promotions during credits, and public service announcements. This yielded a data base of more than 19,000 commercials from 251 movies. For 151 films broadcast from May 1 through September 16, 1995, Nielsen information on ratings by demographic audience were also available.

The *1993 Simmons Study of Media and Markets* (1994), based on a survey of 22,468 adults in the United States, provided data on consumer demographics of products advertised on these films. This study gives a breakdown by age, income, education, and gender of product users. The Simmons data provide product usage demographics for specific products, for example, the Buick Le Sabre automobile. For those advertised products that were not found in the Simmons study, the commercial was linked to the closest product category information. For example, since there was no product-specific information on Golden Crisp Cereal in the Simmons study, demographic information was collected on the general users of cold breakfast cereal.

Products were linked to parent companies through information from *Company Brand $, 1993* (1994). For each parent company, total advertising expenditures for 1993 were collected from *Ad $ Summary, 1993* (1994), which lists firm expenditures for advertising across ten media, including network television, syndication, spot, and cable television. Together these data link advertised products to particular programs, consumers, and parent companies.

Prime-Time Network Movie Results

Movie Sample Analysis

From May 1, 1995, through February 29, 1996, there were 357 movies scheduled for broadcast in prime time by ABC, CBS, Fox, and NBC. These movies were spread across a wide variety of genres: drama, 54 percent; comedy, 14 percent; crime-drama, 10 percent; adventure, 4 percent; thriller, 4 percent; comedy-drama, 4 percent; science fiction, 4 percent; fantasy, 3 percent; western, 2 percent; mystery, 1 percent; and other, 1 percent. This genre distribution is similar to that for prime-time network movies broadcast from 1987 through 1993.[29] Prime-time films broadcast during 1995–96 did differ in some dimensions from those broadcast in earlier seasons. The 1995–96 movies were more likely to be films first released in theaters (36 percent for 1995–96 vs. 29 percent for 1987–93), to deal with family crime (9 percent vs. 4 percent), and to be based on true stories (22 percent vs. 18 percent). In the 1995–96 sample 23 percent of the films dealt with murder, a drop from 30 percent for the 1987–93 seasons.

Beyond the genre information and plot descriptions available in publications such as *TV Guide,* viewers had some additional indicators of the content of prime-time broadcast films. MPAA ratings were available for all the theatrical films.[30] The distribution of MPAA ratings for the films broadcast from May

1995 through February 1996 is 2 percent G, 12 percent PG, 10 percent PG-13, 15 percent R, and 62 percent unrated (nearly all of which are made-for-television movies).[31] Those films rated by the MPAA also carried program content indicators in the viewer guide *What's on Tonite,* although the guide did not distinguish between the content of the theatrical release and the potentially edited version shown on network television. For the sample as a whole, 21 percent of the movies had a content indicator for violence, 9 percent for nudity, 21 percent for adult situations, and 25 percent for adult language. These figures may be lower bounds for the presence of these types of content, however, since made-for-television movies are not categorized by viewer guides on these dimensions. For the sample of theatrical films shown in prime time by ABC, CBS, Fox, and NBC, 59 percent had an indicator for violence, 24 percent for nudity, 55 percent for adult situations, and 72 percent for language.

The broadcast networks placed viewer warnings on 18 out of the 230 made-for-television films and 33 out of the 127 theatrical films aired from May 1995 through February 1996. By MPAA rating, the breakdown of theatrical films that received warnings was 0 out of 5 G, 1 of 38 PG, 2 of 31 PG-13, and 30 of 52 R films. Judging whether all movies that contained violence of concern (e.g., harmful to children) carried viewer warnings is difficult without a detailed examination of the content of each film. As discussed above, the UCLA Center for Communication Policy (1995) conducted such a study for the 1994–95 season and concluded that 50 out of 118 theatrical films and 23 out of 161 made-for-television movies they examined had violence that raised concerns. For those films with problematic uses of violence, the networks placed warnings on 28 out of the 50 violent theatrical films and 6 of the 23 violent made-for-television films. By this measure, nearly half of the violent films that should have carried a viewer warning did not in the 1994–95 season. The use of warnings, though imperfect, has increased markedly from earlier eras. Between 1987 and 1993 only 2 percent of the films broadcast by the networks during prime time contained viewer discretion warnings.

Nielsen ratings for these prime-time films provide information on the demographic makeup of their audiences. For 151 films shown on broadcast television from May 1, 1995, through September 16, 1995 (a sample for which Nielsen data were available), the average rating for children 2 to 11 was 3.0. This translates into 1.4 million children on average viewing these prime-time network movies. Children in this age group had a 4.2 rating for prime-time network movies from 1987 through 1993. The increase in competition in the television market has thus lowered the number of children watching prime-time broadcast network movies. Note that 68 percent of these films started at 9 P.M., so that concerns about content may lessen as the starting time of the film progresses. Teens 12 to 17 averaged a 4.2 rating for prime-time network films, which translated into 900,000 viewers in this age group.

TABLE 8.1. Broadcast Network Prime-Time Movie Audiences

Viewing Population	1987–93 Mean Ratings ($N = 2,295$)	1995 Mean Ratings ($N = 151$)	1995 Mean Viewers (Millions)
Children, 2–11	4.2 (2.8)	3.0 (1.8)	1.4
Teens, 12–17	5.5 (3.4)	4.2 (2.4)	0.9
Women, 18 and up	9.0 (3.7)	6.4 (2.8)	6.3
Women, 18–34	7.1 (3.4)	5.0 (2.7)	1.6
Women, 18–49	7.8 (3.3)	5.5 (2.6)	3.4
Women, 25–54	8.5 (3.5)	6.0 (2.8)	3.4
Women, 55 and up	11.2 (5.6)	8.0 (4.3)	2.4
Men, 18 and up	7.0 (3.0)	4.7 (2.3)	4.3
Men, 18–34	5.4 (2.9)	3.5 (2.3)	1.1
Men, 18–49	6.1 (3.3)	3.9 (2.5)	2.4
Men, 25–54	6.7 (3.0)	4.4 (2.5)	2.4
Men, 55 and up	9.3 (4.4)	6.6 (3.2)	1.5
Household ratings	11.7 (3.9)	8.7 (3.2)	8.3

Note: Standard deviations are in parentheses.

Table 8.1 indicates that ratings for prime-time broadcast movies have also declined for adult demographic groups such as males 18+ and females 18+.[32] For some of these adult groups, ratings for prime-time movies dropped by nearly a third from 1987–93 to the 1995–96 season. Competition from cable would be especially intense for movie viewers, since premium channels air recent releases more readily than broadcast networks. Overall, the films in the 1995–96 sample averaged a 15.3 share (down from 19.6 for 1987–93), which indicates that approximately 1 in 6 households watching television at the time the programs were aired were watching these movies. For each age group women had higher ratings than men, which suggests that products aimed at women may be likely sponsors of these programs.[33] As is true for television in general, ratings among those aged 55+ were much higher than those for young adults. Since older consumers are less likely to be targeted by advertisers, however, the large number of elderly viewers may not translate into a significant number of commercials aimed at these consumers.

Differences in audiences across films will create different incentives for advertisers, for example, sponsors with products aimed primarily at males might find it more attractive to advertise on a movie with higher male ratings. Research based on Nielsen data indicates that men in all age groups have higher ratings for movies that are particularly violent, that women are more likely to watch movies about family crime, and that women and men age 55+ have higher ratings for mystery films.[34] Movie audiences and hence advertisers will vary by content. If there is a backlash among product customers from sponsoring violent television, there may be an independent impact of the warning label on the incentives of advertisers. Isolating this effect involves comparing commercials on movies that are similar in audience but differ in labeling. For 88 theatrical films, the analysis will focus on comparing the 28 violent theatrical films that received viewer warnings with the 25 violent theatrical films that did not receive a warning and the 35 films that did not have a violent content indicator.[35] Among the 164 made-for-television films, it is more difficult to identify a "violent" comparison set since the shows are not categorized by viewer guides as violent. For the 146 made-for-television films that did not carry warnings, I selected the films that were in a subset of violent genres (science fiction, thriller, westerns) or that had the words "dead" or "murder" in their titles. This resulted in a "violent" subset of 18 made-for-television movies to compare with the 17 that carried viewer discretion warnings.[36]

Advertising Analysis

Broadcaster reactions to warning labels are initially analyzed in table 8.2. Even if the price of advertising were to drop on programs with warnings, broadcasters should still maintain the same number of "nonprogram" minutes per show (hypothesis H_4). Table 8.2 indicates that for theatrical films broadcast in prime time by the networks, violent movies with warnings did have a higher number of nonprogram minutes (15.0) than nonviolent theatrical films (14.4). This may reflect the ability of broadcasters to charge audiences a higher "price" for the content of these films. Warnings do not, however, have an independent impact on nonprogram minutes. The number of nonprogram minutes on violent films without warnings (15.1) was nearly identical to the number of minutes on violent movies with warnings (15.0). Nonprogram minutes were also similar across the three made-for-television movie categories (14.4 minutes for those with warnings, 14.6 for those without warnings, and 14.7 for the "violent," no-warning subset). Thus warnings do not have a separate impact on the number of nonprogram minutes broadcasters insert in prime-time movies.[37]

If the price of advertising drops for advertisements on movies with warnings, then broadcasters may substitute network promotions and public service announcements for commercial advertisements (H_5). In order to test this, each advertisement was assigned to a unique category: product advertisement (all commercial products and services, except for those broken down into finer categories noted below); commercials for movies showing in theaters; commercials for videos; health service, utility, military, or nonprofit advertisements; public service announcements; advertisements for television shows on the local stations (e.g., local news, syndicated programs); and advertisements for network programs.[38] Table 8.3 shows that for theatrical movies, programs with warnings had a lower proportion of general product advertisements (60.2 percent) than

TABLE 8.2. Nonprogram Minutes per Hour

	Mean	Standard Deviation	N	Difference of Means Test (*T* stat) 1 vs. 2	2 vs. 3
Theatrical movies					
(1) nonviolent	14.4	1.1	34		
(2) violent, warning	15.0	1.5	28		
(3) violent, no warning	15.1	1.6	25		
				−2.24**	−0.32
Made for television movies					
(1) no warning	14.6	1.0	140		
(2) warning	14.4	1.2	17		
(3) "violent," no warning	14.7	0.6	18		
				0.69	−1.08

*** = statistically significant at 1%; ** = at 5%; * = at 10%.

movies without warnings (64.8 percent) or movies that were violent but did not carry warnings (63.4 percent). Violent movies with warnings had a higher percentage of network promotions (24.1 percent) than violent movies without warnings (22 percent) or nonviolent movies (20.8 percent). These differences of proportion, which are all statistically significant, indicate that advertiser pullout may lead broadcasters to show less advertising for general products and substitute network promotions for the unsold advertising. Note that the percentage of advertisements devoted to public service announcements is very similar across the subsamples (1.4 percent for nonviolent films, 1.3 for violent with warnings, and 1.1 for violent without warnings). The broadcasters do not appear to respond to advertiser pullout by running more public service announcements on violent films with warnings.

The predicted pattern does not hold true for made-for-television movies that carry viewer warnings (see appendix table 8.1). The percentage of general product advertisements on made-for-television movies with warnings (61.7 percent) is similar to that for movies without warnings (62.9 percent) and the "violent" made-for-television subset that did not carry warnings (62.3 percent). In difference-of-proportion tests, the difference between the made-for-television films with warnings and those in the other two samples is not statistically significant for general product advertisements or network promotions. This suggests that advertiser pullout may not be as great a problem for made-for-television films carrying warnings.

If warnings increase the probability for some firms that they will experience fewer sales, the model predicts that the products and firms advertising on movies with warnings should differ. Appendix table 8.2 uses the industry clas-

Table 8.3.   Percentage Distribution of Advertisements on Theatrical Movies

Advertisement Category	Movies Subsamples			Difference of Proportion Test (Z stat)	
	(1) Nonviolent Movies	(2) Violent, Warning Movies	(3) Violent Movies, No Warning	1 vs. 2	2 vs. 3
Product	64.8	60.2	63.4	3.35***	−2.22**
Movie	1.4	4.3	1.8	−5.81***	4.68***
Video	1.3	0.6	1.4	2.32**	−2.36**
Health services	0.2	0	0	1.46	0
Utility	0.1	0.1	0.3	0	−1.30
Military	0.2	0.6	0.1	−1.82*	2.30**
Nonprofit	0.1	0.1	0	0	0.98
Public service	1.4	1.3	1.1	0.18	0.61
Network	20.8	24.1	22.0	−2.74***	1.64*
Local station	9.6	8.5	9.6	1.31	−1.24
Total	99.9	99.7	99.7		
Network, local station PSA	31.8	33.9	32.7	−1.55	0.76
Commercial advertisements	68.1	65.8	67	1.69*	−0.83
Total number of advertisements	2,731	2,176	2,128		

*** = statistically significant at 1%; ** = at 5%; * = at 10%.

sification system developed by the Simmons survey to detail the differences in consumer product demographics between nonviolent theatrical films and violent theatrical films with warnings. Movies with warnings had a higher percentage of products that did not fit into the Simmons classification system, consistent with newer products or products with a smaller audience having less to fear in terms of brand-name backlash. The percentage of sports and leisure advertisements and alcohol advertisements was higher on movies with warnings, consistent with targeting younger consumers. Products with "family" brand identities, such as those in baking, cereals, and other food items made up a lower percentage of advertisements on movies with warnings.

Table 8.4 attempts to isolate the independent impact of warnings by examining differences in advertiser mix between violent theatrical films with warnings and those without. Automobiles, trucks, and vans, sports and leisure products, and alcohol products constituted a higher percentage of advertisements on movies with warnings. Backlash may be lower for some of the firms in these industries because they are targeting younger or male consumers.[39] Products where firms may have family images, such as those in food industries (e.g., cereals, baking, condiments) and kitchen products, accounted for a lower

TABLE 8.4. Percentage Distribution of Advertisements across Simmons Product
Categories, Theatrical Movies

Product Category	Violent, Warning	Violent, No Warning	Difference Test (Z stat)
Product unclassified	10.2	8.8	1.3
Automobiles, cycles, trucks, & vans	13.4	10.4	2.5**
Automotive products and services	0.8	0.8	0.2
Travel	1.8	1.1	1.4
Banking, investments, insurance, credit cards & contributions, memberships & public activities	1.8	1.6	0.4
Games & toys, children's and babies' apparel & specialty products	0.9	1.5	−1.4
Computers, books, discs, records, tapes, stereo, telephones, TV & video	4.7	5.7	−1.2
Appliances, garden care, sewing & photography	3.6	4.9	−1.8*
Home furnishings & home improvements	2.0	2.0	0.1
Sports & leisure	3.6	2.0	2.5**
Restaurants, stores & grocery shopping	15.0	20.0	−3.5***
Direct mail & other in-home shopping, yellow pages, florists, telegrams, faxes & greeting cards	0.5	0.2	1.3
Jewelry, watches, luggage, writing tools and men's apparel	0.8	0.6	0.5
Women's apparel	1.1	1.1	−0.2
Distilled spirits, mixed drinks, malt beverages, wine & tobacco products	2.7	1.6	1.9*
Coffee, tea, cocoa, milk, soft drinks, juices & bottled water	4.2	2.9	1.8*
Dairy products, desserts, baking & bread products	0.6	1.8	−2.8***
Cereals & spreads, rice, pasta, pizza, mexican foods, fruits & vegetables	1.8	3.4	−2.7***
Soup, meat, fish, poultry, condiments, dressings & sauces	1.6	2.9	−2.4**
Chewing gum, candy, cookies & snacks	4.6	3.7	1.2
Soap, laundry, paper products & kitchen wraps	2.2	3.9	−2.6**
Household cleaners, room deodorizers, pest controls & pet foods	2.2	3.0	−1.3
Health care products & remedies	7.6	6.0	1.7*
Oral hygiene products, skin care, deodorants & drug stores	5.9	4.7	1.4
Fragrances, hair care & shaving products	4.0	3.7	0.4
Women's beauty aids, cosmetics & personal products	2.5	1.8	1.3
Total	100.1	100.1	

*** = Statistically significant at 1%; ** = Statistically significant at 5%; * = Statistically significant at 10%.

percentage of advertisements on films with warnings relative to violent films without warnings.

Appendix table 8.3 indicates that for made-for-television movies the differences between advertisers on movies with versus without warnings are consistent with the backlash theory. Sports and leisure and alcoholic beverage products constitute higher percentages of advertisements on films with warnings, while those associated with food industries constitute a lower percentage of advertisements on these films. When advertisement distributions are compared in appendix table 8.4 for made-for-television programs with warnings and made-for-television films without warnings that may be "violent," some patterns are consistent with the table 8.4 results for theatrical films. Sports and leisure products were more likely to be on programs with warnings, while cereals were less likely. Women's apparel and women's beauty aids, however, were more likely to be on made-for-television movies with warnings. This may be related to the fact that made-for-television movies in general have higher ratings among women, as do family crime movies. If backlash is lower for sponsoring these programs than for sponsoring the action-adventure theatrical films, then advertiser reactions may differ to warnings on theatrical films versus warnings on made-for-television films.

Since violent films with warnings and nonviolent films attract different audiences, one expects that the products advertised on the two subsets of films will differ (e.g., by H_1 violent films should be more likely to have products aimed at younger viewers or men). If there is a backlash against advertising on films with warnings, then within the set of violent theatrical films, products with lower expected backlashes such as those aimed at men and younger consumers should be more likely to be advertised on films with warnings (H_2). Table 8.5 bears out both of these predictions for theatrical films. The differences in consumer demographics are statistically significant but small in magnitude. This is what one would expect, however, for at least two reasons. Since advertising on broadcast network television is bought by companies seeking broad audiences, one may expect a degree of similarity across films in product target audiences. If advertiser pullout affects firms differentially, then only a small percentage of firms may pull out with a warning. The small number of advertisements affected by advertiser pullout would translate into small changes in the advertiser mix on films with warnings. A small number of advertiser pullouts on a movie would still translate into significant lost revenues given that 30-second commercials sell for between $90,000 and $150,000 for prime-time broadcast movies.

Relative to products sponsoring nonviolent theatrical films, table 8.5 reveals that products advertised on violent films with theatrical warnings were more likely to be used by individuals aged 18–24, males, households without children, and those with incomes of $40,000+.[40] Products advertised on violent theatrical films with warnings were less likely to be used by individuals age 55–64 or 65+, those with incomes $10–19,000, or high school graduates. These differences in product demographics may arise from differences in program audiences or advertiser reactions to viewer warnings. To isolate the independent impact of advertiser reactions to viewer discretion warnings, I compare the advertisements on violent theatrical films with warnings to advertisements on violent theatrical films without warnings (two subsets that may be relatively sim-

Table 8.5. Consumer Demographics of Products Advertised on Theatrical Movies

Mean % of Product Consumers in Category	Movies Subsamples			Difference of Means Test (*T* stat)	
	(1) Nonviolent Movies	(2) Violent, Warning Movies	(3) Violent Movies, No Warning	1 vs. 2	2 vs. 3
Age					
18–24	12.1	13.0	12.4	−5.84***	3.66***
25–34	24.4	24.6	24.5	−1.42	0.62
35–44	24.6	24.5	24.6	1.04	−0.62
45–54	16.0	15.8	15.9	1.40	−0.86
55–64	10.4	10.1	10.3	3.63***	−2.24**
65 up	12.6	12.1	12.4	3.47***	−2.0**
Male	49.2	49.6	49.1	−1.69*	1.96**
Female	50.8	50.5	50.9	1.60	−1.90*
Income					
<10,000	8.0	7.9	8.0	0.97	−1.26
10–19,000	14.1	13.9	14.1	2.32**	−2.00**
20–29,000	16.2	16.2	16.3	−0.20	−0.99
30–39,000	15.1	15.0	15.1	2.58***	−2.04**
40,000+	46.7	47.1	46.6	−2.06**	2.29**
50,000+	34.2	34.5	34.0	−1.45	2.01**
60,000+	24.3	24.5	24.1	−0.88	1.67*
Education					
Not HS graduate	16.1	16.0	16.1	1.13	−0.61
HS graduate	35.7	35.3	35.7	3.08***	−2.75***
Attended college	25.9	26.2	26.0	−2.53***	1.38
College graduate	22.3	22.6	22.3	−1.55	1.43
No children in household	55.4	56.1	55.7	−2.94***	1.88*
Total adult use	20.9	18.1	20.3	3.73***	−2.90***
Number of total ads	2,282	1,665	1,725		

*** = statistically significant at 1%; ** = at 5%; * = at 10%.

ilar in audience). Products advertised on films with viewer discretion warnings were more likely to be used by those age 18–24, by men, and by those in households with no children. Products on films with warnings were less likely to be used by those age 55–64 and 65+ and by women.

Each of these results is consistent with a backlash effect. Since younger consumers and males are less likely to view violent television as a problem, companies with products aimed at these consumers will be less likely to face a backlash. If other companies withdraw from advertising, the demographics of products advertising on movies with warnings will tilt more toward men and younger consumers. These firms may even be more likely to buy the advertising time of those companies that pull out, which would accentuate this trend. Products with higher percentages of older consumers and women, two groups that report greater dissatisfaction with television violence, face greater backlash and hence are less likely to advertise on violent programs with warnings. If potential brand image damage from advertising on a film with a warning is greater for products with a "family" brand image, this would explain why products on violent movies with warnings had a higher percentage of consumers with no children in the household than those on violent films without warnings. Note that products on violent movies with warnings had a lower percentage of total use by adults (18.1 percent) than that for products on violent movies without warnings (20.3 percent). This too is consistent with companies trying to reach larger audiences facing a greater potential for backlash.[41]

The evidence of advertiser reactions to warnings is more mixed for made-for-television movies. There are statistically significant differences in the consumer demographics of products on made-for-television movies with warnings versus those without warnings. Appendix table 8.5 indicates that products on these movies with warnings were more likely to be consumed by those age 18–24 or 25–34 and by males. They were less likely to be consumed by those 45–54, 55–64, 65+, and by females. It is more difficult with the made-for-television movies to judge the independent impact of warnings since one needs to define an alternative set of movies without warnings that should be similar in audience. If one compares made-for-television movies with warnings with the subset of "violent" no-warning films, the predicted differences in product age do arise. Products advertised on the films with warnings were more likely to be used by those age 18–24 or 25–34 and less likely to be used by those 45–54, 55–64, or 65+. Differences in use of the products by males and females are not statistically significant between the two subsamples. Products advertised on movies with warnings actually have a lower percentage of households without children as a percentage of customers than those on movies without warnings, which is the opposite pattern expected if "family" products faced a backlash from advertising on made-for-television films.

Another way to examine differences in program audiences is to examine advertising for products aimed directly at male consumers (e.g., Hair Club for Men) or female consumers (e.g., Maybelline Revitalizing Makeup). For each movie subsample, the percentage of these "gender-focused" products aimed at men was calculated. For nonviolent theatrical films, 29 percent of the gender-focused products were aimed at men, while for violent theatrical films with warnings the percentage was 39 percent and for violent theatrical films without warnings the percentage was 38 percent.[42] These figures suggest that even on violent films the majority of gender-focused products are aimed at women. Made-for-television movies without warnings have a similar percentage of their gender-focused products aimed at men (32 percent) compared to those movies with warnings (31 percent).

The model of advertiser backlash predicts that, holding product-level characteristics constant, larger firms may be more reluctant to advertise on violent programs with warnings because their actions may be more likely to be scrutinized by interest groups. The companies advertising on network prime-time broadcast movies are large firms with familiar brand identities. For theatrical movies, for example, the top three advertisers were Procter and Gamble, General Motors, and Pepsico for nonviolent films in the sample; Pepsico, Warner-Lambert, and Unilever for the violent films with warnings; and Sears, McDonald's, and Pepsico for violent films without warnings (see appendix table 8.6). Though all of these companies are "large," the differences in firm size predicted in the backlash model do appear in the data. Table 8.6 defines firm size along two dimensions, advertising expenditures by the parent companies associated with the advertisements on particular types of movies and the number of products in the network advertising sample associated with the parent companies sponsoring advertisements on these films. Companies that advertised on violent films with warnings did have lower average media expenditures ($316,925,000) than firms sponsoring advertisements on violent movies without warnings ($380,182,000). The difference-of-means tests for expenditures on network television, syndicated television, and cable television were also statistically significant for companies advertising on violent films with warnings versus those without warnings. Advertisements on violent movies with warnings came from companies with an average of 19.7 different products advertised on prime-time movies in the sample, versus a mean of 22.6 for advertisements on violent movies without warnings. As predicted by the backlash theory, products advertised on violent theatrical films with warnings are associated with parent companies with lower media expenditures and fewer advertised products. Larger firms may try to avoid theatrical films with warnings because of their greater potential to generate scrutiny of their advertising policies.

The analysis of the impact of advertiser backlash has rested in part on the assumption that violent movies with warnings and violent movies without warnings draw similar audiences and are similar in controversial content, so that firm incentives to advertise will relate to reputation effects caused primarily by the application of the warning label to the films. Ideally, one would like detailed information on movie content and audience composition so that one could control for these factors in analysis of advertising decisions. Table 8.7 addresses part of these concerns by using logistic analysis to identify the factors that distinguish advertisements on movies with warnings. The logits in table 8.7 use the sample of advertisements on theatrical films with violence and analyze the factors that predict whether a product will be on a movie with a warning. The inclusion of the Nielsen ratings for women 18–49 and men 18–49 allows one to control for the nature of the audience captured by a film (and in part the nature of the content, since content and audience are related). The results indicate

TABLE 8.6. Mean Company Media Expenditures and Products Advertised for Advertisements on Theatrical Movies

1993 Mean Parent Company Expenditures ($000s)	Advertisements on Violent Movies, Warning	Advertisements	Advertisements on Violent Movies, No Warning	Advertisements	Difference of Means Test (*T* Statistic)
Total media	316,925	689	380,182	727	3.68***
Network television	134,178	689	161,321	727	3.27***
Spot television	73,080	689	78,699	727	1.44
Syndicated Television	16,321	689	21,700	727	2.34**
Cable television	18,826	689	24,859	727	3.97***
Average number of products advertised in movie sample by the parent company	19.7	727	22.6	765	2.52***

Note: Media expenditures information come from *Ad $ Summary, 1993* (1994). Products were linked to parent company information using *Company/Brand $, 1993* (1994). Total media expenditures are the sum of expenditures on network television, spot television, syndicated television, cable TV networks, network radio, national spot radio, magazines, Sunday magazines, newspapers, and outdoor advertising as reported in *Company/Brand $*.

*** = Statistically significant at the .01 level; ** = significant at the .05 level.

TABLE 8.7. Determinants of Advertising on Theatrical Movies with Warnings

Variable	(a)	(b)	(c)	(d)
Intercept	−2.90	1.12	−2.15	0.90
	(2.60)	(3.45)	(3.80)	(5.12)
% 18–24	−0.01	−0.03	−0.003	−0.04
	(0.02)	(0.02)	(0.03)	(0.04)
% 25–34	−0.03	−0.03	−0.03	−0.002
	(0.02)	(0.03)	(0.04)	(0.05)
% 45–54	0.02	0.03	0.38	0.05
	(0.03)	(0.03)	(0.04)	(0.05)
% 55–64	−0.12***	−0.18***	−0.11***	−0.13**
	(0.03)	(0.04)	(0.04)	(0.06)
% 65 up	−0.02	−0.002	−0.03	−0.03
	(0.03)	(0.03)	(0.04)	(0.05)
% <$10,000	0.06	0.04	0.07	−0.00001
	(0.04)	(0.05)	(0.06)	(0.07)
% $10–19,000	0.05	0.02	0.05	0.06
	(0.04)	(0.04)	(0.05)	(0.07)
% $30–39,000	−0.03	−0.10**	−0.07	−0.16***
	(0.04)	(0.05)	(0.05)	(0.06)
% $40,000 up	0.02	−0.02	0.0009	−0.04
	(0.02)	(0.03)	(0.03)	(0.04)
% Male	0.01*	0.02	0.03**	0.03*
	(0.01)	(0.03)	(0.01)	(0.02)
% No children	0.05***	0.04***	0.05***	0.05**
	(0.01)	(0.02)	(0.02)	(0.02)
Rating men 18–49		0.36***		0.29***
		(0.04)		(0.06)
Rating women 18–49		−0.23***		−0.19***
		(0.03)		(0.04)
Company total			−8.46e-7**	−1.46e-6***
media expenditures			(3.56e-7)	(4.75e-7)
Number of company			0.007	0.007
advertised products			(0.005)	(0.007)
Log likelihood	−1708.9	−1057.4	−914.3	−554.4
Number of advertisements	2,499	1,647	1,356	865

Note: Dependent variable = 1 in logit analysis if ad was on a theatrical movie with a warning. Sample consists of all ads on theatrical violent movies (i.e. those with and without warnings). Standard errors are in parentheses.
*** = statistically significant at 1%; ** = 5%; * = 10%.

that products aimed at attracting men 18–49 will advertise on films with warnings, while those aimed at women 18–49 are less likely to advertise on films with warnings. In addition, products with a higher percentage of users 55–64 were less likely and products with a higher percentage of households with no children were more likely to advertise on theatrical films with warnings. Controlling for the rating of who shows up in the audience for a film, products with higher use among males were more likely to advertise on the films with warnings. These results are consistent with products facing different incentives to react to warnings based on the gender, age, and family status of their target customers. Products from firms with higher media expenditures were less likely to advertise on movies with warnings, consistent with the notion that these firms may try to avoid movies with warnings because they have a higher potential for attracting interest group scrutiny.

Market Segmentation in Violent Cable Programs

Cable television provides another avenue to test theories of advertiser support for violent programming. The *NTVS* research indicates that basic cable programming is more likely to contain violence than broadcast network programming and that when it is violent basic cable programming will be more likely than broadcast network programming to contain multiple violent interactions.[43] Ratings for cable networks are much lower than those for broadcast network programs, raising the possibility that programmers may adopt a strategy of niche programming to reach particularly narrow audiences through their violent shows. Basic cable channels are less likely than the industry average to provide advisories or content codes on violent programs, in part because unlike the premium cable channels (which are the most likely to provide viewers with content information) these networks may be concerned about advertiser backlash. Advertising on cable is not monitored by interest groups such as the AFA, however, so the relative "anonymity" of cable sponsorship may mean that advertisers are less likely to believe that sponsoring shows with warnings on basic cable will lead to controversy.

To examine how advertising audiences vary across types of violent programming on cable, one first needs to select a sample of programs and adopt a definition of violent shows. Three basic cable channels were selected, TNT, USA, and TBS, which ranked 1, 2, and 3 in terms of Nielsen prime-time audience ratings for basic cable networks for June 1995.[44] In addition, a local independent broadcast station in the Raleigh–Durham market, WKFT, was selected. The shows from this outlet are included in the sample of basic cable programs since many viewers would only be able to see its programming through basic cable subscription (because of its weak broadcast signal on channel 40). For the week of April 1 to 7, 1995, all programming from noon until midnight was taped for these four stations. Commercials were coded for all series programming in violent genres, defined as action-adventure, science fiction, mystery, and dramas that dealt with crime, official police, or detectives. For movie programming, all movies in action-adventure, horror, mystery, science fiction, thriller, and western genres were included in the commercial coding sample. Movies that were dramas were included if viewing guides indicated through content indicators or descriptions that the films were violent. To supplement the sample of movies from April 1 to 7 that contained viewer discretion warnings, all movies from April 8 to 30 on these four channels that contained viewer discretion warnings in viewer guides or were preceded by on air warnings were included. This added a total of 21 movies to the sample. The series programming on these cable channels consisted primarily of programs previously aired on broadcast network television. For analysis, these violent series were divided into three groups: "crime" series, which dealt with crime, science fiction, and western themes; mystery series; and children's series (i.e., *Tattooed Teenage Alien Fighters* and *VR Troopers*).[45] Overall, there were a total of 104 separate episodes of series programming and 63 movies that were coded, which yielded a sample of 5,700 commercials on "violent" cable programming.

One way to describe the audience segmentation across violent cable programming is to examine the variation across programs in the percentage of gender-focused products (i.e., those used primarily by one gender) that are aimed at males. Table 8.8 shows that there is no statistical difference in the percentage of gender-focused products aimed at males on violent movies with warnings versus those without warnings, which may indicate that the backlash against advertising on labeled programs is not as significant a factor for movies on basic cable. The percentage of male products on crime series (52 percent) is much higher than that for mystery series (39.4 percent), consistent with women being a more likely target audience for the mystery programming. There is a wide range in the percentage of male products across channel outlets. TNT and TBS, both owned by Turner Broadcasting, had significantly different percentages of male products. TNT, which at the time had an established violent movie night on Saturdays that the channel advertised as "*Saturday Nitro*," had 53.4 percent of gender-focused products that were aimed at males.[46] In contrast, TBS had only 30.1 percent of its gender-focused product advertisements aimed at men. These differences are consistent with programming models that suggest that when channels are owned by the same firm they will, other things being equal, be less likely to target the same audience at the same time.[47] The local independent broadcast station had a male-product percentage of 69.7 percent, the highest of the four outlets. This accords with the evidence that programming on local independents tends to be more violent and when violent contain a greater number of violent interactions. Ratings data indicate that across all age groups men exhibit higher ratings for programs that critics describe as particularly violent.[48]

The distribution of advertisements across product categories again provides another way to describe audience segmentation and test for advertiser reactions to the placement of program warnings on cable movies. Table 8.9 indicates that there are fewer changes in the pattern of advertisers when warnings are placed on cable movies than when warnings are placed on prime-time

TABLE 8.8. Percentage of Gender-Focused Products Aimed at Males, by Cable Subsample

	% Male Products	N	Difference Test (Z stat)
Violent movies with warnings	38.8	116	
			−1.2
Violent movies without warnings	46.1	165	
Violent movies	48.9	262	
			1.4
Violent series	43.1	281	
Crime series	52.0	196	
			1.8*
Mystery series	39.4	66	
TNT programming	53.4	146	
			4.1***
TBS programming	30.1	143	
USA programming	42.1	178	
			−4.3***
WKFT programming	69.7	76	

Note: Gender-focused products are those which Simmons presents data only for female use (e.g., Maybelline Revitalizing Makeup) or male use (e.g., Hair Club for Men). The table reports the fraction of these gender-focused products that are aimed only at males. N = Number of advertisements for gender-focused products in the program sample.

*** = Statistically significant at 1%; * = Statistically significant at 10%.

broadcast theatrical movies (analyzed in table 8.4). Both cable movies with and without warnings had approximately 20 percent of product advertisements that did not fit into the general Simmons product categories, a figure which is double that for theatrical movies on broadcast television. This may be because products advertised on cable are less likely to be the traditional goods marketed to a broad audience through a mass medium such as broadcast network television. If one compares cable movies with and without warnings, there are fewer shifts in the distribution of products caused by the placement of the warnings on cable movies. For cable movies, there are a higher proportion of sports and leisure products advertised on films with warnings, consistent with these products having a lower potential backlash among target consumers for sponsoring violent programming. Unlike the case with broadcast network movies, movies with warnings on basic cable did not have a higher proportion of advertisements for alcoholic beverages. On broadcast network films, those with warnings had a higher percentage of product advertisements for automobiles and trucks, yet this effect was not observed for the cable films with warnings. While products in four "family brand" categories (i.e., dairy products, cereals, soup, and soap) were less likely to advertise on broadcast theatrical network films with warnings, for the cable movies those with warnings only had lower percentages of adver-

TABLE 8.9. Percentage Distribution of Advertisements across Simmons Product Categories, Violent Cable Movies

Product Category	Violent, With Warning	Violent, No Warning	Difference Test (Z stat)
Product unclassified	19.4	20.0	−0.4
Automobiles, cycles, trucks, & vans	10.3	9.9	0.3
Automotive products and services	0.9	2.3	−2.5**
Travel	1.4	1.4	−0.0
Banking, investments, insurance, credit cards & contributions, memberships & public activities	4.1	2.9	1.5
Games & toys, children's and babies' apparel & specialty products	0.9	1.3	−0.9
Computers, books, discs, records, tapes, stereo, telephones, TV & video	3.0	2.0	1.4
Appliances, garden care, sewing & photography	5.5	2.5	3.4***
Home furnishings & home improvements	2.5	4.2	−2.2**
Sports & leisure	2.3	0.8	2.7***
Restaurants, stores & grocery shopping	9.0	11.0	−1.5
Direct mail & other in-home shopping, yellow pages, florists, telegrams, faxes & greeting cards	2.7	4.0	−1.7*
Jewelry, watches, luggage, writing tools and men's apparel	0.2	0.3	−0.3
Women's apparel	0.5	0.8	−0.9
Distilled spirits, mixed drinks, malt beverages, wine & tobacco products	1.9	1.3	1.1
Coffee, tea, cocoa, milk, soft drinks, juices & bottled water	2.8	3.3	−0.6
Dairy products, desserts, baking & bread products	0.7	1.6	−2.1**
Cereals & spreads, rice, pasta, pizza, mexican foods, fruits & vegetables	4.0	4.5	−0.5
Soup, meat, fish, poultry, condiments, dressings & sauces	1.6	1.7	−0.1
Chewing gum, candy, cookies & snacks	4.0	4.1	−0.1
Soap, laundry, paper products & kitchen wraps	1.3	3.4	−3.3***
Household cleaners, room deodorizers, pest controls & pet foods	8.0	6.7	1.1
Health care products & remedies	5.0	4.2	0.9
Oral hygiene products, skin care, deodorants & drug stores	2.7	2.2	0.7
Fragrances, hair care & shaving products	2.7	2.0	1.1
Women's beauty aids, cosmetics & personal products	2.3	1.8	0.9
Total	99.7	100.2	

*** = Statistically significant at 1%; ** = Statistically significant at 5%; * = Statistically significant at 10%.

tisements from the dairy and soap industries. In sum, the product distribution of advertisements does change when warnings are placed on cable films, but these changes are less pronounced than those observed for broadcast network films. This is what would be predicted if advertising on cable and local independents was not likely to generate scrutiny, which in turn would mean that firms would be less likely to change their advertising decisions because of the addition of a warning to a movie.

Table 8.10 underscores that market segmentation for advertising on violent cable programming is evident from the distribution of products across industries. Cable series (crime, mystery, and children) contain advertisements that may be much more likely to be targeted to female viewers, who may be the principal shoppers for their families. Dairy products, soups, soap and laundry, health care products, and oral hygiene and skin care products accounted for a higher percentage of the advertisements on violent cable series. Cable movies, in contrast, had a higher percentage of advertisements from automobiles, travel, banking and insurance, home improvements, and men's apparel.

The target audience segmentation in advertising on violent cable programs is also evident in table 8.11, which details the consumer demographics of the products advertised on these shows. Relative to products advertised on violent cable movies, products advertised on violent cable series had a higher percentage of customers among those 55–64 or 65+, a higher percentage of female consumers, and a greater fraction of consumers among those with incomes less than $30,000. Products advertised on violent movies were more likely to have a higher percentage of users 18–24 or 35–44, a larger fraction of male consumers, and a greater percentage of consumers with incomes greater than $30,000. Products advertised on violent series were also used by a larger proportion of the adult population (21.4 percent) than those on violent movies (17.7 percent). These results are consistent with advertisements on violent cable series being more likely to be aimed at older or female consumers, while advertisements on violent cable movies are aimed at younger or male consumers.[49]

Violent programs also may vary by the nature of the firms advertising on them. Table 8.12 reveals that the total company media expenditures and total number of products advertised in the sample of network programs are nearly identical for advertisements on cable movies with and without warnings. For broadcast theatrical films, products on movies with warnings came from firms with lower media expenditures and fewer products, consistent with the pullout of larger firms concerned about interest group scrutiny. For cable movies, however, the differences in company characteristics between products on movies with and without warnings are not statistically significant, providing further evidence that advertiser backlash may be less common on cable films because anticipated interest group scrutiny is lower.[50] Advertisements for products on violent series come from firms with larger media expenditures and more products

TABLE 8.10. Percentage Distribution of Advertisements across Simmons Product Categories, Cable Series versus Movies

Product Category	Cable Series	Cable Movies	Difference Test (Z stat)
Product unclassified	19.2	19.7	−0.4
Automobiles, cycles, trucks, & vans	4.5	10.1	−6.9***
Automotive products and services	0.3	1.7	−4.9***
Travel	0.6	1.4	−2.6***
Banking, investments, insurance, credit cards & contributions, memberships & public activities	1.9	3.4	−2.9***
Games & toys, children's and babies' apparel & specialty products	3.0	1.1	4.1***
Computers, books, discs, records, tapes, stereo, telephones, TV & video	2.3	2.4	−0.3
Appliances, garden care, sewing & photography	3.4	3.7	−0.6
Home furnishings & home improvements	1.5	3.5	−4.1***
Sports & leisure	1.2	1.4	−0.6
Restaurants, stores & grocery shopping	11.3	10.2	1.2
Direct mail & other in-home shopping, yellow pages, florists, telegrams, faxes & greeting cards	3.2	3.5	−0.5
Jewelry, watches, luggage, writing tools and men's apparel	0	0.3	−24.5***
Women's apparel	0.6	0.7	−0.5
Distilled spirits, mixed drinks, malt beverages, wine & tobacco products	1.9	1.5	1.1
Coffee, tea, cocoa, milk, soft drinks, juices & bottled water	3.8	3.1	1.2
Dairy products, desserts, baking & bread products	2.6	1.3	3.2***
Cereals & spreads, rice, pasta, pizza, mexican foods, fruits & vegetables	4.7	4.3	0.6
Soup, meat, fish, poultry, condiments, dressings & sauces	3.0	1.7	2.8***
Chewing gum, candy, cookies & snacks	5.0	4.0	1.5
Soap, laundry, paper products & kitchen wraps	4.6	2.5	3.6***
Household cleaners, room deodorizers, pest controls & pet foods	6.7	7.2	0.6
Health care products & remedies	6.1	4.6	2.2**
Oral hygiene products, skin care, deodorants & drug stores	4.3	2.4	3.4***
Fragrances, hair care & shaving products	2.0	2.3	−0.6
Women's beauty aids, cosmetics & personal products	2.1	2.0	0.3
Total	99.8	100.0	

*** = Statistically significant at 1%; ** = Statistically significant at 5%; * = Statistically significant at 10%.

Table 8.11. Consumer Demographics of Products Advertised on Cable Movies versus Cable Series

Mean % of Product Consumers in Category	(1) Violent Movies	(2) Violent Series	Difference of Means Test (T stat) 1 vs. 2
Age			
18–24	10.9	10.6	2.13**
25–34	23.8	23.8	0.46
35–44	24.4	24.1	3.29***
45–54	16.6	16.1	5.84***
55–64	10.9	11.1	−1.87*
65 up	13.4	14.3	−6.43***
Male	50.2	47.8	9.95***
Female	49.8	52.2	−9.91***
Income			
<10,000	8.0	8.7	−7.20***
10–19,000	14.3	14.8	−5.00***
20–29,000	16.0	16.2	−3.49***
30–39,000	15.0	14.7	4.11***
40,000+	46.8	45.6	5.42***
50,000+	34.2	33.2	5.04***
60,000+	24.5	23.7	5.05***
Education			
Not HS graduate	16.1	16.7	−3.58***
HS graduate	35.4	36.0	−4.36***
Attended college	26.1	25.6	4.59***
College graduate	22.4	21.8	3.33***
No children in household	56.6	56.3	0.18
Total adult use	17.7	21.4	−5.19***
Number of total ads	2,382	2,081	

*** = statistically significant at 1%; ** = significant at 5%; * = significant at 10%.

advertised than those on violent cable movies, adding to the evidence that movies may be aimed at a narrower market segment than the series. Similarly, the products on mystery series come from firms with more media expenditures and advertised products than those on crime series, which may have a narrower audience. While there is no statistically significant difference in the figures for TNT and TBS in table 8.12, firms advertising on USA had more products advertised overall than those on the local independent WKFT.

Conclusions

The industry committee charged with developing a television program rating system in 1996 had many potential goals: the provision of parents with program

TABLE 8.12. Comparing Media Expenditures, by Cable Subsample

	1993 Mean Parent Company Total Media Expenditures ($000)	Average # of Parent Company Products	Difference of Means Test (*T* Statistic)	
			$	#
Violent movies with warnings	315,528	18		
Violent movies without warnings	293,385	17	1.0	0.8
Violent movies	307,967	18		
Violent series	350,133	22	−2.7***	−3.5***
Crime series	332,471	20		
Mystery series	385,435	25	−1.8*	−2.4**
TNT programming	277,963	17		
TBS programming	298,072	16	−1.2	1.1
USA programming	389,664	24		
WKFT programming	364,332	20	0.9	2.4**

Note: Media expenditures information come from *Ad $ Summary, 1993* (1994). Products were linked to parent company information using *Company/Brand $, 1993* (1994). Total media expenditures are the sum of expenditures on network television, spot television, syndicated television, cable TV networks, network radio, national spot radio, magazines, Sunday magazines, newspapers, and outdoor advertising as reported in *Company/Brand $.*
*** = Statistically significant at the .01 level; ** = significant at the .05 level; * = significant at the .10 level.

information; the protection of broadcaster, cable, advertiser, and producer profits; the encouragement of creative expression by the entertainment community; the heading-off of the development of a more detailed ratings system by the government; and the creation of a system credible enough to keep the issue of ratings from encouraging groups to push for an auction of the broadcast spectrum. The research presented in this volume, which was submitted to the committee head Jack Valenti during the development of the ratings system, indicates the factors one would take into account if effective provision of information about program content were the paramount goal of the ratings system. Chapter 2 indicates that research does indicate how different types of program content give rise to different types of harm for children. Chapters 3 and 4 demonstrate that a coding system based on potential harms is available and has been implemented to describe the differences in violent content in broadcast and cable programs. Chapter 7 shows that how program information affects the viewing decisions of children and parents can be studied, and that the form of the information does make a difference in the efficacy of the information. Many media researchers used such results to conclude that a ratings system that provides specific content information is superior to the age-based category system initially chosen by the industry. This chapter provides evidence on why the committee may have faced incentives to design a ratings system that responded to the interests of advertisers rather than parents.[51]

Program warnings do change the mix of advertisers supporting prime-time movies in systematic ways. In response to program warnings, broadcasters do not change the number of "nonprogram" minutes in shows. They are more likely, however, to run promotions for network shows on theatrical films with warnings, consistent with a drop in price because of advertiser pullouts. For theatrical films, it is clear that warnings have an independent impact on which types of products are advertised on films. The placement of a warning on a violent theatrical film changes the incentives for particular products to advertise. Within the set of violent theatrical films, products aimed at younger consumers, males, and households without children are more likely to advertise on shows with warnings. Products from industries such as sports and leisure or alcoholic beverages play a larger role in supporting programs with warnings, while those products in industries with "family" images such as food or kitchen products are less likely to advertise on theatrical films with warnings. Some of these patterns are also present for warnings on made-for-television movies, although the reactions to these warnings are harder to measure because of the absence of a comparable made-for-television subset to compare the warning movies with. Reactions to warnings on made-for-television movies may differ because these films may be less violent than those theatrical films that receive viewer warnings.

The advertising differences identified as arising from viewer warnings are statistically significant and small in magnitude. In a market where a 30-second advertisement on a prime-time movie may cost $150,000, however, a small number of advertiser pullouts on a movie may translate into significant sums if multiplied across many broadcast movies. The results identified here such as the increase in network promotions on movies with warnings suggest that viewer advisories do translate into lost advertising revenues for prime-time broadcast networks. For example, the shift of 2 percent of advertisements on prime-time broadcast movies with warnings from paid advertising to network promotions could have cost networks approximately $8 million in lost revenues over the course of the sample period (May 1995–February 1996).[52]

These potential losses provide networks with multiple incentives. They will be less likely to place warnings on movies that are truly violent, as evidenced by the UCLA finding that networks had placed viewer advisories on less than half of the prime-time movies that raised issues of concern with respect to violence in the 1994–95 season. In the development of the television ratings systems, networks may have been less willing to give viewers detailed information about violence since this could would raise the probability of advertiser backlash. In the implementation of the ratings system, broadcasters may be more likely to give a film a TV-PG than a TV-14 if advertisers fear that the higher rating translates into greater advertiser pullouts. All these effects point to the importance of outside evaluation by interest groups, nonprofits (e.g., Federman 1996; Rideout

1996), and academics of the content of the television ratings system and the implementation of these ratings.

In the long term, the reduction in advertising returns to violent programs may also affect the mix of programming offered. Evaluating this outcome from a social welfare perspective is difficult, in part because of the uncertainty of the magnitude of negative effects of violent programs on children *and adults.* Current policies such as the V-chip and ratings system are aimed at reducing consumption of violent programming by children. Yet the research in chapter 2 indicates that violent programming may affect both children and adults. Advertiser reactions to warnings may reduce programming that is harmful to both groups, but this may also reduce the utility of adults who would like to consume the programming and are not affected by its content.

Warnings on broadcast network films do change advertiser behavior. These changes in behavior are based not on the distribution of altruism among companies but on the distribution of incentives for firms to respond based on their consumer demographics. These results demonstrate the importance of recognizing the incentives for broadcasters and advertisers in supporting violent programming and of incorporating these incentives into assessments of the television program rating system.

The results of the analysis of cable advertising also confirm the model of advertiser decisions to sponsor violent programs. Advertisements on different types of violent cable programming are targeted at different consumer groups. Products on mystery series are aimed at older or female consumers relative to those on crime series. Advertisements on violent series in general are for products used more by females, older consumers, and those with lower incomes relative to advertisements for products on violent movies. The differences between products advertised on violent cable movies with and without warnings are much less stark, however, than those for movies with and without warnings on prime-time network broadcast television. This suggests that the prospects for advertiser backlash are less likely to influence firms' decisions about sponsoring violent cable programming since interest groups are much less likely to monitor these advertisements than those on prime-time broadcast television. This also indicates that firms' concerns about reputations for sponsoring violent programming may diminish if the division of the television audience into many different audiences makes monitoring of advertising by interest groups less likely.

NOTES

I have benefited from the excellent research of Rob Carscadden, Nancy Torre, Madhuri Bhat, Dan Lipinksi, Robert Malme, Aaron Miller, Matthew Schruers, and Theodore Tatos. Research support from the New York Times Company Foundations and is gratefully acknowledged.

1. Joanne Cantor, Suzanne Stutman, and Victoria Duran, *What Parents Want in a Television Rating System: Results of a National Survey* (Madison: University of Wisconsin, 1996).

2. Jack Valenti, "The Television Ratings System is Simple and User-Friendly," *Los Angeles Times,* January 3, 1997: B9.

3. Nancy Mathis. 1996. "TV Remote Goes Back to Parents; Clinton Applauds Rating Guide Plan," *Houston Chronicle,* March 1, 1996: A1.

4. Mathis, "Clinton Applauds Rating Guide Plan," A1.

5. Richard Zoglin, "Chips Ahoy; As a New Study Warns that Violence Saturates the Airwaves, a Technological Quick Fix Promises to Help. But Will the V Chip Really Protect Our Children?" *Time,* February 18, 1996: 58.

6. Mark Landler, "TV Turns to an Era of Self-Control." *New York Times,* March 17, 1996: B1.

7. James T. Hamilton, *Channeling Violence: The Economic Market for Violent Television Programming* (Princeton: Princeton University Press, 1998).

8. See the reanalysis of Times Mirror polling data in Hamilton 1998. The original polling information was published in Times Mirror 1993.

9. Hamilton, *Channeling Violence.*

10. *National Television Violence Study: Executive Summary 1994–1995* (Studio City, CA: Mediascope, Inc., 1996), 20.

11. Joanne Cantor and Kristen Harrison, "Ratings and Advisories for Television Programming: University of Wisconsin, Madison Study." In *National Television Violence Study: Scientific Papers 1994–1995* (Studio City, CA: Mediascope, 1996), III-14.

12. Diane Mermigas, "Cable Hot in '96 Upfront Sales, BCPM Panel Says." *Electronic Media.* May 27, 1996: 2.

13. Nielsen Media Research, *Household and Persons Cost Per Thousand, November 1995* (New York: Nielsen Media Research, 1995).

14. Landler, "TV Turns," B1.

15. Hamilton, *Channeling Violence.*

16. Landler, "TV Turns," B1.

17. Federman (1996, 19) notes, "According to Don Ohlmeyer, West Coast President of NBC, the network loses between a quarter of a million to a million dollars in advertiser pull-out whenever an advisory is placed on a movie of the week. He also notes that some of that loss is made up by other advertisers who aren't bothered by an advisory."

18. As noted in chapter 4, the figures for violent programs on network-affiliated broadcast stations include both programming they receive from the network and the other fare such as syndicated shows that they air.

19. For the fall 1993 sweeps period, the AFA's top 12 sponsors of violence on prime time were Chrysler Corp. (#1), ConAgra, Burroughs Wellcome, Grand Metropolitan, Unilever, Miles Inc., Helene Curtis Industries, Campbell Soup, Pepsico, Ciba-Geigy, J. C. Penney, and Clorox. For the May 1995 sweeps the AFA based its "Dirty Dozen" ratings on incidents of sex, violence, and profanity in the shows that companies sponsored. The group listed the "12 Top Sponsors of Prime-Time Filth" as Visa USA, Anheuser-Busch, Sara Lee, Toyota Motor Sales, MasterCard International, Paramount Communications, Maybelline, Adolph Coors, MCI Communications, Bristol-Myers Squibb, Unilever, and Coca-Cola. See American Family Association, 1993, 1995.

20. The AFA called for a boycott of Unilever, maker of Elizabeth Arden cosmetics and Close-Up toothpaste, for sponsoring *NYPD Blue,* a show that Rev. Wildmon described as an attempt to "open the doors of sexual nudity on prime-time television." The AFA "claims to have changed the advertising policies of some of the mightiest corporations in America, including Burger King, Clorox, and SC Johnson. Pepsi pulled a 'sacrilegious ad' featuring Madonna and cancelled sponsorship of her world tour after AFA lobbying." See Olins 1995.

21. This is a simplified description of advertising decisions. For models of advertising purchases that take into account the frequency of exposures of a given group to particular messages, see Rust 1986.

22. A rating for a demographic group is defined as the percentage of the number of people in that group watching a program. A program's share for a demographic group is the percentage of the members of that group watching television at a given time that are watching the particular program.

23. The placement of a warning on a program may or may not cause the advertising price received by the broadcaster to drop. First, consider ads that have already been sold in the "upfront" market. The warning may cause some companies that fear controversy to withdraw from their commitment close to airtime. If the network is able to find advertisers who are indifferent to the warning that are willing to buy this time, the price will not drop. If there are not advertisers willing to pay the previous price, then the broadcaster will have to lower the price to sell the commercial time. In terms of spot market sales, assume there are a set of firms just willing to pay a price X to advertise on the movie. The addition of the warning may then deter some of these companies, but there may still be a number of firms willing to pay this price. If not, the broadcaster may have to lower the price to sell the time on the program with an advisory.

24. In 1994 broadcast television donated $113.9 million in time to Advertising Council public service campaigns. See Elliott 1995, D-9.

25. See Spitzer 1996 for a discussion of the impact of the V-chip on programming.

26. See UCLA Center for Communication Policy 1995, 77.

27. Federal Document Clearing House, Inc., "Senator Simon and Others Discuss an Audit of Television Violence," September 20, 1995. News conference transcript available in Lexis CURNWS file.

28. *National Television Violence Study,* I-45. Note that the description of movie genre data is based on films aired on broadcast television (which are often edited), basic cable, and premium cable (which are often unedited). The results did not further distinguish between movies shown on broadcast versus cable.

29. The distribution by genre of prime-time network broadcast movies for 1987 to 1993 was drama 46 percent, comedy 13 percent, crime-drama 13 percent, adventure 6 percent, comedy-drama 5 percent, mystery 4 percent, fantasy 3 percent, western 3 percent, thriller 3 percent, other 3 percent, and science fiction 2 percent (see Hamilton, *Channeling Violence*). Film genre was determined by the program's listing in *TV Guide.*

30. Note that for nine of the films listed as originally made for television, the Internet viewer's guide also listed MPAA ratings for these films and indicators of film content.

31. For the theatrical films shown in prime time, the distribution by rating is 1 percent unrated, 4 percent G, 30 percent PG, 24 percent PG-13, and 41 percent R.

32. A difference of means test between ratings for 1987–93 versus 1995 is statistically significant at the .01 level for each of the ratings categories in table 8.1.

33. Media buyers explicitly describe programs such as Sunday night movies as often more oriented toward women than men. Describing the shift of the science fiction program *X-Files* by Fox to Sunday evening, one media buyer said, "I think '*X-Files*' will get creamed. That move is a big mistake, because in the fourth quarter of the year TNT and ESPN will have sports to lure male viewers from '*X-Files*,' and the other networks' movies are pretty female-oriented." See Littlefield 1996, F9.

34. Hamilton, *Channeling Violence*.

35. Of the 357 movies scheduled between May 1, 1995, and February 29, 1996, a total of 252 were coded for commercial content. All movies were recorded and coded that aired during prime time on the four major broadcast networks from May 1 through December 31, 1995 (except for those that were preempted or experienced a recording error). From January 1 through February 29, 1996, only those movies that had a violence indicator or warning were coded. These additional films were coded to increase the size of the comparison sets to test the impact of warning labels. The results in the paper are thus presented as subsample comparisons rather than for the sample as a whole because the sample is intentionally weighted to focus on violent films.

36. Cole (UCLA Center for Communication Policy 1995, 72) notes that a "large number of made-for-television movies have ominous or threatening titles that imply the show will be violent, whether or not it actually is violent."

37. These figures are comparable to previous estimates of nonprogram minutes. In November 1992 there were 13.5 minutes of nonprogram content per hour of prime time on the four major networks. See Jensen 1993, 33.

38. Movies and videos were distinguished from the category of product ads because the Simmons data collected for product ads was much more detailed than the data available on consumer demographics for the particular films advertised. Data on general movie and video use were used in analysis of the consumer demographics for movie and video ads.

39. According to an official at Coors Brewing, the company tries to avoid advertising on "family shows" so that they avoid advertising to children and pregnant women. Supporting violent programs may ironically be part of a policy to reduce exposure of children to alcohol advertising. See Bhat 1996, 25.

40. Table 8.5 and appendix table 8.5 report the consumer demographics of individuals using the product or goods in the product category for the product advertised.

41. Since the Simmons data were used at the product-specific level (e.g., what percentage of consumers use a particular brand) and category level (e.g., what percentage of consumers use this category of good), the figure on mean adult usage represents an average of both product-specific and category-specific use.

42. The Z statistics for the difference of proportion of male products are: theatrical nonviolent (29 percent) versus theatrical violent with warnings (39 percent) $Z = -2.5$; theatrical violent with warning versus theatrical violent without warnings (38 percent) $Z = .2$; made-for-television without warning (32 percent) versus made-for-television with warning (31 percent) $Z = .2$; made-for-television with warning versus "violent" made-for-television without warning (28 percent) $Z = .8$.

43. *National Television Violence Study: Executive Summary,* 20.

44. Second quarter prime-time ratings based on coverage homes for each network for May 29, 1995, through June 25, 1995, were 2.4 for TNT, 2.2 for USA, and 1.9 for TBS. See Brown 1995, 20.

45. The "crime" series included were on TNT *Chips, How the West Was Won, Kung Fu, Starsky and Hutch,* and *Wild, Wild West,* on TBS *Matlock,* on USA *Knight Rider, Macgyver, Magnum, P.I., Silk Stalkings,* and *Tekwar,* and on WKFT *High Tide, Legendary Journeys of Hercules, Renegade, The Extraordinary,* and *Vanishing Son.* The mystery series were *Forever Knight* (WKFT), *In the Heat of the Night* (TNT), *Murder, She Wrote* (USA), and *Perry Mason* (TBS). The children's series were *Tattooed Teenage Alien Fighters* (USA) and *VR Troopers* (WKFT).

46. Assessing TNT's programming in June 1995, *Mediaweek* noted: "Arguably the boldest stroke made by Siegel [the network president] et al. came last January when TNT yanked its *Bugs Bunny* cartoon block in access (6–8 P.M.) in favor of more-adult fare, such as the '70s period piece *Starsky and Hutch* and *In the Heat of the Night.* The latter . . . has hit somewhat of a nerve at the net, increasing the number of adults 25–54 tuning in to the daypart by 52 percent, and women 25–54 by 58 percent. 'It's not just a bunch of blue-hairs watching,' notes Siegel . . . TNT's '*Saturday Nitro,*' which features an action movie—often of a campy nature—scheduled from 10 p.m. to midnight, is up 24 percent in men 18–49, 21 percent in women 18–49 and 23 percent in adults 18–49." See Burgi 1995, 25.

47. For discussion of the impact of channel ownership on program diversity, see Owen and Wildman 1992, chapters 3 and 4.

48. Hamilton, *Channeling Violence.*

49. Within cable series there are also evident audience differences. Ads on cable crime series had a higher mean percentage of product users in the 18–24 and 25–34 demographic categories, while ads on mystery programs had a higher mean percentage of product users in the 55–64 and 65+ age groups.

50. Additional evidence that warnings on basic cable movies do not generate the advertiser backlash observed in broadcast films includes the fact that for products advertised on violent cable movies with and without warnings the percentage of male consumers is identical (50.2 percent) and that there is no statistical difference in the percentage of users without children in the home (56.7 percent for movies without warnings versus 56.6 percent for those with warnings). In contrast, for broadcast films movies with warnings had products advertised that had a higher percentage of male users and a higher percentage of users without children than violent movies without warnings.

51. The legal analysis in chapter 11 stresses that while the FCC could appoint a commission to develop a ratings methodology if it were dissatisfied with the system developed by the industry, under the V-chip legislation the industry would not be required to use this alternative methodology. This in effect gave the industry committee greater assurance that the system they adopted would be unlikely to be supplanted even if interest groups, legislators, and parents expressed dissatisfaction with the proposal.

52. Consider: 357 (the number of films over the sample period) × .14 (that carry warnings) × .02 (shift in ads from paid advertising to promos) × 77 (ads per movie) × $100,000 (per ad) = $7.7 million (forgone ad revenue). This calculation is an approximation, for it ignores the fact that advertiser backlash could cause some ads to be sold at

a lower price rather than shifted to promos and ignores the additional revenues that network promotions for shows may generate as they translate into more viewers in the long run.

REFERENCES

American Family Association. 1993. *The 12 Top Sponsors of Violence on Prime-Time TV.* Tupelo, MS: American Family Association.

American Family Association. 1995. *AFA Dirty Dozen, The 12 Top Sponsors of Prime-Time Filth.* Tupelo, MS: American Family Association.

Bhat, M. 1996. *How Should Advertising Agencies Advise Corporate Sponsors About Advertising on Violent Television in the Era of the Vchip?* Master's Memo. Durham, NC: Duke University, Sanford Institute of Public Policy.

Brown, R. 1995. "If It's Monday, It Must Be Wrestling: TNT Goes to Mat with USA over New Pro-Wrestling Series." *Broadcasting and Cable,* August 21: 32.

Burgi, M. 1995. "Weathering Heights." *Mediaweek,* June 19: 25.

Bushman, B., and A. D. Stack. 1996. "Forbidden Fruit Versus Tainted Fruit: Effects of Warning Labels on Attraction to TV Violence." *Journal of Experimental Psychology: Applied* 2(3): 207–26.

Cantor, J., and K. Harrison. 1996. "Ratings and Advisories for Television Programming: University of Wisconsin, Madison Study." In *National Television Violence Study: Scientific Papers 1994–1995,* III-1–III-26. Studio City, CA: Mediascope.

Cantor, J., K. Harrison, and M. Krcmar. 1996. *Ratings and Advisories: Implications for a New Rating System for Television.* Paper prepared for Duke Conference on Media Violence and Public Policy, June 28–29. Durham, NC: Duke University, Sanford Institute of Public Policy.

Cantor, J., and M. B. Krcmar. 1996. "Part II: Effects of Advisories and Ratings on Parent-Child Discussions of Television Viewing Choice." In *National Television Violence Study: Scientific Papers 1994–1995,* III-27–III-50. Studio City, CA: Mediascope.

Cantor, J., S. Stutman, and V. Duran. 1996. *What Parents Want in a Television Rating System: Results of a National Survey.* Madison: University of Wisconsin Communication Arts.

Cowan, J. 1979. *See No Evil; The Backstage Battle over Sex and Violence on Television.* New York: Simon and Schuster.

Elliot, S. 1995. "Donations Up in '94 for Public Service." *New York Times,* July 24: D9.

Federal Document Clearing House, Inc. 1995. "Senator Simon and Others Discuss an Audit on Television Violence." *FDCH Political Transcripts,* September 20.

Federman, J. 1996. *Media Ratings; Design, Use and Consequences.* Studio City, CA: Mediascope.

Hamilton, J. T. 1995. *Marketing Violence: The Impact of Labeling Violent Television Content.* Dewitt Wallace Center for Communications and Journalism Working Paper Series. Durham, NC: Duke University, Terry Sanford Institute of Public Policy.

———. 1998. *Channeling Violence: The Economic Market for Violent Television Programming.* Princeton: Princeton University Press.

Jensen, J. 1993. "Prime-Time Clutter Falls Slightly; But Commercial Time Rises." *Advertising Age,* March 8: 33.

Kunkel, D., B. J. Wilson, D. Linz, J. Potter, E. Donnerstein, S. L. Smith, E. Blumenthal, and T. Gray. 1996. "Violence in Television Programming Overall: University of California, Santa Barbara Study." In *National Television Violence Study: Scientific Papers 1994–1995,* I-1–172. Studio City, CA: Mediascope.

Landler, M. 1996. "TV Turns to an Era of Self-Control." *New York Times,* March 17: B1.

Leading National Advertisers. 1994a. *Ad $ Summary 1993.* New York: Leading National Advertisers, Inc.

———. 1994b. *Company Brand $ 1993.* New York: Leading National Advertisers, Inc.

Littlefield, K. 1996. "Ad Buyers Not Excited by Fall Schedules." *Orange County Register,* May 26: F9.

Mathis, N. 1996. "TV Remote Goes Back to Parents; Clinton Applauds Rating Guide Plan." Houston Chronicle, March 1: A1.

Mermigas, D. 1996. "Cable Hot in '96 Upfront Sales, BCPM Panel Says." *Electronic Media,* May 27: 2.

Montgomery, K. C. 1989. *Target: Prime Time: Advocacy Groups and the Struggle Over Prime Time.* New York: Oxford University Press.

National Television Violence Study: Executive Summary 1994–1995. 1996a. Studio City, CA: Mediascope.

National Television Violence Study: Scientific Papers 1994–1995. 1996b. Studio City, CA: Mediascope.

Nielsen Media Research. 1996. *Nielsen Television Index: Household and Persons Cost per Thousand, November 1995.* New York: Nielsen Media Research.

Olins, R. 1995. "Moral Crusade Hits Unilever." *Sunday Times,* June 18: Business.

Olson, M. 1971. *The Logic of Collective Action: Public Goods and the Theory of Groups.* Cambridge: Harvard University Press.

Owen, B. M., and S. S. Wildman. 1992. *Video Economics.* Cambridge: Harvard University Press.

Rideout, V. 1996. *Making Television Ratings Work for Children and Families: The Perspective of Children's Experts.* Santa Monica, CA: Children Now.

Roper Organization, Inc. 1993. *America's Watching: Public Attitudes toward Television.* Roper Organization.

Rust, R. T. 1986. *Advertising Media Models, A Practical Guide.* Lexington, MA: Lexington Books.

Simmons Market Research Bureau. 1994. *Simmons Study of Media and Markets 1993.* New York: Simmons Market Research Bureau.

Spitzer, M. L. 1996. *The Constitutional Law and Economics of the V Chip.* Paper prepared for Duke Conference on Media Violence and Public Policy, June 28–29. Durham, NC: Duke University, Sanford Institute of Public Policy.

TV Parental Guidelines Oversight Monitoring Board. 1996. *The TV Parental Guidelines.* Washington, DC: TV Parental Guidelines Oversight Monitoring Board.

UCLA Center for Communication Policy. 1995. *The UCLA Television Violence Monitoring Report.* Los Angeles: UCLA Center for Communication Policy.

Valenti, J. 1997. "The Television Ratings System Is Simple and User-Friendly." *Los Angeles Times,* January 3: 9.

Zoglin, R. 1996. "Chips Ahoy; As a New Study Warns that Violence Saturates the Airwaves, a Technological Quick Fix Promises to Help. But Will the V Chip Really Protect Our Children?" *Time,* February 18: 58.

APPENDIX 1

A Model of Advertising on Violent versus Nonviolent Programs

A firm considering the purchase of advertising time on violent and nonviolent programs will consider the sales generated by advertising, the possible consumer backlash from advertising on violent programs, and the costs of advertising. To model this decision, let

Q_v, Q_{nv} = Amount of minutes of advertising time purchased on violent or nonviolent programs

R_v, R_{nv} = Average ratings for the violent or nonviolent programs

P_v, P_{nv} = Average price per minute of advertising time on violent or nonviolent programs

α_i = Demographics of a product's consumers. This may include the percentage of a product's customers that are 18–34 or the percentage of a product's customers that are male

I = Amount of information that people have on whether a firm advertises on violent programs

VS = Sales revenue generated by advertisements on violent programs

NS = Sales revenue generated by advertisements on nonviolent programs

BL = Change in sales revenue if a product's consumers are fully informed about a firm's advertising purchases of violent programming

A = Probability that consumers will be fully informed about a firm's advertising purchases.

Note that $VS(Q_v, R_v, \alpha_i)$ and $NS(Q_{nv}, R_{nv}, \alpha_i)$. By assumption $VS_Q, NS_{Q_{nv}}, VS_{R_v}, NS_{R_{nv}} > 0$. The demographic characteristics α_i are defined so that as α_i increases VS increases and NS decreases. Thus as the proportion of a product's customers that are young increases, for a given level of other variables (such as program ratings), sales generated by violent programs will increase and those from nonviolent programs will decrease ($VS_{\alpha_i} > 0$, $NS_{\alpha_i} < 0$). Similarly, as the percentage of a product's customers that are male increases, the sales generated by advertising on violent programs will increase. The expected value of the change in sales from advertising on violent programs is $A(I)BL(Q_v, R_v, \alpha_i)$, where A_p BL_Q, $BL_{R_v} > 0$. Note that $BL_{\alpha_i} < 0$ since as the percentage of a product's users that are male increases the loss in sales will be lower since males are less likely to view television violence as a significant problem. Only advertising costs are considered (e.g., production costs are ignored here).

The firm will choose Q_v and Q_{nv} to maximize Z, where $Z = VS(Q_v, R_v, \alpha_i)$ $+ NS(Q_{nv}, R_{nv}, \alpha_i) - A(I)BL(Q_v, R_v, \alpha_i) - P_v Q_v - P_{nv}Q_{nv}$. The first order conditions are

$$Z_{Qv} = VS_{Qv} - A(I)BL_{Q_v} - P_v = 0$$

$$Z_{Q_{nv}} = NS_{Q_{nv}} - P_{nv} = 0,$$

which indicates that when the firm is maximizing profits from advertising that $\dfrac{VS_{Q_v} - A(I)BL_{Q_v}}{P_v} = \dfrac{NS_{Q_{nv}}}{P_{nv}}$ This means that the net return per dollar spent on advertising on violent programs will equal the return on a dollar spent on advertising on nonviolent programs. The Hessian is

$$|H| = \begin{vmatrix} VS_{Q_v Q_v} - A(I)BL_{Q_v Q_v} & 0 \\ 0 & NS_{Q_{nv} Q_{nv}} \end{vmatrix}.$$

The second order sufficient condition for a maximum will be satisfied if we assume that $VS_{Q_v Q_v} - A(I)BL_{Q_v Q_v}$ is negative and $(VS_{Q_v Q_v} - A(I)BL_{Q_{nv} Q_v})(NS_{Q_{nv} Q_{nv}})$ is positive. This also implies that $NS_{Q_{nv} Q_{nv}}$ is negative.

We can explore how changes in the exogenous variables $(\alpha_i, R_v, R_{nv}, P_v, P_{nv})$ affect a firm's selection of $\bar{Q}_v$ and $\bar{Q}_{nv}$ by using Cramer's rule. As α_i increases, we find that

$$\frac{\delta \bar{Q}_v}{\delta \alpha_i} = \frac{(-VS_{Q_v \alpha_i} + A(I)BL_{Q_v \alpha_i})NS_{Q_{nv} Q_{nv}}}{|H|} \text{ and}$$

$$\frac{\delta \bar{Q}_{nv}}{\delta \alpha_i} = \frac{(VS_{Q_v Q_v} - A(I)BL_{Q_v Q_v})(-NS_{Q_v \alpha_i})}{|H|}.$$

Note that from the assumption that the second order condition is satisfied we know that the denominator $|H|$ is positive. Since $NS_{Q_{nv} Q_{nv}}$ is negative from the second order condition assumption, $\dfrac{\delta \bar{Q}_v}{\delta \alpha_i}$ will be positive if $VS_{Q_v \alpha_i} > A(I)BL_{Q_v \alpha_i}$ and negative if $VS_{Q_v \alpha_i} < A(I)BL_{Q_v \alpha_i}$. Thus as the percentage of male consumers for a product increases, the purchase of advertising on violent programs will increase if the increase in sales caused by an additional advertisement as the male percentage increases is higher than the change in expected value of the backlash from an additional advertisement as the male percentage increases.

$(VS_{Q_v Q_v} - A(I)BL_{Q_v Q_v})$ is negative from the second order condition, and $NS_{Q_v \alpha_i}$ is negative by assumption. This means that $\dfrac{\delta \overline{Q}_{nv}}{\delta \alpha_i}$ is negative, i.e., that as the male percentage of product customers increases fewer advertisements will be bought on nonviolent programs.

Use of Cramer's rule also demonstrates the changes in advertising purchases as I increases, which would occur if warning labels were placed on violent films so consumers were more likely to be aware of firm's advertising actions:

$$\frac{\delta \overline{Q}_v}{\delta I} = \frac{(A_I BL_{Q_v})NS_{Q_{nv} Q_{nv}}}{|H|} \quad \text{and}$$

$$\frac{\delta \overline{Q}_{nv}}{\delta I} = 0.$$

A_I is positive, since by assumption the probability that people will associate a company with its advertising on violent programs increases if warning labels are placed on violent films. BL_{Q_v} is positive and $NS_{Q_{nv} Q_{nv}}$ negative, so $\dfrac{\delta \overline{Q}_v}{\delta I}$ is negative. A firm will place fewer advertisements on violent programs as I increases. Note that this impact would be lower for firms with smaller backlash changes.

As ratings increase for violent programs, purchases of advertisements on the programs will depend on the relationship between sales increases and consumer backlash. Note that

$$\frac{\delta \overline{Q}_v}{\delta R_v} = \frac{(-VS_{Q_v R_v} + A(I)BL_{Q_v R_v})NS_{Q_{nv} Q_{nv}}}{|H|} \quad \text{and}$$

$$\frac{\delta \overline{Q}_{nv}}{\delta R_v} = 0.$$

If the sales term outweighs the backlash term, the firm will purchase more advertisements on violent programs as ratings go up. If the backlash term is dominant, then the firm will purchase fewer advertisements on violent shows. The model also indicates that as the price of advertising on violent programs goes up, the firm will purchase fewer advertisements on these shows.

TABLE A8.1. Percentage Distribution of Advertisements on Made-for-Television Movies

Advertisement Category	Movie Subsamples			Difference of Proportion Test (*Z* stat)	
	(1) No Warning	(2) Warning	(3) "Violent" No Warning	1 vs. 2	2 vs. 3
Product	62.9	61.7	62.3	0.86	−0.32
Movie	1	2.8	1.4	−3.99***	2.50**
Video	0.9	1	1.1	−0.41	−0.38
Health services	0.1	0.2	0	−1.14	1.63
Utility	0.1	0.2	0.1	−0.19	0.66
Military	0.2	0.4	0.3	−1.21	0.55
Nonprofit	0.2	0.1	0.1	1.08	0.00
Public service	1.3	1.5	1.3	−0.48	0.37
Network	21.6	22.7	22.2	−0.87	0.33
Local station	11.7	9.5	11.2	2.62***	−1.43
Total	100	100	99.9		
Network, local station PSA	34.6	33.7	34.7	0.65	−0.55
Commercial advertisements	65.4	66.3	65.2	−0.65	0.60
Total number of advertisements	10,700	1,318	1,408		

*** = Statistically significant at 1%; ** = at 5%; * = at 10%.

TABLE A8.2. Percentage Distribution of Advertisements across Simmons Product Categories, Theatrical Movies

Product Category	Nonviolent	Violent, Warning	Difference Test (Z stat)
Product unclassified	8.5	10.2	−1.6
Automobiles, cycles, trucks, & vans	12.2	13.4	−1.0
Automotive products & services	0.4	0.8	−1.6
Travel	1.3	1.8	−1.1
Banking, investments, insurance, credit cards & contributions, memberships & public activities	2.0	1.8	0.4
Games & toys, children's and babies' apparel & specialty products	1.6	0.9	1.8*
Computers, books, discs, records, tapes, stereo, telephones, TV & video	5.6	4.7	1.1
Appliances, garden care, sewing & photography	3.5	3.6	−0.1
Home furnishings & home improvements	2.3	2.0	0.5
Sports & leisure	0.8	3.6	−5.2***
Restaurants, stores & grocery shopping	17.8	15.0	2.1**
Direct mail & other in-home shopping, yellow pages, florists, telegrams, faxes & greeting cards	0.8	0.5	1.2
Jewelry, watches, luggage, writing tools and men's apparel	1.3	0.8	1.4
Women's apparel	1.2	1.1	0.3
Distilled spirits, mixed drinks, malt beverages, wine & tobacco products	0.5	2.7	−4.7***
Coffee, tea, cocoa, milk, soft drinks, juices & bottled water	3.7	4.2	−0.7
Dairy products, desserts, baking & bread products	2.0	0.6	3.5***
Cereals & spreads, rice, pasta, pizza, mexican foods, fruits & vegetables	3.4	1.8	2.9***
Soup, meat, fish, poultry, condiments, dressings & sauces	3.1	1.6	2.9***
Chewing gum, candy, cookies & snacks	3.7	4.6	−1.3
Soap, laundry, paper products & kitchen wraps	2.7	2.2	0.9
Household cleaners, room deodorizers, pest controls & pet foods	3.0	2.2	1.5
Health care products & remedies	6.2	7.6	−1.6
Oral hygiene products, skin care, deodorants & drug stores	3.8	5.9	−2.7***
Fragrances, hair care & shaving products	6.2	4.0	2.9***
Women's beauty aids, cosmetics & personal products	2.6	2.5	0.1
Total	99.9	100.1	

*** = Statistically significant at 1%; ** = Statistically significant at 5%; * = Statistically significant at 10%.

TABLE A8.3. **Percentage Distribution of Advertisements across Simmons Product Categories, Made-for-Television Movies without and with Warnings**

Product Category	No Warning	Warning	Difference Test (Z stat)
Product unclassified	7.3	10.2	-2.7***
Automobiles, cycles, trucks, & vans	13.2	10.0	2.9***
Automotive products & services	0.6	0.7	-0.3
Travel	1.1	0.2	4.4***
Banking, investments, insurance, credit cards & contributions, memberships & public activities	1.7	1.3	1.0
Games & toys, children's and babies' apparel & specialty products	0.6	1.6	-2.4**
Computers, books, discs, records, tapes, stereo, telephones, TV & video	4.9	6.0	-1.3
Appliances, garden care, sewing & photography	4.3	3.4	1.4
Home furnishings & home improvements	2.6	1.0	3.9***
Sports & leisure	0.8	2.7	-3.3***
Restaurants, stores & grocery shopping	16.7	16.6	0.1
Direct mail & other in-home shopping, yellow pages, florists, telegrams, faxes & greeting cards	0.7	0.1	3.6***
Jewelry, watches, luggage, writing tools and men's apparel	0.9	0.9	-0.1
Women's apparel	1.5	2.3	-1.6
Distilled spirits, mixed drinks, malt beverages, wine & tobacco products	0.8	2.1	-2.7**
Coffee, tea, cocoa, milk, soft drinks, juices & bottled water	3.3	3.4	-0.1
Dairy products, desserts, baking & bread products	2.5	1.3	2.9***
Cereals & spreads, rice, pasta, pizza, mexican foods, fruits & vegetables	4.0	0.7	8.9***
Soup, meat, fish, poultry, condiments, dressings & sauces	3.0	2.0	2.1**
Chewing gum, candy, cookies & snacks	3.3	3.5	-0.3
Soap, laundry, paper products & kitchen wraps	3.3	2.5	1.3
Household cleaners, room deodorizers, pest controls & pet foods	3.1	2.2	1.6
Health care products & remedies	7.3	10.3	-2.8***
Oral hygiene products, skin care, deodorants & drug stores	4.5	5.8	-1.5
Fragrances, hair care & shaving products	5.7	5.6	0.2
Women's beauty aids, cosmetics & personal products	2.5	3.7	-1.8*
Total	100.1	99.9	

*** = Statistically significant at 1%; ** = Statistically significant at 5%; * = Statistically significant at 10%.

TABLE A8.4. Percentage Distribution of Advertisements across Simmons Product Categories, Made-for-Television Movies with Warnings and "Violent" Made-for-Television Movies without Warnings

Product Category	Warning	"Violent," No Warning	Difference Test (Z stat)
Product unclassified	10.2	9.2	0.7
Automobiles, cycles, trucks, & vans	10.0	13.0	−2.0**
Automotive products & services	0.7	0.5	0.4
Travel	0.2	1.3	−2.6**
Banking, investments, insurance, credit cards & contributions, memberships & public activities	1.3	1.3	−0.1
Games & toys, children's and babies' apparel & specialty products	1.6	0.5	2.2**
Computers, books, discs, records, tapes, stereo, telephones, TV & video	6.0	5.9	0.1
Appliances, garden care, sewing & photography	3.4	4.4	−1.1
Home furnishings & home improvements	1.0	2.2	−1.9*
Sports & leisure	2.7	1.0	2.6**
Restaurants, stores & grocery shopping	16.6	17.1	−0.3
Direct mail & other in-home shopping, yellow pages, florists, telegrams, faxes & greeting cards	0.1	0.4	−1.3
Jewelry, watches, luggage, writing tools & men's apparel	0.9	0.9	0.1
Women's apparel	2.3	1.1	2.0*
Distilled spirits, mixed drinks, malt beverages, wine & tobacco products	2.1	1.4	1.1
Coffee, tea, cocoa, milk, soft drinks, juices & bottled water	3.4	4.1	−0.8
Dairy products, desserts, baking & bread products	1.3	2.1	−1.3
Cereals & spreads, rice, pasta, pizza, mexican foods, fruits & vegetables	0.7	3.3	−4.0***
Soup, meat, fish, poultry, condiments, dressings & sauces	2.0	2.4	−0.6
Chewing gum, candy, cookies & snacks	3.5	2.4	1.3
Soap, laundry, paper products & kitchen wraps	2.5	3.6	−1.3
Household cleaners, room deodorizers, pest controls & pet foods	2.2	2.7	−0.7
Health care products & remedies	10.3	6.7	2.7***
Oral hygiene products, skin care, deodorants & drug stores	5.8	3.9	1.8*
Fragrances, hair care & shaving products	5.6	6.4	−0.7
Women's beauty aids, cosmetics, & personal products	3.7	2.1	2.0**
Total	99.9	99.9	

*** = Statistically significant at 1%; ** = Statistically significant at 5%; * = Statistically significant at 10%.

Table A8.5. **Consumer Demographics of Products Advertised on Made-for-Television Movies**

Mean % of Product Consumers in Category	Movies Subsamples			Difference of Mean Test (T stat)	
	(1) No Warning	(2) Warning	(3) "Violent" No Warning	1 vs. 2	2 vs. 3
Age					
18–24	11.8	12.9	12.1	−6.56***	3.92***
25–34	23.9	24.6	24.1	−4.58***	2.92***
35–44	24.5	24.4	24.4	0.56	0.20
45–54	16.1	15.8	16.1	3.74***	−2.95***
55–64	10.6	10.2	10.6	5.32***	−3.62***
65 up	13.1	12.2	12.9	5.31***	−3.01***
Male	49.0	49.5	49.4	−1.84*	0.51
Female	51.0	50.5	50.7	1.86*	−0.55
Income					
<10,000	8.1	8.1	8.0	0.30	0.55
10–19,000	14.1	14.0	14.0	1.77*	−0.05
20–29,000	16.2	16.2	16.2	−0.76	−0.20
30–39,000	15.0	15.1	15.0	−1.67*	1.56
40,000+	46.6	46.7	46.8	−0.38	−0.51
50,000+	34.1	34.0	34.2	0.40	−0.91
60,000+	24.2	24.1	24.3	0.61	−0.91
Education					
Not HS graduate	16.1	16.2	16.0	−0.70	1.20
HS graduate	35.7	35.8	35.5	−0.84	1.42
Attended college	25.8	26.1	26.0	−2.47**	0.78
College graduate	22.5	22.0	22.6	2.17**	−1.97**
No children in household	56.2	55.4	56.3	3.49***	−3.41***
Total adult use	20.6	19.7	20.0	1.05	−0.30
Number of total ads	8,728	999	1,141		

*** = Statistically significant at 1%; ** = at 5%; * = at 10%.

TABLE A8.6. Top Ten Advertisers by Theatrical Movie Subsample

A. Nonviolent ($N = 843$ Matched Advertisements)

Advertiser	Total Advertisements
1. Procter & Gamble	44
2. General Motors Corp.	42
3. Pepsico Inc.	38
4. Sears Roebuck & Co.	35
5. McDonald's Corp.	33
6. Chrysler Corp.	29
7. AT&T Corp.	23
8. Ford Motor Co.	21
9. Nissan Motor Co.	20
10. General Mills Inc.	19

B. Violent, Warning ($N = 689$ Matched Advertisements)

Advertiser	Total Advertisements
1. Pepsico Inc.	45
2. Warner-Lambert Co.	28
3. Unilever PLC	24
4. General Motors Corp.	23
4. McDonald's Corp.	23
6. Procter & Gamble	18
7. Ford Motor Co.	17
7. Subway Franchising Co.	17
9. Wendy's International	16
10. Time-Warner Inc.	15

C. Violent, No Warning ($N = 727$ Matched Advertisements)

Advertiser	Total Advertisements
1. Sears Roebuck & Co.	48
2. McDonald's Corp.	41
3. Pepsico Inc.	39
4. Procter & Gamble	38
5. Walt Disney Co.	20
6. General Motors Co.	19
6. Wendy's International	19
8. AT&T Corp.	18
8. Warner-Lambert Co.	18
10. Philip Morris Co.	17

Note: Of the products advertised on theatrical movies in the sample, 2,259 matched with information in *Company/Brand $ 1993* that linked products with parent company information.

Chapter 9

Stop the Violence: Lessons from Antiviolence Campaigns Using Mass Media

Myra Gregory Knight, Karen Kemp, Jane D. Brown, and Frank Biocca

Introduction

In the early 1980s, an animated dog character named McGruff urged television audiences nationwide to "take a bite out of crime." Viewers sat up and took notice of the funny, trench-coated canine. Almost a quarter of those who saw the dog responded by changing their behaviors in accord with his suggestions. They locked their doors, turned on their lights, and helped their neighbors form community crime-watch programs. In some cases, they went even further and bought guard dogs to aid in their crime prevention efforts (O'Keefe 1985). The McGruff campaign, as the project came to be called, helped discredit the idea that the mass media could do little to positively shape human behavior. It demonstrated that, with carefully defined goals and attention to empirically supported communication principles, the mass media could figure prominently in addressing public health and safety issues.

Since McGruff, evidence has continued to mount that such campaigns can be highly successful (DeJong and Winsten 1990). Many successful campaigns employing the mass media have targeted issues of significant public concern. Many also have benefited from an improved understanding of the complex, psychological processes underlying behavior change. In the public health arena, for example, mass media campaigns have tackled stubborn social problems such as unhealthy lifestyles (Fortmann et al. 1995; Farquhar et al. 1977, 1985), drug and alcohol abuse (May and Mintz 1988), and teenage pregnancy (Vincent, Clearie, and Schlucheter 1987).

Meanwhile, the issue that prompted the McGruff campaign remains a salient public concern. Levels of violent crime in the United States stand close to their all-time high: between 1974 and 1993, violent crime grew to 14 percent from 10 percent of all reported crime (Russell 1995). Violence against women and teens is particularly pervasive (Apfel 1995; Seufert-Barr 1995). In a recent survey, almost three-quarters of U.S. teens said they are afraid of violent crimes among their peers. That fear appears justified: Approximately 3,100 teens aged 15–19 were murdered in 1993, and 18 percent of all murderers were teens aged 15–19 (Apfel 1995). Since 1984, gun homicides by teenagers have tripled, and an estimated 100,000 children carry guns to school each day (Owens 1994).

The fictional world contains parallel threats. The most comprehensive assessment of televised violence to date found that violence—defined as credible threats, aggressive acts, or harmful consequences of unseen violence—occurs in a majority (57 percent) of programs. One-fourth of the violent interactions on television involve a handgun, and in 73 percent of violent scenes perpetrators suffer no consequences for their behavior. These circumstances make it more likely that viewers become desensitized to violence and perceive violence as a risk-free means to an end (Kunkel et al. 1996).

In an early, dramatic display of how life can imitate "art," a group of San Francisco schoolchildren sexually assaulted a nine-year-old girl after watching the 1974 TV movie "Born Innocent," in which reform school residents use a mop handle to rape a young girl (Cowan 1978; Montgomery 1989). Research confirms what that incident and others like it imply: Although not all viewers are inclined to model violent behaviors depicted on television, watching televised violence is one pathway for social learning of aggressive behavior (Heath et al. 1989; Comstock and Paik 1990). Some researchers estimate that television contributes as much as 10 percent to the level of real-life violence (Strasburger 1995). If this statistic is valid, then television may be implicated in roughly 2,500 U.S. homicides annually.

The public's concern over the connection between televised and real-life violence has continued since the 1950s, when the first congressional hearings on television violence were convened. In 1977 the National Parent-Teachers Association led a large antiviolence campaign, a potent blend of advertiser boycotts, license challenges, a grassroots monitoring campaign, and nationwide media coverage (Montgomery 1989). More recently, the American Academy of Pediatrics condemned television violence and called for parents to restrict their children's television viewing (American Academy of Pediatrics 1990).

Over the years, broadcasters and producers have frequently used First Amendment arguments to resist overt regulatory controls on content. Some have responded to public, advertiser, and congressional pressures by instituting a "family viewing hour," providing content advisories, beefing up content screening processes, and changing content. In the late 1990s, public and political pressure for improvement has intensified and brought new opportunities for change. In 1994, the National Cable Television Association and the networks commissioned large-scale studies of violence on television to monitor their pledges to reduce the frequency and glamorization of violence on television. In 1996, the entire television industry pledged to create a television violence ratings system that will be used in conjunction with a channel-blocking device called the V-chip and agreed to an FCC ruling that would require at least three hours of educational programming for children each week.

Activism has led to some clear improvements, but Kunkel et al.'s (1996) content analysis underscores that the television environment remains essentially unchanged. Violence is pervasive, and programs with an antiviolence theme are rare, making up only 4 percent of all programming. Peggy Charren, founder of the advocacy group Action for Children's Television, said content is "worse now than when I started" (Hall 1996). Similarly, David Britt, president and CEO of Children's Television Workshop, testified to Congress that "if we are just a special interest, we are not very good at it—because there really isn't any more quality children's programming now than there was [20 years ago]" (Britt 1996).

Amid these new opportunities and continuing concern, then, the question remains: Can television be employed to alter attitudes about violence or help people learn alternatives to violent behaviors? A number of different groups, such as the Children's Defense Fund, the Center for the Study and Prevention of Violence, and even private companies such as The Body Shop, have developed antiviolence campaigns that use the media (National Organizations for Youth Violence Prevention Information 1996).

The television industry also has produced antiviolence programming and public service announcements. A national campaign initiated by the National Cable Television Association (NCTA) aired in March 1995 and was dubbed "Voices against Violence Week." The week-long, 51-channel effort was the most comprehensive televised effort ever to address violence in America, during which each cable channel devoted a portion of its programming to some aspect of violence (NCTA 1995). As part of their National Television Violence Study, the NCTA commissioned a team of researchers at the University of North Carolina at Chapel Hill to assess the effectiveness of the programming and PSAs aired in that and other televised antiviolence campaigns. Some individuals involved in that and other current campaigns have expressed the need for additional guidance on how best to construct antiviolence messages and the need for funding to conduct pretests and evaluations of effectiveness (Fenley 1996; E. Littleton 1996; Schmidt 1996).

In this chapter we present the initial findings of the UNC-CH studies and examine these results in the context of other antiviolence campaigns that have used mass media in attempts to reduce violence. Table 9.1 gives an inventory of the antiviolence media campaigns that have been conducted since the early 1980s that will be referred to. In this chapter *violence* is defined as an exertion of physical force meant to injure or abuse. The campaigns we examined were re-

TABLE 9.1. Attributes of Antiviolence Campaigns that Included Media, 1980 to Present

Campaign	Year Reported	Target Audience	Messages	Channels	Funding	Outcome Measures	Outcome
Alberta Anti-Crime Campaign, (Sacco and Silverman)	1981	Potential offenders, potential victims	"Let's not give crime a chance."	PSAs, newspapers and billboard ads	Government	Knowledge, attitudes, incidence of violence	Knowledge
Barron Assessment and Counseling Center, Jamaica Plain, MA	Ongoing	Boston students who bring guns to school	Not specified	Videos	?	?	?
Building Conflict Solving Skills Topeka, KS	Ongoing	Elementary and middle school students	"Talk to me." "Listen to me."	Videos	Kansas Child Abuse Prevention Council	?	?
Channeling Children's Anger, Washington, DC	Ongoing	Children	Anger management	Video, PSA edutainment	Institute for Mental Health Initiatives	?	?
Children's Creative Response to Conflict, Nyack, NY	Ongoing	Children	Not specified	Videos	?	?	?
Community Youth Gang Services, Los Angeles, CA	Ongoing	Youth gangs	Not specified	Video	Community Youth Gang Services, Inc.	?	?
Conflict Management/ Mediation Program, St. Louis, MO	Ongoing	Potential offenders, potential victims	Conflict resolution	Videos	?	?	?
Dating Violence Intervention Program, Cambridge, MA	Ongoing	Potential offenders potential victims	"Can't be beat."	Video, TV	?	?	?
Eisenhower Foundation Campaign (Bennett and Laverakas)	1989	Community	Varied	Varied	Eisenhower Foundation	Knowledge, attitudes, violent incidents	Knowledge, attitude change

Program	Date	Target audience	Message	Media	Sponsor	Evaluation	Result
ESR National Conflict Resolution Program, Cambridge, MA	Ongoing	Students, teachers, administrators	Not specified	Videos	Schools	?	?
Facing History and Ourselves, Brookline, MA	Ongoing	Potential victims, potential offenders	Not specifeid	Audio tapes, films	?	?	?
Families and Schools Together (FAST), Seattle, WA	Ongoing	High-risk children, families, schools, neighborhoods	Not specified	Videos	?	?	?
Family Maasai, Atlanta, GA	Ongoing	Black youth, schools, families, communities	Not specified	Television, videos	?	?	?
Felony Firearm Statute Campaign (Loftin, Heumann, and McDowall)	1983	Potential offenders	Fear—cost of committing felony with firearm	PSAs—television billboards, bumperstickers	Government	Violent incidents	No change
Gang Intervention Program, Albuquerque, NM	Ongoing	Youth gangs	Not specified	Video, television, news media	Youth Development Inc.	?	?
Gulf War Interventions (Raviv)	1993	Potential offenders, potential victims	Reassurance: "All responses are normal; it is the situation that is abnormal."	Television, telephone	Government	Knowledge, attitudes, behavior change	Knowledge, attitude, behavior
McGruff (O'Keefe)	1985	Potential victims	"Take a bite out of crime."	PSAs, magazines, newspapers	Advertising Council	Knowledge, attitude, behavior	Knowledge, attitude behavior change
Massachusetts, Adolescent Violence Prevention Project, Boston, MA	Ongoing	Adolescents	Anger management	Videos	Massachusetts Department of Public Health	?	?
Mat. Child Health, Violence Prevention Activities, Sante Fe, NM	Ongoing	High-risk males, community	Not specified	Videos	New Mexico Department of Health	?	?

(continued)

TABLE 9.1.—Continued

Campaign	Year Reported	Target Audience	Messages	Channels	Funding	Outcome Measures	Outcome
Mental Health Foundation Campaign (Abbot)	1992	Opinion leaders	Importance of reducing violent television content	Television, newspapers, pamphlets, reports, PR, lobbying	New Zealand Health Foundation	Attitudes, incidents of violent content	Attitude change, reduction in violent content
National School Safety Center, Westlake Village, CA	Ongoing	School-age children and youth	Not specified	Films	National School Safety Center	?	?
NCTA Initiatives (Biocca et al.)	1995	Potential offenders	Varied	Cable television	NCTA	Knowledge, attitude	Knowledge change
Old Colony Y Girls' Secure Detention Unit Brockton, MA	Ongoing	At-risk girls	Not specified	Videos, films, peer-taped videos	Old Colony YMCA	?	?
One-Day and Three-Day Youth Come-Togethers, Los Angeles, CA	Ongoing	Youth gangs	Not specified	Videos, peer-made videos, photos	LA County Probation Department	?	?
Outreach and Tracking, Brockton, MA	Ongoing	Potential offenders	Not specified	Varied	Old Colony YMCA	?	?
PACT (Hammond and Yung)	1991	African-American at-risk youth	"Givin' it, takin' it, workin' it out."	Videos, peer-taped videos	Schools	Knowledge, attitudes, behavior	Knowledge, attitude, behavior change
PACT Violence Prevention Project, Pleasant Hills, CA	Ongoing	Middle, high-school aged youth, community	Not specified	Videos, posters, written materials, PR, public info	Contra Costa County Health Services	?	?
Pediatrician Counseling Program for Firearm Injury Prevention, Washington, DC	Ongoing	Youth, parents, service providers	Not specified	Videos	Center to Prevent Handgun Violence	?	?

Program	Date	Audience	Topic	Media	Organization	Knowledge, attitudes, behavior intent	Changes in knowledge, attitude, behavior intent
Prevention of Violence in Intimate Relationships (Jaffe et al.)	1992	Potential offenders	Not specified	Videos	Schools, courts	?	?
Project Stress Control, Atlanta, GA	Ongoing	Students, parents, teachers	Anger management	Videos	Wholistic Stress Control Institute	?	?
Squash-It (Edwards, 1995)	Ongoing	Potential offenders, potential victims, opinion leaders	"It's not worth it, let's squash it."	PR, edutainment, PSAs, posters, fact sheets	Foundations, private companies	?	?
STAR (Coben et al.)	1994	Potential offenders, potential victims, communities, parents, opinion leaders	"Kids + Guns: A Deadly Equation"	PR, PSAs, posters, fact sheets, educational media, political involvement	Center to Prevent Handgun Violence	?	?
Teen Dating Violence Project, Austin, TX	Ongoing	Teens	Not specified	Videos, interpersonal	Austin Center for Battered Women	?	?
Teen Program, Concord, CA	Ongoing	Potential offenders, potential victims, concerned adults	Not specified	Movie	Battered Women's Alternatives	?	?
Teens on Target, Oakland, CA	Ongoing	Teens	Not specified	Videos, movies, radio, television, peer-produced videos	Summit Medical Center	?	?
Victim Services Program, Chicago, IL	Ongoing	Victims, Potential victims	Not specified	Videos	Community Mental Health Council	?	?
Violence Prevention Coalition,	Ongoing	Potential offenders, potential victims	Not specified	Television, film	LA County Department	?	?

(continued)

TABLE 9.1.—Continued

Campaign	Year Reported	Target Audience	Messages	Channels	Funding	Outcome Measures	Outcome
Los Angeles, CA					of Health Services		
Violence Prevention Curriculum for Adolescents (Coben et al.)	1994	School-age teens	Not specified	Educational media, interpersonal	Schools	Knowledge, incidences of violence	Changes in knowledge
Violence Prevention Curriculum (Second Step), Seattle, WA	Ongoing	Children	Not specified	Videos	Committee for Children	?	?
Violence Prevention Project (Spivak, Hausman, Prothrow-Stith)	1989	Children and adolescents, community	"Friends for life, don't let friends fight."	PSAs, posters, brochures, educational media, billboards	Advertising Club of Boston, schools	Knowledge, attitudes, behavior	Knowledge, attitude change; limited behavior change
Washington Community Violence Prevention Program, Washington, DC	Ongoing	Community	Unspecified	News media	Washington Hospital Center	?	?
Youth Program Oakland, CA	Ongoing	Potential offenders, potential victims	Not specified	News media, public information campaign	Oakland Men's Project	?	?

Note: Ongoing campaigns for which no citation is given are drawn from a list compiled by the National Network of Violence Prevention Practitioners, available from the Education Development Center in Boston, MA.

stricted to those dealing with violence directed toward other people rather than against one's self or personal property. For example, school-based programs to prevent teen suicide were excluded. However, campaigns meant to discourage breaking and entering, during which many violent injuries occur, or date rape, an often unreported crime of violence against women, were included. We define an *antiviolence campaign* as an organized, purposive effort involving the use of mass media to promote awareness and knowledge of violence, to increase preference for nonviolence, or to encourage and support nonviolent behavior. *Mass media* encompass not only the traditional forms of media employed to reach large audiences, such as television and radio, but also educational media such as audio and videotapes, which typically are meant for smaller audiences.

The first section of the chapter describes the studies conducted at UNC-CH. In the second and third sections we discuss audiences and messages in more detail and finally consider aspects of production and distribution that can help to optimize the effectiveness of antiviolence campaigns. We recommend that producers of antiviolence messages invest more effort in defining their audiences and objectives. Specifically, they should consider targeting preteens, opinion leaders, potential victims of violence, and peers, families and communities of potential offenders rather than the young, violent males who have constituted the traditional audience for such messages. Second, messages should be based on formative research and should reflect the audience's size, diversity, and stage of change. Alternatives to celebrity endorsements should be considered, as should the use of multiple media, purchased airtime and careful coordination with other media and interpersonal channels. Evaluation criteria should reflect the goals of the messages.

Changes in the production and distribution of antiviolence messages also are needed. We recommend that industry and government sponsors place more emphasis on well-coordinated, national campaigns and on funding evaluations for such campaigns. Industry and government also should search for ways to place economic value on programming that is not purely entertainment. The Children's Television Act should be strengthened to specify the hours educational programming must air and to allow for the inclusion of PSAs and edutainment in the mix that would satisfy CTA requirements. Finally, the Centers for Disease Control should assume a greater role in coordinating national, antiviolence media campaigns.

The UNC-CH Studies of the Television Industry's Antiviolence Messages

In June 1994, the National Cable Television Association commissioned the National Television Violence Study (NTVS), the largest industry-sponsored study of television. As part of the project's mission, the UNC-CH research team studied antiviolence educational initiatives, including both programs and public service announcements, most of which were developed by the television industry. The team began by looking at message and viewer variables related to effectiveness. Below we briefly summarize five studies conducted in the first year. A more detailed report can be in found in Biocca et al. 1995.

Sample of the TV Industry's Antiviolence Campaigns and Target Audiences

The UNC-CH Center for Research in Journalism and Mass Communication assembled an archive of antiviolence programming from the 1994–95 television season. When the center's experimental research began, the archive included 89 PSAs and 64 antiviolence educational programs produced by a total of 33 organizations. Many of these had aired during Voices against Violence Week. Programming formats varied by channel. For example, the Showtime movie channel offered the movie *Zooman*, about a family's search for justice after their daughter is killed; ESPN showed *Our Violent Games*, a documentary about sports violence; the Family Channel aired *Break the Silence: Kids against Child Abuse;* and talk shows brought on crime experts.

The center tested a systematic probability sample of the PSAs and one longer educational program from the archive. The test materials included *Kids Killing Kids*, an hour-long educational program; and 15 PSAs. The materials were shown to three diverse groups of youth: (1) seventh grade students in a suburban middle school; (2) college males; and (3) 12 to 19-year-old males incarcerated in a state-run training school for serious offenders. Teens were selected as the target audience because of widespread concern over the increase in youth violence (Butterfield 1996) and because the majority of the PSAs in the sample appeared to target this group.

Because this phase of the research was exploratory, nonprobability sampling of study participants was used. More than 200 youths participated in five studies. To explore a broad range of issues, the studies employed both quantitative and qualitative methods. Quantitative methods included a continuous response measure of viewer interest, as well as pencil-and-paper pre- and posttests of recall and attitudes toward violence. Qualitative methods were focus groups and in-depth interviews. The effectiveness of the PSAs and programs was judged by the degree to which intended audiences were:

1. interested in the messages;
2. emotionally affected by the messages;
3. able to understand and remember the messages; and
4. moved to change their attitudes and norms about violence after viewing the messages.

Findings

The findings across five studies suggest that the television industry's antiviolence PSAs and programs had minimal effects on adolescent viewers. There was no evidence of any significant effect on attitudes about violence.

Quantitative and Experimental Results

Interest. 75 percent of training school students and 46 percent of middle school students who saw the PSAs reported at least slight interest based on average second-by-second ratings. However, neither the training school group nor the middle school group considered the award-winning one-hour program on conflict resolution, *Kids Killing Kids*, any more interesting than a fire safety video. Viewing antiviolence PSAs failed to change college students' level of interest in violent scenes that immediately followed the PSAs.

Emotional response.   Based on self-reports of emotional response, PSAs depicting the threat or results of violence were more effective than those employing other tactics. Training school students felt significantly more aroused after viewing the antiviolence PSAs, but reported no change in feelings of pleasure or dominance. Dominance was defined as a feeling of being in control or empowered and is closely tied to the concept of self-efficacy. Middle school students also felt more aroused, but felt less pleased and less dominant after viewing the PSAs.

Attitude change.   The study found no evidence of change in attitudes about violence after viewers saw either the hour-long program or a violent movie interspersed with antiviolence PSAs as well as regular advertisements.

Unintended effects.   The experiments found no negative unintended effects in tests for anxiety, depression, or hostility among college-age viewers. After viewing the antiviolence programming, none of the test groups reported increased tendencies to view the world as a violent place.

Qualitative Results

Attention.   From the focus group and one-on-one interviews we learned that the network promotions and sponsor identifications included in the PSAs probably had a negative effect: They competed for audience attention and reduced time available for the antiviolence message.

Comprehension.   Messages promoting pacifist themes, such as "Just walk away," did not seem credible to the training school students, most of whom had personal experience with violence. However, these messages scored higher with middle school students, who as a rule had less direct experience with violence. PSAs and program segments that portrayed paralysis or the death of innocent victims as a consequence of violence seemed to disturb adolescents more than the possibility that they themselves might die.

Narrative or story formats generally were more arousing than the celebrity speakers/testimonial format. Narratives also were more frequently misinterpreted than those in which celebrities spoke. Narrative formats stimulated more discussion among the middle and training school groups, and more association with life experiences among the training school group. Although some celebrity speakers aroused interest, some also lacked credibility, especially those who were perceived as violent in real life or in their jobs. Those spokesmen and women with questionable credibility left the audience confused or discounting the antiviolence message.

Attitudes.   Most of the antiviolence campaign slogans, such as "Stop the violence," promoted attitudes that apparently were already held by target audiences.

Conclusions

The studies found that antiviolence PSAs could attract the interest and attention of teen audiences, but the PSAs tested in the studies varied significantly on most measures of effectiveness, suggesting that many could have been improved. Coupled with previous antiviolence research, the finding that an award-winning, hour-long program had no effect on short-term attitudes suggests that by itself, one television show may be only modestly helpful in decreasing violent attitudes or behavior. The finding that exposure to *nine* 30- to 60-second antiviolence PSAs during an hour-long movie did not diminish interest in subsequent violent scenes suggests that antiviolence PSA campaigns may not air frequently enough to achieve their objectives. Viewers simply may be overwhelmed by messages that glamorize violence.

Because the effect of the "Voices against Violence" campaign was evaluated only in an experimental situation involving teenage subjects, it is unclear whether the campaign influenced the attitudes or behaviors of other audiences in the real world. As we will discuss in more detail in the next sections, such campaigns may affect other audiences or have other unintended effects. These messages, may, for example, have reinforced existing nonviolent behavior among preteens or helped to keep television violence on the political agenda, but other research designs would have been necessary to have documented these effects.

How Can We Make Television a More Effective Antiviolence Tool?

Comparing Successful and Unsuccessful Antiviolence Campaigns

A review of other antiviolence campaigns shows that some have had modest success while others have not had much effect at all. Why do we find such variation? First, these campaigns have varied not only in quality but also in their objectives and messages. In addition, although the goal of each is to reduce violence in America, they may be functioning in a paradoxical context. The more a campaign attempts to use direct, explicit antiviolence messages to reach those who commit the most violence, *the less effective they may be.* We suggest some reasons for this paradox below and consider how future campaigns could be improved by targeting other audiences as well.

Whom Should We Reach? Audience Analysis and Segmentation

The people we would most like to reach with antiviolence messages are those who commit violence. Around the world and in America, the most violent segment of society is men between 15 and 30 years old (Archer 1994; Federal Bureau of Investigation 1991; Reiss and Roth 1993). But young men are not always the targets of antiviolence messages. Some campaigns seek to reach them indirectly by influencing others in their environment: family, girlfriend, peer, the larger community (see fig. 9.1).

Primary audiences.   Most of the broadcast and cable television messages examined in the UNC Center's study targeted primary audiences: male teens or preteens. Primary audiences also have been the focus of many other antiviolence campaigns, including Ontario, Canada's, Prevention of Violence in Intimate Relationships program and Detroit's Felony Firearms Statute Campaign. If the goal is to reduce the incidence of violence, targeting such audiences may appear both direct and logical. Evaluations of programs taking this route, however, suggest that influencing young men predisposed to violence is particularly challenging.

As part of the NTVS, researchers at UNC-CH sought to measure the effectiveness of antiviolence PSAs and programs targeted to male teens aged 12 to 18 years. Two of the studies were conducted with some of the most troubled training school students in the state of the North Carolina. Most were felons, and a number were incarcerated for murder. Among these subjects, 77 percent reported having shot a gun at someone one or more times (Biocca et al. 1996). If there is any group we would want to dissuade from violence, this is the one.

How did male teens respond to the television's antiviolence messages we tested? No short-term attitude change occurred. Both incarcerated and middle school teens found narrative PSAs more arousing than testimonials, for example, but middle school teens found the narrative PSAs less pleasurable. The incarcerated teens were particularly aroused by scenes consistent with their personal life experiences and were more responsive than the middle school audience to young rap artists and attractive female musicians. Neither audience was significantly interested in an Emmy Award–winning conflict-resolution program, *Kids Killing Kids,* and neither audience showed significant attitude change as a result of

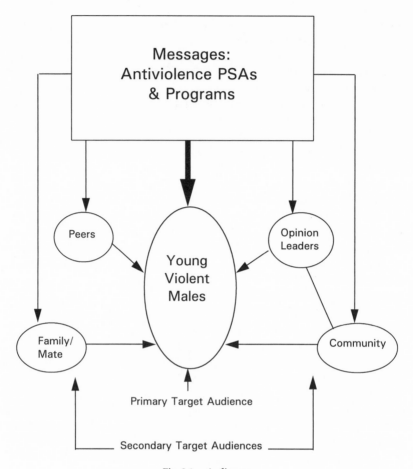

Fig. 9.1. Audiences

viewing the program. Still, the incarcerated group showed greater interest than the middle school group during the final segment of the show, possibly because the segment featured people, scenes, and messages with which it was already familiar. The primary audience of violence-prone teens, then, might best be approached as a specific audience segment rather than as part of an undifferentiated group of teens.

Other approaches have been used with different target audiences. The *Positive Adolescents Choices Training (PACT)* campaign in Dayton, Ohio, used peer models to teach high school students communication, negotiation, and problem-solving skills (Hammond and Yung 1991). Participants in this small-scale study, most of whom were African-American, videotaped themselves and their peers demonstrating their new skills. Other program components included small-group training sessions, role-plays and psychodramas, and an incentive system of "success dollars" that participants could exchange for T-shirts, tapes, jewelry, or games. Based on teacher and observer evaluations, the program improved the students' interpersonal and problem-solving skills and helped reduce violence-related school suspensions and expulsions.

Ontario, Canada, also targeted high school students in its *Primary Prevention Program on Violence in Intimate Relationships* and found some audience segments less receptive to its message than others (Jaffe, Sudermann, Reitzel, and Killip 1992). The Ontario campaign focused on wife assault and dating violence, and featured a video dealing with the effects of violence on women and families. Other components of the program included speeches by representatives of the police department and school board, student and professional plays, and talks by victims of violence and professionals who work with victims. Evaluations indicated significant positive attitude, knowledge, and behavioral intent changes at posttest and at delayed follow-up. Researchers, however, noted a "backlash" effect among some male students and postulated that those students already were engaged in violence. This finding suggests that children or younger teens may be more susceptible to antiviolence messages than older teens who already have developed conflict resolution strategies.

The *Felony Firearm Statute Campaign* targeted potential criminals in Detroit with fear-inducing messages to spread the word of sentencing reform meant to reduce violent crime (Loftin, Heumann, and McDowall 1983). The reform imposed a two-year mandatory add-on sentence for defendants convicted of possession of a firearm in the commission of a felony. Although the campaign employed a variety of media and the messages seemed clear, gun crime in Detroit failed to decline. Evaluators suggested that potential offenders may have been more willing to risk a stiffer sentence than to face armed resistance without a gun. Thus, even campaigns with clear messages may fail if the disadvantages of the recommended actions outweigh the advantages.

For many violence-prone teens, such antiviolence efforts may come too late. Several longitudinal studies indicate that children as young as six who are rated as aggressive or antisocial by parents, teachers, or peers continue to exhibit these characteristics in adulthood (Eron and Huesmann 1984; Olweus 1991). Aggressive behavior in childhood is the single best predictor of aggression later in life.

The pattern of findings suggests that the primary target audience, young violent males, may be resistant to attitude change messages and may respond only to those that are carefully tailored for them. Messages that work well with secondary target audiences like peer groups may be completely ineffective and counterproductive when directed at the primary target audience.

Secondary audiences. Secondary audiences include individuals or groups with whom potentially violent individuals interact or individuals or groups who otherwise can alter the environment surrounding potentially violent individuals (see fig. 9.1). Through their words or actions, secondary audiences can help to make violence a more difficult or less attractive solution to problems. Examples of such audiences include peers and family members of violence-prone children, potential victims of violent crime, communities or neighborhoods with significant incidences of violent crime, and opinion leaders such as legislators and television executives.

Peers or family members.   *Cease Fire,* an ongoing campaign, targets family members—the wives and girlfriends of potential gun owners (Schmidt 1996). Based on survey research, campaign planners believe that these influential women, if sufficiently motivated, could contribute substantially toward countering society's progun messages by persuading their partners not to bring guns home. The campaign stresses the danger to children when guns are kept in homes, and seeks to change commonly held beliefs about handguns as tools for residential security. The campaign has not been formally evaluated.

Potential Victims

Potential victims of violence represent another important secondary audience. The *McGruff* campaign, for example, urged neighbors to keep an eye on one another's homes to deter unlawful and potentially dangerous intrusions. Israel's *Gulf-War Interventions* campaign offered families advice and counseling to prevent stress-related violence, while, in Canada, Alberta's *Let's Not Give Crime a Chance* campaign targeted both potential victims and offenders to reduce the incidence of violent crime. In each case, potential victims were urged to take actions that could prevent or lessen the effects of attacks.

In the *McGruff* campaign, the trench-coated cartoon dog was coupled with the on-screen appearance of human role models who demonstrated assorted anticrime techniques, including locking doors, turning on lights, and reporting suspicious activities to police (O'Keefe 1985). Related community programs varied by locale but often included the distribution of anticrime literature and the formation of community watch groups. Almost one-fourth of those who saw the dog responded by changing their behaviors in accord with his suggestions.

As part of its *Gulf War Interventions,* Israel attempted to deter anxiety, aggression, and other psychological effects of the war with Iraq by targeting Israeli families trapped within the country during Iraq's air attacks (Raviv 1993). The government-owned Israel Education Television and Israel General Television dispensed warnings, instructions, interviews with psychiatrists, and special programs for children on a 24-hour basis. Messages for adults were delivered by an army spokesman, nicknamed "the national pacifier"; those for kids, by Sesame Street–type puppets. The highly motivated audiences received legitimization for their feelings of anxiety and anger, learned a variety of coping techniques, and cultivated greater sensitivity and tolerance toward the reactions of family members. In a telephone survey, 83 percent of viewers said the programs fostered behavioral adjustment, and 79 percent said they helped reduce tension or stress.

Alberta's well-funded, provincewide, *Let's Not Give Crime a Chance* campaign, however, produced uneven results (Sacco and Silverman 1981). Perhaps too ambitious in its goals, Alberta sought to influence both potential victims and potential offenders. It targeted potential victims of vandalism, auto theft, and residential breaking and entering, and potential offenders for auto theft and for hitchhiking-related assaults and rapes. Radio and television public service announcements and newspaper and billboard advertising were used. The campaign was deemed successful only in that residents could recall its theme; criminal behavior and crime statistics did not change. Thus, the two campaigns that targeted only potential victims were somewhat more successful than the one targeting a combination audience.

Communities

Communities represent yet another audience for antiviolence messages. Campaigns enlisting community involvement can provide an environment that reinforces behavior change, promote participation among residents, and foster a sense of ownership in the antiviolence message (Eng and Hatch 1991; Flora and Cassady 1990). Community residents may be willing to help fine-tune messages for local audiences and provide advice about the likely success of various communication channels. In underfunded campaigns, their time and talents can help stretch limited resources. Examples of antiviolence campaigns that have targeted communities include the *Violence Prevention Project* in Boston and the *Eisenhower Foundation's Neighborhood Program* in nine cities across the United States. Other antiviolence efforts with limited media involvement also have enlisted communities. These include late-night basketball programs such as *Midnight Hoops* in Columbia, South Carolina (Coben, Weiss, Mulvey, and Dearwater 1994), jobs programs such as *Community Youth Gang Services* in Los Angeles (Coben et al. 1994), antidrug programs such as D.A.R.E. (Kennedy School 1990), and mentoring programs (Rowe 1990).

The *Violence Prevention Project* coupled a public information campaign with a community-based education program (Hausman, Spivak, Prothrow-Stith, and Roeber 1992; Spivak, Hausman, and Prothrow-Stith 1989). The public information campaign included posters, brochures, and television PSAs with the theme, "Friends for life don't let friends fight." Other program components included a youth leadership development program, counseling and referral services for at-risk youth, and training and educational materials for teachers, hospitals, and communities. Evaluators measured changes in knowledge and attitudes among youth who completed the education program and limited shift in self-reports of fighting. In a telephone survey, 59 percent of black youths in the campaign area recalled the project theme. Black youths were more likely than their white peers to participate in the classes, discussions, and workshops that were offered, possibly because they watched more television and received more exposure to the campaign's PSAs. In similar situations, program visibility among white youths might be bolstered with PSAs aired on radio. Among agencies solicited by the project, 40 percent conducted some form of violence prevention education, an encouraging level of participation in the tough neighborhoods the campaign targeted.

Like the Violence Prevention Project, the *Eisenhower Foundation's Neighborhood Program* emphasized neighborhood ownership of the antiviolence effort (Bennett and Lavrakas 1989). Community groups in nine U.S. cities defined the local crime problem and decided how to tackle it. The groups employed "awareness activities," which sometimes included mass media, but the nature of their activities and the message content differed in different communities. More than one-fifth of residents participated in their community's activities. The 1989 evaluation documented an increase in residents' knowledge of and participation in anticrime activities, but did not find a reduction in crime. In both the *Violence Prevention Project* and the *Eisenhower Foundation* program, then, targeting the community at least reaped the reward of increased program participation.

Opinion Leader

A fourth alternative to targeting primary audiences is to target opinion leaders who can help change laws, regulations, or media content that contribute to violence. Several theorists have argued that such social changes also are necessary to support individual efforts at improving healthy behavior (Milio 1985; Sacco and Trotman 1990; Wallack 1990). Efforts to affect the content of television shows to provide nonviolent role models and to counter the general idea that violence is an effective solution to problems is one example of this strategy. In some countries, laws and regulations favoring less violent (non-U.S.) entertainment have been adopted. Examples of antiviolence campaigns that have enlisted opinion leaders include the *Mental Health Foundation Campaign* in New Zealand and the *Squash-It Campaign* developed by the Harvard School of Public Health.

The *New Zealand Mental Health Foundation Campaign* was directed toward reducing violent content on New Zealand's two, government-controlled television networks (Abbot 1992). Phase I of the 10-year project involved a content analysis based on George Gerbner's ratings system (Gerbner et al. 1977; Gerbner 1989; Morgan 1990). The foundation assumed that once violent content was documented, broadcasting authorities would take steps in the public interest to change programming. The analysis revealed an average rate of nine violent episodes per hour on New Zealand television, the highest in the world on public (government-sponsored) networks. However, broadcasting authorities reacted angrily to that assessment, challenging the findings and resisting programming changes.

Phase II of the project involved a public information campaign targeting politicians, professional and community organizations, and the general public. Components included publicity, news releases, reports of the analyses, professional papers, pamphlets, teaching units for schools, and lobbying activities. A newspaper helped fund part of the project. Public opinion favoring reductions in violent programming increased to 71 percent from 62 percent within two years and stabilized at the higher level. Several national organizations made public statements calling for change. In response, a national regulatory organization, the Royal Commission on Broadcasting, sided with the foundation against the broadcasters and endorsed virtually all of the foundation's recommendations. A governmental advisory group, the Ministerial Committee of Inquiry into Violence, also criticized the broadcasters and endorsed the Royal Commission stance. The committee observed that further study was unnecessary and would only delay the remedies needed. With the replacement of top broadcasting officials by the new Labor government, programming changes were made that reduced the incidence of violent episodes per hour to four compared with the previous nine.

Squash-It, a current campaign designed by the Harvard University School of Public Health, has enlisted both broadcasting executives and celebrities in its efforts against violence (Edwards 1995). The title of the campaign is taken from a phrase used by African-American urban teens as shorthand for "Let's not fight." The campaign's recruits so far have included producer Quincy Jones, who has pledged to get the music industry involved in the campaign, and the ABC and Fox television networks, which have incorporated the campaign's message in special episodes of regular television programs. Although evaluations of the campaign have not been completed, it seems clear from both the *Squash-It* and *New Zealand Mental Health Foundation* campaigns that the entertainment industry can function either as an ally or opponent in the antiviolence struggle.

Recommendations

Based on this review of issues surrounding target audiences, the following recommendations are offered:

1. Television industry antiviolence efforts should be coordinated into better-targeted campaigns meant for highly specific audiences (Lefebvre and Flora 1988).

2. Children should be targeted more often in antiviolence campaigns since they may be more responsive than older audiences.
3. Audiences that can promote environmental change should be considered as important targets because they can help change the context in which individual behavior occurs. For example, parents might be the focus of information about the V-chip or media literacy.
4. Communities should be targeted to help increase participation in antiviolence campaigns and ultimately decrease violence by supporting individual behavior change.

What is the Message? Message Themes and Design Considerations

Once target audiences are chosen, campaign designers must fashion messages that will reach and move the audience. What can we learn from the NTVS analysis and these other campaigns about improving antiviolence messages?

One approach is to examine messages according to a model of health behavior called the Stages of Change model (DiClemente 1993; Prochaska and DiClemente 1992; Prochaska, Redding, Harlow, Rossi, and Velicer 1994). This model provides a useful way to conceptualize the target audience, as well as a theoretical foundation for construction and evaluation of antiviolence messages. The model suggests that the cessation of violence or adoption of alternative behaviors does not occur automatically, with one bold action or effort. Instead, change requires movement through discrete stages to achieve maintained cessation or initiation of alternative behavior. The stages are precontemplation, contemplation, preparation, action, maintenance, relapse, and recycle (see fig. 9.2). The model incorporates two intervening variables—self-efficacy and decisional balance, or the weight given to the pros and cons of change. The model thus helps explain why some audiences are more receptive than others to certain antiviolence messages and why campaigns incorporating messages for several audiences at different stages of change may produce broader-based effects than those that rely on only one.

At any stage, change may be assisted by processes of change, or cognitive and behavioral activities relevant for that particular stage (Prochaska et al. 1994). For example, teens at the first stage—precontemplation—have not yet recognized violence as a problem. They may be uninformed, underinformed, or demoralized about their ability to avoid violence, or they may simply avoid thinking about the subject. In the UNC-CH study, for example, one incarcerated teen insisted that the nonviolent response suggested in a PSA narrative "ain't realistic—somebody bump into you like that, it won't be that much talking." Middle school students, however, often expressed doubts about the scope of the problem. "The reason I can't relate to any of these [PSAs] is because it

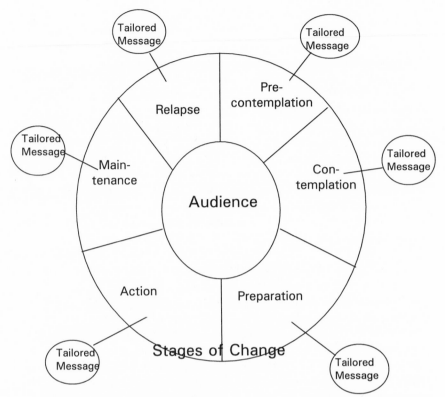

Fig. 9.2.   At each stage of behavioral change, messages need to be tailored to the audience's psychological and information needs

looked like a place like New York," one youth said. "I think it's really startling that every 20 seconds someone is injured by a handgun," another said. Their progress toward confronting and dealing with the problem could be aided by processes of change such as consciousness-raising, or acquiring information related to violence prevention; by experiencing and releasing their feelings about violence; and by "environmental reevaluation," or envisioning a better world without violence.

On the other hand, teenagers at the action stage of change require coping skills. They are more likely to be helped by suggestions for substitute behaviors or demonstrations of conflict resolution skills. None of the PSAs tested in the UNC-CH study assisted viewers toward action by presenting clear recommendations about how to stop violence. Two PSAs that used fear appeals aroused viewers but left them feeling little sense of control or self-efficacy. The incarcerated teens were particularly disturbed by images of paralyzed victims in "Before and After Hospital." Both incarcerated and middle school teens were aroused and disturbed by "Stray Bullet," which depicted a baby threatened by a single gunshot.

Different communication tools also are likely to be appropriate during different stages of change. In the precontemplation and preparation stages, mass media can provide information to increase general awareness of the problem of violence. At stages that require the use of coping skills, media can play an instructional role. Videos, for example, are ideal vehicles for demonstrating alternatives to violent behavior. In the maintenance stage of behavior change, mass media can help create an environment that supports nonviolence by targeting the community, and through their agenda-setting capabilities, promote better schools, improved job opportunities, and decent wages in violence-prone neighborhoods. Media campaigns also could support other antiviolence efforts, such as school and community programs that encourage alternatives to gang membership and discourage the acquisition or use of weapons.

Messages for Precontemplation/Contemplation

Antiviolence messages targeting the first and second stages of change—precontemplation and contemplation—would seek to add to awareness and knowledge of violence and violence-related issues. Based on theory, the most receptive audiences for such messages are likely to be those that have little experience with violence and have not yet formed opinions (Petty and Cacioppo 1984a, 1984b). Such groups would include children, preteens, and residents of safer, less violence-prone neighborhoods. Groups that have personal experience with violence or who already have rejected the possibility of nonviolence would be harder to persuade and require different types of messages.

Messages for these less-involved audiences are more likely to succeed if they reinforce widely held beliefs. Among incarcerated teens interviewed as part of the UNC-CH portion of the NTVS, for example, a message suggesting that violence threatens innocent children was better received than one urging teens to walk away from confrontations. Special attention should be paid to selecting sources, channels, and messages that are appropriate to the audience. For example, rap-music artists Chuck D. and Redman were credible sources for many incarcerated teens, but those same sources were unfamiliar and occasionally incomprehensible to middle school teens. Backgrounds and motivations of the sources also should be carefully considered. Incarcerated teens laughed at President Clinton, who one youth recalled had "smoked but not inhaled" marijuana; some middle school teens did not recognize basketball player Derrick Coleman, and others thought he looked violent or advocated nonviolence only because he was paid to convey that message.

Media tools appropriate to the precontemplation/contemplation stages of change would be directed toward a mass audience, though the messages they carry might be tailored to specific segments of that audience. The messages could be intended to increase knowledge and awareness of violence, or they could dramatize the issue, allowing for the release of feelings and emotions that provide impetus for change. Such messages also could help viewers envision the prospects of a world without violence, further enhancing incentives for change. Gloria Estefan's PSA telling viewers to "stop the violence" exemplifies a precontemplation/contemplation message. Messages intended solely for a precontemplation/contemplation audience would not include a recommendation to take action. Since awareness and knowledge are the primary goals of precontemplation/contemplation messages, evaluations of campaigns employing such strategies should seek to measure awareness and knowledge rather than some other outcome.

Examples of such precontemplation/contemplation messages include most of the PSAs evaluated in the NTVS and those of the *Let's Not Give Crime a Chance* campaign in Alberta, Canada. None of these messages resulted in significant behavior change, although some aroused interest and awareness among some audiences.

In the *Let's Not Give Crime a Chance* campaign, the communication message did not suit the goal. Evaluators criticized the campaign for failing to take into account the predispositions of audience members, most of whom did not view the selected crimes as major problems. The campaign also overused PSAs and newspaper advertising with this uninvolved audience and neglected to differentiate audience segments. In addition, it failed to specify the mechanisms through which its goals would be achieved. The campaign probably would have worked better by adhering to recommended techniques for designing messages and by testing messages on a small audience before taking them to the entire province.

Further support for the likely ineffectiveness of poorly targeted messages is cited by Prothrow-Stith in her book *Deadly Consequences* (1991). In the process of developing the Violence Prevention Project, she and her colleagues received firsthand experience about how little most Americans understand about the causes of violence, not to mention the motivations of adolescents. The ad agency that created their ads at first came up with the slogan, "Blow the Whistle on Crime," which vaguely suggested that teens were passive bystanders rather than possible victims or offenders. After more advice from Prothrow-Stith and her team, the agency's next effort used narrative message formats to depict the grievous emotional consequences of violence and to highlight the roles friends and acquaintances play as catalysts to violence. PSAs featuring the new slogan, "Friends for Life Don't Let Friends Fight," were coupled with posters and T-shirts reinforcing the message.

Messages for Preparation/Action

The primary goal of messages targeting audiences in the preparation/action stages of change is to promote antiviolence attitudes or intentions to take action. Audiences at these stages already are knowledgeable about the negative effects of violence and need help rethinking their attitudes or acquiring antiviolence skills. According to theory, this help would best come through authorities or opinion leaders. Media are appropriate, but probably work better if combined with interpersonal communication, which allows for feedback from the audience. Media typically are used for instruction, such as teaching anger management, conflict-resolution skills, or empathy for victims.

Messages are likely to be subtle: "Here's what knowledgeable people think about violence" and "Here's what people like us can do about it." If such messages are poorly received, the reasons for audience rejection of the attitudes and skills advocated need to be assessed and solutions tailored to audience objections. The backlash noted with some audiences exposed to preparation/action communication (Biocca et al. 1995; Schewe and O'Donohue 1993) suggests that some audience members may not have advanced beyond the precontemplation/contemplation stages of change. Examples of campaigns using preparation/action communication messages are the *Sexual Abuse Prevention Project,* which tested two techniques for discouraging date rape, the *PACT* program designed to teach communication, negotiation, and problem-solving skills to African-American teens, and Israel's *Gulf-War Interventions.* In addition, *Kids Killing Kids,* the 30-minute antiviolence video tested as part of the NTVS, might be used as a preparation/action tool in an instructional setting.

The *Sexual Abuse Prevention Project* at Northern Illinois University was intended to help prevent date rape on a college campus. This project screened older teens and young adults taking an introductory psychology course to determine those at risk of becoming offenders (Schewe and O'Donohue 1993). Men deemed to be at high risk were shown one of two videos. One video featured women victims of rape, child sexual abuse, or sexual harassment talking about their experiences; the other video featured researchers and treatment providers presenting factual information to counter common rape myths. Evaluations showed attitude change—increased empathy for victims—only in the group that had viewed the video featuring victims. Empathy induction thus was viewed as superior to fact presentation as a technique for effecting attitude change. These findings support communication theory on the importance of source selection and on the use of emotional as opposed to factual appeals. Women victims of sexual abuse were more effective conveyors of information than researchers and treatment providers. Moreover, the audience—most of whom were probably not rapists and thus were uninvolved with the issue of date rape—apparently preferred the emotional appeal.

PACT also demonstrated the importance of choosing sources and the importance of message timing. In the *PACT* program, as in the *Sexual Abuse Prevention Project,* participants had been evaluated as at-risk for violence. Those who had not already rejected the concept of nonviolence would likely be receptive to information that could help support change, such as recommendations for avoiding conflict. In the NTVS, the video *Kids Killing Kids,* which offered such recommendations, was more interesting to the incarcerated teens than the middle school teens, many of whom lived in relatively safe homes and neighborhoods. That the incarcerated teens did not find the video more interesting than they did might be attributed to the presence of peers who had rejected nonviolence as unrealistic or who did not relate to the role models presented.

Israel's *Gulf-War Interventions* illustrated the value of combining media to advance behavior change. In that campaign, television was used to disseminate advice to the largest possible audience, but then telephone hotlines were used to allow for questions and elaboration. The calm army spokesman proved a good role model for adults; puppets helped to soothe and calm children.

Other examples of antiviolence campaigns that emphasize preparation/action messages include the London (Ontario, Canada) *Primary Prevention Program on Violence in Intimate Relationships* (Jaffe, Sudermann, Reitzel, and Killip 1992) and the *Violence Prevention Curriculum for Adolescents* (Coben, Weiss, Mulvey, and Dearwater 1994).

Quite a few researchers have published extensive guidelines for targeting audiences and communicating health and prosocial messages. Among the most comprehensive are Maibach and Parrott (1995), Backer, Rogers, and Sopory (1992), Rice and Atkin (1989), and Salmon (1989). McGuire (1989) offers helpful suggestions on theoretical foundations of campaigns, Rice and Atkin (1994) on characteristics of successful campaigns, and Romer and Kim (1995) on targeting African-American and Latino youth. The following recommendations, taken from these and other guidelines, seem particularly relevant:

1. The use of a nonviolent role model is likely to be effective in antiviolence messages. The model should have power, high social status with the target audience, and demonstrate nonviolent approaches to resolving interpersonal conflict in his or her life. Messages that increase the potential power of peer-driven shame and social stigma also may be effective.
2. Messages should provide examples of specific, feasible, and concrete behaviors that teens can use to decrease their likelihood of engaging in violence.
3. Messages that contain frightening elements should include clear and realistic suggestions for reducing fear and resolving conflict, to avoid leaving viewers feeling powerless to change (Job 1988).

Messages for Behavior Maintenance

The goal of messages aimed at audiences in the maintenance stage of change would be to alter the audience's environment to make nonviolent behavior easier to practice. Audiences would include individuals who accept the concept of nonviolence and possess the skills to make it work, but who need support from other people, social institutions, or the prevailing culture to sustain their nonviolent behavior. Communication research suggests that media help to shape society's concepts of appropriate behavior (Gerbner, Gross, Morgan, Signorielli, and Jackson-Beck 1979). Thus, the violent incidents and characters so prevalent in mass media today would tend to reinforce the idea that "real" men settle problems by force or violence. Similarly, avoiding violent confrontations might be perceived as "unmanly." Messages targeting advanced stages of change, then, would seek to discourage depiction of violence in the media and to promote depiction of alternatives to violence. Certainly, a major thrust would be the reduction of gun-toting, macho-men role models.

Changes of such a nature must be accomplished indirectly, through the cooperation of executives, producers, and others who can influence media production. Communication tools such as public relations, media advocacy, creative epidemiology, and edutainment provide the means for securing this cooperation. *Creative epidemiology* is the use of new or interesting scientific data to draw media attention to a public health issue. *Media advocacy* focuses attention on the way a health problem is framed or perceived in an effort to change policy. *Edutainment,* or educational entertainment, is the embedding of prosocial messages in entertainment programming (Montgomery 1990).

Examples of messages for behavior maintenance are the *Parent Teacher's Association Campaign* against television violence and the *New Zealand Mental Health Foundation Campaign.*

The *PTA Campaign* to reduce violent television programming used confrontational tactics to discourage violence on U.S. television. The project led to these results: a number of targeted series were canceled; networks intensified their internal screening activities; portrayals of aggressive personal violence in prime time declined 9 percent; and nine of the top 12 sponsors of hard-action television shows greatly reduced their advertising support for such programs. Despite the campaign's success, the PTA shifted its efforts in the 1980s to teaching parents and children critical viewing skills (Montgomery 1989; PR Newswire 1995).

Based in part on the *PTA Campaign,* the *New Zealand Mental Health Foundation Campaign* accomplished a similar reduction in violent programming after changing its message to target different audiences. Rebuffed by the media industry after documenting unusually high levels of violent programming, the foundation next targeted media consumers and elected officials. Its new message—that violent programming defeated the country's best interests—fell on more receptive ears.

Edutainment, a technique that has helped to support health-related goals in developing countries (Brown and Singhal 1993; Brown, Singhal, and Rogers 1989; Henry J. Kaiser Family Foundation 1995), also fits the behavior maintenance category. The *Squash-It* campaign discussed previously, for example, has succeeded in incorporating its campaign slogan and hand signal into *Beverly Hills, 90210,* a syndicated television program popular among teen viewers. Another antiviolence campaign with edutainment components is *Channeling Children's Anger (CCA),* an Institute for Mental Health Initiatives project based in Washington, DC.

Messages for Sustained Change

These campaigns involve some combination of the message types discussed previously. For example, a combination of all three message types might be used to help a diverse audience move further toward nonviolent behavior change. Such a technique would support the efforts of individuals regardless of their position in the stages of change cycle. Similarly, preparation/action and maintenance strategies might be combined to assist individuals who need to acquire conflict-resolution skills and who would be more likely to use them in a less violence-prone neighborhood. All media tools associated with the messages to be combined would be appropriate. Campaigns intended to influence a diverse audience, to produce long-term behavior change or to generally "fix the problem" of some form of violence would likely require messages for multiple audiences. Several promising or highly successful antiviolence campaigns fit this category.

Examples include the *Southeastern Michigan Spinal Cord Injury System (SEMSCIS),* which seeks to prevent a devastating result of violence; *Straight Talk about Risks (STAR),* a national campaign based in Washington, DC; and the National Crime Prevention Council's *Take a Bite Out of Crime* campaign, also known as the McGruff campaign. The development of the *Violence Prevention Project* also provides a valuable lesson about combining message types.

SEMSCIS, developed in Detroit, intends to help prevent spinal cord injuries, many of which result from violent behavior (Weingarden and Graham 1991). The program focuses on a video, *Wasted Dreams,* in which five teenage paraplegics tell their stories. The video is presented in schools, supported with an anatomy lesson of the spinal cord, role-playing and, sometimes, appearances by paraplegic teens. Related activities involve the use of newspapers and television. Each school holds a poster contest, and winners are announced at a luncheon to which the local media are invited. Buttons and bumper stickers with the slogan "Ban the Handgun" also are distributed. Evaluations based on a written quiz given as a homework assignment showed short-term increases in knowledge of dangers and consequences. *SEMSCIS* demonstrates the value of credible sources, an emotional appeal, and community support in moving what was probably an uninvolved audience a step closer to attitude and behavior change. Its messages hold promise for long-term behavior change, particularly if the media component is expanded to keep its lessons fresh in audience members' minds. The campaign's developers should seek to measure changes in behavioral intent or behavior.

Straight Talk about Risks (*STAR*), a campaign of the Center to Prevent Handgun Violence in Washington, DC, uses a combination of messages in its efforts to teach alternatives to using guns (Coben et al. 1994). *STAR* targets school-aged children and teens, their parents, and their communities using videos, educational curricula, and community-awareness materials. The campaign also incorporates counseling, mentoring, and crisis intervention. In cooperation with Gun Control Inc., the Center to Prevent Handgun Violence also engages in data gathering, edutainment projects, media briefings, physician education and motivation activities, and joint lobbying with police organizations.

Although most famous for its public service announcements, the *Take a Bite Out of Crime* campaign also incorporated community projects, "real-life" role models, and recommendations for action (O'Keefe 1985). It thus combined three types of messages. The trench-coated McGruff watchdog in cartoon format functioned effectively as an attention-getting device and helped the campaign reach both young and old viewers with its messages.

The *Violence Prevention Project* highlights the possibilities of campaigns that combine messages for different audiences. That project, discussed previously, combined an educational core curriculum with a community awareness and involvement campaign. Used alone and presented by teachers, the core curriculum failed to achieve its goals. It achieved more impressive results with expanded community and media components.

Evaluation of Effectiveness

The antiviolence campaigns examined in this review used a variety of measures of effectiveness. Israel's Gulf-War Interventions, for example, asked audience members whether its telephone hotlines and psychological self-help television programs helped them cope with the stresses of the war. Judged on those criteria, the campaign was deemed a success (Raviv 1993). Other projects set standards that were harder to achieve. New Zealand's Mental Health Foundation campaign sought to reduce violent content on television and gauged its progress based on an annual content analysis of programming. After 10 years, the campaign achieved a substantial reduction. Nevertheless, evaluators expressed concern that changes in the availability of nongovernment programming threatened to erode that gain (Abbot 1992). In both campaigns, the standards for evaluation were appropriate to the campaign's goals.

In some other campaigns, however, the measure of success was inappropriate for the stated goal. Alberta's *Let's Not Give Crime a Chance* campaign sought to reduce the incidence of crime, or effect behavioral change, primarily through PSAs and billboard advertising. Such techniques used alone have a questionable track record for influencing behavior (Backer et al. 1992). Predictably, the Alberta campaign came up short on behavior change but did succeed in increasing awareness of the campaign and its overall theme (Sacco and Silverman 1981). The *SEMSCIS* campaign, in contrast, set a goal of reducing spinal cord injuries, but measured only knowledge and awareness in its end-of-program evaluation. Evaluators did not report plans for follow-up evaluations (Weingarden and Graham 1991). Thus, it appears that antiviolence campaigns can succeed, but that measurements of effectiveness should reflect stated goals. In addition, campaigns that seek behavior change should do evaluations repeatedly over a period of weeks or months rather than simply before and after the campaign, to allow for differing rates of behavior change within the target audience.

Media Channels

Many of the campaigns we have discussed relied primarily on television or videos to reach their teen target audiences. Visual media appear ideal for demonstrating skills or promoting empathy for victims. When the goal is to promote awareness and knowledge among large numbers of teens, however, radio or a combination of radio and television may be more effective (Klein et al. 1993). In the one instance in which educational media were used alone to promote behavior change, the Violence Prevention Curriculum, the campaign failed to achieve its goal (Coben et al. 1994). When the same materials were later used along with traditional mass media such as PSAs and posters, the campaign was more successful (Spivak, Hausman, and Prothrow-Stith 1989).

Only a handful of campaign evaluations offered statistics on how many people actually saw the messages, or discussed whether the campaigns had used paid or unpaid media time or space—a factor that affects exposure. At least some of the NTVS PSAs were aired over cable television without charge, and the *Mental Health Foundation* campaign attracted newspaper sponsorship for some of its efforts (Biocca et al. 1995; O'Keefe 1985). In addition, the fact that the McGruff campaign was endorsed by the Advertising Council suggests that it also may have received at least some free airtime.

Because these campaigns differed in their effectiveness, few generalizations can be drawn from them about the relative merits of the paid and unpaid time. As part of a study commissioned by the National AIDS Information and Education Program, the Research Triangle Institute found that in some instances buying media time helped to ensure stations' continued provision of free public service airtime as well as maintenance of records on the airing of both paid and unpaid spots. The institute also found that some campaigns have increased their donated time by as much as four times by buying some airtime. It recommended the use of edutainment as another means of increasing free airtime (Gibbs, Rizzo, and Dunteman 1990).

Recommendations

In view of the NTVS findings and the examination of other campaigns, the following recommendations are offered for future antiviolence campaigns regarding messages, sources, channels and evaluation:

Strategies/Messages
1. Communication strategies should reflect the target audience's most likely stage of change. For example, a precontemplation/contemplation strategy might be inappropriate for students in a training school, because many of the students already have engaged in violent behavior. A preparation/action strategy would provide a better fit.
2. PSAs should be submitted to formative evaluation and testing before they are aired to improve their quality and effectiveness (Atkin and Freimuth 1989; Biocca et al. 1995).
3. Messages for large audiences should focus on changing accessible subsets of a problematic behavior. For example, rather than overtly attempting to put a stop to all smoking, antismoking advocates have reduced the social acceptability of smoking by targeting the dangers to nonsmokers when smokers light up in grocery stores, restaurants, and other public places.
4. If goals are multiple and the audience diverse, multiple messages are indicated. The *McGruff* campaign brought about behavior change, attitude change, and awareness change by using a cartoon character for attention, "real-life" role models for preparation, and by making specific recommendations for action. Furthermore, the message selected was not controversial, virtually guaranteeing a receptive audience.
5. Campaign messages should be coordinated and should reinforce one another. Two of the least effective campaigns varied their antiviolence messages. The Alberta *Let's Not Give Crime a Chance Campaign* used a single message for part of the campaign, then changed to varied messages to address varied target crimes (Abbot 1992). The *Eisenhower Campaign* employed "awareness activities," which may have included

mass media, but the nature of these activities and the message content differed in different neighborhoods (Bennett and Lavrakas 1989). These campaigns' lack of success suggests that message variation may be confusing and that messages are more likely to succeed if they reinforce one another.

6. Empathy-inducing messages are likely to be more effective than factual messages in antiviolence campaigns.

7. Communicators should increase their use of messages that portray outcomes of violent behavior such as paralysis, death of innocent victims, or negative consequences to the perpetrator's family. The content analysis done by Kunkel et al. (1996) showed that only 16 percent of televised violence showed long-term negative consequences of violent behavior.

Sources

1. Sources of messages should be chosen carefully. Victims of violence were particularly well-received as sources (Jaffe et al. 1992; Schewe and O'Donohue 1993; Weingarden and Graham 1991). So were humorous cartoon or puppet sources among younger audiences (Raviv 1993; O'Keefe 1985). Same-race peers and teachers proved effective for an ethnic audience (Hammond and Yung 1991).

2. Campaigns should decrease reliance on testimonials/celebrity endorsers and avoid using any celebrity who has been publicly associated with violence, even fictional violence. The testimonial format was used far more often in the *NTVS* campaigns, although narrative formats were more effective (see also Wilde 1988).

Media Channels

1. Campaign planners should consider using multiple media, including radio, to facilitate knowledge and awareness of violence among teens.

2. Campaigns should consider buying airtime and should increase the use of edutainment as a means of increasing their messages' exposure.

3. Large-scale antiviolence television campaigns are more likely to be effective if coordinated with other media and interpersonal channels such as intervention programs in schools and youth groups.

Evaluations

1. Evaluation criteria should reflect the goals of the campaign. For example, crime incidence is a better indicator of behavior change than of awareness. (For more about campaign evaluation, see Flay and Cook 1989.)

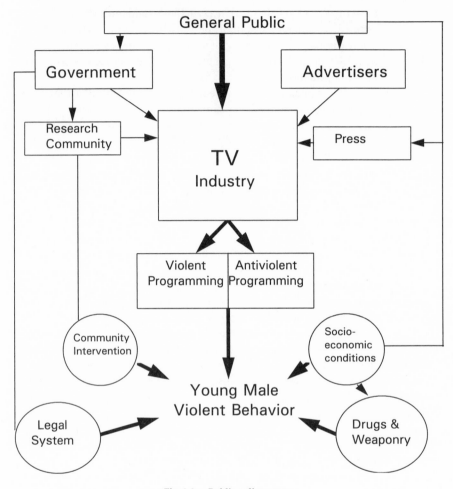

Fig. 9.3.   Public policy actors

Production and Distribution: Actors and Actions

So far, we have discussed guidelines for targeting audiences and constructing effective antiviolence messages and campaigns. But even if these and other recommendations are considered in the campaign design stage and well-designed antiviolence messages or programs are created, they must work their way through a maze of often competing forces if they are to be seen on television. Decisions about whether to air antiviolence programming are affected by interactions among people in the television industry, politicians, advertisers, special interests, the media, researchers, and the general public. Figure 9.3 depicts these interactions, which all potentially affect violent behavior among youth. The actual delivery of antiviolence messages often is hampered by prevailing paradigms about media, by political and economic forces, and by insufficient communication between researchers and creative teams. Here we address some of these barriers.

Prevailing Paradigms

Research strongly suggests that violent behavior grows out of interactions among an individual's psychosocial development, neurological and hormonal characteristics, and social influences such as media. Conversely, no research suggests that any one of these factors is more fundamental than the others in creating a violent individual (Reiss and Roth 1993, 102). Nevertheless, many of those involved in violence prevention place more value on direct interventions such as school-based programs to teach conflict resolution skills and see media campaigns as a sidecar attached to the "real" vehicle for change—if there is any money left over. Often, there is not (Fenley 1996). Although public health professionals agree that violence is a complex problem requiring multiple solutions (Mercy et al. 1993; Prothrow-Stith 1991), the well-coordinated national media campaign seems to be an often overlooked part of the response.

The perception that antiviolence media campaigns are an optional but not integral element is tied to the idea that they cannot be expected to accomplish much. That idea, in turn, is tied to insufficient funding for evaluating antiviolence campaigns, evaluations that would explain why some campaigns fail and others succeed. Our review of the academic literature showed that evaluations are the exception rather than the norm, and that even when they are done they frequently set up inappropriate measures of success.

The assumption that the individual bears the primary responsibility for filtering, understanding, interpreting, and reacting to what he sees in the media also hampers broader dissemination of antiviolence messages. For example, the program-blocking V-chip requires parents to take control of the content entering the home but does not tackle the content itself. Although television activists generally see the V-chip as a positive development, they also point out that it does nothing to foster programming improvements and may even lead to more hours of violent programming (Hall 1996).

Media literacy—teaching viewers how to interpret violent content—is another approach that stresses individual rather than societal responsibility (Wallack 1990). Although it is essential to teach parents how to lessen violent television's potential for harmful effects on their children, this approach downplays the responsibility of networks, producers, distributors, and toy marketers to provide beneficial alternatives. In addition, media literacy may be less effective than other approaches with the youngest children, who are developmentally unable to distinguish fact from fantasy despite careful instruction in the differences between real and cartoon violence. Even teenagers can find that distinction difficult. Nathan McCall recalled seeing the movie *The Godfather,* and being "mesmerized by the movie's shoot-outs, retaliatory murders and the ruthless gangster code." He wrote:

> I eventually got my chance to do the Godfather thing when an older guy in the neighborhood threatened my girl . . . I was 19 and it didn't take much to push me into reckless action. When I ran into that man, I gunned him down. It was like one great fantasy, as glorious as the gangland slayings in the movie. After he collapsed, I stood over him, proud that I'd upheld the Godfather code. But later that night, as I was fingerprinted and booked in a police station, the fantasy faded. . . . if he died, I'd be charged with murder, yet I would have denied to the end that I was a murderer. Why wasn't I prepared to accept the consequences of my actions? Because on some level, I was certain that the person who shot that guy was not really me— it was some person I'd thought I wanted to be. I'd been fantasizing, and fantasies don't deal with consequences. (McCall 1994)

Perhaps the young McCall would have reacted differently to the movie if he'd learned critical viewing skills. Nevertheless, media literacy aims to change the fish, rather than the ocean in which the fish swims. Lacking evidence that the individual is the appropriate primary focus for antiviolence efforts, it makes sense to use as many tools as possible to deter violent behavior, including improving the television environment.

A third paradigm hampering antiviolence media messages is that broadcast television is primarily an entertainment medium in which "responsibility doesn't pay." This belief, shared by industry and audience alike, crops up in articles about television violence (Aufderheide and Montgomery 1994; Richmond 1995). Afraid to tamper with proven formulas for entertainment success, the industry and advertisers understandably resist change. But a glance at burgeoning sales of educational computer software for children suggests that many have already discovered that consumers can learn new patterns of consumption. Children's television advocate Emily Littleton believes that television producers have become "lazy and complacent" and that if they return to their creative roots, they will find ways to "make money and serve kids too" (Littleton 1996). *Sesame Street*'s product licensing successes, without which the show would not remain on the air, demonstrate that prosocial themes are salable (Britt 1996).

Political Forces

Voices against Violence Week was one attempt by the television industry to demonstrate responsibility. Yet this campaign illustrated how political pressures can stifle the potential effectiveness of a campaign. Critics decried Voices against Violence Week as an attempt to forestall congressional regulatory action—nothing more than "a video fig leaf"—while advocates saw it as emblematic of a shifting attitude in the industry. Tony Cox, leader of the cable industry's antiviolence effort and former senior vice president of Viacom, said that even among broadcasters, there is no longer debate about whether television violence contributes to violence in our society. He said the campaign demonstrated a new willingness to assume some responsibility for the problem (Kolbert 1995).

Although the campaign probably would not have been initiated if not for congressional pressure, that pressure also contributed to message dilution. The stated goals of the campaign were raising public awareness about violence and fostering debate about solutions, but unstated goals clearly included cleaning up the cable industry's public image. Cox complained that "television has been scapegoated by politicians unwilling or unable to address the real causes of violence" and wished for "somebody to acknowledge that violence in society isn't our fault" (as quoted in Cerone 1995). Many of the PSAs used in the campaign seemed most concerned with the message, "see what we're doing about violence," leading to obtrusive channel identifications that distracted viewers from the antiviolence message.

Although some materials used in the campaign were pretested with focus groups (Jusang 1996), there was no evidence that the campaign was guided by effectiveness principles. Cox reported that the PSAs featuring President Clinton aired because the White House phoned and asked the cable industry to air the already recorded ads. No research was done to discover whether Clinton would be seen as a credible source by the target audience. Many of the celebrity PSAs used in the campaign were filmed in a temporary studio set up outside an industry awards ceremony, where passing stars were stopped and asked to read the antiviolence message off a TelePrompTer. Again, no preproduction evaluations were conducted (Cox 1995). Thus, political pressure sparked action, but also promoted hastily constructed messages with multiple missions. As in the case of the television industry's proposed rating system, the industry's PSA campaign reflected considerations beyond that of preventing violence.

The Children's Television Act

The Children's Television Act of 1990 (codified at U.S.C. § 303b(a)(2)) illustrates the difficulty of crafting effective regulations (Center for Media Education 1992; Montgomery 1989). The act required broadcasters to serve the educational and informational needs of children, partly through programming specifically designed to meet those needs, but did not spell out exactly what kinds of programming would satisfy the requirement or when the programs should air. It also tied renewal of a station's broadcast license to its children's programming efforts. Although children's advocates saw passage of the act as a watershed event because it codified a previously unstated responsibility to serve young viewers, it took six years for advocates, industry, and the Federal Communications Commission to agree on a method for measuring if a station had met that responsibility (Aufderheide and Montgomery 1994; Federal News Service 1996; Mendoza 1996; Mifflin 1996a, 1996b). Advocates argued that the act fell short because it lacked quantifiable performance measures and was inadequately enforced, leading stations to count cartoons such as *Yogi Bear* and *The Jetsons* as educational programming (Center for Media Education 1992). Broadcasters argued that attempts to impose specific, externally defined standards of behavior are unconstitutional and not desired by Congress (Quello 1996). Before it was strengthened in mid-1996, the act's vagueness allowed educational shows to be shunted to predawn hours where they were doomed to tiny audiences (Aufderheide and Montgomery 1994).

After pressure from the White House, the industry agreed to new FCC steps to strengthen the act in mid-1996. A minimum of three hours per week of regularly scheduled, 30-minute educational programs is now required, and shows must air between 7 A.M. and 10 P.M. In a concession to broadcasters, the FCC allowed some flexibility in meeting the three-hour rule: specials, short programs, or PSAs that add up to an equivalent amount of programming are acceptable. Changes also were made to the definition of educational programming, such that educators will be involved with setting informational goals for programs before they are produced.

These improvements in the act could help increase the small share of television time children's educational programming now has. And the rules that specifically mention PSAs as a type of programming that can help stations meet the CTA standard may stimulate increased funding for more antiviolence media campaigns and access to expensive television airtime.

Edutainment

The decision to link license renewals to a minimum of three hours per week of educational programming also could renew interest in edutainment, a comparatively cheap method for increasing prosocial content on television. Using existing characters in dramas or situation comedies has worked well to promote better images for African Americans, Hispanic Americans, gay people, and other groups, and as a way to air controversial viewpoints on abortion and other social issues (Montgomery 1989). This approach has several advantages over creating new, informational programming. Audiences already have established relationships with the characters and actors. In addition, a demand for story lines creates avenues for advocates who can creatively mesh their messages with the established structure of the medium (Daves 1995).

Harvard's *Squash-It* campaign exemplifies how this method is being used for antiviolence themes. It is too early to discuss the effect of *Squash-It,* and, given television's dependence on conflict as a central storytelling force, a pacifist theme faces a difficult challenge. A similar approach, however, worked well with drunk driving, a far less regular feature of the television world than violence. As a result of that campaign, the phrase "designated driver" has been added to the American lexicon and alcohol-related traffic deaths declined from 57.2 percent of all traffic deaths in 1982 to 43.5 percent in 1993. Because of its relative affordability and potential effectiveness, "edutainment" deserves greater attention as a vehicle for antiviolence information. Strengthening and defining the Children's Television Act is likely to spur more activity in this area as well.

Although the Children's Television Act provides some opportunities for improving television content, regulation is typically fraught with political pitfalls, and, historically, politicians are far less interested in helping foster quality programming than in battling, or appearing to battle, negative content (Britt 1996; Danish and Donahue 1996; Mendoza 1996; Rowland 1983). Critics suggest this is because it is far easier to target television than to seriously combat other correlates of violence, such as poverty and drug abuse (e.g., Danish and Donahue 1996; Hall 1996). Although 82 percent of Americans polled believe there is not enough educational children's television (see *Public Attitudes about Children's Television* 1995), politicians have not been as quick to recognize the need for it and even planned to cut funds to PBS, the nation's leading outlet for educational programming. In this political context, regulatory steps can be expected to have only limited ability to improve the television environment. Regulatory efforts clearly help create pressure to which the television industry responds, but greater emphasis should be placed on generating funds to produce and market better programs.

Economic Forces

The multimillion-dollar, action-figure–saturated toy industry represents the strongest force in children's programming, and it has virtually shouldered out educationally oriented programming not linked with product promotions. The Federal Trade Commission currently is investigating toy companies' retail distribution practices. Its recommendations present an opportunity to give educational programming a fighting chance. Under current market conditions, instead of broadcasters buying shows, toy companies purchase commercial airtime—"spot commitments"—on stations that agree to air toy-based children's shows. Television analysts say this pattern exists only in the children's market (Farhi 1996a; C. Littleton 1996). Although since 1990 the FCC has barred stations from running commercials for a toy during a program based on that toy, there is no restriction on spot commitments. As a result, the toy industry is setting the agenda for what children see, programs are aired based on economic clout rather than quality, and educational programs lacking product links are at a severe disadvantage in the competition for broadcaster commitments (Jeff Chester, as quoted in Farhi 1996b).

Broadcasters say the practice is exacerbated by competition from child-oriented cable channels and by merchandising, which can be more lucrative than advertising. For example, *Mighty Morphin Power Rangers* merchandise linked to the television show has generated more than $1 billion in retail sales (Kelly 1995), with portions of the revenue going to distributors, producers, and stations (Freeman 1993). Prosocial programs rarely offer such opportunities. Although the existence of the Children's Television Act slightly improves the marketability of educational shows, the dollars behind toy-based shows ensure that the latter get the best time slots. PSAs aimed at educating the public about violence are launched into this same competitive environment and stand about the same minimal chance of airing. If educational programs and PSAs are to compete, they must look for acceptable marketing options (pacifist action figures?), secure public or private underwriting, or seek regulatory remedies.

Awards have been widely used by advocates to encourage programming that promotes a particular view, and advocacy groups often have given awards to shows for which they served as "technical consultant" (Montgomery 1989). Some of the awards became Hollywood status symbols and led to short-term programming changes, but it is questionable whether that translated into economic benefits for the industry. A few have offered cash rewards to producers and writers. A far greater economic benefit could be realized if viewers were as well-informed about these awards as they are about the Emmys. Symbols printed in television guides to denote award-winning nonviolent programs would raise viewer awareness and make the programs easier to find. If awards were coupled with public recognition for advertisers and foundations that supported such programming, they would be more likely to become an economic incentive.

Communication among Violence-Prevention Actors

Another barrier to effective placement of antiviolence messages in the mass media is insufficient coordination among antiviolence communication efforts. In a policy-oriented review of U.S. violence prevention efforts, a CDC team noted that "To learn from and fully capitalize on these ongoing prevention experiences, federal agencies, foundations and communities will need to significantly improve their ability to share information and coordinate activities" (Mercy et al. 1993, 22). The same need was echoed by individuals interviewed for this paper.

"There are a lot of local efforts, but they don't tie into any big national effort," said the CDC's Mary Ann Fenley. Cease Fire Executive Director Elizabeth

Schmidt agreed. "People are not talking to one another," she said. "A lot of these groups are very competitive with one another." A multitude of groups are producing antiviolence messages aimed at domestic violence, gang violence, gun owners' spouses, potential victims, and so on. This array of messages lacks the clearly defined, behavior-oriented national focus of the highly successful "designated driver" campaign, for example. Without sustained consistency and clarity the messages may be too diluted to lead to measurable results.

The Violence Prevention Division of the U.S. Centers for Disease Control has begun planning for the public awareness component of its prevention strategy. The $250,000 effort is beginning with an inventory of private resources and public resources in the CDC, the U.S. Department of Justice (the main funding source for the private National Crime Prevention Council), Health and Human Services, the National Institutes of Mental Health, and state and local health agencies. After identifying a subject focus and taking stock of existing messages, the CDC plans to devise a public awareness plan (Fenley 1996). "We may find that the best target is not the one at risk," Fenley said.

If adequately funded, the effort will provide an overdue opportunity for the CDC to formulate and lead a long-term, national, public-health–based, antiviolence campaign as well as to serve as a clearinghouse for currently scarce antiviolence campaign design information. The CDC's Violence Prevention Division could serve as an archivist for antiviolence PSAs and educational material, and it could provide funding for a research project that would produce a handbook for creation of such material, easing the way for groups that lack resources to conduct preproduction research. Although funding fluctuates, the CDC is the largest, most stable national organization involved in the antiviolence effort, and therefore it has the best ability to play a leadership role and to mount and sustain a consistent national campaign.

Recommendations

This section considered a few of the interactions among the groups depicted in figure 9.3 that influence what airs on television, leading to the following recommendations:

1. Violence prevention efforts should place more emphasis on well-coordinated, national media campaigns.
2. Funding for evaluation of campaigns is needed so campaign developers can benefit from lessons learned from prior campaigns.
3. The television industry has recognized its significance as a teacher in society. Both the industry and government should continue to look for ways to place economic value on programming that is not purely entertainment.

4. The CDC should assume a greater role in coordinating national antiviolence media campaigns.

Conclusions

At the time of this writing the NTVS has completed only one year of a three-year study. But the results from the first year and the history of antiviolence campaigns point to some general conclusions, which we have reviewed here. Antiviolence efforts are, for the most part, sporadic and unsystematic. Unfortunately, goodwill and significant effort are sometimes squandered by poor coordination across campaigns, among actors, and across persuasion channels such as schools, television, and interpersonal communication. Careful campaign pretesting and evaluation are rare, even though the cost is small compared to the cost of production and airtime. But there are signs of strategies that can be more effective.

We are entering a period when most of the actors depicted in figure 9.3 agree with the Surgeon General's office that violence is an epidemic. The nation is spending billions of dollars treating the victims of gun violence, but the cost in human misery is much higher. Under these conditions it may be unconscionable not to use television as an important vehicle for the prevention of violence.

The successful campaigns reviewed above suggest that more systematic and coordinated use of this powerful medium can help curb some of the behavioral precursors of violence. But campaigns must be carefully planned, targeted, coordinated across institutions, and delivered across multiple channels. Evaluation at various stages must be a key component. The experience of past campaigns has been summarized in this article. We hope that this collective experience may give us some guidance on how to better implement future antiviolence campaigns in which television is a major player in the prevention of violence.

REFERENCES

Antiviolence Campaigns from the Literature

Abbott, M. W. 1992. "Television Violence: A Proactive Prevention Campaign." In *Primary Prevention of Psychopathology: Vol. 14: Improving Children's Lives: Global Perspectives on Prevention,* ed. G. W. Albee, L. A. Bond, and T. V. Cook Monsey, 263–78. Newbury Park, CA: Sage.

Bennett, S. F., and P. J. Lavrakas. 1989. "Community-based Crime Prevention: An Assessment of the Eisenhower Foundation's Neighborhood Program." *Crime and Delinquency* 35(3): 345–64.

Coben, J. H., H. B. Weiss, E. P. Mulvey, and S. R. Dearwater. 1994. "A Primer on School Violence Prevention." *Journal of School Health* 64(8): 309–13.

Hammond, W. R., and B. R. Yung. 1991. "Preventing Violence in At-Risk African-American Youth." *Journal of Health Care for the Poor and Underserved* 2(3): 359–72.

Hausman, A. J., H. Spivak, D. Prothrow-Stith, and J. Roeber. 1992. "Patterns of Teen Exposure to a Community-based Violence Prevention Project." *Journal of Adolescent Health* 13(8): 668–75.

Jaffe, P. G., M. Sudermann, D. Reitzel, and S. M. Killip. 1992. "An Evaluation of a Secondary School Primary Prevention Program on Violence in Intimate Relationships." *Violence and Victims,* 7(2): 129–46.

Loftin, C., M. Heumann, and D. McDowall. 1983. "Mandatory Sentencing and Firearms Violence: Evaluating an Alternative to Gun Control." *Law and Society Review* 17(2): 287–318.

O'Keefe, G. J. 1985. "'Taking a Bite out of Crime': The Impact of a Public Information Campaign." *Communication Research* 12:147–78.

Raviv, A. 1993. "The Use of Hotline and Media Interventions in Israel during the Gulf War." In *The Psychological Effects of War and Violence on Children,* ed. L. A. Leavitt and N. A. Fox. Hillsdale, NJ: Lawrence Erlbaum.

Sacco, Vincent F., and R. A. Silverman. 1981. "Selling Crime Prevention: The Evaluation of a Mass Media Campaign." *Canadian Journal of Criminology* 23:191–202.

Schewe, P. A., and W. O'Donohue. 1993. "Sexual Abuse Prevention with High-Risk Males: The Roles of Victim Empathy and Rape Myths." *Violence and Victims* 8(4): 339–51.

Spivak, H., A. J. Hausman, and D. Prothrow-Stith. 1989. "Practitioners' Forum: Public Health and the Primary Prevention of Adolescent Violence—The Violence Prevention Project." *Violence and Victims* 4(3): 203–12.

Weingarden, S. I., and P. M. Graham. 1991. "Targeting Teenagers in a Spinal Cord Injury Prevention Program." *Paraplegia* 29:65–69.

Violence, Communication Theory, and Health Campaigns

American Academy of Pediatrics, Committee on Communications. 1990. "Children, Adolescents, and Television." *Pediatrics* 85:1119–20.

Apfel, I. 1995. "Business Reports: Crime: Teen Violence: Real or Imagined?" *American Demographics* 17(6): 22–23.

Archer, J. 1994. "Introduction to Male Violence." In *Male Violence,* ed. J. Archer, 1–22. London: Routledge.

Atkin, C. K., and V. Freimuth. 1989. "Formative Evaluation Research in Campaign Design." In *Public Communication Campaigns,* ed. R. E. Rice and C. D. Atkin, 131–50. Newbury Park, CA: Sage.

Atkin, C. K., and L. Wallack, eds. 1990. *Mass Communication and Public Health: Complexities and Conflicts.* Newbury Park, CA: Sage.

Aufderheide, P., and K. Montgomery. 1994. *The Impact of the Children's Television Act on the Broadcast Market.* Washington, DC: Center for Media Education.

Backer, T. E., E. M. Rogers, and P. Sopory. 1992. *Designing Health Communication Campaigns: What Works?* Newbury Park, CA: Sage.

Biocca, F., J. Brown, S. Fuyuan, J. M. Bernhardt, L. Batista, K. Kemp, G. Makris, M. West,

J. Lee, H. Straker, H. Hsiao, and E. Carbone. 1996. "Assessment of Television's Antiviolence Messages: University of North Carolina, Chapel Hill Study." In *National Television Violence Study, 1994–1995* (IV-1–IV-121). Studio City, CA: Mediascope.

Britt, David. 1996. Testimony to the House Telecommunications and Finance Subcommittee (Nexis electronic information service), February 29.

Brown, W. J., and A. Singhal. 1993. "Entertainment-Education Media: An Opportunity for Enhancing Japan's Leadership Role in Third World Development." *Keio Communication Review* 15:81–101.

Brown, W. J., A. Singhal, and E. M. Rogers. 1989. "Pro-Development Soap Operas: A Novel Approach to Development Communication." *Media Development* 4:43–47.

Butterfield, F. 1996. "Major Crimes Fell in '95, Early Data by F.B.I. Indicate." *The New York Times,* May 6: A1.

Carthey, M., Outreach Manager, UNC Television. Communication with Author. April 1996.

Center for Media Education and Institute for Public Representation, Georgetown University Law Center. 1992. *A Report on Station Compliance with the Children's Television Act.* Washington, DC: Center for Media Education.

Cerone, D. H. 1995. "Cable Joins Together to Take on Violence." *Los Angeles Times,* March 18.

Comstock, G., and H. Paik. 1990. *The Effects of Television Violence on Aggressive Behavior: A Meta Analysis.* Unpublished Report to the National Academy of Sciences Panel on the Understanding and Control of Violent Behavior. Washington, DC.

Cowan, G. 1978. *See No Evil.* New York: Touchstone/Simon and Schuster.

Cox, T. 1996. Personal communication. January.

Danish, S. J., and T. R. Donahue. 1996. "Understanding the Media's Influence on the Development of Antisocial and Prosocial Behavior." In *Preventing Violence in America,* ed. R. L. Hampton, P. Jenkins, and T. P. Gullotta, 133–55. Thousand Oaks, CA: Sage.

Daves, J., Media Project Director, Advocates for Youth. 1995. Communication with Author. September.

DeJong, W., and J. A. Winsten. 1990. "Recommendations for Future Mass Media Campaigns to Prevent Preteen and Adolescent Substance Abuse." *Health Affairs* 9(2): 30–46.

DiClemente, C. C. 1993. "Changing Addictive Behaviors: A Process Prospective." *Current Directions in Psychological Science* 2:101–6.

Edwards, E. 1995. "'Squash It' Campaign Gets New TV Zip." *Washington Post,* April 12: C1.

Eng, E., and J. W. Hatch. 1991. "Networking Between Agencies and Black Churches: The Lay Health Advisor Model." In *Prevention in Human Services,* ed. K. Pargament and K. Maton, 123–46. Binghamton, NY: Haworth Press.

Eron, L. D. 1986. "Intervention to Mitigate the Psychological Effects of Media Violence on Aggressive Behavior." *Journal of Social Issues* 42(3): 155–69.

Eron, L. D., and L. R. Huesmann. 1984. "The Relation of Prosocial Behavior to the Development of Agression and Psychopathology." *Aggressive Behavior* 10:201–11.

Farhi, P. 1996a. "Action Man Stars but Merchandisers Call the Toon." *Washington Post,* February 8: A1.

————. 1996b. "Media Group Attacks Toy-based Children's TV Shows." *Washington Post,* February 23.

Farquhar, J. W., S. P. Fortmann, N. Maccoby, W. L. Haskell, P. T. Williams, J. A. Flora, C. B. Taylor, B. W. Brown Jr., D. S. Solomon, and S. B. Hulley. 1985. "The Stanford Five City Project: Design and Methods." *American Journal of Epidemiology* 122:323–34.

Farquhar, J. W., N. Maccoby, P. D. Wood, J. K. Alexander, H. Breitrose, B. W. Brown Jr., W. L. Haskell, A.L. McAlister, A. J. Meyer, J. D. Nash, and M. P. Stern. 1977. "Community Education for Cardiovascular Health." *Lancet* 1:1192–5.

Federal Bureau of Investigation. 1991. *Uniform Crime Reports.* Washington, DC: Government Printing Office.

Federal Communications Commission. 1991. *Policies and Rules Concerning Children's Television Programming, Revision of Programming and Commercialization Policies, Ascertainment Requirements, and Program Log Requirements for Commercial Television Stations.* 6 FCC Rcd 5098, 5101.

Federal News Service. 1996. "Hearing of the Telecommunications and Finance Subcommittee of the House Commerce Committee." *Federal News Service* (Nexis), March 27.

Fenley, M. A., Public Information Officer for the Division of Violence Prevention of the U.S. Centers for Disease Control. 1996. Communication with Author. April.

Flay, B. R., and T. D. Cook. 1989. "Three Models for Evaluating Prevention Campaigns with a Mass Media Component." In *Public Communication Campaigns,* ed. R. E. Rice and C. D. Atkin, 175–96. Newbury Park, CA: Sage.

Flora, J. A., and D. Cassady. 1990. "Roles of Media in Community-based Health Promotion." In *Health Promotion at the Community Level,* ed. N. Bracht, 143–57. Beverly Hills, CA: Sage.

Fortmann, S. P., et al. 1995. "Community Intervention Trials: Reflections on the Stanford Five-City Project Experience." *American Journal of Epidemiology* 42(6): 576–86.

Freeman, M. 1993. "Power Rangers Represent Mega Merchandising Clout for Saban." *Broadcasting and Cable,* December 20.

Gerbner, G. 1977. "Comparative Cultural Indicators." In *Mass Media Policies in Changing Cultures,* ed. G. Gerbner, 199–205. New York: Wiley.

————. 1989. "Cross-Cultural Communications Research in the Age of Telecommunications." In *Continuity and Change in Communications in Post-Industrial Society,* ed. The Christian Academy, vol. 2. Seoul, Korea: Wooseok.

Gerbner, G., L. Gross, M. Morgan, N. Signorielli, and M. Jackson-Beck. 1979. "The Demonstration of Power: Violence Profile No. 10." *Journal of Communication* 29(3): 177–96.

Gibbs, D. A., N. P. Rizzo, and G. P. Dunteman. 1990. "Feasibility Study Regarding Paid Advertising." In *Evaluation Design Studies Final Report, Volume 2* (Contract No. 200-88-0643). Research Triangle Park, NC: Research Triangle Institute for the Centers for Disease Control.

Hall, S. 1996. "Kids TV is Abysmal, Crusader Says." *Indianapolis Star,* February 13: C1.

Heath, L., L. B. Bresolin, and R. C. Rinaldi. 1989. "Effects of Media Violence on Children." *Archives of General Psychiatry* 46:376–9.

Henry J. Kaiser Family Foundation. 1995. *The Use of Mainstream Media to Encourage So-*

cial Responsibility: The International Experience. Menlo Park, CA: Henry J. Kaiser Family Foundation.

Huesmann, L. R. 1986. "Psychological Processes Promoting the Relation Between Exposure to Media Violence and Aggressive Behavior by the Viewer." Journal of Social Issues 42(3): 125–39.

Information Access Company. 1996. "FCC Commissioner Says Strengthen Kid's TV Rules." Newsbytes. Information Access Company, Inc. (Nexis), April 1.

Job, R. 1988. "Effective and Ineffective Use of Fear in Health Promotion Campaigns." American Journal of Public Health 78(2): 163–67.

Jusang, I., President of MEE Productions, Philadelphia, PA. 1996. Communication with Author. April.

Kelly, L. 1995. "The Lure of Kids Merchandising." Electronic Media, April 24: 21.

Kennedy School. 1990. Spreading the Gospel: The Origin and Growth of the Drug Abuse Resistance Education Program. J. F. Kennedy School of Government Case Program. Cambridge: Harvard University.

Klein, J. D., J. D. Brown, K. W. Childers, J. Oliveri, C. Porter, and C. Dykers. 1993. "Adolescents' Risky Behavior and Mass Media Use." Pediatrics 92(1): 24–31.

Kolbert, E. 1995. "In Mounting Campaign against Violence, Is the Cable Industry Practicing What It Preaches?" New York Times, March 13.

Kunkel, D., B. S. Wilson, D. Linz, J. Potter, E. Donnerstein, S. Smith, E. Blumenthal, T. Gray. 1996. "Violence in Television Programming Overall: University of California, Santa Barbara Study." In National Television Violence Study, 1994–1995, (I-1–I-172.) Studio City, CA: Mediascope.

Lefebvre, R. C., and J. A. Flora. 1988. "Social Marketing and Public Health Intervention." Health Education Quarterly 15(3): 299–315.

Littleton, C. 1996. "Syndicators Battle for Custody of Kids." Broadcasting and Cable, January 22.

Littleton, E., Director of the Campaign for Children's Television of the Center for Media Education. 1996. Interview with Author. April.

Maibach, E., and R. L. Parrott, eds. 1995. Designing Health Messages: Approaches from Communication Theory and Public Health Practice. Thousand Oaks, CA: Sage.

May, C., and J. H. Mintz. 1988. Action on Drug Abuse, Really Me: Canada's Social Marketing Program on Alcohol and Other Drugs. Paper presented at the 35th International Congress on Alcoholism and Drug Dependence, August, Oslo.

McCall, N. 1994. "My Rap against Rap." Washington Post, May.

McGuire, W. J. 1989. "Theoretical Foundations of Campaigns." In Public Communication Campaigns, ed. R. E. Rice and W. J. Paisley, 41–70. Beverly Hills, CA: Sage.

Mendoza, M. 1996. "Quotas for Educational Shows Reexamined." Dallas Morning News, March 14: 1C.

Mercy, J. A., M. L. Rosenberg, K. E. Powell, C. V. Broome, and W. L. Roper. 1993. "Public Health Policy for Preventing Violence." Health Affairs, Winter: 7–29.

Mifflin, L. 1996a. "FCC Urged to Strengthen Children's TV." New York Times, April 2: A16.

———. 1996b. "TV Broadcasters Agree to 3 Hours of Children's Educational Programs a Week." New York Times, July 29: A8.

Milio, N. 1985. "Health Education = Health Instruction + Health News: Media Experiences in the United States, Finland, Australia and England." In The Media, Social

Science and Social Policy for Children, ed. E. A. Rubinstein and J. D. Brown. Norwood, NJ: Ablex.

Montgomery, K. C. 1989. *Target: Prime Time: Advocacy Groups and the Struggle Over Prime Time.* New York: Oxford University Press.

———. 1990. "Promoting Health through Entertainment Television." In *Mass Communication and Public Health,* ed. C. Atkin and L. Wallack, 114–29. Newbury Park, CA: Sage.

Morgan, M. 1990. "International Cultivation Analysis." In *Cultivation Analysis: New Directions, in Media Effects Research,* ed. N. Signorielli and M. Morgan, 225–48. Newbury Park, CA: Sage.

Morgan, M., and N. Signorielli. 1990. *Cultivation Analysis.* Newbury Park, CA: Sage Publications.

National Cable Television Association. 1995. "President Clinton Lends His Voice to the Cable Industry's Voices Against Violence Week Initiative." Press release, March 2.

National Organizations for Youth Violence Prevention Information. 1996. *Fact Sheet from the Children's Safety Network.* (Available from the Education Development Center, Inc., 55 Chapel Street, Newton, MA 02158-1060.)

Olweus, D. 1991. "Victimization Among School Children." *Advances in Psychology* 76:45.

Owens, M. R. 1994. *Joint Hearing on H.R. 4086, The Youth Development Block Grant Act Hearing.* August. Washington, DC: U.S. Government Printing Office.

Petty, R. E., and J. T. Cacioppo. 1984a. "The Effects of Involvement on Responses to Argument Quantity and Quality: Central and Peripheral Routes to Persuasion." *Journal of Personality and Social Psychology* 46:69–81.

———. 1984b. "Source Factors and the Elaboration Likelihood Model of Persuasion." *Advances in Consumer Research* 11:668–72.

PR Newswire. 1995. "Take Control of the Family Television, Cable TV, and the National PTA Join Forces to Combat TV Violence." *PR Newswire,* February (Machine-readable data file).

Prochaska, J. O., and C. C. DiClemente. 1992. "Stages of Change in the Modification of Problem Behaviors." In *Progress in Behavior Modification,* vol. 28, ed. M. Hersen, R. M. Eisler, and P. M. Miller. Sycamore, IL: Sycamore.

Prochaska, J. O., C. A. Redding, L. L. Harlow, J. S. Rossi, and W. F. Velicer. 1994. "The Transtheoretical Model of Change and HIV Prevention: A Review." *Health Education Quarterly* 21(4): 471–86.

Prothrow-Stith, D. 1991. *Deadly Consequences.* New York: HarperPerennial.

Public Attitudes about Children's Television. 1995. October 5. Washington, DC: Center for Media Education.

Quello, J. H. 1996. "The FCC and the Children's Television Act: Relying on the Discretion of Broadcasters." *Legal Times,* February 19: 28.

Reiss, A. J., Jr., and J. A. Roth, eds. 1993. *Understanding and Preventing Violence.* Washington, DC: National Academy Press.

Rice, R. E., and C. Atkin, eds. 1989. *Public Communication Campaigns.* 2d ed. Newbury Park, CA: Sage.

Rice, R. E., and C. Atkin. 1994. "Principles of Successful Public Communication Campaigns." In *Media Effects: Advances in Theory and Research,* ed. J. Bryant and D. Zillman, 365–87. Hillsdale, NJ: Lawrence Erlbaum.

Richmond, R. 1995. "Cable's Antiviolence Week: For Ruse or For Real?" *Daily News,* March 19.

Romer, D., and S. Kim. 1995. "Health Interventions for African American and Latino Youth: the Potential Role of Mass Media." *Health Education Quarterly* 22(2): 172–89.

Rowe, P. 1990. "Volunteer Mentors Empower Inner-City Youths." *Children Today* 19(1): 20.

Rowland, W. D., Jr. 1983. *The Politics of TV Violence.* Beverly Hills, CA: Sage.

Russell, C. 1995. "True Crime." *American Demographics* August: 22–26, 28–31.

Sacco, V. F., and M. Trotman. 1990. "Public Information Programming and Family Violence: Lessons from the Mass Media Crime Prevention Experience." *Canadian Journal of Criminology* 32(1): 91–105.

Salmon, C. T., ed. 1989. *Information Campaigns: Balancing Social Values and Social Change.* Newbury Park, CA: Sage.

Schmidt, E., Executive Director, Cease Fire, Inc. 1996. Communication with Author. April.

Seufert-Barr, N. 1995. "Fourth World Conference on Women: Seeking Action for Equality, Development, Peace." *UN Chronicle* 32(2): 39–43.

Singhal, A., E. M. Rogers, and W. J. Brown. 1993. "Harnessing the Potential of Entertainment-education Telenovelas." *Gazette* 51:1–18.

Strasburger, V. C. 1995. "Adolescents and the Media: Medical and Psychological Impact." In *Developmental Clinical Psychology and Psychiatry,* vol. 33, ed. A. E. Kazdin. Thousand Oaks, CA: Sage.

Vincent, M. L., A. F. Clearie, and M. D. Schlucheter. 1987. "Reducing Adolescent Pregnancy through School and Community-based Education." *Journal of the American Medical Association* 57(24): 320–1.

Wallack, L. 1990. "Improving Health Promotion: Media Advocacy and Social Marketing Approaches." In *Mass Communication and Public Health: Complexities and Conflicts,* ed. C. Atkin and L. Wallack. Newbury Park, CA: Sage.

Wilde, G. J. 1988. "Effects of Mass Media Communications on Health and Safety Habits: An Overview of Issues and Evidence." *Addiction* 88(7): 983–96.

Chapter 10

Framing of the Television Violence Issue in Newspaper Coverage

Cynthia Hoffner

Introduction

Television violence has been a topic of concern since the introduction of the medium, but the current decade has seen a resurgence of interest in the social impact of such content. Recent concern seems to reflect fears that increasingly accessible and/or graphic violence in many forms of entertainment, including television, is linked to societal violence. While there are clearly many other causes of violent crime and social problems (e.g., guns, drugs, gangs), television violence is undoubtedly a contributing factor. A large and diverse body of research demonstrates that, for many children, adolescents, and adults, exposure to televised violence contributes to fear, desensitization, acceptance of violence, and aggressive behavior (see Donnerstein, Slaby, and Eron 1994; Paik and Comstock 1994).

The resonance of this issue in today's society is illustrated by the fact that the 1996 U.S. presidential candidates, President Clinton and Senator Dole, expressed similar concerns about media violence despite markedly different views on other issues. Moreover, under pressure from Congress to address the problem of televised violence, the networks recently implemented a controversial system for rating program content. However, there is no clear consensus among interested groups regarding the extent of the problem or, more importantly, the appropriateness and effectiveness of various solutions. Much of what the public and, to some extent, policymakers know about the issue of television violence is undoubtedly derived from the news media.

This study examines coverage of the television violence issue in five major U.S. newspapers during 1994 and 1995. The chapter follows the traditional format of a quantitative research report, including a literature review, methodology (i.e., sampling and coding procedures), results, and discussion. To highlight the key points of the study, this introduction summarizes the major results and their implications.

Of the three major topics identified (content, effects, solutions), violent content and solutions received the most attention, with the effects of televised violence addressed much less frequently. The most common content-related theme was excessive violence, which was mentioned more than twice as often as the context or nature of violent portrayals. This emphasis is misleading, because context is more important than sheer amount in determining effects. When the effects of televised violence were discussed, evidence was often not provided, and specific examples were cited more often than research findings. A substantial minority of articles suggested (inaccurately) that effects are minimal or controversial. These aspects of the coverage may lead readers to conclude that affected individuals are unique and thereby to deny the susceptibility of themselves or their children. Discussion of solutions gave little consideration to how individuals can personally cope with televised violence. Rather, the struggle between industry self-regulation and government involvement was emphasized. Markedly different viewpoints were attributed to these two groups. Whereas government officials tended to express concern about televised violence and to favor government intervention, the television industry was more likely to minimize the problem and to equate various solutions with censorship.

In general, news coverage did not appear to adequately reflect the current research consensus regarding the harmful effects of televised violence, or the importance of context in determining effects. In part, important research may be overlooked by the press simply because journalists are unaware of the work. To help ensure more extensive and accurate coverage, researchers need to take initiative in communicating their findings and interpretations in a manner that is understandable to journalists and the public.

Literature Review

News coverage of television violence can be placed within the context of media communication about risk (e.g., Goshorn and Gandy 1995; Singer and Endreny 1987). The study of risk has traditionally focused on hazards to health and well-being posed by natural forces, technologies, risky behaviors, and diseases, and on ways of reducing these risks. Television violence is a news topic primarily because it is believed to cause harm to individuals and society, and because society is seeking ways of reducing the harm. Clearly not everyone is similarly affected, but the potential for harm translates into some degree of risk for individuals, either from direct exposure to televised violence, or through contact with others who have been affected. Perception of risk is influenced by the availability and use of relevant information (e.g., Kahneman and Tversky 1984). Personal experience and interpersonal communication are vivid and easily accessible sources of information. The news media also provide much information about aspects of the television violence issue, such as research evidence and industry and legislative responses. Goshorn and Gandy (1995) argue that how risk is *framed* by the news media influences perception of risk, particularly the risk faced by others.

"Framing," as used in many disciplines, refers to the selection and emphasis of certain aspects of information over others. News frames can function both as cognitive structures that guide information processing and as characteristics of news texts (Entman 1991). The present study focuses on news texts, but it should be noted that news frames can be internalized and guide processing of subsequent news stories (Pan and Kosicki 1993).

Analyses of news coverage have utilized many different definitions of framing (e.g., Entman 1993; Gamson 1989; Goshorn and Gandy 1995; Iyengar and Simon 1993; Pan and Kosicki 1993). One useful definition is offered by Entman (1993, 52): "To frame is to select some aspects of a perceived reality and make them more salient in a communicating text, in such a way as to promote a particular problem definition, causal interpretation, moral evaluation, and/or treatment recommendation for the item described." In a related discussion, Pan and Kosicki (1993, 58–59) differentiate between a topic, which they define as "a summary label of the domain of social experiences covered" and a theme or frame, which "connects different semantic elements of a story . . . into a coherent whole . . . [and] has the capability of directing attention as well as restricting the perspectives available to audiences." Thus, a theme or frame connects ideas within a news story in a way that suggests a particular interpretation of an issue. To illustrate, a theme/frame on the topic of "solutions to television violence" might portray the V-chip as a way to reduce societal harm or as a form of censorship.

Research on framing indicates that news frames can shape the way the audience interprets issues, affect the perceived legitimacy of particular groups, and influence the outcome of public policy debates (Edelman 1993; Entman and Rojecki 1993; Herman 1985; Iyengar 1990; Iyengar and Simon 1993; Pan and Kosicki 1993). Consequently, political or advocacy groups often strive to influence the frames employed in news coverage (e.g., Dionisopoulos and Crable 1988; Wallack, Dorfman, Jernigan, and Themba 1993). Because the news media are the source of much of what the public knows about the television violence issue, news framing of the issue has the potential to impact public opinion and public policy about televised violence.

One important function of framing is to characterize or define a problem (e.g., Dionisopoulos and Crable 1988; Edelman 1993). What aspects of the issue are most important, and how are they presented? Public concern about television violence depends primarily on the negative effects that are presumed to result from viewing. The relative emphasis on effects versus other aspects of the issue may influence the degree to which television violence is perceived as a significant public health problem. The manner in which content and effects are framed also may have important consequences. News discussion of violent content, for example, may focus on the sheer amount of violence or on the context and portrayal of violence. Much evidence indicates that the effects of violence vary depending on the nature of the depictions (as noted in chapter 2; Kunkel et al. 1995), but it is not known whether this message is communicated to the public.

Public perception of television violence as a public health problem may also be influenced by the types of effects discussed and the potential mediators identified. For example, news coverage may focus on behavioral effects to the exclusion of less observable (but perhaps more pervasive) attitudinal and emotional effects, or may suggest (incorrectly) that adverse effects are limited to particular vulnerable subgroups. The nature of the evidence provided may also shape perceptions. Evidence for effects could include examples of affected individuals (e.g., an adolescent who copied a violent act), or research studies and conclusions. Specific exemplars are likely to be more vivid and memorable than research conclusions, and they may influence beliefs about the effects of televised violence on others (Iyengar 1990, 1991). But it is also easier to differentiate oneself from specific, often atypical, individuals. Thus, when evidence is presented in the form of examples and illustrations, readers may find it easier to blame affected individuals and to deny the susceptibility of themselves or similar others (Perloff 1993).

Another function of framing is the assignment of responsibility for social problems (Goshorn and Gandy 1995; Iyengar 1990, 1991). The notion of responsibility involves both cause (who/what caused the problem?) and treatment (who should solve the problem?), but treatment is a more pressing concern for television violence. Those often described as responsible for dealing with televised violence are the television industry, the government, and the audience. Is the television industry or the government primarily responsible for regulating the amount or availability of violent programming; or is the audience responsible for making appropriate choices and monitoring what children view? By assigning responsibility and framing solutions in particular ways, the news media may partially determine public support for various treatment options, which in turn may benefit particular groups (Dionisopoulos and Crable 1988; Edelman 1993; Entman and Rojecki 1993; Wallack et al. 1993). Freedom of expression versus censorship is an issue that is often raised when mass media content is questioned. Given that mass media providers value independence and self-regulation, framing potential solutions (e.g., government regulation, the V-chip) as censorship would be beneficial to the television industry. In contrast, government officials may benefit if the debate over solutions is framed as a political is-sue, but mainly if their own party is shown as more concerned about the pub-lic welfare.

The role of research in news coverage deserves further attention, because social science research should form the basis for public opinion and policy deci-sions about television violence. News reports about television violence research can contribute to public understanding or misunderstanding of scientific con-clusions, depending on the nature of the coverage (Eron 1986; Rubinstein and Brown 1985). In general, journalists and the public tend to regard the social sci-ences as less valid and scientific than the natural sciences (Dunwoody 1986; Evans 1995). For issues within the realm of everyday experience, like television violence, journalists may feel that reporting of research is not necessary to com-municate effectively about the topic. However, understanding relevant research is essential for people to form accurate beliefs based on more than opinion, speculation, and personal experience. When research is mentioned, the per-ceived value of the conclusions may vary depending on the information pro-vided about the researchers and the specific studies cited.

The degree of controversy associated with research conclusions, and also with potential solutions, is an important aspect of news coverage to consider. Journalists may sometimes emphasize disagreements in order to generate con-troversy and attract attention (Dunwoody 1986; Mazur 1981). They also may pre-sent alternative viewpoints in the interest of fairness, even if those viewpoints are not supported by the preponderance of evidence. Yet this approach may con-vey the wrong message to the public. For example, research is highly consistent in demonstrating the adverse effects of televised violence on emotions, atti-tudes, and behaviors (Donnerstein et al. 1994; Paik and Comstock 1994). Sug-gesting that research conclusions are a matter of debate may lead to public mis-perception of the evidence. In contrast, the varied agendas of interested parties make controversy over appropriate solutions to television violence inevitable. Reporting of controversy in this context may serve to engage the public in learn-ing about and considering the various alternatives (Olien, Donohue, and Tichenor 1995).

Summary of Issues Addressed

In addition to providing descriptive information about news coverage of tele-vision violence, the present study addressed issues in several areas, based on the above analysis. First, in defining the television violence issue, what has been the relative emphasis on content, effects, and solutions? Second, what specific themes have been included within each of these topic areas? In particular, how are violent content and effects presented, how are solutions portrayed, and to what extent are aspects of the issue depicted as controversial? Third, how have three specific frames been used: television violence as a public health problem, as a partisan political issue, and as a censorship issue? Fourth, how often are the views of key groups depicted, and what are their motivations regarding the television violence issue? And finally, how is research on television violence reported?

Methodology

Sample

This study examined newspaper articles about the television violence issue that appeared in five major U.S. newspapers during 1994 and 1995. The selected newspapers were: the *Chicago Tribune,* the *Los Angeles Times, The New York Times, USA Today,* and the *Washington Post.* According to a recent report in Advertising Age (Skews 1995), these newspapers are among the seven newspapers with the largest U.S. circulation (the others are the *Wall Street Journal* and the *New York Daily News*). The five selected newspapers were chosen because of their wide circulation and because they cover different geographical regions of the United States.

Using the key words "television" and "violence," four computerized data bases were searched: DataTimes, Newspaper Abstracts, National Newspaper Index, and Readers Guide to Periodical Literature. This process identified 405 articles. All of these articles were located and examined, with the exception of three articles that were unavailable.[1] Forty-eight articles were subsequently eliminated because they did not refer to television violence (i.e., "television" and "violence" both appeared in the article, but not as a unit).[2] Four cartoons were also excluded. Thus, a total of 350 articles contained some reference to the television violence issue. Photocopies of these articles from print or microfilm were used in the coding process.

Training of Coders

Four coders (3 females, 1 male) with varied political affiliations (2 Republicans, 1 Democrat, 1 independent) participated in at least 10 hours of training and practice. They first reviewed and discussed the coding scheme and then independently applied the scheme to television violence articles from the selected newspapers published in 1993. Coders met several times during the training period to discuss their coding decisions and achieved at least 70 percent agreement on the practice materials. During the coding process, each coder was assigned some articles that were being classified by another coder. A total of 59 randomly chosen articles (16.7 percent) were coded by two coders, and disagreements were resolved by a third coder. Reliabilities were calculated using Scott's pi or Krippendorf's alpha. Most reliabilities for the variables reported in this paper ranged from .76 to 1.00, with a few as low as .68.[3]

Coding Procedures

Basic information coded for each article included the newspaper, date, placement of the article, and column inches.[4] Coders also classified the article type, the author, and the role of television violence in the article (primary topic, secondary topic, brief reference).

Following Pan and Kosicki's (1993) analysis of the differences between a topic and a theme (frame), both topics and themes were coded. The major television violence topic(s) on which the articles focused were classified as content, effects, and/or solutions, and the primary themes mentioned in the article were also coded. A list of themes was developed inductively based on an examination of the sample. Themes included evaluative positions or claims about content, effects, and solutions, as well as references to controversy (see table 10.1). Coders checked the themes on the list that appeared in each article.

Three ways of framing the television violence issue were examined in more detail: as a public health problem, a partisan political issue, and a censorship issue. Television violence was framed as a public health problem if the article indicated that violence has negative effects on individuals and/or society. If so, coders noted whether children were described as particularly vulnerable, whether any mediating factors were identified, and what type of evidence for effects was provided (e.g., examples, research). Television violence was framed as a partisan political issue if the article explicitly contrasted the two political parties, defined positions as "republican" or "democrat" (rather than simply attributing positions to specific individuals), or described the issue as a political controversy. Coders also judged which (if either) political party was portrayed as more concerned. Television violence was framed as a censorship issue if any solutions to the problem of television violence were described as censorship or a threat to free speech. Which solutions were so described, and who regarded them as censorship, were also recorded.

The study also examined how the articles portrayed the motivations of three key groups with interest in the issue of television violence: the television industry (e.g., network and cable representatives, creators), government officials (e.g., the president, Congress), and researchers. Coders classified whether or not the views of each group were presented, and if so, what views or motivations were depicted. Motivations included being concerned about or denying problems associated with television violence, avoiding or supporting government regulation, and seeking monetary/political/personal gain. Coders also recorded whether each article cited average citizens or reported the results of public opinion polls. The specific views of average citizens were not coded be-

TABLE 10.1. Television Violence Themes in Three Article Types and the Total Sample

	Article Type			
	News Reports (%)	Features (%)	Opinion/ Editorials (%)	Total (%)
Violent television content				
Amount excessive/increasing	48.0	61.8	46.2	49.8
Portrayals are problematic	18.2	18.2	24.6	21.5
Amount is decreasing	13.5	20.0	6.2	12.3
Popular	7.4	16.4	9.2	10.2
Portrayed responsibly	8.1	3.6	6.2	7.8
Whether television is too violent is controversial	4.7	3.6	4.6	4.1
Effects of television violence				
Causes crime/agression/imitation	18.9	21.8	26.2	21.2
Affects attitudes/values	10.8	18.2	21.5	15.0
Causes fear/desensitization	8.1	23.6	13.8*	12.3
Other factors more important causes of social problems	2.0	10.9	21.5***	9.2
Effects are controversial	4.1	1.8	7.7	4.4
No/minimal negative effects	2.0	5.5	6.2	3.8
Solutions to television violence				
Regulation should be done by the television industry	38.5	30.9	20.0*	29.4
Government should not be involved in regulation	31.1	21.8	29.2	27.0
V-chip will be useful/give parents control	31.8	21.8	18.5	24.6
Ratings/warnings recommended	25.7	16.4	10.8*	18.8
V-chip bad idea/ineffective/ impractical	16.2	18.2	27.7	17.4
Government should be involved in regulation	18.9	10.9	9.2	14.0
Government's role is controversial	16.2	5.5	6.2*	10.9
V-chip is controversial	12.2	10.9	6.2	9.6
Limit violence to late hours	14.9	1.8	4.6**	9.6
Parents should regulate children's viewing	6.1	16.4	15.4*	9.6
How/by whom programs will be rated is controversial	2.7	14.5	10.8**	6.5
Viewers should pressure television industry to reduce violence	2.7	3.6	7.7	3.8
Media literacy training will reduce television violence problem	1.4	10.9	1.5**	3.1
Number of articles	148	55	65	293

Note: The table values reflect the percentage of articles of each type, and in the total sample, that included each theme. The total sample includes an additional 25 articles of other types (e.g., reviews, letters). Asterisks indicate the significance of chi square analyses comparing the three article types.

*** = Statistically significant at .001 level, ** = significant at .01 level, * = significant at .05 level.

cause preliminary examination of the sample revealed that these were mentioned rarely.

Finally, the presentation of research was examined in greater depth. References to specific studies were coded for the primary topic of the research (content, effects, solutions, other), how the research was evaluated, whether methods were described, and whether the article functioned primarily to report research. When research findings were cited (without reference to a specific study), the primary topic and evaluation were also coded. For all researchers named, coders recorded their identified field of expertise and the topics on which they were cited. Only individuals explicitly identified as researchers were included, on the assumption that this is the only way the general public would be aware of their role.

Results

The results reported below are primarily descriptive, intended to provide information about how the television violence issue was presented during 1994 and 1995 in major U.S. newspapers. Some articles received codes in multiple categories for certain variables. Thus, percentages for those variables total to more than 100 percent. The basis for calculating percentages is either the total number of articles or the number of articles that received a particular code (e.g., depicted the views of government officials), as indicated. All means in the text with no subscript in common differ at $p < .05$ by the Scheffé method.

Sample Description

Of the 350 articles coded, television violence was the primary topic in 226 (64.6 percent), a secondary topic in 67 (19.1 percent), and a brief reference in the remaining 57 (16.3 percent).[5] The final sample used in this study included the 293 articles with television violence as a primary or secondary topic.

More articles in the final sample appeared in the *Los Angeles Times* ($n = 80$) than in the other four newspapers: the *Washington Post, n = 58*; *USA Today, n = 55*; the *New York Times, n = 54*; and the *Chicago Tribune, n = 46*. A single-sample chi-square revealed that this difference was significant, $\chi^2(4) = 11.11, p < .05$. Half of these articles were news reports (50.5 percent), which essentially dealt with breaking news. The others were classified as opinion/editorials (22.2 percent), feature articles that explored the issue in some depth (18.8 percent), program reviews (6.1 percent), letters to the editor (1.0 percent), and other (e.g., a book review, 1.4 percent). Four-fifths of the articles (80.5 percent) were authored by journalists, with an additional 12.3 percent attributed to no author, typically indicating the work of a newspaper staff writer. The remaining articles were written by television industry representatives (2.1 percent), researchers (.7

percent), and other individuals (4.4 percent; e.g., educator, clergy). The average story length was 23.5 column inches (range = 0.5 to 264.0). Fully 10.2 percent of the articles appeared on the front page, which is a relatively high percentage, given that about five percent of all newspaper stories appear on page one (Weiss and Singer 1988).

Major Topics and Themes

Most of the articles focused on one topic area (content, effects, or solutions), but about 15 percent had more than one focus. Over half (56.7 percent) of the articles focused on solutions, such as government regulation and the V-chip. The amount/portrayal of violence was the focus of 43.3 percent of the articles. Only 16.7 percent of the articles focused on the effects of televised violence.

The specific themes in each article were also examined. On average, there were 3.7 themes per article. Table 10.1 presents the percentage of articles in the total sample, and in the three most frequent article types, that included 26 specific themes on the television violence issue. Only themes that appeared in at least 3 percent of the articles are included. To clarify the discussion of the findings, percentages (rounded to whole numbers) are repeated in the text when relevant.

The percentages for the total sample (see table 10.1) reveal that the single most common theme, mentioned in 50 percent of the articles, is that there is too much violence on television. The excessive amount of violence was a much more common theme than concern regarding how violence is portrayed (e.g., graphic, glamorous), although violent portrayals were criticized in 22 percent of the articles. Favorable evaluation of content, emphasizing a decrease in the amount of violence (12 percent) or responsible violent portrayals (8 percent), was less frequent. Whether television is too violent was rarely described as controversial (4 percent).

When the effects of television violence were addressed, the negative impact on behavior was the most common theme, in 21 percent of the articles, followed by negative effects on attitudes (15 percent) and emotions (12 percent). Nearly one-tenth of the articles (9 percent), however, noted that other factors, such as poverty, guns, and drugs, were more important determinants of social problems than television violence. Few articles denied that televised violence has negative effects (4 percent) or described effects as controversial (4 percent). However, even these small numbers constitute a relatively substantial proportion of the articles that *focused* on the effects of violence. In fact, nearly one-quarter of the articles (24.5 percent) that focused on effects included claims that the negative effects of television violence are minimal or controversial.

Many different solutions to television violence were discussed, with the bulk of references dealing with the relative value of government's involvement in regulation or with the V-chip. The two most common themes emphasized that the industry (29 percent) and not government (27 percent) should be responsible for regulating violent content on television. However, 14 percent of the articles indicated that the government should be involved, and 11 percent described the government's role as controversial. Discussion of the government's role was typically associated with coverage of legislation for the V-chip and other solutions. The V-chip was depicted favorably in one-quarter of the articles (25 percent), but it was also criticized (17 percent) and described as controversial (10 percent). Nearly 19 percent of the articles recommended ratings and/or warnings as potential solutions, but a smaller proportion (7 percent) noted that how a ratings system would be implemented is controversial. In addition, 10 percent of the articles mentioned limiting violence to later hours. To some extent, ratings, warnings, and the V-chip are solutions that involve individual responsibility (once the information or technology is in place), but other solutions that rely on audience involvement were mentioned less frequently. Only 10 percent of the articles discussed parental responsibility for children's viewing, and less than 4 percent recommended public pressure on the television industry or media literacy training as solutions.

The three most frequent types of articles (news reports, features, and opinion/editorials) were compared on the inclusion of each theme. As table 10.1 shows, there were no significant differences in coverage of violent content, but several differences emerged in discussion of effects and solutions. Attitudinal effects of violence were discussed least often in news reports and most often in feature articles. An examination of the percentages shows that news reports also tended to discuss behavioral and emotional effects less often than the other article types. In fact, when all references to negative effects (behavioral, attitudinal, emotional) were combined, negative effects were mentioned significantly less often in news reports (29.7 percent) than in features or opinion/editorials (43.3 percent), $\chi^2(1) = 4.76$, $p < .03$. The argument that society's problems are due less to television violence than to other factors was made most often in opinion/editorials and least often in news reports.

News reports were more likely than other article types to argue that regulation should be done by the television industry, and to advocate ratings, warnings, and limiting violence to later hours. Although the article types did not differ significantly in arguments for or against government involvement, news reports were more likely to note that the government's role is controversial. In contrast, controversy over a ratings system was mentioned more often in features and opinion/editorials. Parental regulation as a solution was also discussed more often in features and opinion/editorials, and the value of media literacy was mentioned mainly in feature articles.

Public Health Problem, Partisan Political Issue, Censorship Issue?

Three specific ways of framing of the television violence issue were examined in more detail.

1. *Public health problem.*   Television violence was portrayed as a negative influence on individuals or society in a little more than one-third of the articles (39.6 percent). Of these articles, 73.3 percent described children as particularly vulnerable to adverse effects, and 18.1 percent identified other factors as potential mediators of negative effects. Specifically, family characteristics, such as working parents and children's unsupervised viewing, were mentioned in 12.1 percent, social conditions, such as neighborhood crime, were cited in 6.9 percent, and personal traits, such as aggressiveness, were identified in only 3.4 percent. More than half of the articles (53.5 percent) provided no evidence for negative effects other than the opinion of the author. In 20.2 percent of the articles, evidence was based on examples or illustrations, such as a mother's description of her son imitating the Power Rangers. Researchers or experts were quoted as evidence in 16.7 percent of the articles, and research studies or findings were cited in 15.8 percent.

2. *Partisan political issue.*   Although over half of the articles discussed the views of government officials (see next section), only about one-tenth (10.6 percent) explicitly depicted television violence as a political issue about which the two parties differed. More often positions were associated with individuals, and differences were among members of the same party (e.g., Democrats who favored government regulation versus ones who wished to avoid it). In articles that presented television violence as a partisan issue, Democrats were shown as more concerned than Republicans in nearly a third (32.3 percent), but only 6.4 percent showed Republicans as more concerned than Democrats. In the remaining articles, the relative concern of the two parties was equal (41.9 percent) or could not be determined (19.4 percent).

3. *Censorship issue.*   In about one-quarter (27.3 percent) of the articles, certain solutions to television violence were depicted as censorship or a threat to free speech. The solutions described this way were government regulation in general (in 58.5 percent of the articles), the V-chip (38.8 percent), a ratings system (22.5 percent), and limits on when violence can air (5.0 percent). The three latter solutions were typically criticized within the context of legislation requiring their implementation. Fully 61.3 percent of these articles indicated that individuals affiliated with the television industry regarded certain solutions as censorship. Other groups portrayed similarly were journalists (15.0 percent), Republicans (13.8 percent), civil libertarians (7.5 percent), average citizens (6.3 percent), and Democrats (5.0 percent).

Motivations of Key Groups: Television Industry, Government Officials, Researchers

The motivations of several key groups, as conveyed by the articles in the sample, were examined. The views of the television industry were depicted in 66.9 percent of the articles, those of government officials in 58.0 percent, and those of researchers in 14.3 percent. In comparison, only 5.8 percent of the articles cited average citizens (usually parents), and 5.1 percent reported the results of public opinion polls on the topic.

Table 10.2 presents the motivations depicted for members of the three most frequently cited groups. First, as can be seen in table 10.2, representatives of the television industry were portrayed as less concerned about televised violence and its effects, and more inclined to minimize or deny these problems, than members of the other groups. A substantial proportion of articles, however, did portray industry representatives as concerned about violence. Researchers were depicted as most concerned about negative effects; in fact, their motivations were limited almost exclusively to concern about violent content and effects. With regard to government regulation, industry representatives were nearly always depicted as opposing government control. In contrast, government officials were more often shown as supporting government regulation, although in a substantial proportion of articles, they expressed a desire to avoid government involvement. In a small number of articles, both industry representatives and government officials were described as motivated by monetary or political gain.

TABLE 10.2. Television Violence-Related Motivations of Three Key Groups

| | Key Groups | | |
Motivations	Television Industry (%)	Government Officials (%)	Researchers (%)
Concern about amount/portrayal	34.7	62.4	64.3
Concern about negative effects	8.7	18.8	35.7
Deny/minimize problem of amount/portrayal	28.1	1.2	4.8
Deny/minimize negative effects	8.2	0.0	0.0
Protect free speech/avoid government regulation	47.4	25.3	2.4
Advocate/facilitate government regulation	4.6	53.5	0.0
Seek monetary/political/ personal gain	16.3	10.0	0.0
Number of articles depicting the views of each group	196	170	42

Note: The table values are the percentage of articles depicting the views of each group that portray group members as having each motivation.

The Presentation of Research

Altogether, approximately one-quarter of the articles (25.9 percent) cited research studies, findings, and/or researchers. A total of 66 specific research studies were discussed in 52 (17.7 percent) of the articles. Nearly two-thirds (62.1 percent) of these studies were content analyses, about one-quarter (28.8 percent) dealt with the effects of television violence, 4.5 percent dealt with solutions (e.g., warnings), and 4.5 percent dealt with the popularity of violent television programs. Although most of the studies were unevaluated, a substantial proportion were criticized or described as controversial: content analyses, 29.3 percent; effects, 15.8 percent; solutions, 0.0 percent; and violence popularity, 100.0 percent. Explicit praise was given only to a few content analyses (12.2 percent). Information about research methodology was provided for nearly half of the studies (45.5 percent), and the researchers who conducted the studies were cited by name about as often (54.5 percent).

As an indicator of the emphasis given to studies, it was determined whether the primary function of the article was to report study results. Some articles simply cited studies briefly in support of a point, whereas others focused on reporting research, such as a *Chicago Tribune* story headlined "Study: TV Violence Rises 41 Percent in 2 Years." Just under half of the articles that referenced studies (46.2 percent) functioned primarily to report research. Nearly all of these (91.7 percent) reported content analyses, with the remaining two articles (8.3 percent) focusing on effects.

In 24 articles (8.2 percent), research findings were discussed without reference to specific studies (e.g., "Research shows that . . . "). These findings dealt with effects (75.0 percent) more often than with content (25.0 percent), but never with solutions. In most cases the findings were unevaluated, but 16.7 percent were criticized or described as controversial, and 4.2 percent were praised.

Individuals identified as researchers were mentioned 51 times in 42 (14.3 percent) of the articles. Four individuals accounted for 34 of these mentions: George Gerbner (12), Jeffrey Cole (10), Robert Lichter (7), and Leonard Eron (5). Nearly half of the researchers named (47.1 percent) had no identified field of expertise, 29.4 percent were in the communication field, 7.8 percent were psychologists, 3.9 percent were education professors, and 11.8 percent were in some other field (e.g., social science, child development). Researchers were cited on the topic of violent content in 61.9 percent of the articles, on effects in 35.7 percent, and on solutions in 11.9 percent. It should be noted that some experts who were cited were undoubtedly researchers but were not so identified in the articles.

Discussion

This study provides an initial examination of newspaper coverage of the television violence issue. The emphasis of the coverage was on violent content and solutions, with the effects of televised violence receiving much less attention. To some extent, this distribution of topics probably reflects the nature of news, with events such as speeches, press conferences, and congressional debates receiving the most coverage (Weiss and Singer 1988). For example, during the time period covered, Congress considered several bills designed as potential solutions, and analyses of violent content were announced or released by the networks, the cable industry, and independent action groups. It may also be that negative effects were considered a given by many journalists and thus were not the focus of news coverage. Clearly the current debate centers around the question of what to do about television violence.

The single most common news theme was the excessive amount of violence on television. This theme was mentioned more than twice as often as any discussion of the context or nature of violent portrayals (e.g., graphic, glamorous). How violence is portrayed, however, is more important than sheer amount in determining effects (as noted in chapter 2; Kunkel et al. 1995). The general public certainly recognizes some differences among portrayals (e.g., animated versus live-action), but may misunderstand the factors that interact to determine viewer responses. For example, fantasy violence may be regarded as unrealistic by mature viewers, but not by young children who have difficulty distinguishing fantasy and reality. However, this type of information has received relatively little press coverage. For example, recent news coverage of the National Television Violence Study's 1994–95 content analysis results (as noted in chapter 4) focused on the sheer amount of violence (e.g., 57 percent of programs contained violence), rather than the contextual variables that were emphasized in the report.

The analysis of news coverage also revealed that favorable evaluations of violent content (i.e., decreasing, portrayed responsibly) were not mentioned often. Many of the references to responsible portrayals singled out specific programs, such as *NYPD Blue*'s emphasis on the tragic aftermath of violence and other television series that altered bomb-related plotlines following the Oklahoma City bombing.

The emphasis on excessive violent content and the need for solutions suggests that televised violence is potentially harmful, but effects were infrequently the focus of news coverage. When effects were discussed, it was encouraging to note that attitudinal and emotional effects were mentioned nearly as often as more observable behavioral effects such as aggression and crime. Some articles identified mediating factors, but fortunately did not give the impression that *only* certain vulnerable subgroups were likely to be affected by televised violence. However, despite the high degree of consensus among researchers (e.g., Donnerstein et al. 1994), nearly one-quarter of these articles suggested that the negative effects of television violence are minimal or controversial. This conveys a misleading impression regarding the state of scientific knowledge about television violence.

Over half of the articles that dealt with effects provided no evidence other than the authors' opinions. When evidence was included, examples and illustrations were cited slightly more often than research. These aspects of the coverage may lead readers to conclude that affected individuals are in some way unique and thereby deny their own susceptibility. Research shows that the majority of the public believes there is too much violence on television, and that television violence has harmful effects on viewers, particularly children (e.g., Gunter and Stipp 1992; Moore and Saad 1993). However, a growing body of evidence on the so-called third-person effect shows that people believe that others are more affected by media messages than they are themselves (Perloff 1993). Recent studies on media violence have found that people regard violent portrayals as much less harmful to themselves and their own children than to others (Duck and Mullin 1995; Gunter 1994; Hoffner et al. 1997). This raises the concern that people may support certain solutions with "others" in mind, but may not be motivated to take precautionary measures themselves, either by modifying their own viewing habits or monitoring those of their children.

Solutions to the problem of television violence received the most news attention. The coverage of solutions emphasized the struggle between self-regulation by the industry and government involvement, undoubtedly due in part to the extensive coverage of congressional debates about television violence legislation. The specific solution that was discussed most often, in both favorable and unfavorable terms, was the V-chip. The V-chip was portrayed by some as an ideal solution that would put control in the hands of the viewing public. But concerns were raised not only about whether the V-chip should be required by law, but about the violence ratings that are necessary for the device to function. The key questions were: Who should rate programs, and how can the ratings be done fairly, accurately, and efficiently?

News coverage gave little consideration to how individuals can cope with the issue of television violence. The focus on government and the television industry seemed to convey the impression that the primary responsibility for solutions lies with these groups. Parental regulation of children's viewing was recommended in about one-tenth of the articles, primarily features and opinions/editorials. However, these were generally brief references, rather than more in-depth explanations of how parents can mitigate the negative effects of televised violence. Research shows that many parents have few rules for children's television use and do not discourage viewing of many program genres that are high in violence, such as police shows and superhero shows. Although parent–child communication about television can increase benefits and reduce harms, parents often do not utilize this type of viewing guidance (Wright, St. Peters, and Huston 1990). For the most part, the news media have missed the opportunity to inform the public about the benefits of active coviewing with children, educational interventions, and ways of providing input to the FCC or the television industry (Donnerstein et al. 1994).

Although the forces that shape news coverage cannot be readily identified in a content analysis, comparisons among the viewpoints attributed to different groups offer some interesting insights. Clearly, the contrasting agendas of the two most frequently cited groups, the television industry and government officials, received ample coverage. There was a tendency for some in the television industry to minimize the problem of television violence, which contrasted markedly with the views of government officials (and also researchers). Clearly, the industry benefits from conveying the impression that violence on television is not a serious problem, a view that many (but not all) in the industry have maintained for years (Rubinstein and Brown 1985). The concern expressed by many government officials is undoubtedly genuine, but presumably also appeals to the public as evidence that those in power are confronting the forces that may contribute to society's problems.

With regard to solutions, the television industry was most likely to oppose government involvement and to equate various solutions with censorship. Clearly these positions are favorable to the industry's preference for independence and self-regulation. Framing government involvement as censorship should help move public sentiment toward the industry position, since censorship is very unpopular concept in our free society. Similar strategies have been used by other groups, such as the tobacco industry, which has tried to frame the debate about smoking as a free speech/individual choice issue (Wallack et al. 1993). This approach shifts the focus away from the potential harms associated with the product (e.g., television violence, cigarettes). Not surprisingly, government officials were relatively favorable toward government involvement, although a substantial proportion also expressed concern about protecting freedom of speech. Clearly, the government should have an interest in shielding society, especially children, from negative influences. But it is also advantageous for government officials if legislative intervention is viewed as a way of achieving valued societal objectives.

Part of the reason that the views of the industry and government officials received such extensive coverage is that these groups undoubtedly have greater access to journalists and more skill at influencing the news agenda than do citizens or researchers. Government officials, in particular, are also more likely to be involved in events that are considered "breaking news," such as legislative debates or press conferences. And the views of industry representatives may often be included by journalists in an effort to present all sides of the issue. For example, Weiss and Singer (1988) described a television reporter who prepared a story about the causal link between television violence and aggressive behavior, and included an opposing view from the industry mainly to show that he was being fair.

Research studies were mentioned in approximately one-sixth of the articles, and researchers were cited slightly less often. It could be argued that this is a substantial amount of coverage, especially given that many articles focused on congressional debates about solutions. However, research on the effects of television violence received very little press attention. Nearly all of the articles that focused on research studies reported content analyses, such as the 1994 Center for Media and Public Affairs study of a single day of television, and the 1995 UCLA analysis of network programming. Large, well-funded studies like these are often the subject of press releases and press conferences arranged by the sponsoring organizations. Haskins (1985) notes that much important research, with potential policy implications, is overlooked by the press simply because journalists are unaware of the work.

The importance of communicating researchers' perspectives is illustrated by the recent controversy over the age-based ratings system (e.g., unsuitable for children under 14) recently introduced by the networks. Many scholars believe that content-based ratings, which would provide specific information about violent and sexual content, would be more useful to parents and more effective in discouraging children from viewing problematic programs. To provide the public with all relevant information regarding the choice of a ratings system, the news media must cover not only the networks' perspective, but also the views of experts on televised violence and the relevant research findings (as noted in chapter 7).

Haskins (1985) suggests that researchers and professional organizations have a responsibility to publicize findings that may have important implications for the public and policymakers. Gaining attention for research may prove to be difficult, however, if the findings appear highly specialized or lacking in public relevance (Weiss and Singer 1988). Moreover, journalists unfamiliar with scientific methodology may have difficulty interpreting research reports. Social scientists are used to communicating the complexity of research studies to their peers, and they tend to qualify the conclusions they draw from individual studies. Journalists, in contrast, must write clear, succinct, readable narratives that will interest the general public. With these issues in mind, Haskins (1985, 82) makes some important recommendations to social scientists seeking to communicate effectively with the news media:

> First, they must make available a short and vivid document summarizing their findings in plain English. Second, they must draw the policy implications that seem most appropriate and express these in a similarly unadorned fashion. Third, if necessary, they must make themselves available to the media to answer questions about the results and conclusions.

At the Duke Conference on Media Violence and Public Policy (June 1996), Joanne Cantor reported that she followed these steps and was pleased with the accurate and substantial articles about her research (Cantor and Harrison 1996) that appeared in the *Philadelphia Inquirer* and *USA Today*. If researchers doing important work heed Haskins's recommendations, perhaps research will receive more extensive coverage, and the articles will more accurately reflect researchers' conclusions and interpretations.

The present study has provided some insight into how the television violence issue has been covered by the press. Some speculations have been offered regarding the impact of this coverage on public opinion, but a content analysis cannot reveal how readers respond to news depictions. Research on other topics, such as poverty and nuclear power, has shown that news framing can impact public opinion and ultimately exert an influence on public policy (e.g., Entman and Rojecki 1993; Iyengar 1990). Future research needs to examine the link between the news media framing of the television violence issue and how the audience conceptualizes the issue. Public concern about the role of mass media in our society makes it likely that news coverage will play a continuing role in the current debate.

NOTES

The author would like to thank Stacy Schneider and Ken Smith for their invaluable assistance in developing the coding scheme, coding the articles, and data entry, and Becky Bixby for participating as a coder.

1. The unavailable articles included two that appeared only in the international edition of *USA Today* (the U.S. edition is microfilmed) and one that appeared only in the national edition of the *New York Times* (the late edition is microfilmed).

2. For example, articles identified in the search that did not deal with "television violence" included stories about: (a) whether violent criminals should be allowed luxuries such as television in their prison cells; (b) President Clinton discussing street violence during an appearance on MTV; and (c) a television documentary about spousal abuse.

3. The lower reliabilities were obtained for two themes reported in table 10.1 (violent portrayals are problematic, pi= .68; warnings/ratings recommended, pi = .72) and two motivations reported in table 10.2 (government officials' concern about amount/portrayal of violence, pi = .68; the television industry's desire to protect free speech/avoid government regulation, pi = .68).

4. Because the process of photocopying (especially from microfilm) often involves enlargement or reduction, column inches had to be estimated. First, the number of lines per inch in the copy were divided by the typical number of lines per inch in the original newspapers (judged to be about 7.5, based on examination of print editions). This number was multiplied by the column inches in the photocopy. Reliability for estimated column inches was $r = .98$.

5. Television violence was considered a secondary topic if a substantial proportion of the article was devoted to the issue, but one or more other issues were addressed at length as well. For example, several articles discussed violence in television, movies, and music videos. Television violence was considered a brief reference if the topic was referred to in only one or two sentences. For instance, an article about an earthquake stated

that students were emotionally affected, despite being "calloused . . . by age, circumstance, or television violence."

REFERENCES

Cantor, J., and K. Harrison. 1996. "Ratings and Advisories for Television Programming: University of Wisconsin, Madison Study." In *National Television Violence Study: Scientific Papers 1994–1995* (III-1–III-50). Studio City, CA: Mediascope.

Dionisopoulos, G. N., and R. E. Crable. 1988. "Definitional Hegemony as a Public Relations Strategy: The Rhetoric of the Nuclear Power Industry after Three Mile Island." *Central States Speech Journal* 39:134–45.

Donnerstein, E., R. G. Slaby, and L. D. Eron. 1994. "The Mass Media and Youth Aggression." In *Reason to Hope: A Psychosocial Perspective on Violence and Youth,* ed. L. D. Eron, J. H. Gentry, and P. Schlegel, 219–50. Washington, DC: American Psychological Association.

Duck, J. M., and B. A. Mullin. 1995. "The Perceived Impact of the Mass Media: Reconsidering the Third Person Effect." *European Journal of Social Psychology* 25:77–93.

Dunwoody, S. 1986. "When Science Writers Cover the Social Sciences." In *Reporting Science: The Case of Aggression,* ed. J. H. Goldstein, 67–81. Hillsdale, NJ: Erlbaum.

Edelman, M. J. 1993. "Contestable Categories and Public Opinion." *Political Communication* 10:231–42.

Entman, R. M. 1991. "Framing U.S. Coverage of International News: Contrasts in Narratives of the KAL and Iran Air Incidents." *Journal of Communication* 41(4): 6–28.

———. 1993. "Framing: Toward Clarification of a Fractured Paradigm." *Journal of Communication* 43(4): 51–58.

Entman, R. M., and A. Rojecki. 1993. "Freezing out the Public: Elite and Media Framing of the U.S. Anti-Nuclear Movement." *Political Communication* 10:151–67.

Eron, L. D. 1986. "The Social Responsibility of the Scientist." In *Reporting Science: The Case of Aggression,* ed. J. H. Goldstein, 11–20. Hillsdale, NJ: Erlbaum.

Evans, W. 1995. "The Mundane and the Arcane: Prestige Media Coverage of Social and Natural Science." *Journalism and Mass Communication Quarterly* 72:168–77.

Gamson, W. A. 1989. "News as Framing." *American Behavioral Scientist* 33:157–61.

Goshorn, K., and O. H. Gandy Jr. 1995. "Race, Risk and Responsibility: Editorial Constraint in the Framing of Inequality." *Journal of Communication* 45(2): 133–51.

Gunter, B. 1994. "The Question of Media Violence." In *Media Effects: Advances in Theory and Research,* ed. J. Bryant and D. Zillmann, 163–211. Hillsdale, NJ: Erlbaum.

Gunter, B., and H. Stipp. 1992. "Attitudes about Sex and Violence on Television in the United States and in Great Britain: A Comparison of Research Findings." *Medienpsychologie* 4:267–86.

Haskins, R. 1985. "From the Social Policy Perspective: Comment and Critique." In *The Media, Social Science, and Social Policy for Children,* ed. E. A. Rubinstein and J. D. Brown, 78–89. Norwood, NJ: Ablex.

Herman, E. S. 1985. "Diversity of News: 'Marginalizing' the Opposition." *Journal of Communication* 35(3): 135–47.

Hoffner, C., R. S. Plotkin, M. Buchanan, J. D. Anderson, S. Schneider, L. A. Ricciotti, L.

Kowalczyk, K. Silberg, and A. Pastorek. 1997. *The Third-person Effect in Perceptions of the Influence of Television Violence.* Paper presented to the meeting of the International Communication Association, Montreal, Canada, May.

Iyengar, S. 1990. "Framing Responsibility for Political Issues: The Case of Poverty." *Political Behavior* 12:19–40.

———. 1991. *Is Anyone Responsible? How Television Frames Political Issues.* Chicago: University of Chicago Press.

Iyengar, S., and A. Simon. 1993. "News Coverage of the Gulf Crisis and Public Opinion: A Study of Agenda-Setting, Priming, and Framing." *Communication Research* 20:365–83.

Kahneman, D., and Tversky, A. 1984. "Choices, Values, and Frames." *American Psychologist* 39:341–50.

Kunkel, D., B. J. Wilson, E. Donnerstein, D. Linz, S. L. Smith, T. Gray, E. Blumenthal, and J. Potter. 1995. "Measuring Television Violence: The Importance of Context." *Journal of Broadcasting and Electronic Media* 39:284–91.

Kunkel, D., B. J. Wilson, D. Linz, J. Potter, E. Donnerstein, S. L. Smith, E. Blumenthal, and T. Gray. 1996. "Violence in Television Programming Overall: University of California, Santa Barbara Study." In *National Television Violence Study: Scientific Papers 1994–1995* (I-1–I-172). Studio City, CA: Mediascope.

Mazur, A. 1981. "Media Coverage and Public Opinion on Scientific Controversies." *Journal of Communication* 31(2): 106–15.

Moore, D. W., and L. Saad. 1993. "Public Says: Too Much Violence on TV." *The Gallup Poll Monthly* August: 18–20.

Olien, C. N., G. A. Donohue, and P. J. Tichenor. 1995. "Conflict, Consensus, and Public Opinion." In *Public Opinion and the Communication of Consent,* ed. T. L. Glasser and C. T. Salmon, 301–22. New York: Guilford.

Paik, H., and G. Comstock. 1994. "The Effects of Television Violence on Antisocial Behavior: A Meta-analysis." *Communication Research* 21:516–46.

Pan, Z., and G. M. Kosicki. 1993. "Framing Analysis: An Approach to News Discourse." *Political Communication* 10:55–76.

Perloff, R. M. 1993. "Third-Person Effect Research 1983–1992: A Review and Synthesis." *International Journal of Public Opinion Research* 5:167–84.

Rubinstein, E. A., and J. D. Brown. 1985. "Television and Children: A Public Policy Dilemma." In *The Media, Social Science, and Social Policy for Children,* ed. E. A. Rubinstein and J. D. Brown, 93–117. Norwood, NJ: Ablex.

Singer, E., and P. Endreny. 1987. "Reporting Hazards: Their Benefits and Costs." *Journal of Communication* 37(3): 10–26.

Skews, R. K. 1995. "Dailies Still on Losing Trend in Circulation." *Advertising Age* 66 (November 6): 34.

Wallack, L., L. Dorfman, D. Jernigan, and M. Themba. 1993. *Media Advocacy and Public Health.* Newbury Park, CA: Sage.

Weiss, C. H., and E. Singer. 1988. *Reporting of Social Science in the National Media.* New York: Russell Sage Foundation.

Wright, J. C., M. St. Peters, and A. C. Huston. 1990. "Family Television Use and Its Relation to Children's Cognitive Skills and Social Behavior." In *Television and the American Family,* ed. J. Bryant, 227–52. Hillsdale, NJ: Erlbaum.

Chapter 11

A First Glance at the Constitutionality of the V-Chip Ratings System

Matthew L. Spitzer

Introduction

The Telecommunications Act of 1996 requires that all television sets sold in the United States contain a special computer chip—popularly called a "V-chip"—that will allow the viewer to program his or her television's receiver section. In particular, this V-chip will allow the viewer to program the television to reject any show that has been rated too sexual or too violent or too offensive in some other way. Television shows' ratings will be electronically encoded in the signal that is transmitted to the set, so the viewer will be able to program the television to reject entire classes of shows, rather than be required to make individual decisions about every program.

A television ratings system now appears to be in place.[1] Television programs will be rated in a hierarchy: TV-G (for all ages), TV-PG (parental guidance suggested), TV-14 (may be inappropriate for children under 14), and TV-MA (for adults).[2] Once large numbers of people purchase sets (or add-on boxes)[3] with the V-chip, we will likely alter our television viewing habits substantially. In reaction, the nature of the television market may change, and the fare available to children and adults may, in turn, transform.

Reactions to the V-chip have varied from ecstatic[4] to indifferent[5] to outraged.[6] Legal analysis of the V-chip has been uneven.[7] Some of those who like the idea of the V-chip have trouble paying even the most cursory attention to the question of possible constitutional problems,[8] while one commentator who is outraged sees obvious constitutional violations.[9]

This chapter provides an introduction to some of the constitutional issues surrounding the V-chip.[10] Now that the broadcast and cable industries have announced their ratings system, enough can be discerned to allow us to sketch out the major issues under the First Amendment. Before we can proceed to the constitutional law and economics of the V-chip, however, we need to explain the statutory background.

Section 551 of the Telecommunications Act of 1996 creates an administrative system for rating and regulating violence and sex on television.[11] Section 551(e) gives the industry's "distributors of video programming" one year from the date of passage of the act to:

> (A) establish [...] voluntary rules for rating video programming that contains sexual, violent, or other indecent material about which parents should be informed before it is displayed to children, . . . ; and
> (B) agree voluntarily [...] to broadcast signals that contain ratings of such programming.[12]

I will refer to this year-long period as "Stage One." The "voluntary" ratings system implemented during Stage One must be "acceptable to the [Federal Communications] Commission."[13] The FCC is to determine whether an acceptable voluntary ratings system has been adopted by the distributors of video programming by consulting with "appropriate public interest groups and interested individuals."[14] At this time we are waiting for the FCC's decision to approve or not the industry's ratings system.

If, at the end of a year, the distributors of video programming have failed to adopt an acceptable ratings system, the administrative system enters Stage Two. During Stage Two the FCC is authorized to create a special advisory committee. The advisory committee is to mirror the polity and the industry,[15] and it must submit a report to the FCC recommending a ratings system.[16] Based on the report and recommendations of the advisory committee, the administrative system enters Stage Three. In Stage Three the FCC must prescribe two different types of regulations. First, the FCC must promulgate "guidelines and recommended procedures" for rating video programming containing "sexual, violent, or other indecent material about which parents should be informed."[17] These regulations will not require anyone to rate programming. Instead, the regulations are only a recommended system for anyone who might choose to rate programs. Second, with respect to any video programming that has been rated, the FCC must promulgate rules "requiring distributors of such video programming to transmit" the rating in a way that would allow the V-chip to block the rated programming. These regulations will require distributors of video programming to transmit the ratings.

To summarize the V-chip administrative system in Stage Three, the FCC's recommendations for how to rate video programming *will not be* binding rules, while the FCC's rules for transmitting any such ratings *will be* binding. The V-chip administrative system in Stage Three says to the industry "you need not rate, but if you do you *must* transmit the rating." The conference report accompanying the act directly supports this interpretation:

> The rules prescribed for transmitting a rating are requirements. In contrast, the guidelines and recommended procedures for a rating system are not rules and do not include requirements. They are intended to provide industry with a carefully considered and practical system for rating programs if industry does not develop such a system itself. However, nothing in subsection (b)(1) authorizes, and the conferees do not intend that, the Commission require the adoption of the recommended rating system nor that any particular program be rated.[18]

Regardless of what happens about rating television programs, all new television sets with screens at least 13 inches in diagonal must have a V-chip installed.[19] Nothing in the act seems to cover the tuner section in a VCR.

In sum, then, the act's plan looks something like table 11.1. Does such a plan violate the First Amendment to the Constitution? To answer that question I will analyze the question under alternative assumptions. First, I will assume that the ratings system is done in Stage One and resembles the one already proposed by the industry. Second, I will assume that Stage One fails and that the FCC must promulgate recommendations and rules in Stage Three.

In part I of this chapter I will first outline the "state action" doctrine—the rules that govern when "private behavior" will be treated as if it were behavior of the state and hence subject to the requirements of the First Amendment. I then apply the state action rules to the V-chip ratings system adopted in Stage One. This part concludes that the industry's decision to adopt a V-chip ratings system in Stage One will be treated as state action and hence will be subject to scrutiny under the First Amendment. The form of the system, however, may well be regarded as private behavior. In part II, I conduct a similar analysis, but focus on a V-chip ratings system adopted in Stage Three. I conclude that the V-chip ratings system will be subject to the First Amendment if the system is adopted in Stage Three. Part III of this chapter concludes that the Court will likely find the V-chip system constitutional under substantive First Amendment

TABLE 11.1.   Telecommunications Act of 1996 V-Chip Plan

	Stage One	Stage Two (max one year)	Stage Three
Ratings	Voluntary	Advisory Committee Report	FCC "guidelines"
Transmission	Voluntary	Nothing	FCC rules require
Chip	Must be installed	Must be installed	Must be installed

analysis. The reasons for my conclusion will differ depending on the precise nature of the First Amendment claim. A producer claiming that the entire V-chip system produces a chilling effect will fail, at this point, to demonstrate the chill.[20] A producer complaining about his individual rating will fail, possibly because of special state action problems, and possibly because of the justifications for the ratings system.

I.   The State Action Requirement in Stage One: "Voluntary" Ratings

Under this alternative (Stage One) I will analyze the system already adopted by the broadcast and cable industry, including the studios. Television programs designed for the entire audience will be rated in a hierarchy: TV-G (for all ages), TV-PG (parental guidance suggested), TV-14 (may be inappropriate for children under 14), and TV-MA (for adults).[21] Considerations of violence, sex and language will be collapsed into one variable, coded for age-appropriateness. All of the major broadcast and cable networks will encode a program's ratings and transmit them with the program to the viewer. If, for example, the viewer sets a V-chip for TV-PG, then no program with a rating of TV-14 or TV-MA will appear on that viewer's set.

Let us assume that someone, either a program producer or a viewer's group, objects to the V-chip plan as a violation of the First Amendment. Further, assume that such a person or group has standing to bring the objection before a federal court.[22] The first and most important defense that such a litigant will face is termed the "state action" requirement.

The First Amendment begins "Congress shall make no law. . . ." As a consequence, the First Amendment restricts only the actions of the government and does not restrain private behavior.[23] When a private party restrains another private party's speech the First Amendment provides no impediment to the practice, at all. In fact, in certain circumstances, such as when the editor of a newspaper chooses not to print certain content, the First Amendment protects the private party's right to "restrict" the speech of another private party.[24] The need to find government action before the First Amendment controls the case is called the "state action" requirement.

As applied to this situation, the government and (presumably) the distributors of video programming will claim that the ratings and the transmission of the ratings within shows result only from private, not government, action.[25] After all, they will say, the ratings are being done by program producers or by studios or by video distributors, all of whom are private actors. The decision to rate a television program for violence and sex, like a newspaper editor's decision to print an article, is not constrained by the First Amendment and cannot be challenged on that constitutional basis in court. As a consequence, they will argue, we need not even discuss First Amendment doctrine or policy. The case ends before it begins.

How should we evaluate this claim by the government? To provide a sophisticated and nuanced evaluation, we must first explore part of the doctrinal and theoretical background about the state action doctrine and then apply this analysis to the V-chip rating facts.

A.   Background on the State Action Doctrine

The state action doctrine applies to more than just the First Amendment. Most of the Constitution's protections for individual rights apply only to the state.[26] Constitutional guarantees of freedom from racial discrimination,[27] the right to be represented by counsel at criminal trial,[28] freedom from unlawful search and seizure,[29] and the right to a fair procedure before important rights are taken away[30] all apply only to state action. If private individuals discriminate on racial grounds, interfere with the right to counsel, unlawfully search or seize evidence, or refuse to give someone a fair procedure, the Constitution is not violated. The aggrieved parties must look to some other source of law, such as the 1964 Civil Rights Act, for protection.

The state action doctrine attempts to draw the line between private action—which is unconstrained by most constitutional guarantees—and state action—which must comply with the requirements of the Constitution.[31] This chapter will not try to explain and rationalize state action, in general. Instead, I will note a couple of the major themes involved and then concentrate on cases dealing with the First Amendment, particularly as it applies to mass media.

1.   Rationale for State Action and the First Amendment

Why have a "state action" requirement for the guarantees of freedom of speech and press in the First Amendment? Two answers suggest themselves. First, the First Amendment reads, in part, "*Congress* shall make no law . . . abridging the freedom of speech, or of the press. . . ." Quickly perusing the text suggests that the First Amendment was aimed at restraining the government, not individuals.[32] This language has been interpreted to apply to state and local governmental actors, as well, through the operation of the Fourteenth Amendment.[33] But even with this expansion, it would seem that there is much activity that the First Amendment does not, by its terms, cover. When one individual destroys another individual's writings, the First Amendment would seem to have little to say.

This "textualist" argument has some appeal, but is not without problems. The main problem is that it is never clear when the government has taken "action." Put differently, should the government's decision to allow certain behavior count as government action? If the government, for example, allowed individuals to destroy each other's writings, would a subsequent destruction of writings count as state action?[34] Usually the answer has been "no." Psychological framing of the issues, aided and abetted by the structure of the English language, has seemingly prevented the Court from taking this path.[35] Sometimes, however, when the appeal of finding state action has been very strong, the court has flirted with finding governmental permission to be state action. Again, these cases tended to involve racial discrimination, particularly in the period prior to the passage of the 1964 Civil Rights Act.

A second argument for the state action requirement for the First Amendment is based in an understanding of some of the basic policies behind having guarantees of freedom of speech and press. Courts and commentators have traditionally justified these freedoms in two different ways. First, many have argued that freedom of speech and press are valuable because they promote general social goals. In particular, freedom of speech and press may promote the search for truth, by allowing for an open, robust marketplace of ideas. In addition, these freedoms may also promote effective self-government through democracy. Second, many commentators and courts also believe that freedom of speech and press help safeguard the exercise of individual liberties that are particularly important. Freedom of speech, in particular, may be central to identity and self-definition.[36]

The state action requirement essentially lets private parties trade off the important interests served by the guarantees in the First Amendment for other values. These other values might be interests external to the First Amendment, such as economic efficiency, or might be internal, such as when private parties adjust expressive freedoms between themselves. Two examples follow.

In some disputes that involve state action and freedom of expression, the purposes of the First Amendment would appear to push in favor of finding state action. For example, when the owner of a fast food franchise forbids employees (including those with no client contact) from wearing political buttons (e.g., "Reelect the President" or "Ban the Bomb"), the courts would likely find no state action.[37] Yet if we are interested in an effective marketplace of ideas, effective self-government, or self-identity, the First Amendment should protect wearing political buttons. Indeed, the owner of the fast-food franchise would likely forbid wearing such buttons precisely because encouraging a robust marketplace of ideas, attention to self-government, or the assertion of self-identity while *on the job* would slow down work and reduce efficiency. The law allows the employer and the employees to agree to trade off First Amendment interests for increased efficiency.

In other disputes that involve state action and freedom of expression, the First Amendment seems to push in more than one direction. For example, where the owner of a newspaper hires reporters to write stories, but retains the right to edit the stories to be acceptable to the owner, the expressive interests of the reporters are limited, but the expressive interests of the newspaper owner are enhanced. The only way for the newspaper owner to assemble a paper with particular qualities and editorial viewpoint is to assert control over the reporters' writings. Are the marketplace of ideas, the drive for effective self-government, and the assertion of self-identity helped or hindered by the newspaper owner's control of the reporters? The answer is far from clear. If the courts were to find state action in the newspaper owner's contracts with reporters and were to outlaw the control over the reporters' expression, the reporters' freedoms might expand, but the newspaper owner's opportunity to assemble and publish newspapers would be diminished, if not extinguished. The law deals with this situation by refusing to find state action, and leaving the allocation of responsibility for the newspaper's content up to agreements between the private parties.

2. Racial Discrimination Cases

In the last 45 years the Supreme Court has been much more willing to find state action in cases involving racial discrimination than in any other type of case. For example, in Reitman v. Mulkey,[38] the Supreme Court considered the constitutionality of an amendment to California's constitution. The amendment to Article I, section 26, guaranteed owners of real property the right to rent or not rent real property for any reason, including racial prejudice. Despite the amendment's appearance of preserving a sphere of private autonomy in renting real property, the Supreme Court found state action and struck down the amendment. The new Article I, section 26 gave racial discrimination a type of protected status and hence amounted to impermissible state involvement. Similarly, in Shelley v. Kraemer,[39] the Supreme Court ruled that court enforcement of racially restrictive private covenants constituted state action. Private individuals had formed contracts according to which they promised not to sell their private homes to black people. The Supreme Court held that enforcing these contracts in court would violate the equal protection clause of the Fourteenth Amendment. The logical implication of Shelley is that the equal protection clause applies to all private contracts. However, the Supreme Court has refused to extend Shelley beyond the racial discrimination context.[40]

3. Cases without Racial Discrimination Issues

The Supreme Court will sometimes find that the behavior of "private" entities is state action even where racial discrimination is not an issue. The Court is most willing to do so when either of two different theories applies. First, if a private party performs a function that has traditionally and exclusively been a government function, then the Court is more likely to find state action. Second, if the government has become entangled in private conduct by providing strong incentives or encouragement for private individuals to behave in some way, then the private parties' behavior may be deemed "state action."

The government function theory is designed to prevent the government from eluding constitutional restrictions on government action by delegating its functions to private actors. In cases raising no obvious racial discrimination issue the Court has been skeptical of the claim that a private entity was performing a traditional and exclusive government function.[41] When a private company owned and ran an *entire* town, the company performed a public function and had to comply with the Constitution.[42] However, in most less extreme situations, the Court has been unwilling to find a government function. Thus, when a private utility, with a state-granted monopoly, provides service to customers, the "Constitution [is] inapplicable."[43] Similarly, when a private shopping center provides a place for people to shop and stroll, it does not trigger state action.[44] Running schools,[45] regulating intercollegiate athletics,[46] and regulating the U.S. Olympic program[47] have all failed to qualify as state action.

The government entanglement "theory" is far more complicated, confused, and unsatisfying. Here the question is whether the government has so involved itself, either by providing incentives, encouragement, or resources, with private behavior, that the actions of a private party must be deemed that of the state.[48]

The Court is often unwilling to find state action in cases involving no racial discrimination, though sometimes the Court does so.[49] Most important for purposes of this chapter, the Court appears to have established that granting a license to a private party does not make the private party's actions into state action.[50] State subsidies to private actors also seem not to trigger state action.[51] For example, in Rendell-Baker v. Kohn,[52] a school that received over 90 percent of its income from the state fired a teacher because she had been critical of school administration. The Supreme Court refused to find state action, stating that the firing was not "compelled or even influenced by any state regulation."[53] In Blum v. Yaretsky government Medicaid funding rules essentially required the transfer of hospital patients to less well-equipped care facilities under certain circumstances. Despite the fact that Medicaid provided over 90 percent of the funds for the patients, the decision to transfer remained, according to the Court, a private one.

4.   Broadcasting and Cable Cases

There are several cases involving attempts by the federal government to "persuade" broadcasters or cable companies to volunteer to change their behavior. These cases involve the government's attempt to reduce the amount of violent programming,[54] sexually explicit programming,[55] or drug-oriented rock and roll.[56] These cases raise the issue of whether the broadcasters' or cable operators' refusal to carry particular material constitutes state action.

The most recent of these cases is Denver Area Educational Telecommunications Consortium v. FCC.[57] Cable television operators control the content on almost all of the channels on the cable system. On a few channels—termed "access" channels—the cable operator may not control the content. Leased access channels are those that have been set aside, pursuant to requirements in the Cable Act of 1984, for lease by commercial entities not affiliated with the cable operator. Public, educational, and governmental ("PEG") access channels are those that are set aside, pursuant to contract with the local municipality, for use by members of the public, educational institutions, or governmental bodies. In the 1992 Cable Act[58] Congress changed the rules for leased access and PEG access channels on cable television systems. Under Section 10(a) of the 1992 Cable Act, a cable operator gained authority to refuse to carry indecent programming on leased access channels.[59] If a cable operator decided to carry indecent programming on leased access, it had to put the indecent programming on a single channel, block the channel from cable subscribers, and only unblock the channel in response to a written request from a particular subscriber.[60] Section 10(c) of the 1992 Cable Act required the FCC to allow cable operators to prohibit "any programming which contains obscene material, sexually explicit conduct, or material soliciting or promoting unlawful conduct."[61] Section 10(d) removed the cable operators' previously granted immunity from criminal liability for carrying obscenity on access channels.

In response to a claim by program producers and viewers that the statutory scheme violated the First Amendment, the Court of Appeals for the District of Columbia Circuit, sitting *en banc*, analyzed the state action issue. The majority held that there was no state action as to either Section 10(a) or Section 10(c). Because Section 10(a) allowed but did not require cable operators to exclude indecent programming, the cable operator's decision to refuse leased access to indecent programs was only private behavior. The majority rejected three basic arguments: (1) giving cable operators permission to exclude *only* this type of program represented too much government encouragement and manipulation; (2) the burden of requiring that all indecent programming that is carried be segregated and blocked essentially coerced cable operators into refusing carriage for indecent programming; and (3) removing cable operators' immunity for carrying obscene material on access channels coerced the cable operators' carriage decisions. The majority thought that permission, though limited to a particular topic, was still permission. The extra burdens from segregating and blocking indecency were termed "speculative." And the removal of immunity by Section 10(d) seemed a natural companion to the permission granted by Section 10(a).[62]

The Supreme Court issued three opinions in *Denver Area*. Justice Breyer, writing for Stevens, O'Connor, and Souter, seemed to find state action in Sections 10(a) and 10(c). The conclusion is only slightly uncertain because Justice Breyer first stated the issue rather clearly and then, without explicitly answering the state action question, proceeded to a lengthy discussion of the substantive First Amendment claims.[63] The substantive discussion would have been quite irrelevant unless Justice Breyer had implicitly found that a cable operator's decision to refuse to carry indecency would have been state action.

Justice Kennedy, writing with Justice Ginsburg, explicitly found state action as to both sections 10(a) and 10(c):

> The plurality at least recognizes this as state action, ante, at 6, avoiding the mistake made by the Court of Appeals. . . . State action lies in the enactment of a statute altering legal relations between persons, including the selective withdrawal from one group of legal protections against private acts, regardless of whether the private acts are attributable to the State.[64]

Justice Thomas, writing for the Chief Justice and Justice Scalia, did not confront the state action issue. Instead, he asked to what extent the First Amendment protects cable operators, programmers, and viewers from state action. Justice Thomas argued that all of the speech rights start with the cable operator, and that access channels represent a (constitutionally questionable) infringement of cable operators' rights. Creating the access channels does not, consequently, create any First Amendment interests in programmers or viewers. Hence, they cannot object to the regulations. Only cable operators may object.[65]

B.   Application of State Action to V-Chip Ratings in Stage One

To apply the state action doctrine to the V-chip we must make a distinction. The plaintiff producer's claim might be that the existence of any ratings system, in and of itself, chills speech and stifles the marketplace of ideas. If this is the claim then the issue is whether there is state action in bringing the ratings system into existence. The plaintiff producer's claim might, however, be more specific. The producer might object to a ratings system that is age-based rather than content-based.[66] In that case, the producer would object to the *form* of the ratings system adopted by the industry. Last, the producer might object to the rating that was given to one of his shows. The producer's show might have been given a TV-MA, but the producer thinks that the show deserves only a TV-G. In this case the question will be whether there is state action in the assignment of a particular rating to a show. The three different types of producer claims may get different answers to the question of state action.

There are several possible arguments as to why the "voluntary" ratings and transmission scheme is actually government action. All of these arguments refer to the "excessive entanglement" branch of the doctrine.

1. Political Economy and the "Free" Digital Channel
for Broadcasters

One change facing broadcasting in the near future is that broadcasters will have to give up the 6 Mz of spectrum that they are now using for analog broadcasting. New digital broadcasting channels, also most likely 6 Mz, will be allocated for digital broadcast transmissions. These new licenses will give the broadcasters the flexibility to deliver one high definition picture with 6 channel sound, or to deliver several lower quality signals.

Existing broadcasters want the federal government to give each of them a 6 Mz "digital" license (for free) and allow the broadcasters to keep the existing analog licenses for as long a period as possible before surrendering the analog licenses to the FCC.[67] Many in the House and Senate, including former Senator Dole, have suggested auctioning off the new digital licenses to the highest bidders.[68] The public treasury, rather than existing broadcasters, would reap the benefits from the new spectrum. Such a prospect has terrified existing broadcasters and has compelled them to give Congress whatever is wanted. What is wanted, in short, is a "voluntary" ratings system.[69]

This trade of "free" spectrum for good behavior in restraining broadcast violence has occasionally reached the level of explicit public musings by FCC officials or Congressmen.[70] These public musings almost always take the form of a veiled threat. The broadcasters' good behavior is described as a "quid pro quo" or part of a "social compact" for free spectrum.[71] The argument is that the carrot of a "free" digital channel, combined with the stick of surrendering the analog channel, has overwhelmed the broadcasters' free will on ratings. As a consequence, the "voluntary" ratings system is really government action.

The description is absolutely correct as a matter of political economy, and it might also serve to establish state action, *at least as to the industry's agreeing to create and implement a ratings system*. Note that none of these carrots or sticks have been offered in exchange for rating any particular show in any way. Hence, the political economy argument will not help an individual producer who is objecting to the way in which his program was rated establish state action in the individual exercise of discretion. Rather, the political pressure has been directed at getting a ratings system. Hence, this may help establish state action for a plaintiff whose theory objects to the existence of the ratings process.

There has been at least one case holding that official threats and links between broadcast violence and licenses constitutes state action.[72] On the other hand, there has been no explicit statutory or administrative link between the two issues. It remains perfectly possible for the broadcasters to gain the free channel without instituting a ratings system. Hence, the Court may be more likely to view the digital channel as political background, but not legal entanglement or coercion.

2.   Requiring the Chip in the Set

The next argument focuses on the undisputed state action of requiring that the V-chip be installed in the set. This is more, goes the argument, than just requiring an "on/off" switch be installed in television sets. The only purpose of a V-chip is to facilitate a ratings and screening system. By requiring one part of the ratings and screening system, the government has so injected itself into the process as to constitute excessive encouragement as to the entire enterprise. Requiring the chip may also put the government's imprimatur on whatever system evolves.

This argument, standing by itself, is weak. A Court that is loath to find government action where Medicare rules virtually coerce the transfer of an elderly patient is also unlikely to find government action, based solely on requiring the chip, when program producers decide to implement a ratings scheme. However, in combination with other factors this argument may gain importance. After all, the producers' and networks' decision to implement a ratings scheme can only come after the requirement of V-chips in the sets.[73] Hence, we have clear state action in the first step in implementing a ratings system. What is more, this argument would seem to work equally well for a plaintiff objecting to either an individual instance of rating a program, or for one objecting to the entire ratings system. However, to complete the state action argument we must rely on other considerations, such as the political economy argument discussed immediately above, or the other concerns to which we turn in the sections below.

3.   Governmental "Approval"

The government might have become so involved in the process that its approval and encouragement for ratings have stepped over the line into impermissible entanglement. I believe that this argument has considerable power as to the industry's decision to adopt a ratings system. However, recent events have greatly blunted this argument's force as to the type of ratings system adopted.

The federal government has pressured the industry to adopt a ratings system. Consider the meeting between Bill Clinton and leaders of the broadcast and cable industry[74] at the White House. President Clinton called the industry leaders to the White House, asked for a commitment to implement a "voluntary" ratings system, and got it on the spot. In addition, President Clinton, while trying to verbally distance himself from the process, has indicated that he intends to stay involved:

Q (Los Angeles Times): What kind of a role do you foresee for yourself, for the White House, in monitoring the implementation of this system and making sure it's done right?

A (President Clinton): Well, the first thing I think is that the government should not be involved in the process by which the system is developed and then implemented. Just like we're not involved in the movie ratings. I don't believe we should be involved.

I think the industry, if you look at the movie ratings or even if you look at the advisories that we see now on television before certain programs, I think it's clear that once the industry decides to do this and hold itself publicly accountable, that there's a very high probability that a good job will be done on this.

What I think I can do is to, first of all, receive the results of their efforts since they sort of kicked it off here. If they'd like to come back, I invited them to come back and make a report to me and to bring in the members of Congress, and I'm trying to keep this in a very nonpolitical way.

So one of the things we might be able to do is to highlight the work once it's done, to emphasize it, and then to make sure that we do everything we can to explain to people how the V-chip works and how they should access it as they buy new televisions. And for those who do not have the V-chip— and for several years there will be millions of Americans who won't have it—to encourage them still to become familiar with the rating system and to use it at home anyway.

Q (Los Angeles Times): Is there a place for jawboning or exhortation about overall quality in programming?

A (President Clinton): Well, I think that's the next follow-up.[75]

In addition, one could also consider government involvement left over from implementation of the Television Violence Act.[76] When the networks were slow to implement a standard, Senator Paul Simon told the industry that if it failed to reduce violence within the following 60 days congressional action would follow.[77]

In a recent televised meeting between Senator Joseph Lieberman (D-Connecticut) and Representative Edward Markey (D-Massachusetts) and Hollywood producers Steven Bochco (*NYPD Blue*), John Wells (*ER*), Marta Kaufman (*Friends*), and others, the discussion of the V-chip boiled over into threats. Producer Lionel Chetwynd attacked the politicians by saying, "It's all a charade. They've made Hollywood a target of opposition in a political season. . . . Never before in the history of the republic has the coercive power of the state been enlisted to control or in any way limit the First Amendment."[78] In response, Senator Lieberman said, "I find these comments to be dispiriting. . . . Folks, if you keep on down this road in a state of denial, there's a group of folks behind me and [Representative] Markey that don't have the same concern for the First Amendment that we do."[79]

As to the *type* of ratings system actually adopted, different factors push in opposite directions. Consider the requirement that the FCC find the voluntary ratings system acceptable, or else the process proceeds to the second phase.[80] This appears to border on the government adopting the private system as its own, indicating that there is state action. On the other hand, recent events seem to suggest that there is no state action in the adoption of the TV-Y, TV-G, etc., system. Prior to the industry's choice of the age-based ratings system, interest groups and politicians pressured the industry to adopt a content-based system. A content-based system would give the information about the level of sex, violence, and strong language in a program, and permit the viewer to filter based on those factors. Academics,[81] interest groups,[82] and congressmen[83] argued that the public wanted and needed a content-based system. The pressure was strong enough that Vice President Al Gore met with representatives from several interest groups that wanted President Clinton to intervene in the process.[84] The industry, however, coalesced around an age-based ratings system[85] and then refused to give in to pressure. Through Jack Valenti, the chairman of the industry ratings committee, the industry has been moderately pugnacious:

> Referring to Rep. Edward J. Markey (D-Mass.), who joined [Senator] Lieberman in strongly criticizing the TV industry's system Thursday, Valenti said, "Ed Markey wants the government to be Big Brother . . . and have us do what he wants to do. If Congressman Markey leads the troops on the White House floor to pass any legislation that we believe torments the 1st Amendment, we'll see him in court."
>
> Valenti also dismissed suggestions from industry critics that the Federal Communications Commission, which must give its approval to the ratings system, could reject the industry's plan and impose one of its own.
>
> "If the FCC says that what we present is unsuitable, we're under no obligation to use any other design," he said. "We will not use any other TV ratings guidelines except the ones that we are going to announce next week."[86]

The combination of these factors provides a reasonably strong argument for finding state action, at least as to the creation of the ratings system. The involvement of President Clinton, the required approval of the ratings system by the FCC, and threats by Lieberman and Markey provide a reasonably strong case that the intensity of government involvement has passed the point where the ratings can be thought of as private, voluntary behavior. Telling the president "no" after you have been summoned to the White House, particularly if you are a firm in a partially regulated industry, requires great courage. Continuing to resist when members of Congress are issuing veiled threats and the FCC must approve your ratings system is, in short, too much to expect. In sum, the level of involvement by the government is, in total, so great that the industry's behavior should be viewed, in part, as government behavior.[87]

In contrast, the factors do not suggest state action in the *type* of ratings system that has been chosen. The industry has resisted substantial pressure and steadfastly stuck to its age-based system. Despite the need for subsequent FCC approval, the facts[88] suggest that the industry's age-based system should be viewed as a private, independent choice.[89]

4.   Ratings vs. Transmission of Ratings

To the extent that the Court is willing to consider the transmission of ratings apart from the ratings system, it is more likely that the voluntary transmission of ratings will be regarded as state action. This conclusion follows from the *requirement* in Stage Three that any ratings *must* be transmitted. If program distributors refuse to "voluntarily" transmit the ratings in Stage One, they will be forced to transmit in Stage Three. Hence, the form of the regulation is "volunteer to do X now, or in a year we will force you to do X." As a consequence, there is no real private choice.

There are at least two possible responses. The first response is that the decision to transmit the ratings during Stage One is still voluntary. The law does not impose any penalty for failing to transmit the rating during Stage One. Once we reach Stage Three transmission will be required by the law, and then there will be state action. The second response is that under the act the distributor will only be required to transmit ratings in Stage Three if the program producers have adopted a ratings system. If not, there will be nothing to transmit. Hence, the actual form of the regulation is "volunteer to do X now, or in a year we might force you to do X." This is not sufficient encouragement or coercion to constitute state action.

C.   Putting All of the Stage One State Action
Arguments Together

When one combines the effects of the various arguments—requiring the chip in the set, requiring the transmission of ratings in Stage Three, the carrot of 6

MHz of "free spectrum," pressure from President Clinton, threats from congressmen, and the requirement of FCC approval of a "voluntary" system—it is hard to conclude that the system is voluntary. In the absence of these factors no V-chip ratings system would likely be created, and virtually all of these pressures have been brought to bear for the purpose of pushing the industry to adopt a ratings system. In other words, I suggest that the Court should find state action present in the creation of a Stage One V-chip ratings system.[90]

This does not imply that the Court should (or would) find state action in the decision to use an age-based ratings system, or to impose any particular rating on a particular program. The pressures for a content-based ratings system have failed, and there was no pressure from government to choose the age-based system. Further, government actors have not (to my knowledge) been trying to get any particular show rated in a particular way. Blum v. Yaretsky[91] would seem to be the natural comparison. In Blum the government clearly created the reimbursement system that created the entirely forseeable consequence of transferring patients to facilities with fewer capabilities. However, no particular decision to transfer was made by the government, and the Court declined to find state action in a particular transfer. Here the government may be free to argue that although the ratings system was produced by state action, the operation of the ratings system as to individual cases is still private action. The V-chip ratings system could apply any rating to any particular show, without government involvement.

II.   State Action in Stage Three: The FCC's "Suggested" Ratings System

The existence of state action, or its absence, will depend in part on the continued behavior of President Clinton and of other powerful politicians.[92] Let us assume that the "voluntary" system from Stage One fails, that political involvement decreases, that the FCC forms an advisory committee, and that the committee submits a report within one year. Next, assume that the FCC issues two different types of directive. With respect to ratings the FCC promulgates "guidelines and recommended procedures." With respect to transmission, the FCC requires that the ratings be transmitted when the ratings have been implemented. Under these assumptions, what are the arguments for state action (different from the arguments elucidated above)?[93]

A.   Requiring Transmission

If a ratings plan has been adopted by the studios and networks,[94] then the transmission of those ratings would be required. This would almost certainly qualify as sufficient compulsion to turn the networks' actions (regarding transmission) into state action.

Note that this will probably suffice to establish "state action" for different

sorts of complaints. A producer complaining of the "chill" from the entire ratings system will be able to show that *all* of the ratings under the system must be
transmitted. And a producer complaining about the rating his show was given
by a review board may show that the law requires that the rating of *the producer's*
show be transmitted.

B. The FCC's "Suggested" Ratings System

Perhaps the act of constituting an advisory committee, taking their report, and
promulgating "guidelines and recommended procedures" so involves the government that private action becomes public. This involves the government in
the ratings system far more than did just finding the "voluntary" system in Stage
One "acceptable." (Clearly that did not happen here, for if it had we would not
have gotten to Stage Three.) When put together with the admitted requirements
of installing V-chips and transmitting ratings, the entire system becomes government action.

I will spend little time evaluating this argument because the courts will
likely find state action in the requirement of transmission, and the substantive
First Amendment analysis of requiring transmission will also require an analysis of the ratings system. To see this, just try to answer the question Why require
transmission? without referring to the arguments for and against the substance
of the ratings that are being transmitted. I contend that this cannot be done. For
example, assume that the FCC's suggested system rated *only* stories involving
explicit descriptions of intercourse as appropriate for all ages, and it attached
ratings to shows based on this idea. Programs with explicit descriptions of intercourse would be rated "family fare," while programs lacking such material
would be given "adults only" ratings. Such ratings, once attached to a program,
would have to be transmitted. A producer or broadcaster objecting to the requirement of transmitting ratings, based on the First Amendment's general un-
friendliness to forced speech,[95] would likely prevail. The government's attempt
to justify requiring transmission would likely fail, because the underlying ratings system is useless. The government could neither claim that the transmission was needed to protect children, nor that rational parents would use the
transmitted ratings to choose shows (because shows including explicit descriptions of intercourse always go through the filter). In just this way, any attempt
to evaluate under the First Amendment the requirement of transmitting ratings
will end up focusing on the substance of the V-chip ratings system.[96]

III. The Substantive First Amendment Claim against the V-Chip

Assuming that a litigant can get past the state action requirement, he must still
convince a court that the V-chip ratings system violates the substantive re-

quirements of the First Amendment. Proving that the V-chip rating constituted state action, but losing the claim that the First Amendment was violated, would provide the litigant no relief.

Any court evaluating such a First Amendment claim would need to cover many issues to fully treat the case. I will attempt no such thorough treatment in this section.[97] Instead, I will discuss only a subset of the issues. I will divide the analysis, once again, according to whether the suit challenges a system devised in Stage One or Stage Three.

A. Substantive First Amendment Analysis in Stage One

1. The Nature of the Infringement of Speech

To analyze the substantive First Amendment claim we must first spell out the nature of the claim of infringement. This claim will differ, at least in Stage One, based on the nature of the producer's claim. If the producer is attacking the entire V-chip ratings system he will likely claim that the system, in general, chills speech. This could be a claim about any ratings system, or, more likely, a claim about the type of ratings system actually adopted. In either case, the producer will claim that the existence of the system causes producers, networks, and others to alter their speech in ways to satisfy the system.[98] The mix of speech produced by the market will, in turn, change. And disfavored speech (sexual, violent) will be produced less.[99]

An alternative theory of infringement will likely be advanced by a producer who is complaining about the rating his particular program receives. Such a producer will claim that the rating for his program burdens his individual speech, much like a tax or a license would burden his speech. When his programs have ratings that will cause more V-chips to reject the program, his speech is limited.[100]

2. Chilling Effect

I will discuss the chill argument first and then return to the license argument. To evaluate the chill argument we will need some way to analyze the likely effect of the V-chip on the market. *Broadcasting and Cable Magazine* seems to think that the effects have already arrived:

> Hollywood's broadcast network producers and programmers say they are stoically bracing themselves for the future under a new television ratings system they contend will place a premium on blandness rather than creativity.
>
> Although most are taking a wait-and-see attitude, some have stepped up

production or orders for family-friendly shows since the passage last February of legislation mandating a V-chip device that will allow parents to block certain programming, and Hollywood's subsequent agreement to develop a companion ratings system.

At least one prominent producer thinks that the atmosphere already is restricting creative freedom, although the ratings system is still six months away and it will be at least two years before the V-chip is introduced.[101]

Broadcasting and Cable Magazine may or may not be right about the V-chip. I have shown elsewhere that the market effects of the V-chip will depend crucially on details about which it would be unreasonable to expect knowledge from governmental officials,[102] and perhaps even from members of the industry. Depending on these details, the V-chip ratings system may or may not change the level of sex and violence on television, and may even destroy our ability to characterize the likely offerings in the market.[103] Hence, whoever has the burden of proof in showing a chill will likely fail.

The nature and source of the appropriate burden of proof on this issue lies beyond the scope of this chapter. However, I must point out that the Supreme Court, starting with Ginsberg v. New York[104] and going to the present[105] has utilized a very light burden of proof for the connection between children's exposure to indecent material and ill effects from the exposure. The Court has been willing to presume bad effects, or accept rather thin evidence as satisfying any burden. Such an attitude could produce an analogous result in the case of the V-chip, leading the Court to require a large burden of proof to show a chill from regulations designed to shelter children from "inappropriate" material.

3.   The License Theory of Infringement[106]

A complaining producer's argument would be straightforward.[107] The V-chip ratings system prevents him from distributing his product to everyone who might otherwise be able to receive it. The program's rating will cause it to be filtered out of the sets of many homes. In this way, the V-chip ratings system is standing between the producer and otherwise able (and willing?) recipients.

First Amendment "licensing" cases represent the closest analogy to the producer's claims. The licensing cases consider various circumstances in which the government, through an administrative apparatus, makes governmental permission a prerequisite to communication. Representative cases have struck down schemes requiring the permission of a city manager to distribute literature,[108] requiring a permit to use a sound amplification system on a motor vehicle,[109] or requiring a permit—to be issued at the unfettered discretion of the mayor—for placing a newspaper vending machine on public property.[110] Although some licensing cases have been upheld,[111] the Court remains very skeptical of licensing schemes.[112]

Many of the licensing cases considered attempts by state and local governments to create permit systems for motion pictures. The federal courts have tended to treat governmental regulations that license motion pictures very harshly. These regulations, which restricted the ability of motion picture theaters to show sexual or violent fare to children and teenagers, were routinely struck down.[113] Because these film ordinances were undoubtedly passed, in part, for the purpose of protecting children, and because the film licensing ordinances attempted to filter children out of the audience, the film ordinances and the V-chip ratings system bear a certain similarity.

The Court should find that the V-chip ratings scheme differs from the film licensing scheme in two important ways. First, the film licensing schemes were designed to prevent children (and sometimes adults)[114] from seeing harmful material, regardless of the views of the families involved. In contrast, the V-chip will allow families to make decisions for themselves. This both greatly reduces the burden on distributing the rated material and also allows more precise filtering of material to children according to parents' wishes.[115] Second, a motion picture ratings system could allow children to see movies if accompanied by a parent or guardian, much as the private MPAA ratings system allows with R rated movies.[116] This imposes substantial costs on any parent wishing to let his or her child see the rated motion picture. In contrast, the V-chip ratings scheme will impose very low costs on any such parent.

My guess—that these two reasons will serve to distinguish the film licensing cases—rests in part on the federal courts' attitude toward "time zoning" indecent broadcast material.[117] Indecency, which has much more to do with sex and language than with violence, can be regulated so as to keep it away from children. Broadcast indecency may therefore be restricted to certain portions of the day.[118] As Judge Harry Edwards and Mitchell Berman have forcefully pointed out, this represents a burden to those parents who wish to expose their children to indecent broadcasts.[119] And despite this burden, such restrictions on broadcast indecency have been upheld. Where better filtering can be implemented, such as with indecency over the telephone (also known as "dial-a-porn"), the government must implement better filters.[120] Once children, but not adults, are screened out, the regulation of telephonic indecency passes constitutional muster.

The V-chip ratings system compares very favorably to the indecency regulations that have been upheld. The V-chip ratings are not nearly as intrusive as the time zoning regulations for broadcast indecency.[121] Under the V-chip ratings system very violent, sexual, or profanity-laced programming may be broadcast or cablecast at any hour of the day. It will be up to adults (parents for their children and other adults for themselves) to filter out the content. The V-chip ratings also compare favorably to the filtering approaches (e.g., requiring a credit card) adopted for dial-a-porn. The cost and potential risk from setting a V-chip is clearly lower than that involved in giving out a credit card number over the telephone.[122]

The grounds on which the V-chip ratings scheme can be distinguished from the motion picture licensing precedents—parental autonomy and low cost—match closely the ways in which the V-chip is less burdensome than the indecency regulations that have been approved. As a consequence I expect the Court to distinguish, as a general matter, the motion picture precedents when ruling on the constitutionality of the V-chip.

4.   Sufficient Justification for the Infringement?

Assuming that the Court concludes that the V-chip ratings system, and perhaps its application, constitutes state action, and that the system infringes speech in some judicially cognizable fashion, the Court must still confront the questions of whether the infringements are sufficiently justified. More particularly, the Court must decide whether the government has a good enough reason for infringing this sort of speech, and whether the V-chip ratings system is closely enough connected to the government's good reasons.

a.   Finding the Standard of Review
In theory a court must first choose a standard of review with which to evaluate a regulation of speech. Usually the choice of a standard is crucial, for the more demanding the standard, the less likely the regulation will pass muster. However, as I will explain in detail below, I believe that the choice of a standard in this case will not be particularly important. *The V-chip regulations are likely to pass the most demanding level of scrutiny, and hence will also pass less demanding levels of review.*

The two standards of review that will contend for the court's choice are "strict" scrutiny and "intermediate" scrutiny. Strict scrutiny generally requires that the regulation of speech be designed to serve a "compelling state interest" and that the regulation must be "carefully tailored to achieve" the compelling interest.[123] This formulation, which is supposed to express skepticism about the validity of the regulations at issue, is to be applied to regulations that are "content-based."[124] Such regulations, which reward or punish speakers based, in part, on the content of speech, are presumptively invalid.[125] Intermediate scrutiny, in contrast, demands only an "important" governmental interest to justify the regulation. In addition, the regulation of speech must directly implement the important governmental interest, but need not be as narrowly tailored to the task as those that are tested under strict scrutiny.[126] Intermediate scrutiny is often used to test content-neutral regulations[127] or content-based regulations in the field of broadcasting,[128] as well as regulations that have incidental effects on speech.[129]

In Denver Area Educational Tele-Communications Consortium v. FCC[130] the Supreme Court split five to four on the issue of whether the federal courts should apply traditional formulations of First Amendment doctrine in the field of telecommunications. Justice Breyer, writing for himself and three other justices, claimed not. The field of telecommunications is changing too rapidly, said Justice Breyer, to allow the Court to use one of the traditional verbal formulations for testing federal regulations under the First Amendment.

> [N]o definitive choice among competing analogies (broadcast, common carrier, bookstore) allows us to declare a rigid single standard, good for now and for all future media and purposes. That is not to say that we reject all the more specific formulations of the standard—they appropriately cover the vast majority of cases involving Government regulation of speech. Rather, aware as we are of the changes taking place in the law, the technology, and the industrial structure, related to telecommunications, we believe it unwise and unnecessary definitively to pick one analogy or one specific set of words now. . . .
>
> Rather than decide these issues, we can decide this case more narrowly, by closely scrutinizing [section] 10(a) to assure that it properly addresses an extremely important problem, without imposing, in light of the relevant interests, an unnecessarily great restriction on speech.[131]

Note that Justice Breyer appears to be substituting a new formulation—"properly addresses an extremely important problem, without imposing, in light of the relevant interests, an unnecessarily great restriction on speech"—for the old standards. However, he took such pains to deny that he was picking a standard that I will take him at his word. I will assume that Justice Breyer's plurality opinion chose no doctrinal structure that can be applied directly to the next case.[132]

In contrast, Justice Kennedy, joined by Justice Ginsburg, applied traditional First Amendment doctrine. "When confronted with a threat to free speech in the context of an emerging technology, we ought to have the discipline to analyze the case by reference to existing elaborations of constant First Amendment principles."[133] Justice Kennedy rejected the plurality's reliance upon technological and economic change to delay developing standards. "The plurality seems distracted by the many changes in technology and competition in the cable industry. . . . The laws challenged here, however, do not retool the structure of the cable industry. . . ."[134] Justice Kennedy applied strict scrutiny and found all aspects of the statute unconstitutional.

Justice Thomas, writing for the Chief Justice and Justice Scalia, also embraced traditional First Amendment standards and rejected the plurality's reliance upon technological and economic change to justify any other course of action.[135]

b.   Finding a Good Reason

Regardless of whether the Court chooses one of the traditional standards, strict or intermediate scrutiny, or pursues Justice Breyer's formulation—looking for extremely important problems and regulations that do not unnecessarily restrict speech—the government will likely claim that the V-chip ratings system helps parents control children's diet of violent, sexually explicit, or profanity-laced programming. Will such a purpose—empowering parental control of children's television viewing—be regarded as *compelling?* If so, then the purpose will suffice for strict scrutiny and also for intermediate scrutiny and (probably) for Justice Breyer's "approach" as well.

I think that the recent trends in judicial reasoning on closely analogous subjects will push the Court to regard empowering parents as a compelling justification. The Court of Appeals for the Eighth Circuit held that protecting the "physical and psychological well-being of minors" from violence in videotapes represented a compelling state interest.[136] And the Court of Appeals for the District of Columbia Circuit has already ruled that "helping parents supervise their children" is a compelling governmental interest.[137] In addition, the Supreme Court has in the past been solicitous of protecting children and empowering parents, at least in the somewhat analogous area of indecent telecommunications.[138] Justice Thomas recently characterized the law in the following language: "Our precedents establish that government may support parental authority to direct the moral upbringing of their children by imposing a blocking requirement as a default position."[139] The trend, in short, is for the Court to approve governmental allocation of control of offensive television programming to parents. Given the political tenor of our times, I would give odds that the Supreme Court will continue down this line[140] and find that empowering parents to control children's viewing provides a compelling government interest. A fortiori, empowering parents would also be an important governmental interest and therefore would satisfy intermediate scrutiny.

c.   Finding a Close Connection between the V-Chip and Empowering Parents

Is the V-chip ratings system, approved in Stage One, sufficiently "narrowly tailored" to pass strict scrutiny? If so, then the V-chip ratings system will also pass the "directness" requirement of intermediate scrutiny.

The answer to the narrow tailoring inquiry will depend, in part, on the details of implementing the V-chip. The harder the V-chip is for adults to work, and the easier it is for children to circumvent, the less well tailored is the ratings system. If we assume that the V-chip will be easy for adults and hard for children, then I suspect that the Court should regard the ratings system as narrowly tailored. The Court should find that the V-chip places little burden on adults' choice of shows, but effectively empowers parents.[141] Those adults without children in the house can just turn the V-chip off, thereby allowing the set to receive everything. Those adults with children in the house can set the V-chip to screen out the unwanted matter for children.

Are there less intrusive alternatives to the V-chip that accomplish the same purpose? There are three obvious alternatives to the V-chip ratings system's approach. First, parents could closely monitor their children's viewing. This might require sitting and watching the shows, or at least frequently monitoring what is on the set. Second, the V-chip could allow only blocking by day, time, and channel, thereby forcing parents to make an independent judgment about the worth of individual shows. Third, the V-chip ratings system could be content-based, rather than age-based. The Court should find the first two alternatives to the V-chip ratings system to be too costly and time-consuming for parents, or not sufficiently effective, to invalidate the V-chip ratings system.[142] The alternative of content-based ratings, however, might prove troublesome. Requiring parents to closely monitor their children's viewing sounds ideal on the surface. However, many (most?) parents cannot afford to spend large amounts of time sitting with their children and monitoring what is on the set. In the lower income strata there is often no parent present to do the monitoring. Even when the parent is in the house, he or she must often perform other tasks to keep the household running. Once a child has learned to use the channel control, turning the set to a child-friendly show and leaving the room is quite risky. One leaves the child with *Sesame Street*, and returns to find him or her watching MTV.

The second alternative, requiring the parent to program the set by date, time, and channel, is likely to be ineffective. First, it would be quite costly. Any household that gets, for example, 50 channels of cable television, will have to monitor and decide about $(50)(24) = 1200$ hours of television *every day*. This is likely to be a time-consuming task, even with the repetition in show lineup on some channels. Further, the programming task may well be beyond the competence of many parents. As a consequence, few parents will actually do the programming. Together these arguments suggest that the first two alternatives to the V-chip ratings system are much more costly and likely to be less effective. Hence, the government should not be required to use one of the first two alternatives.[143]

The third alternative, content-based ratings, may prove troublesome for a narrow tailoring analysis.[144] Assuming that parents generally wish to restrict their children's diet of violence, sex, and language, perhaps the V-chip system should give this information directly to parents in the ratings. An age-based ratings system that filters the information through the "one size fits all" judgments of the producers[145] implements the purposes of the law less directly. In addition, parents may care about other categories of material, such as respect for God or portrayals of women. Perhaps the system should be constructed to cater to the desires of such parents, as well. Assuming that suitable empirical research documents the preferences of parents,[146] tailoring the ratings system to parents' interests would seem to be straightforward. The responses to this argument will depend on cost and technology issues, as well as data about parental preferences, that are, to my knowledge, unresolved. Do most parents really prefer using a content-based rather than an age-based ratings system? Would a content-based system be so complex that significant numbers of parents would be deterred from using it? Would including more categories of material, perhaps from non-producer ratings, greatly increase the cost of the system? If the answers to these issues suggest that the cost of going to a content-based system is sufficiently high, or perhaps that the demand for a content-based system is sufficiently low, perhaps an age-based ratings system will pass narrow tailoring analysis.[147]

5. First Amendment Process and the V-Chip

If the Supreme Court finds the V-chip ratings system to be enough like film licensing so as to apply the precedents, it may well conclude that some form of First Amendment due process guarantees applies to the system.[148] The form that the guarantees take will depend on whether the Court follows the film licensing cases directly or engages in a more free-form sort of balancing suggested by Matthews v. Eldridge.[149]

a.   Freedman v. Maryland
The film precedents define the process rights of producers who are unhappy with the ratings their motion pictures get. Assume for the moment that the Court will apply these precedents to the V-chip ratings system. Because the V-chip ratings system has a process for reversing producer ratings, perhaps where someone deems them to be "unreasonable," the appeals process issue may be central.[150]

   In Freedman v. Maryland[151] the Court considered the criminal conviction of a motion picture exhibitor who had refused to submit his film to the Maryland State Board of Censors for prior approval. The Court first held that a state had the authority to require films to be submitted to a state review board. However, the Maryland statute violated the First Amendment because the procedures for acting upon and reviewing an adverse censorial finding were too slow and costly to the film exhibitor. In particular, the Freedman Court ruled that (1) the film censor must bear the burden of proof; (2) any restraint on speech prior to a judicial determination must be limited to preserving the status quo and must be for as short a period of time as is possible for a reasonable judicial process; and (3) a final judicial determination on the censor's ruling *must* be guaranteed to issue promptly.[152] Failure to provide such procedural safeguards would amount to giving unlimited discretion to an administrative official to disallow speech—something that the Court has consistently ruled unconstitutional.[153] The Court was particularly sensitive to the economic needs of film distributors for quick procedures so as not to interfere with their incentives to distribute the film.[154]

As applied to any V-chip ratings system that contains a process for reversing an "unreasonable" initial rating that a program producer assigns to his or her own product, the Freedman procedural requirements might require a lot.[155] The rationale—that the economics of the medium will give the rater unfettered discretion unless review is very quick and inexpensive—would seem to apply directly. A program producer who is unhappy with an "adults only" type of V-chip rating, such as TV-MA, will need a quick and inexpensive process to help him position his product and make whatever changes, if any, are needed to attain the desired V-chip rating. As a consequence, I would expect the Court to hold that (1) the burden of proof must be on the V-chip rater who is reversing a program producer's rating of his own show; (2) prompt[156] judicial resolution of the ratings dispute be guaranteed; and (possibly) (3) the producer's own rating will apply until the process is complete.[157] Of course, it might be difficult for the "voluntary" system to guarantee speedy *judicial* review without some further legislative action by Congress. The Telecommunications Act of 1996 gave disappointed producers no right to jump to the front of the line in court. Perhaps applying for temporary restraining orders and preliminary injunctions would suffice, but I doubt it. The substantive requirements for these procedures includes demonstrating likelihood of success on the merits. This may represent too much of a burden. If so, then processes currently available to disappointed producers would fail the Freedman requirements. In the absence of further congressional action that improves review procedures in court, the Stage One system might be put to a stark choice: either allow "unreasonable" ratings by program producers to stand unchallenged, or else risk the entire ratings system foundering on Freedman's requirement of a speedy process.

Any Stage One V-chip system that satisfies the Freedman requirements is likely to be quite expensive. The V-chip system will have to rate huge numbers of hours of programs. Consider the following quote by Jack Valenti:

> Let me put it to you in stark terms. A single cable system today, with 70 channels on the average, operating 24 hours a day, will produce 611,520 hours of programming a year. That amounts to 2,000 hours a day. Now, if you cut that in half and say half of it is going to be non-rateable—news, sports—you get down to a thousand hours a day. That's the equivalent of rating 500 motion pictures a day. The movie ratings system rates two

movies a day, sometimes three. So you have three movies a day versus 500.[158]

If there are disputes regarding only 3 percent of the episodes rated, that will amount to 15 movies worth of time per day that must be rerated by some administrative process and then put onto a fast judicial track. What is more, these 15 movies of time per day might well turn into 20 or 25 separate cases, because many television programs are only 30 minutes long. Further, the V-chip ratings system must be prepared to deal with peak load problems; some weeks will have 30 movies worth of time per day that must be rerated, while other weeks will have none. The system must be able to deal with the periods of peak demand for rerating without slowing up. This means that the system will have to maintain excess capacity most of the time, and along with it a substantial expense. In practical terms it means that the V-chip ratings system will have to hire many reraters and lawyers (for the subsequent judicial process).

There may be some ways of reducing these costs. First, once a show has been rated for exhibition in one market, that rating could be used for exhibiting the same show in other markets. An old episode of *The Mary Tyler Moore* show that is rated as appropriate for children over a cable system in Charleston, South Carolina, should also be rated appropriate for children over a local broadcast in Ithaca, New York. Second, one could try rating series programming by sampling several episodes of the series and then presumptively using the rating derived from the sample for the entire series.[159] Producers would be responsible for notifying the raters of any surprises in particular episodes. Third, distribution contracts could specify arbitration of any disputes. Such clauses might raise antitrust or First Amendment process concerns, but if such concerns were overcome the monetary savings could be substantial.

b.   *Matthews v. Eldridge*

Is there any possible response on the part of the government to the process requirements outlined above? Yes. The government might be able to persuade the Court to apply the modern balancing approach to procedural due process, rather than the First Amendment process approach from film cases, to the V-chip ratings system. In Matthews v. Eldridge[160] the Court defined a balancing test for deciding which procedures are required under the Fourteenth Amendment.

> First, the private interest that will be affected by the official action, second, the risk of an erroneous deprivation of such interest through the procedures used, and the probable value, if any, of additional or substitute procedural safeguards; and finally, the Government's interest, including the

function involved and the fiscal and administrative burdens that the additional or substitute procedural requirement would entail.[161]

In the 1980s and 1990s the Court has been somewhat deferential to the government's choice of procedures under this test.[162] As applied to the V-chip ratings system there would seem to be significant interests on both sides of the balance. The producer's First Amendment rights are at stake, and the economics of the business makes a speedy determination of the proper rating very valuable to the producer. However, the great expense involved will count as a reason to reduce the procedural protections under Matthews v. Eldridge. I have no idea how the Court would or should do the balancing. But I am certain that this approach will give the government a better chance of victory than will the film licensing cases.

6.   Summary of Stage One and the First Amendment

In Stage One, given current doctrine, the Court should probably find the V-chip ratings system to be constitutional. The Court should probably regard empowering parents to control their children's television viewing as a compelling state interest and find the V-chip narrowly tailored to that purpose. The only significant problem may be the choice of an age-based rather than a content-based system; the age-based system may not be narrowly tailored to the purpose of empowering parents. However, a plaintiff will have great difficulty showing that the choice of an age-based system was state action. Hence, a First Amendment claim based on the type of V-chip ratings system should fail. Further, the Court may require the V-chip ratings system to satisfy the procedural requirements of Freedman v. Maryland, and doing so may require further congressional action.

B.   Substantive First Amendment Analysis
in Stage Three

I will have very little to say in this section, mainly because I think the substantive First Amendment analysis is quite similar to that described above. One point needs elaboration, however. Recall that in Stage Three we established state action, in part, by the requirement that if a show is rated then the broadcasters *must* transmit the rating. Hence, as to the transmission, there is clear state compulsion.

  To evaluate the constitutionality of compelling transmission, one must evaluate the ratings system. To see this, ask what the state interest in compelling transmission might be. As I pointed out previously, the government will have to show that parents will want to use the ratings to control their children's viewing to justify forcing broadcasters and cable systems to transmit the ratings. This leads us directly back into the analysis of justifications from Stage One of the V-chip ratings system.

Conclusion

In Stage One the industry's decision to adopt a ratings system should likely be regarded as state action. The Court, however, should probably view the particular age-based system that has been adopted as private action. And the rating assigned to any particular show will likely also be regarded as private action. In Stage Three the state action calculus may change. The Act's requirement that ratings be transmitted probably establishes state action across the board.

The V-chip ratings system may well be constitutional under the First Amendment. The litigant bearing the burden of proof of showing or negating a chill from the ratings system should probably lose at this point. Also, the government may be able to justify the V-chip ratings system, even under strict scrutiny, as supporting parental authority to control children's diet of television. The age-based form of the ratings system, however, may be vulnerable.

NOTES

This essay was prepared for the Duke Conference on Media Violence and Public Policy. I thank the participants at the Duke conference, in an Olin Workshop at Cornell University, and in a Law and Economics Workshop at the University of Chicago: Erwin Chemerinsky, Richard Craswell, Larry Simon, Jean Spitzer, and Eric Talley. Research assistance was provided by James Mixon, Alec Harrell, Young Dae Moon, Janene Bassett, and Brian Hickey. Errors remain my own. I can be reached at mspitzer@law.usc.edu.

1. Jane Hall and Brian Lowry, "Industry Unveils Its Ratings System for TV Programs," *Los Angeles Times*, Home Edition, December 20, 1996: A1. As I explain later in the chapter, this system may or may not survive administrative review.

2. Hall and Lowry, "Ratings System," A1. There are also two other ratings, TV-Y (appropriate for all children) and TV-Y7 (designed for children age 7 and above), that apply to programs designed for children. It is currently not clear if a program rated TV-Y7 will pass through a V-chip set for TV-PG.

3. Add-on boxes will likely retail for around $40. See "V-Chip Technology Waits for Washington," *Broadcasting and Cable*, December 30, 1996: 8 (reporting that Soundview Technology will sell a "V Chip Converter" for around $40).

4. "Why the Markey Chip Won't Hurt You," *Broadcasting and Cable*, August 14, 1995: 10 (interview with Rep. Edward J. Markey (D-Mass.); Reed E. Hundt, "The Public's Airwaves: What Does the Public Interest Require of Television Broadcasters?" *Duke Law Journal* 45 (1996): 1089, 1126; for a more sophisticated and satisfying defense of the V-chip on policy grounds, *see* James T. Hamilton, "Private Interests in 'Public Interest' Programming: An Economic Assessment of Broadcaster Incentives," *Duke Law Journal* 45(1996): 1177. *See also* Mark M. MacCarthy, "Broadcast Self-Regulation: The NAB Codes,

Family Viewing Hour, and Television Violence," *Cardozo Arts and Entertainment Law Journal* 13(1995): 667 (explaining why "self-regulation" does not work); and Kevin W. Saunders, "Media Self-Regulation of Depictions of Violence: A Last Opportunity," *Oklahoma Law Review* 47(1994): 445 (same).

5. Ronald J. Krotoszynski Jr., "Into the Woods: Broadcasters, Bureaucrats, and Children's Television Programming," *Duke Law Journal* 45(1996): 1193, 1194. *See also* David B. Kopel, "Massaging the Medium: Analyzing and Responding to Media Violence Without Harming the First Amendment," *Kansas Journal of Law and Public Policy* 4(1995): 17.

6. Ted Hearn, "Lawmaker Fields Calls V-Chip Unconstitutional," *Multichannel News,* November 27, 1995: 152; Robert Corn-Revere, "'V' Is Not for Voluntary," *Cato Institute Briefing Paper* No. 24, August 3, 1995; and Robert Corn-Revere, "Television Violence and the Limits of Voluntarism," *Yale Journal on Regulation* 12(1995): 187. *See also* Rep. Tom Coburn, "V-Chipping Away at Parental Responsibility Is Not the Solution to TV's Morality Crisis," ROLL CALL, Oct. 23, 1995 (opposing version of V-chip that would have governmental body do ratings, but supporting one that had parents making decisions). Bob Dole, Sen. Paul Simon (D-Illinois), and Rep. Jack Fields (R-Texas) all opposed the V-chip before passage, though they stopped short of outrage. Christopher Stern, "Industry Battles Ratings, V-Chip," *Broadcasting and Cable,* June 26, 1995: 16.

7. There have been some very good pieces discussing, in general, the constitutionality of regulating violence on television. *See* Thomas G. Krattenmaker and L.A. Powe Jr., "Televised Violence: First Amendment Principles and Social Science Theory," *Virginia Law Review* 64(1978): 1123; Harry T. Edwards and Mitchell N. Berman, "Regulating Violence on Television," *Northwestern University Law Review* 89(1995): 1487; James A. Albert, "Constitutional Regulation of Televised Violence," *Virginia Law Review* 64(1978): 1299; Dennis L. DeLeon and Robert L. Naon, Note, "The Regulation of Televised Violence," *Stanford Law Review* 26(1974): 1291; and Ian Matheson Ballard Jr., "See No Evil, Hear No Evil: Television Violence and the First Amendment," *Virginia Law Review* 81(1995): 175 (student note). For a first-rate analysis of the constitutional problems involved in regulating indecent political speech, see Lili Levi, "The FCC, Indecency, and Anti-Abortion Political Advertising," *Villanova Sports and Entertainment Law Journal* 3(1996): 85.

8. See Hundt, "Public Interest," 1089, 1126; Krotoszynski Jr., "Into the Woods," 1193, 1994; David V. Scott, Comment, "The V-Chip Debate: Blocking Television Sex, Violence, and the First Amendment," *Loyola of Los Angeles Entertainment Law Journal* 16(1996): 741.

9. See Corn-Revere, "Television Violence," 187. Although clearly not outraged by the V-chip, Edwards and Berman ("Regulating Violence," 1487, 1513–15) analyze the V-chip in a way suggesting that it has constitutional problems. They state, "The regulation will raise problems only if the government ordains the program characteristics upon which a lockout mechanism could operate, thereby disadvantaging speech by content or subject matter." *Id.* As we will see later in this analysis, *infra,* the Telecommunications Act of 1996 seems to have done just that.

This chapter will not discuss the question of why governmental coercion is needed, rather than relying on the voluntary actions of industry members. The answer may be that there is a coordination game, where no single set of actors wants to proceed unless they are reasonably certain that the rest of the industry will proceed with a ratings system. The producers will not bother to rate programs and embed the ratings in the programs, for example, unless the producers are certain that the set manufacturers will install chips that can read and filter on the basis of the ratings.

A completely voluntary system for internet sites is currently being developed by the Recreational Software Advisory Council. This voluntary system, which relies on the "Platform for Internet Content Selection" ("PICS" codes) system for embedding codes into internet sites, relies on voluntary ratings of sites by the operators. *See* Hiawatha Bray, "Rated P for Preemptive: System to Shield Kids from Adult Web Material Also Seeks to Keep Censors Off Net," Boston Globe, July 25, 1996, available at http://www. rsac.org/press/960725.html. *See also* Whit Andrews, "Site-Rating System Slow to Catch On," WebWeek, July 8, 1996, available at http://www.webweek.com/96July8/comm/rating.html; and RSAC, "USWeb Affiliate Network to Use RSAC Internet Rating System," July 16, 1996, available at http://www.rsac.org/press/960716.html.

10. In Hundt, "Public Interest," 1089, 1126 (implicitly assuming away the constitutional issue) the chairman of the Federal Communications Commission concludes that there is no constitutional issue worth discussion relating to the V-chip. Krotoszynski Jr., "Into the Woods," 1193, 1194, agrees. As my discussion below shows, they are almost certainly wrong.

Legal analyses of the V-chip are starting to appear. *See* Note in Scott, "The V-Chip Debate," 741; J. M. Balkin, "Media Filters, the V-Chip, and the Foundations of Broadcast Regulation," *Duke Law Journal* 45(1996): 1131.

11. Throughout this chapter the term *television* should be understood to include broadcast and cable television, unless the context makes it clear that this is not the case. In addition, I will often use *violence* as a shorthand for violent, sexually explicit, or laced with strong language.

12. Telecommunications Act of 1996, § 551(e), amending 47 U.S.C. § 303.

13. *Id.*

14. *Id.*

15. The FCC must "ensure that such committee is composed of parents, television broadcasters, television programming producers, cable operators, appropriate public interest groups, and other interested individuals from the private sector and is fairly balanced in terms of political affiliation, the points of view represented . . . " *Id.* § (b)(1).

16. The advisory committee's report must be submitted within one year of the appointment of the committee's "initial members." *Id.*

17. *Id.*

18. H. R. Conference Report 104–458, Section 551—Parental Choice in Television Programming, Conference agreement.

19. Actually, the television must "be equipped with a feature designed to enable viewers to block display of all programs with a common rating." Telecommunications Act of 1996, § 551(c).

20. This assumes that the producer bears the burden of proof.

21. *Id.* There are also two other ratings, TV-Y (appropriate for all children) and TV-Y7 (designed for children age 7 and above), that apply to programs designed for children. It is currently not clear if a program rated TV-Y7 will pass through a V-chip set for TV-PG.

22. The Court has held that a film distributor had standing to object to the U.S. government's labeling his film "political propaganda" because of the potential harm to the distributor's reputation. Meese v. Keene, 481 U.S. 465, 472–77 (1987). Such a theory might apply to give standing to the program producer who may suffer damage to reputation from having his product labeled "violent" or "sexual."

23. San Francisco Arts and Athletics, Inc. v. United States Olympic Committee, 483 U.S. 522 (1987); Lebron v. National Railroad Passenger Corp., 115 S.Ct. 961 (1995).

24. Miami Herald v. Tornillo, 418 U.S. 241 (1974).

25. *See* "Jack of All Trades: The Man in the Middle on the V-Chip," *Broadcasting and Cable,* March 18, 1996: 26, 29 (quoting Jack Valenti, who is spearheading the industry's effort to rate programming, as saying "I'm just saying to you, what we're doing is voluntary. The law does not command us to do it"). This is logically consistent with Valenti's earlier pronouncement about controlling violence on television. Three years earlier Valenti wrote that what "should chill the blood of every citizen is the heavy hand of government slowly, steadily, remorselessly intruding into the outer perimeter of the First Amendment." Jack Valenti, "Whose Children are They, Anyway?" *Los Angeles Times,* October 4, 1993: B7.

26. Erwin Chemerinsky, *Constitutional Law: Principles and Policies* § 6.4 (forthcoming).

27. Virginia v. Rives, 100 U.S. 313 (1879); The Civil Rights Cases, 109 U.S. 3 (1883). See C. Vann Woodward, *Reunion and Reaction: The Compromise of 1877 and the End of Reconstruction* (1966).

28. Polk County v. Dodson, 454 U.S. 312 (1981).

29. Soldal v. Cook County, 113 S.Ct. 538 (1992).

30. Jackson v. Metropolitan Edison Co., 419 U.S. 345 (1974); Memphis Light, Gas and Water Division v. Craft, 436 U.S. 1 (1978); Flagg Bros., Inc. v. Brooks, 436 U.S. 149 (1978).

31. Charles L. Black Jr., Foreword: "'State Action,' Equal Protection, and California's Proposition 14," *Harvard Law Review* 81(1967): 69, 95. See also Edmondson v. Leesville Concrete Co., 500 U.S. 614, 632 (1991) ("cases deciding when private action might be deemed that of the state have not been a model of consistency").

32. Erwin Chemerinsky, "Rethinking State Action," *Northwestern University Law Review* 80(1985): 503, 511–16, explains that at the time of passage of the First Amendment most people assumed that the common law protected individual rights from interference by other individuals. Hence, protections were needed against government interference with rights.

33. Gitlow v. New York, 268 U.S. 652, 666 (1925); Fiske v. Kansas, 274 U.S. 380 (1927); Stromberg v. California, 283 U.S. 359 (1931). Freedom of press case: Near v. Minnesota, 283 U.S. 697, 701 (1931)

34. *See* Chemerinsky, *Constitutional Law* § 6.4.2 (forthcoming).

35. In addition, there is the crucial, practical consideration that counting "failure to prohibit" as state action would turn all individual behavior into state action for purposes of the constitution. *See id.*

36. *See* Martin Redish, *Freedom of Expression: A Critical Analysis,* 9–52 (1984).

37. Hudgens v. NLRB, 424 U.S. 507, 513 (1976) (holding that the First Amendment did not apply to privately owned shopping centers).

38. 387 U.S. 369 (1967). *See also* Burton v. Wilmington Parking Auth., 365 U.S. 715 (1961).

39. 334 U.S. 1 (1948).

40. Chemerinsky, *Constitutional Law* § 6.4 (forthcoming).

41. Most of the cases finding a government function basis for state action involved racial discrimination. This continues the general theme noted in the sections above. For example, Texas attempted to delegate the business of elections to a private political party, which excluded blacks from participating. *See* Nixon v. Herndon, 273 U.S. 536 (1927); Nixon v. Condon, 286 U.S. 73 (1932); Smith v. Allwright, 321 U.S. 649 (1944) *reversing* Grovey v. Townsend, 295 U.S. 45 (1935); and Terry v. Adams, 345 U.S. 461 (1953). Similarly, where a city tried to avoid desegregating a public park by turning control of the park over to a private entity that would refuse to allow blacks into the park, the Supreme Court balked and found state action. Evans v. Newton, 382 U.S. 296 (1966).

42. Marsh v. Alabama, 326 U.S. 501 (1946).

43. Jackson v. Metropolitan Edison Co., 419 U.S. 345 (1974).

44. Hudgens v. National Labor Relations Board, 424 U.S. 507 (1976).

45. Rendell-Baker v. Kohn, 457 U.S. 830 (1982).

46. National Collegiate Athletic Association v. Tarkanian, 488 U.S. 179 (1988).

47. San Francisco Arts and Athletics, Inc. v. United States Olympic Committee, 483 U.S. 522 (1987).

48. As with the government function theory, described in the paragraph above, the archetypal cases finding state action tend to be at least two decades old, and frequently involve racial discrimination. The most famous case in this area is Shelley v. Kraemer, 334 U.S. 1 (1948), in which the Supreme Court held that a court enforcing a racially restrictive covenant in a land sale constituted state action. Prior to the decision in Shelley many residential properties were burdened by promises not to sell the properties to black people. These promises, which were made as part of previous sales of residential property between private parties, were supposed to "run with the land" and be enforceable against any subsequent purchaser. Hence, if a private owner of land burdened by a racially restrictive covenant attempted to sell the land to a black purchaser, a neighbor could sue the seller and have the attempted sale voided. The Supreme Court ruled that the court's enforcement of these covenants would constitute state action, and hence be unconstitutional. Cases involving the racially restrictive use of preemptory challenges have also found state action. *See* Batson v. Kentucky, 476 U.S. 79 (1986); Edmonson v. Leesville Concrete Co., 500 U.S. 614 (1991); and Georgia v. McCollum, 505 U.S. 42, 50 (1992). Subsequent cases involving racial discrimination and that seem to raise the state action question have frequently found the Court ducking the issue. Bell v. Maryland, 378 U.S. 226 (1964) (Justices Douglas and Black debating the issue, while the rest of the Court ducked the issue); Lombard v. Louisiana, 373 U.S. 267 (1963) (overturning trespass convictions of civil rights protestors, but ducking the Shelley issue); and Peterson v. Greenville, 373 U.S. 244 (1963).

49. Compare Flagg Bros. Inc. v. Brooks, 436 U.S. 149 (1978) (refusing to find state action in a private creditor's use of a self-help repossession statute, despite the sheriff's involvement for storage of goods at a warehouse) with Lugar v. Edmondson Oil Co., 457 U.S. 922 (1982) (finding state action when creditor obtained a writ of prejudgment attachment from a court).

50. Moose Lodge Number 107 v. Irvis, 407 U.S. 163 (1972) (refusing to find that a liquor license turned the Moose Lodge's actions into state action, despite the Lodge's explicit racial discrimination); Columbia Broadcasting System v. Democratic National Committee, 412 U.S. 94 (1973) (three justices refusing to find that a broadcasting license turned a broadcaster's refusal to accept paid political advertisements into state action. Note that *no issue* in this case garnered 5 votes); and Jackson v. Metropolitan Edison Co, 419 U.S. 345 (1974) (refusing to find that state-granted monopoly turned electric company into state actor).

51. When racial discrimination is present, the cases tend to find state action. *E.g.* Norwood v. Harrison, 413 U.S. 455 (1973) (free textbooks given to all schools, including racially segregated schools, constituted state action); Gilmore v. City of Montgomery, 417 U.S. 556 (1974) (giving exclusive use of city-owned recreational facilities to segregated private schools created state action).

52. 457 U.S. 830 (1982).

53. *Id.* at 841.

54. Writers Guild of America, West v. FCC, 423 F.Supp. 1064 (C.D. Cal. 1976), *vacated and remanded on jurisdictional grounds sub nom.* Writers Guild of America, West v. ABC, 609 F.2d 355 (9th Cir. 1979), *cert. denied,* 449 U.S. 824 (1980).

55. Illinois Citizens for Broadcasting v. FCC, 467 F.2d 1397 (7th Cir. 1972).

56. Yale Broadcasting Co. v. FCC, 478 F.2d 594 (D.C. Cir.), *cert. denied,* 414 U.S. 914 (1973).

57. Denver Area Education Tele-Communication Consortium v. FCC, 135 L. Ed. 2d 888, 116 S. Ct. 2374, 1996 U.S. Lexis 4261 (June 28, 1996), *reversing in part* Alliance for Community Media v. FCC, 56 F.3d 105 (D.C. Cir. 1995) (*en banc*).

58. Cable Television Consumer Protection and Competition Act of 1992, Pub. L. No. 102-385, 106 Stat. 1460.

59. Sec. 10.

> Children's Protection from Indecent Programming on Leased Access Channels
> (a) Authority to Enforce.—Section 612(h) of the Communications Act of 1934 (47 U.S.C. 532(h)) is amended—
> (1) . . .
> (2) by adding at the end thereof the following: "This subsection shall permit a cable operator to enforce prospectively a written and published policy of prohibiting programming that the cable operator reasonably believes describes or depicts sexual or excretory activities or organs in a patently offensive manner as measured by contemporary community standards."

> Cable Television Consumer Protection and Competition Act of 1992, Pub. L. No. 102-385, § 10, 106 Stat. 1460, 1468 (1992) (codified at 47 U.S.C. § 531).
> 60.   (b) Commission Regulations.—Section 612 of the Communications Act of 1934 (47 U.S.C. 532) is amended by inserting . . . the following new subsection:
> (j)(1) Within 120 days following the date of the enactment of this subsection, the Commission shall promulgate regulations designed to limit the access of children to indecent program-

ming, as defined by Commission regulations, and which cable operators have not voluntarily prohibited under subsection (h) [§ 10(a)] by—

(A) requiring cable operators to place on a single channel all indecent programs, as identified by program providers, intended for carriage on channels designated for commercial use under this section;

(B) requiring cable operators to block such single channel unless the subscriber requests access to such channel in writing; and

(C) requiring programmers to inform cable operators if the program would be indecent as defined by Commission regulations.

Id.

61. *Id.* § 10(c).

62. Judge Wald disagreed on virtually every point, while Judge Edwards, writing separately, found state action as to § 10(a), but not as to § 10(c). Alliance, 56 F.3d 105 at 129. Several cases considering whether a state public utility commission's grant of permission to a franchised monopoly telephone company to refuse to carry dial-a-porn turned the telephone company's subsequent refusal into state action have also refused to equate permission with state coercion. Carlin Communications, Inc. v. Mountain States Tel. and Tel. Co., 827 F.2d 1291 (9th Cir. 1987), *cert. denied,* 485 U.S. 1029 (1988); Carlin Communication, Inc. v. Southern Bell Tel. and Tel. Co., 802 F.2d 1352 (11th Cir. 1986). *See also* Dial Information Servs. Corp. v. Thornburgh, 938 F.2d 1535 (2nd Cir. 1991), *cert. denied,* 502 U.S. 1072 (1992); Information Providers' Coalition v. FCC, 928 F.2d 866 (9th Cir. 1991).

63. Justice Breyer wrote, "[w]e recognize that the First Amendment, the terms of which apply to governmental action, ordinarily does not itself throw into constitutional doubt the decisions of our private citizens to permit, or to restrict, speech. . . ." 1996 U.S. Lexis 4261, *20. He then outlined the petitioner's arguments for finding state action under these circumstances, *id.* at *21-*22 and then proceeded directly to the substantive arguments.

64. Denver Area Educational Tele-Communication Consortium v. FCC, 35 L. Ed. 2d 888, 116 S. Ct. 2374, 1996 U.S. Lexis 4261, *97 (June 28, 1996).

65. *Id.* at *168–*180.

66. A content-based ratings system gives information about the amount of sexual or violent or other types of content in the program.

67. "On their way to being digital, broadcasters feel they are still entitled to cost-free airwaves," *New York Times,* January 22, 1996: D7. "Prepared Statement of Kevin O'Brien, Vice President and General Manager KTVU-TV, Channel 2, San Francisco, CA and Chairman of the Board (The Association of Local Television Stations) before The House Commerce Committee," Federal Information Systems Corp., *Federal News Service,* March 21, 1996. "Fields Chides Broadcasters on Tax Ads," Diversified Publishing Group, *Multichannel News* (March 25, 1996). "Domenici Tunes out TV Auction Plan," *U.P.I., Washington News* (March 14, 1996). This is close to the deal that the FCC had worked out before the passage of the Telecommunications Act of 1996. 142 *Congressional Record* S 1528.

68. "Dole Statement Snags Phone, Cable TV Bill; Senator Fights Free Digital

Broadcast Licenses," *Washington Post,* January 11, 1996: D8. "Dole's Warning To Broad-casters; He'd End Free Licenses," *International Herald Tribune,* January 12, 1996. 142 Cong. Rec. H 1145, H 1150; 142 Cong. Rec. S 684; 141 Cong. Rec. S 14471, S 14513; 141 Cong. Rec. S 7881, S 7898.

69. Newspaper accounts frequently link the two issues. "Dole Statement Snags Phone," *Washington Post,* D8; "On Their Way to Being Digital, Broadcasters Feel They Are Still Entitled to Cost-Free Airwaves," *New York Times,* January 22, 1996: D7. "The Po-litical Battle Grows Over the Use of New Broadcast Technology," *New York Times,* March 18, 1996: D1; "Dole's Warning," *International Herald Tribune.*

70. *See* Corn-Revere, "Television Violence," 187, 199–200 (discussing the comments of former FCC Chairman Alfred Sikes, Congressman Ed Markey, and current FCC Chairman Reed Hundt). On the political economy and its connection to spectrum auc-tions, see Thomas Hazlett, *Assigning Property Rights to Radio Spectrum Users: Why Did FCC License Auctions Take 67 Years?* Working Paper, July 11, 1995.

71. *See* Corn-Revere, "Television Violence," supra, 199–200.

72. Writers Guild of America, West v. FCC, 423 F. Supp. 1064 (C.D. Cal. 1976), *va-cated and remanded on jurisdictional grounds sub nom.* Writers Guild of America, West v. ABC, 609 F.2d 355 (9th Cir. 1979), *cert. denied,* 449 U.S. 824 (1980). *But see* CBS v. Demo-cratic National Committee, 412 U.S. 94 (1973) (a plurality refusing to find state action in the bare licensing of television broadcasters).

73. I am presuming that absent regulation the V-chip would not have been in-stalled.

74. The list of 30 included Ted Turner (TBS), Rupert Murdoch (Fox), Barry Diller (Silver King), Michael Ovitz (Disney), Frank Mancuso (MGM), Kay Koplovitz (USA Network), Alan Levine (Sony), Bob Wright (NBC), Michael Jordan (Westinghouse), Richard Masur (Actor's Guild), Eddie Fritts (NAB), Peter Lund (CBS), Jack Valenti (MPAA), Judith McHale (Discovery), Ray Rodriguez (Univision), Gene Reynolds (Di-rector's Guild), Brian Roberts (Comcast), Ron Meyer (MCA), Bob Iger (Cap Cities/ABC), Lucy Salhany (United Paramount), Rich Frank (C-3), Ervin Duggan (PBS), Haim Saban (Saban Entertainment), Brad Radnitz (President, Writers Guild of Amer-ica, West), Terry Semel (Chairman/co-CEO, Warner Bros., Warner Music Group), Robert A. Daly (Chairman/co-CEO, Warner Bros., Warner Music Group), Jeffrey Katzenberg (Founder, Dreamworks SKG), Jonathan L. Dolgen (Chairman, Viacom), Robert L. John-son (President/CEO, Black Entertainment Television), and Decker Anstrom (President, NCTA). *See* "The Elegant Surrender: Industry Capitulates on V-Chip Without Firing a Shot" (cover story), *Broadcasting and Cable* (March 4, 1996); "President Hears TV Exec-utives Commit to Ratings System," *Los Angeles Times,* March 1, 1996: A1.

75. "Q and A with President Clinton," *Los Angeles Times,* March 2, 1996: F1, 8.

76. Television Program Improvement Act of 1990, 47 U.S.C. § 303c (1994).

77. Jason Moody, *States News Service,* Aug. 1, 1989, available in LEXIS, Nexis Li-brary, Wires File.

78. Greg Braxton, "Confusion, Anger Mark Discussion about V-Chip," *Los Angeles Times,* October 4, 1996: F1, 25.

79. Braxton, "V-Chip," 25. Jack Valenti, who is in charge of putting together the rat-ings system, retorted, "'I'm not worried about those people in back of you because we will be in federal court in a nanosecond' if there is any attempt by lawmakers to impose censorship."

80. The FCC must also approve the technology that will be used in the V-chip itself. This gives another added measure of control. "V-Chip Technology Waits for Washington," *Broadcasting and Cable,* December 30, 1966: 8.

81. Joel Federman, codirector of the Center for Communication and Social Policy at the University of California at Santa Barbara, argued:

> The industry has pledged that its ratings will be useful to parents, helping them to block unwanted shows using the much-heralded V chip. But a recent national survey of parents sponsored by the PTA and conducted by University of Wisconsin researchers found that 80 percent of parents would prefer a system that identifies programs by content rather than the age group for which the programming is appropriate. Parents surveyed said the HBO rating system, which specifies the type and level of sex, violence and language, is significantly more helpful to them and more objective than the MPAA ratings.

Joel Federman, "Let's Pave a High Road for TV Ratings System," *Los Angeles Times,* December 9, 1996: Calendar 3.

82. "But the aggressive strategy chosen by MPAA Chairman Jack Valenti and other entertainment executives could set the stage for a political showdown with a spectrum of critics, from the conservative Traditional Values Coalition to the liberal Center for Media Education, which want information made public in advance about the level of sex, violence and bad language on individual shows." Jube Shiver Jr., "TV Industry to Use Ratings Before Regulatory Review," *Los Angeles Times,* December 19, 1996: A1.

83. Elizabeth Shogren writes,

> [S]ome children's television advocates and members of Congress . . . strongly favor a content-based TV rating system that would give parents more specific information about the sex, violence or foul language found in every entertainment program.
>
> "Parents have reviewed Hollywood's age-based system and given it two thumbs down," said Rep. Edward J. Markey (D-Mass.). "Now is the time for their voices to be heard."
>
> Markey, one of several members of Congress who have spoken out against the industry's design, said he has requested a meeting with the president to try to change his mind.
>
> "We should not spend 10 months trying out a system that child psychologists, pediatricians, religious leaders and educators agree is seriously flawed," Markey said.
>
> Earlier this week the battle between the two sides reached a boiling point. Sen. Joseph I. Lieberman (D-Conn.) threatened to introduce legislation requiring a content-based system. But Valenti, the chief architect of the industry's proposal, countered that he would file a 1st Amendment lawsuit to keep the government from intervening, which would likely stall the introduction of the system.

"Clinton Supports Industry on TV Ratings Proposal," *Los Angeles Times,* Home Edition, December 14, 1996: A1.

84. The vice president apparently told them to take their fight to the FCC. "'The vice president assured us that the White House neither endorses nor condemns the TV ratings system,' said Kathryn Montgomery, president of the Center for Media Education, a Washington communications advocacy group. But, she said, 'there will be an open process at the FCC for debate and comment on this issue.'" Shiver Jr., "TV Industry to Use Ratings," A1.

85. A ratings "committee member acknowledged that an alternative to the MPAA-based system was never seriously considered."

"'This was the only system the whole TV industry would agree to,' the committee member said." Hall and Lowry, "Ratings System," A1.

86. Jane Hall, "TV Ratings Architect Vows to Fight Federal Intervention," *Los Angeles Times*, Home Edition, December 13, 1996: Bus. 1.

87. The response, I suppose, is to focus on the lack of explicit coercion. President Clinton was only making a request, not giving an order. The background legislation does not require ratings. And Lieberman and Markey were only pointing out that *other* congresspersons would not be as friendly as they are. Hence, the decision to rate programs remains private.

The response fails. It does not address the level of government involvement. The Clinton administration and Congress have been deeply and forcefully involved in the V-chip issue. Calling such political behavior "just" a request is silly and wrong. The administration's extremely active involvement in shaping the content of children's television on closely related issues, such as educational television, underscores how seriously broadcasters must regard the administration's pressure. The White House recently brokered a deal for the FCC to require three hours per week of educational programming for children. Again, meetings were held at the White House. *See* Sherry L. Stolberg and Jane Hall, "Educational Children's TV Shows to Air," *Los Angeles Times*, July 30, 1996: A12. The industry's adoption of a V-chip ratings system should, in short, likely be regarded as state action.

88. Subsequent events may well change my conclusion. Some congressmen are pushing to have the FCC approve a V-chip design that will permit content-based systems, and Senator John McCain (R-Arizona), incoming chair of the Senate Commerce, Science and Transportation Committee, plans to hold hearings on television ratings systems early this year. Hall, "Fight Federal Intervention," Bus. 1. President Clinton has urged that the industry's system be given 10 months to see how it works, but seems to be willing to intervene at the end of that period of time. "'Give it 10 months to work,' Clinton said in a nationally televised news conference. 'The parents in the country ought to look at these ratings . . . and then, if they're inadequate or there needs to be some more content in the rating systems, then after a 10-month test period we'll be able to make that argument.'" Shogren, "Clinton Supports Industry," A1.

89. *See generally* Columbia Broadcasting System, Inc. v. Democratic National Committee, 412 U.S. 94 (1973) (refusing to find that federal licensing of broadcasters made their editorial judgments into state action).

90. See also Corn-Revere, "'V' Is Not for Voluntary;" and Corn-Revere, "Television Violence," 187.

91. Blum v. Yaretsky, 457 U.S. 991 (1982).

92. See the discussion above of statements by the president and members of Congress about the rating system.

93. Note that my assumption about decreasing involvement by politicians suggests that the general entanglement theory will be much weaker here.

94. This is probably the only circumstance under which a complaining program producer or viewer could get standing in Stage Three. On the requirement of injury in standing, *see* Enos v. Marsh, 769 F.2d 1363 (1985) (holding that plaintiff lacked standing to bring a claim for relief under the Administrative Procedure Act since plaintiff had presented no fact that actual injury would occur if the Army Corp. of Engineers were to use a lower discount rate in cost-benefit computations for a harbor project); Sierra Club v. Morton, 405 U.S. 727 (1972) (holding that the "injury in fact" test for standing to sue under the Administrative Procedure Act requires more than injury to a cognizable interest and requires that the party seeking review be himself among the injured); Zoslaw v. MCA Distrib. Corp., 594 F. Supp. 1022 (1984) (finding that former operators of a retail record store could have standing to complain of another record retailer's alleged acts of receiving favorable treatment from record distributors who violated price discrimination provisions of the Robinson-Patman Act only if the two record retailers were competitors in the same market); Director Off. of Worker's Comp. v. Perini, 459 U.S. 297 (1983) (holding that the presence of an injured employee as party respondent allowed the petitioner, the Director of the Office of Worker's Compensation Program, to have standing to argue the merits of the case because the respondent's presence assured that the court would be reviewing a case with an actual injury redressable by the court) .

95. Hurley v. Irish-American Gay, Lesbian and Bisexual Group of Boston, 115 S. Ct. 2338; 1995 U.S. LEXIS 4050; 132 L. Ed. 2d 487 (1995); Riley v. National Fedn. of the Blind of North Carolina, Inc., 487 U.S. 781 (1988); Wooley v. Maynard, 430 U.S. 705, 714 (1977).

96. This argument would likely be available to both a plaintiff objecting to the entire V-chip ratings system and to one who is objecting to the rating attached to a particular show. The ratings must be transmitted in general, and as to any particular show that has been rated. Hence, at both levels, there is state action.

97. For example, I will not discuss the "forced speech" issue.

98. The closest analogy would be the "vagueness" and "overbreadth" cases in First Amendment law. The cases on vagueness require that speech regulation be precise, so as to give those subject to the regulations notice of exactly what is prohibited. The Court desires to reign in governmental prosecutorial discretion, Kolender v. Lawson, 461 U.S. 352 (1983); and to avoid "chilling" speech by those who are uncertain as to the reach of the regulations, NAACP v. Button, 3371 U.S. 415 (1963); Smith v. Goguen, 415 U.S. 566 (1974); Baggett v. Bullitt, 377 U.S. 360 (1964); and Houston v. Hill, 482 U.S. 451 (1987). In overbreadth cases the Court invalidates speech regulations that reach substantial amounts of protected speech, in addition to unprotected speech, and allows those challenging the regulations to assert that the protected speech of third parties will be "chilled" by the regulations. See Schad v. Borough of Mt. Ephraim, 452 U.S. 61 (1981); Broadrick v. Oklahoma, 413 U.S. 601 (1973); Secretary of State v. J.H. Munson Co., 467 U.S. 947 (1984).

The Court has often used the (sometimes presumed) change in the mix of speech in the marketplace produced by a change in incentives from government regulations as a basis for invalidating various restrictions on speech. See Miami Herald v. Tornillo, 418 U.S. 241 (1974) (Court struck down a "right of reply" statute in newspapers, in part on the basis that the statute would chill newspapers' editorializing); New York Times v. Sullivan, 376 U.S. 254 (1964) (limiting reach of state defamation laws to reduce potential chill to criticisms of public officials); Simon and Schuster v. Members of the New York State

Crime Victims Board, 502 U.S. 105 (1991) (striking down state law preventing criminals from profiting from sale of story so as to avoid chill to criminals' speech); and United States v. National Treasury Employees Union, 115 S.Ct. 1003 (1995) (declaring unconstitutional a federal law preventing government employees from being paid for off-the-job speeches and writings so as to avoid chill to these expressive activities). For similar concerns about the "fairness doctrine," *see* 1985 Fairness Doctrine Report, .02 F.C.C.2d 143, 58 R.R.2d 1137 (1985).

99. Clearly some government officials, including President Clinton and Rep. Edward Markey (D-Massachusetts) are hoping for a chilling effect. *See* note 102, *infra*.

100. The second theory, of course, suffers from the state action problems reviewed above. There are two additional problems, both resembling state action, that may plague this cause of action. First, producers rate their own shows, at least in the first instance. Hence, a producer unhappy with his rating could rerate himself. The recently announced system will include a 19-member appeals board to resolve ratings disputes, so it is possible that self-help may not be available. Hall, "Fight Intervention," Bus. 1. In addition, viewers must choose to set the V-chip filter before any shows are removed from the set. These actions may serve to cut the link between any government action and individual producer injury.

101. "It's All in the Family TV," *Broadcasting and Cable*, June 3, 1996: 24. See also Howard Rosenberg, "Dick Wolf: Rating TV's New Order," *Los Angeles Times*, Home Edition, January 3, 1997: Calendar 1 (quoting veteran producer as fearing chill of "the 10 o'-clock drama").

102. Clearly some government officials are hoping for a chilling effect. "V-chip proponent Rep. Edward J. Markey (D-Mass.) has said that if even a small percentage of parents take advantage of the technology, ratings would decline for objectionable programming, thus reducing levels of violence." "So, They Fixed TV . . . " *Los Angeles Times*, December 29, 1996: Calendar 3. "President Clinton has said that if enough viewers respond to these initiatives, 'It will change programming, hopefully for the better.'" *Id.*

103. Matthew L. Spitzer, "An Introduction to the Law and Economics of the V-Chip," *Cardozo Arts and Entertainment Law Journal* (forthcoming).

104. 390 U.S. 629 (1968).

105. See previous discussion of the Denver Area Telecommunications case.

106. There is an additional theory that the producer could propound that is beyond the scope of this article. The producer could claim that the V-chip ratings system, which requires the producer to rate the show, represents compelled speech, and as such violates the producer's right not to speak. There are a number of cases that uphold, in general, the right not to speak. West Virginia State Board of Education v. Barnette, 319 U.S. 624 (1943) (invalidating a state requirement that children salute the U.S. flag); Wooley v. Maynard, 430 U.S. 705 (1977) (holding that individuals have constitutional right to obscure the motto "Live Free or Die" on a license plate); and McIntyre v. Ohio Elections Commission, 115 S. Ct. 1511 (1995) (invalidating requirement that campaign literature identify author). The two cases that are likely closest to the V-chip rating system are Lamont v. Postmaster General, 381 U.S. 301 (1965) (invalidating federal statute requiring U.S. Post Office to identify "communist political propaganda" and requiring that those wishing such material request the delivery in writing); and Meese v. Keene, 481 U.S. 465 (1987) (upholding requirement that motion picture exhibitors place the words "political

propaganda" at the start of foreign films that had been identified as propaganda by the U.S. government).

107. Here we must presume that the producer prevailed on his somewhat shaky state action argument in the section before.

108. Lovell v. City of Griffin, 303 U.S. 444 (1938).

109. Saia v. New York, 334 U.S. 558 (1948).

110. City of Lakewood v. Plain Dealer Publishing Co., 486 U.S. 750 (1988).

111. Cox v. New Hampshire, 312 U.S. 569 (1941); Kovacs v. Cooper, 336 U.S. 77 (1949).

112. Forsyth County, Georgia v. Nationalist Movement, 505 U.S. 123 (1992). This should be understood as part of the Court's general hostility toward any regulation that gets classed as a "prior restraint" of speech. *See* Chemerinsky, *Constitutional Law*, § 11.2.3 (forthcoming).

113. *See* Interstate Circuit, Inc. v. Dallas, 390 U.S. 676, 678–81 (1968); Kingsley International Pictures Corp. v. Regents, 360 U.S. 863 (1953); Holmby Productions, Inc. v. Vaughn, 350 U.S. 870 (1955); Commercial Pictures Corp. v. Regents, 346 U.S. 587 (1954); Superior Films, Inc. v. Department of Education, 346 U.S. 587 (1954); Gelling v. Texas, 343 U.S. 960 (1952); Joseph Burstyn, Inc. v. Wilson, 343 U.S. 495 (1952); Paramount Film Distributing Corp. v. City of Chicago, 172 F. Supp. 69 (N.D. Ill. 1959).

State court cases include Police Commissioner v. Siegel Enterprises, Inc., 223 Md. 110, 162 A.2d 727, *cert. denied* 364 U.S. 909 (1960); People v. Kahan, 15 N.Y.2d 311, 206 N.E.2d 333 (1965); People v. Bookcase, Inc., 14 N.Y.2d 409, 201 N.E.2d 14 (1964); Hallmark Productions, Inc. v. Carroll, 384 Pa. 348, 121 A.2d 584 (1956).

114. Criminal prosecution, rather than licensing, has been used to keep material away from consenting adults. *E.g.* New York v. Mature Enterprises, 343 N.Y.S.2d 911 (1973) (finding the film *Deep Throat* obscene).

115. One way of looking at the choices of private parties to utilize the V-chip is that they might "cut the causal chain" between governmental action and the infringement. The producers might respond that the definition of the categories, and the decision to use an age-based system, establishes enough rigidity in the system that the viewer's choice to use the V-chip rating system does not let the government off the First Amendment state action hook. Unfortunately for the producer, it is at exactly this point—the form of the ratings system—that the producer will have the most trouble establishing state action in the first place. Hence, the definition of categories and the choice to use an age-based system, as private action, cannot serve to nullify subsequent private choices of viewers to utilize the categories and ratings.

116. Interstate Circuit, Inc. v. Dallas, 390 U.S. 676, 678–81 (1968).

117. On the regulation of broadcast indecency, *see* Thomas G. Krattenmaker and Lucas A. Powe Jr., *Regulating Broadcast Programming*, chap. 5 (1994); Levi, "The Hard Case of Broadcast Indecency," *New York University Review of Law and Social Change* 20:49.

118. *See* Pacifica Foundation v. FCC, 438 U.S. 726 (1978); Sable Communications, Inc. v. FCC, 492 U.S. 115 (1989); Action for Children's Television v. FCC (ACT I), 852 F.2d 1332 (D.C. Cir. 1988); Action for Children's Television v. FCC (ACT II), 932 F.2d 1504 (D.C. Cir. 1991), *cert. denied sub nom.* Children's Legal Found. v. Action for Children's Television, 503 U.S. 913 (1992); Action for Children's Television v. FCC (ACT III), 58 F.3d 654 (D.C. Cir. 1995) (*en banc*), *cert. denied sub nom.* Pacifica Found. v. FCC, 116 S.Ct. 701 (1996).

119. Edwards and Berman, "Regulating Violence," 1487.

120. Sable Communications, Inc. v. FCC, 492 U.S. 115 (1989). Balkin, "Media Filters," 1131.

121. I am presuming that the two sorts of regulations are substitutes, not comTelevision-ments. *See* Balkin, "Media Filters," 1131, arguing that they must be substitutes.

122. Stephen J. Kim, "'Viewer Discretion is Advised': A Structural Approach to the Issue of Television Violence," *University of Pennsylvania Law Review* 142 (1994): 1383, analyzes part of the First Amendment issue correctly. He perceives that the Court's view of ratings as content-based regulation will lead to strict scrutiny, which will demand that regulations be narrowly tailored to a compelling state interest. Then, unfortunately, Kim gives the reader only the following sentence. "Given the ongoing controversy over the precise effects of media violence and the problem of definition, the government would face a tough battle in demonstrating both its compelling interest and the required fit between means and ends." *Id.* 1406. Kim later acknowledges that the D.C. Circuit did find that enabling parents to control children's television viewing represented a compelling state interest, but fails to follow up with a serious analysis of whether ratings and the V-chip would be narrowly tailored. *Id.* 1408–9.

123. *See* Sable Communications of California, Inc. v. FCC, 492 U.S. 115, 126, 106 L. Ed. 2d 93, 109 S.Ct. 2829 (1989); Consolidated Edison Co. v. Public Serv. Comm'n, 447 U.S. 530, 540, 65 L.Ed.2d 319, 100 S.Ct. 2326 (1980); R.A.V. v. City of St. Paul, 505 U.S. 377 (1992). This standard is also used in many other areas of constitutional analysis. *See, e.g.,* Adarand Constructors v. Pena, 115 S. Ct. 2097 (1995); Sugarman v. Dougall, 413 U.S. 634 (1973); Sherbert v. Verner, 374 U.S. 398 (1963).

124. *See* R.A.V. v. City of St. Paul, 505 U.S. 377, 382, 112 S.Ct. 2538, 2542 (1992).

125. *Id.;* Texas v. Johnson, 491 U.S. 397, 412 (1992). Another implication of this statement is that the government has the burden of proof in such cases. *See* Chemerinsky, *Constitutional Law* § 6.5 (forthcoming).

126. *See* Turner Broadcasting System v. FCC, 129 L. Ed. 2d 497, 114 S. Ct. 2445 (1994); Bellsouth Corp. v. U.S., 868 F. Supp. 1335, 1342 n.10 (N.D. Ala. 1994).

127. *See* the discussion in Turner at 129 L. Ed. 2d 497, 114 S. Ct. 2445 (1994). Sometimes a regulation that is facially "content-based" is regarded as content-neutral if the *motivation* for the regulation is unrelated to suppressing or encouraging particular types of content. *See* Renton v. Playtime Theaters, 475 U.S. 41 (1986).

128. Federal Communications Commission v. League of Women Voters, 468 U.S. 1205 (1984).

129. *See* United States v. O'Brien, 391 U.S. 367 (1968).

130. 1996 U.S. Lexis 4261 (June 28, 1996).

131. *Id.* at *28–*29. In his concurrence Justice Souter echoed Justice Breyer's sentiments about technological uncertainty, counseling against picking a First Amendment doctrine for testing the regulations at issue:

> All of the relevant characteristics of cable are presently in a state of technological and regulatory flux. . . . As cable and telephone companies begin their competition for control over the single wire that will carry both their services, we can hardly settle rules for review of regulation on the assumption that cable will remain a separable and useful category of First Amendment

scrutiny. And as broadcast, cable, and the cyber-technology of the Internet and the World Wide Web approach the day of using a common receiver, we can hardly assume that standards for judging the regulation of one of them will not have immense, but now unknown and unknowable, effects on the others.

Denver Area Educational Tele-Communications Consortium v. FCC, 1996 U.S. Lexis 4261, *86–*88 (footnote omitted).

132. This aspect of Justice Breyer's opinion has received some harsh treatment. *See* Paul M. Barrett, "Cable Ruling May Portend Internet Curbs," *The Wall Street Journal,* July 1, 1996: B1 (quoting Laurence Tribe as saying Breyer's opinion is a "sugar-coated poison pill for the First Amendment"); and James C. Goodale, "Caught in Breyer's Patch," *New York Law Journal* 216(1996): 1 (describing Breyer's opinion as "the nadir of the Court's First Amendment jurisprudence").

133. *Id.* at *95.

134. *Id.* at *103.

135. Justice Thomas wrote, "Curiously, the plurality relies on 'changes taking place in the law, the technology, and the industrial structure, relating to telecommunications,' . . . to justify its avoidance of traditional First Amendment standards. If anything, as the plurality recognizes, . . . those recent developments . . . suggest that local cable operators have little or no monopoly power . . . , thus effectively negating the primary justifications for treating cable operators differently from other First Amendment speakers." *Id.* at *157.

136. Video Software Dealers Association v. Webster, 968 F.2d 684 (8th Cir. 1992). The Eighth Circuit struck down the Missouri law aimed at protecting children because the law was vague and not narrowly tailored. The purpose, however, was conceded to be compelling.

See, in accord, Davis-Kidd Booksellers, Inc. v. McWherter, 866 S.W.2d 520 (Tenn. 1993). For a list of the various interests the state has invoked to justify protecting children from broadcast indecency, see Edythe Wise, "A Historical Perspective on the Protection of Children From Broadcast Indecency," *Villanova Sports and Entertainment Law Journal* 3 (1996): 15, 19.

137. Action for Children's Television v. FCC, 11 F.3d 170, 177 (D.C. Cir. 1993).

138. *See* FCC v. Pacifica Found., 438 U.S. 726 (1978); Sable Communications, Inc. v. FCC, 492 U.S. 115 (1989). In addition, the Supreme Court seems to have coalesced around protecting children from "sexually explicit" material as a compelling state interest. *See* Denver Area Educational Tele-Communications Consortium v. FCC, 1996 U.S. Lexis 4261, *30 (Breyer), *137 ("Congress does have . . . a compelling interest in protecting children from indecent speech") (Kennedy), and *180 ("The parties agree that Congress has a 'compelling interest in protecting the physical and psychological well-being of minors' and that its interest 'extends to shielding minors from the influence of [indecent speech] that is not obscene by adult standards'" (Thomas) (June 28, 1996). Note that this is only slightly different from empowering parents.

139. *Id.* at *180 (while discussing indecency regulation). The Supreme Court also analogized cable to broadcast, finding that cable has a "uniquely pervasive presence" and that patently offensive material can "'confront the citizen' in the 'privacy of the home.'" Denver Area Educational Tele-Communications Consortium v. FCC, 1996 U.S. Lexis

4261, *33. Justice Breyer used this characterization to justify the constitutionality of extending indecency regulation to cable television.

140. *See* James A. Stimson, Michael B. Mackuen, and Robert S. Erikson, "Dynamic Representation," *American Political Science Review* 89(1995): 543; Charles H. Franklin and Liane C. Kosaki, "Republican Schoolmaster: The U.S. Supreme Court, Public Opinion, and Abortion," *American Political Science Review* 83(1989): 752.

141. Note that when the purpose is to empower parents, the question of whether the criteria for age-rating the programming are appropriate becomes an inquiry into the types of programming that most parents would like to control.

142. Justice Breyer mentioned the "lockbox" as an example of a less intrusive alternative to segregating and blocking indecent material in Denver Area Educational Tele-Communications Consortium v. FCC, 1996 U.S. Lexis 4261, *56. As a result, said Justice Breyer, the segregate-and-block requirement of section 10(b) is unconstitutional. The lockbox, however, would likely provide no reason for striking down the V-chip; the V-chip is *easier* to use than the lockbox, whereas the section 10(b) was harder for parents to use than the lockbox.

Justice Breyer mentioned the V-chip in favorable terms in the same case, Denver Area Educational Tele-Communications Consortium v. FCC, 1996 U.S. Lexis 4261, *53, describing the V-chip as a reason to strike down the more intrusive alternative of requiring cable operators to segregate and block all indecent programming on access channels. Although, as Justice Breyer noted, the constitutionality of the V-chip was not at issue in Denver Area, his use of the V-chip indicates a favorable predisposition toward the new technology of program filtering.

143. One caveat should be mentioned here. If, in operation, the V-chip effectively chases all violence, sex, and strong language off of the air, so that adults are reduced to watching only material that is "fit for children," then in operation the V-chip might well offend principles of First Amendment law found in Butler v. Michigan, 352 U.S. 380 (1957).

If the Court were to conceive of the purpose of the V-chip to be reducing the amount of sexual and violent material on the air, rather than helping parents to control their children's diet, and if reducing (but not eliminating) such material were held to be a valid purpose, then the economic analysis of the V-chip presented in Spitzer, "Law and Economics of the V-Chip," supra, would bear directly on the question of narrow tailoring. In order for the V-chip to be lawful it would have to implement, to some degree, the purposes of the law. Depending on the placement and weight of the burden of proof to show narrow tailoring (or "directly implementing" under middle-tier scrutiny), the indeterminacy of the analysis might help establish, or fail to rebut a presumption of, narrow tailoring.

144. Recall that we are assuming that the ratings system constitutes state action.

145. Jane Hall, "Most Sitcoms Given the TV-PG Rating," *Los Angeles Times,* January 11, 1997: F1.

146. Brian Lowry, "Sex on TV's 'Family Hour' Has Increased, Study Finds," *Los Angeles Times,* Home Edition, December 12, 1996: A1. Lynn Smith, "Family Hour Provides No Haven from Sexual Messages," *Los Angeles Times,* Home Edition, December 29, 1996: E3. Shiver Jr., "TV Industry to Use Ratings," A1.

147. I will not discuss in text the possible justification of overriding parents' judg-

ments about what material is appropriate for children, mainly because the V-chip ratings system allows parents to let all material into the home if they wish. Hence the V-chip ratings system seems to be very poorly tailored to the purpose of reversing parental judgment.

148. Note that such a claim of process likely would be brought by a producer who is unhappy with the way in which his product was rated. As I noted below, such a claim would face severe problems with the state action requirement.

149. 424 U.S. 319 (1976).

150. The industry's ratings system includes a review board. "Valenti . . . disclosed that a 19-member board will be established to resolve disputes over the ratings. But the appeals board will consist entirely of people who work in television, rather than including any parents from the outside, as the MPAA uses with its movie ratings." Hall, "Fight Federal Intervention," Bus. 1.

It may be relatively easy to get one person to declare another's rating to be unreasonable. When a large sample of the public was asked to rate current television shows using the MPAA rating system, the sample produced large differences of opinion as to how certain shows should be rated. *See* Michael Schneider, "How 'Bad' Does the Public Think TV Is? Media Executives Have a Committee to Devise a Content Ratings System for Television," *Electronic Media*, 1996 WL 7535273 (July 29, 1996).

151. 380 U.S. 51 (1965).

152. *Id.* at 58–60. *See also* United States v. One Carton Positive Motion Picture Film Entitled "491", 367 F.2d 889 (2nd Cir. 1966) (applying Freedman). *See generally, Annotation: Constitutionality of Regulation of Obscene Motion Pictures—Federal Cases,* 22 L.Ed.2d 949.

153. 380 U.S. 51, 56. For a more recent example of the general principle, see Freeman v. Burson, 504 U.S. 191 (1992).

154. "Particularly in the case of motion pictures, it may take very little to deter exhibition in a given locality. The exhibitor's stake in any one picture may be insufficient to warrant a protracted and onerous course of litigation. The distributor, on the other hand, may be equally unwilling to accept the burdens and delays of litigation in a particular area when, without such difficulties, he can freely exhibit his film in most of the rest of the country;" 380 U.S. 59.

The Court has, in general, followed the procedural requirements outlined in Freedman. *See* FW/PBS, Inc. v. City of Dallas, 493 U.S. 215, 226–230 (1990) (requiring a licensing scheme for sexually explicit businesses to act administratively and provide judicial review within a short period of time, but declining to put the burden of proof on city inspectors); and Southeastern Promotions, Ltd. v. Conrad, 420 U.S. 546, 559–562 (1975) (striking down a city's refusal to allow the musical *Hair* to be staged in a municipal theater because the city's decision making failed to follow the Freedman procedures). *See also* Paris Adult Theater I v. Slaton, 413 U.S. 49, 55 (1973) (commenting favorably upon civil injunction scheme for obscene materials); Heller v. New York, 413 U.S. 483, 489–490 (1973) (approving under Freedman a judge's viewing a film before issuing a warrant for seizure of the film under obscenity statutes); and Riley v. National Federation of Blind of N.C., Inc., 487 U.S. 781 (1988). A recent film case, Meese v. Keene, 481 U.S. 465 (1987), approved a U.S. government film-labeling scheme, but did not address the issue of procedures. For an angry response to Meese v. Keene, *see* Landsbaum, Note, "How to Censor Films Without Really Trying: The Beirut Agreement and the Foreign Agents Registration Act," *Southern California Law Review* 62 (1989): 685.

155. One could argue that the Freedman procedural requirements should not apply to a V-chip ratings system. The Freedman requirements were designed for dealing with administrative suppression of a motion picture, at least as to people under 21. Because the administrative treatment of motion pictures was so harsh, the corresponding procedural protections needed to be great. In contrast, one might argue, a V-chip rating will not suppress a television program to the same degree that motion picture regulation suppressed movies, and the procedural protections can correspondingly be more lax. The rebuttal, I suppose, would focus on the greater speed with which most television products must be brought to market. Because television shows are often created in a very short period of time, and much closer to the time of airing than are motion pictures, the need for speedy and effective review of ratings might be greater in television than in motion pictures. For the purposes of this article, I will assume that the rebuttal will carry the day and that the Freedman procedural requirements will apply.

156. Prompt means less than 8 weeks of administrative process for movies. Teitel Film Corp. v. Cusack, 390 U.S. 139 (1968). Because the lead time for television episodes is much less than for movies, I would expect that the process would have to be faster for V-chip determinations.

157. This might represent preserving the status quo and would certainly give the V-chip ratings system incentives for speedy process.

158. "Jack of All Trades," *Broadcasting and Cable,* 26 (comments of Jack Valenti).

159. "A panel of network and studio representatives led by Motion Picture Association of America President Jack Valenti has been meeting since March to hammer out [V-chip] standards. . . . Shows probably will be rated on a seasonal basis unless there are indications of significant variance by episode." "All in the Family TV," *Broadcasting and Cable,* 24, 28.

160. 424 U.S. 319 (1976).

161. *Id.* at 335.

162. *See* Chemerinsky, *Constitutional Law* § 7.4.3 (forthcoming).

REFERENCES

Albert, J. A. 1978. "Constitutional Regulation of Televised Violence," *Virginia Law Review* 64:1299 (Note).

Andrews, W. 1996. "Site-Rating System Slow to Catch On," *WebWeek,* July 8.

Balkin, J. M. 1996. "Media Filters, the V-Chip, and the Foundations of Broadcast Regulation," *Duke Law Journal* 45:1131.

Ballard, I. M., Jr. 1995. "See No Evil, Hear No Evil: Television Violence and the First Amendment," *Virginia Law Review* 81:175 (student note).

Barrett, P. M. 1996. "Cable Ruling May Portend Internet Curbs," *The Wall Street Journal* July 1: B1.

Black, C. L., Jr. 1967. Foreword: "'State Action,' Equal Protection, and California's Proposition 14," *Harvard Law Review* 81:69, 95.

Braxton, G. 1996. "Confusion, Anger Mark Discussion about V-Chip," *Los Angeles Times,* October 4: F1, 25.

Bray, H. 1996. "Rated P for Preemptive: System to Shield Kids from Adult Web Material Also Seeks to Keep Censors Off Net," *Boston Globe,* July 25.

Broadcasting and Cable. 1995. "Why the Markey Chip Won't Hurt You," *Broadcasting and Cable* August 14: 10.

———. 1996a. "The Elegant Surrender: Industry Capitulates on V-Chip Without Firing a Shot" (cover story), *Broadcasting and Cable* March 4.

———. 1996b. "Jack of All Trades: The Man in the Middle on the V-Chip," *Broadcasting and Cable* March 18: 26, 29.

———. 1996c. "It's All in the Family TV," *Broadcasting and Cable* June 3: 24.

———. 1996d. "V-Chip Technology Waits for Washington," *Broadcasting and Cable* December 30: 8

Chemerinsky, E. 1985. "Rethinking State Action," *Northwestern University Law Review* 80:503, 511–16.

———. 1997. *Constitutional Law: Principles and Policies.* (forthcoming).

Coburn, T. 1995. "V-Chipping Away at Parental Responsibility Is Not the Solution to TV's Morality Crisis," *ROLL CALL,* Oct. 23.

Corn-Revere, R. 1995a. "'V' Is Not for Voluntary," *Cato Institute Briefing Paper No. 24,* August 3.

———. 1995b. "Television Violence and the Limits of Voluntarism," *Yale Journal on Regulation* 12:187.

DeLeon, D. L., and R. L. Naon. 1974. Note, "The Regulation of Televised Violence," *Stanford Law Review* 26:1291.

Diversified Publishing Group. 1996. "Fields Chides Broadcasters on Tax Ads," *Multichannel News* March 25.

Edwards, H. T., and M. N. Berman. 1995. "Regulating Violence on Television," *Northwestern University Law Review* 89:1487.

Federman, J. 1996. "Let's Pave a High Road for TV Ratings System," *Los Angeles Times,* December 9: Calendar 3.

Franklin, C. H., and L. C. Kosaki. 1989. "Republican Schoolmaster: The U.S. Supreme Court, Public Opinion, and Abortion," *American Political Science Review* 83:752.

Goodale, J. C. 1996. "Caught in Breyer's Patch," *New York Law Journal* 216:1.

Hall, J. 1996. "TV Ratings Architect Vows to Fight Federal Intervention, *Los Angeles Times,* Home Edition, December 13: Bus. 1.

———. 1997. "Most Sitcoms Given the TV-PG Rating," *Los Angeles Times,* January 11: F1.

Hall, J., and B. Lowry. 1996. "Industry Unveils Its Ratings System for TV Programs," *Los Angeles Times,* Home Edition, December 20: A1.

Hamilton, J. T. 1996. "Private Interests in 'Public Interest' Programming: An Economic Assessment of Broadcaster Incentives," *Duke Law Journal* 45:1177.

Hazlett, T. 1995. *Assigning Property Rights to Radio Spectrum Users: Why Did FCC License Auctions Take 67 Years?* Working Paper, July 11.

Hearn, T. 1995. "Lawmaker Fields Calls V-Chip Unconstitutional," *Multichannel News* November 27: 152.

Hundt, R. E. 1996. "The Public's Airwaves: What Does the Public Interest Require of Television Broadcasters?" *Duke Law Journal* 45:1089, 1126.

International Herald Tribune. 1996. "Dole's Warning to Broadcasters; He'd End Free Licenses," *International Herald Tribune*, January 12.

Kim, S. J. 1994. "'Viewer Discretion is Advised': A Structural Approach to the Issue of Television Violence," *University of Pennsylvania Law Review* 142:1383

Kopel, D. B. 1995. "Massaging the Medium: Analyzing and Responding to Media Violence Without Harming the First Amendment," *Kansas Journal of Law and Public Policy* 4:17.

Krattenmaker, T. G., and L. A. Powe Jr. 1978. "Televised Violence: First Amendment Principles and Social Science Theory," *Virginia Law Review* 64:1123.

———. 1994. *Regulating Broadcast Programming*, chapter 5.

Krotosynski, R. J., Jr. 1996. "Into the Woods: Broadcasters, Bureaucrats, and Children's Television Programming," *Duke Law Journal* 45:1193, 1194.

Landsbaum, S. L. 1989. "How to Censor Films Without Really Trying: The Beirut Agreement and the Foreign Agents Registration Act," *Southern California Law Review* 62:685.

Levi, L. 1992. "The Hard Case of Broadcast Indecency," *New York University Review of Law & Social Change* 20:49.

———. 1996. "The FCC, Indecency, and Anti-Abortion Political Advertising," *Villanova Sports & Entertainment Law Journal* 3:85.

Los Angeles Times. 1996a. "President Hears TV Executives Commit to Ratings System," *Los Angeles Times*, March 1: A1.

———. 1996b. "Q&A with President Clinton," *Los Angeles Times*, March 2: F1, 8.

———. 1996c. "So, They Fixed TV . . ." *Los Angeles Times*, December 29: Calendar 3.

Lowry, B. 1996. "Sex on TV's 'Family Hour' Has Increased, Study Finds," *Los Angeles Times*, Home Edition, December 12: A1.

MacCarthy, M. M. 1995. "Broadcast Self-Regulation: The NAB Codes, Family Viewing Hour, and Television Violence," *Cardozo Arts and Entertainment Law Journal* 13:667.

Moody, Jason. 1989. *States News Service*, Aug. 1, available in LEXIS, Nexis Library, Wires File.

New York Times Company. 1996. "On Their Way to Being Digital, Broadcasters Feel They Are Still Entitled to Cost-Free Airwaves," *New York Times*, January 22: D7.

———. 1996. "The Political Battle Grows Over the Use of New Broadcast Technology," *New York Times*, March 18: D1

O'Brien, K. 1996. "Prepared Statement of Kevin O'Brien, Vice President and General Manager KTVU-TV, Channel 2, San Francisco, CA and Chairman of the Board (The Association of Local Television Stations) before The House Commerce Committee," Federal Information Systems Corp., *Federal News Service*, March 21.

Redish, M. 1984. *Freedom of Expression: A Critical Analysis* 9–52.

Rosenberg, H. 1997. "Dick Wolf: Rating TV's New Order," *Los Angeles Times*, Home Edition, January 3: Calendar 1.

RSAC, "USWeb Affiliate Network to Use RSAC Internet Rating System," July 16, 1996, available at http://www.rsac.org/press/960716.html.

Saunders, K.W. 1994. "Media Self-Regulation of Depictions of Violence: A Last Opportunity," *Oklahoma Law Review* 47:445.

Schneider, M. 1996. "How 'Bad' Does the Public Think TV Is? Media Executives Have a

Committee to Devise a Content Ratings System for Television," *Electronic Media*, July 29.

Scott, D. V. 1996. "The V-Chip Debate: Blocking Television Sex, Violence, and the First Amendment," *Loyola of Los Angeles Entertainment Law Journal*, Comment, 16:741.

Shiver, J., Jr. 1996. "TV Industry to Use Ratings before Regulatory Review," *Los Angeles Times*, December 19: A1.

Shogren, E. 1996. "Clinton Supports Industry on TV Ratings Proposal," *Los Angeles Times*, Home Edition, December 14: A1.

Smith, L. 1996. "Family Hour Provides No Haven from Sexual Messages," *Los Angeles Times*, Home Edition, December 29: E3.

Spitzer, M. L. 1997. "An Introduction to the Law and Economics of the V-Chip," *Cardozo Arts & Entertainment Law Journal* (forthcoming).

Stern, C. 1995. "Industry Battles Ratings, V-Chip," *Broadcasting and Cable*, June 26: 16.

Stimson, J. A., M. B. Mackuen, and R. S. Erickson. 1995. "Dynamic Representation," *American Political Science Review* 89:543.

Stolberg, S. L., and J. Hall. 1996. "Educational Children's TV Shows to Air," *Los Angeles Times*, July 30: A12.

United Press International. 1996. "Domenici Tunes out TV Auction Plan," *U.P.I.*, *Washington News* March 14.

United States Congress. 1996. H.R. Conference Report 104–458, Section 551—Parental Choice in Television Programming, Conference agreement.

United States Congress. 1996. "Telecommunications Act of 1996." 142 *Congressional Record* S 1528.

Valenti, J. 1993. "Whose Children Are They, Anyway?" *Los Angeles Times*, October 4: B7.

Washington Post. 1996. "Dole Statement Snags Phone, Cable TV Bill; Senator Fights Free Digital Broadcast Licenses," *Washington Post*, January 11: D8.

Wise, E. 1996. "A Historical Perspective on the Protection of Children from Broadcast Indecency," *Villanova Sports and Entertainment Law Journal* 3:15, 19.

Woodward, C. V. 1966. *Reunion and Reaction: The Compromise of 1877 and the End of Reconstruction*. Boston: Little, Brown.

Contributors

Frank Biocca
Director of the Center for Research
  in Mass Communication
University of North Carolina,
  Chapel Hill

Eva Blumenthal
Department of Communication
University of California, Santa
  Barbara

Jane D. Brown
Professor, School of Journalism
  and Mass Communication
University of North Carolina,
  Chapel Hill

Joanne Cantor
Professor, Communication Arts
  Department
University of Wisconsin, Madison

Wayne Danielson
Professor, Department of Journalism
University of Texas, Austin

Edward Donnerstein
Professor, Department
  of Communication
University of California, Santa
  Barbara

Tim Gray
Department of Communication
University of California,
  Santa Barbara

James T. Hamilton
Assistant Professor, Public Policy,
  Economics, and Political Science
Terry Sanford Institute of Public
  Policy
Duke University

Kristen Harrison
Communication Arts Department
University of Wisconsin, Madison

Cynthia Hoffner
Associate Professor, Department
  of Communication
Illinois State University

Karen Kemp
School of Journalism and Mass
  Communication
University of North Carolina,
  Chapel Hill

Marlies Klijn
College of Communication
University of Texas, Austin

Myra Gregory Knight
School of Journalism and Mass
    Communication
University of North Carolina,
    Chapel Hill

Marina Krcmar
Assistant Professor, Department
    of Communication
East Carolina University

Dale Kunkel
Associate Professor, Department
    of Communication
University of California, Santa
    Barbara

Dominic Lasorsa
Associate Professor, Department
    of Journalism
University of Texas, Austin

Daniel Linz
Professor, Department of
    Communication
Director, Law & Society Program
University of California, Santa
    Barbara

Rafael Lopez
College of Communication
University of Texas, Austin

Adriana Olivarez
College of Communication
University of Texas, Austin

James Potter
Professor, Department of
    Communication
University of California, Santa
    Barbara

Stacy L. Smith
Department of Communication
University of California, Santa
    Barbara

Matthew L. Spitzer
Professor of Law and Director of Law
    and Economics Program
University of Southern California

Ellen Wartella
Dean, College of Communication
University of Texas, Austin

D. Charles Whitney
Professor, Department of Journalism
University of Texas, Austin

Barbara J. Wilson
Associate Professor, Department of
    Communication
University of California, Santa
    Barbara

Index

LIBRARY
ST. LOUIS COMMUNITY COLLEGE
AT FLORISSANT VALLEY